RODALE

LOSE WEIGHT THE *SMART*

LOW-CARB WAY

A 7-step diet plan for **STAYING SLIM FOREVER** – with 200 delicious recipes

Bettina Newman RD & David Joachim

recipes by leslie revsin

PREVENTION
Healthy *Cooking*™

All spoon measurements are level: 1 tablespoon = 15 ml; 1 teaspoon = 5 ml

© 2003 Rodale Ltd.
Illustrations © Alan Neider

Printed in Italy by Rotolito Lombarda SpA
Rodale Inc. makes every effort to use acid-free ∞, recycled paper ♻

Designer: Joanna Williams
Cover design: Button Design Co
Photographer: Mitch Mandel/Rodale Images
Food Stylist: Diane Vezza
Cover recipe: Strawberry Cream Cake (page 336)

The recipe for Janet's Roasted Aubergine and Chickpeas (page 291) is adapted from *Higher Choices: Life-Enhancing Recipes* by Janet Lasky. © 1997 by Janet Lasky. Reprinted with permission of Higher Choices Alternative Food Concepts, L.L.C.

ISBN 1–57954–770–2

  4 6 8 10 9 7 5 3   hardcover

Visit us on the Web at www.rodalestore.co.uk

WE **INSPIRE** AND **ENABLE** PEOPLE TO IMPROVE
THEIR LIVES AND THE WORLD AROUND THEM

acknowledgements

After three decades of working with a lower-carbohydrate approach to weight loss, there are many people to thank for this book. Numerous friends, colleagues, researchers and clients have contributed, directly and indirectly, to what you now hold in your hands. In particular, we would like to extend our thanks and warmth to:

Dr Robert C. Atkins, a mentor and good friend who provided a foundation of knowledge and inspired in us a different approach to weight loss.

Leslie Revsin and Carol Munson, who worked magic in the kitchen by translating the principles of smart low-carb eating into truly fabulous recipes.

All of the people who generously shared their weight-loss stories, tips and recipes with us. Special thanks to Jeanne Bennett, Betty Carlucci, Becky Cleveland, Alice Cooper, Amanda Di Pietro, Lindsay Dooley, Norma Gates, Janet Lasky, Joan Lawson, Lynne Peters and Howard Lee Whitehorne.

The wonderful staff at Rodale for their talent, creativity, thoroughness and dedication, especially Neil Wertheimer, Janine Slaughter, Anne Egan, Sindy Berner, Holly McCord, Regina Ragone, Joanna Williams, Mitch Mandel, Jim Gallucci, Jennifer Kushnier, Barbara Thomas Fexa, Kathy Dvorsky, JoAnn Brader, Cindy Ratzlaff and Kathy Hanuschak.

Nancy Hancock for her tireless support.

Jeff Coombs and Mike Napier for patiently tracking down the nutrition information on whole, natural foods.

The Chesapeake General Hospital's Lifestyle Fitness Center for bringing to life the people who are profiled in these pages.

Gene Newman and Christine Bucher, two extraordinary spouses, whose unflagging encouragement and support allowed us to take on the challenges of writing this book. Thanks also to Leonard and Marie Montalbano.

And a big thank you to Rose Marino, who has waited nearly a century to read her granddaughter's book!

— Bettina Newman RD
and David Joachim

In all Rodale cookbooks, our mission is to provide delicious and nutritious recipes. Our recipes also meet the standards of the Rodale Test Kitchen for dependability, ease, practicality, and, most of all, great taste.

contents

INTRODUCTION: WHY LOW-CARB? vii
THE SCIENCE BEHIND LOW-CARB SUCCESS 1
7 STEPS TO SMART WEIGHT LOSS 21
MASTERING CARBS IN AND OUT OF THE KITCHEN 53

EGGS AND BREAKFAST FOODS 81

SNACKS, APPETISERS AND BEVERAGES 105

SOUPS AND SANDWICHES 127

CHICKEN AND TURKEY MAIN DISHES 161

BEEF, PORK AND LAMB MAIN DISHES 199

FISH AND SHELLFISH MAIN DISHES 231

CASSEROLES AND ONE-DISH DINNERS 263

VEGETABLES AND SIDE DISHES 301

BISCUITS, CAKES, PUDDINGS AND FRUIT DESSERTS 329

INDEX 358
STOCKISTS 376

introduction:
why low-carb?

No one can pinpoint the one thing that causes weight gain. For most people, a variety of factors are to blame, including genetics, family history, eating and exercise habits, and lifestyle choices that influence everything from how much sleep you get to how stressed you feel. Fortunately, diet is one of the factors that you can control. Even so, there is great debate about the best dietary changes to make. Eat less fat? Eat fewer calories? Or simply eat less food? Any of these approaches would be better than doing nothing. But years of clinical experience and research make us believe that reducing carbohydrates gets closer to the underlying metabolic problems in weight control than any other dietary modification.

This book is the result of more than 30 years of working with a lower-carbohydrate approach to weight loss. We have talked to and counselled hundreds of people, all of whom have lost weight, kept it off, and improved their health by using the simple plan presented in this book. Most family doctors have been surprised to see that these people – their patients – have reduced their risk of heart disease, diabetes and cancer while losing pounds, boosting their energy levels and getting a new outlook on life.

Becky Cleveland lost 28.6 kg/4½ st and has kept it off for three years and counting. She started with one simple change: she switched from eating refined grains like white flour to eating whole grains like wholemeal flour and oatmeal.

Lindsay Dooley had been a chunky girl since she started school. In her teens, she adopted a smart low-carb approach and dropped four dress sizes. She has stayed slim ever since.

These and many more people share their real-life weight struggles, best slimming strategies and favourite recipes in this book. We've also brought in the expert advice of weight-loss professionals who have studied the health benefits of eating fewer carbohydrate-rich foods. This is a fairly new area of weight-loss research, and the results are exciting. They show that a low-carb approach, when planned wisely, may be one of the most effective and satisfying ways to lose weight and keep it off.

If you're familiar with low-carb eating, you'll notice that our plan is a little different. This book should not be roped into the current stable of low-carb, high-fat diet books and dismissed. When you read it, you'll see that we're not saying you should eliminate carbohydrates altogether. We're not saying that the only starch you can eat is oatmeal. And we're not saying that you can eat all the bacon and cream you want. What we're saying is that the majority of your calories – your daily diet – should come from lean protein foods such as chicken, healthy fats like olive oil and, yes, good-for-you carbohydrates like vegetables and whole grains.

The idea of smart low-carb eating is simple: minimise refined-grain foods and sweets. Replace them with protein-rich, high-fibre meals. And eat sensible portions. For most people, this approach helps to normalise blood sugar levels and curb the impulse to binge eat.

Of course, occasional treats are a key component of long-term success. So we've built a few indulgences into the book. You may notice that a few recipes are slightly higher in carbohydrates (20 to 30 grams or more of carbohydrate for a main dish or dessert). These recipes are meant for those times when you want to indulge – every other week or so. You might also see that some recipes are slightly higher in fat than you might expect (20 grams or more of fat for a main dish or dessert). Don't be scared off. A little bit of fat in your diet can actually help you lose weight. Fat carries flavour and leaves you feeling full and satisfied (because it is slowly digested) so you're less tempted to overeat. Most of the fat used in the recipes is the healthy monounsaturated or polyunsaturated kind, which has been shown to help reduce heart disease risk. The less-healthy saturated fats are kept to a minimum.

After working with hundreds of people trying to lose weight, we've learned that most people want delicious, healthy meals for themselves and their families. Yet almost everyone says they can't spend lots of time in the kitchen. So we've made sure that every recipe in this book comes together easily. Time-Savers and Flavour Tips have been sprinkled throughout so you can take preparation shortcuts when you're busy, or change ingredients to appeal to finicky eaters. And every recipe has been taste-tested at least twice; in some cases, three times. We know that great-tasting food is absolutely critical to reaching your weight goals, so we made sure that every recipe tastes fabulous. In fact, that was the best part of the writing! Flip through the recipes and you'll see that nothing here even remotely resembles diet food. Chocolate Hazelnut Flourless Cake (page 338) is a slice of sheer decadence. Pesto Chicken Sandwich with Roasted Peppers (page 156) is pure eating satisfaction. And Wholemeal Pancakes with Berry Cream Syrup (page 97) – grab the forks!

We hope that you will truly enjoy the food in this book. We believe that, when combined with the simple seven-step plan, these smart low-carb recipes are your quickest route to long-term weight-loss success.

the science behind low-carb success

If you could ask a caveman what he ate yesterday, you'd quickly find out that a low-carbohydrate diet is nothing new. There is little doubt that the palaeolithic diet consisted primarily of meat, vegetables, nuts, fruits and berries. It's true that we don't have records showing how these foods were balanced, but common sense tells us that once an animal was caught and cooked, it yielded a greater number of servings than cavemen could possibly have gathered and consumed from locally available and seasonal vegetables and fruits. Add to this the fact that refined grains, fizzy drinks and sweets were unavailable, and we can safely assume that the invention of the low-carb diet took place long before people began to read about it.

Doctors began to pay formal attention to the effect of carbohydrate restriction in the 1920s, when this diet was used as a treatment option for people with intractable epilepsy. Another 30 to 40 years later, the first public hype about the health benefits of higher-protein, lower-carbohydrate meals began. In the US in the 1960s, Dr Irwin Stillman touted this eating plan in a widely read book and on late-night TV. In the 1970s, Dr Robert Atkins popularised this eating plan when he publicly defied conventional medical wisdom with his 'diet revolution'.

The 1980s and 1990s brought several variations on the low-carb theme, including the Scarsdale Diet, The Zone, Sugar Busters, Protein Power and the Carbohydrate Addict's Diet. Technically, all of these low-carb diets work. People lose weight on them. They might even be able to keep the weight off for a time. However, many of these diets are impractical because they require you to suddenly eliminate your favourite foods – even some of the healthy ones. And some of these low-carb diets are nutritionally inadequate or nearly impossible to sustain over a lifetime.

Our plan takes a whole new approach by starting with your current eating patterns and your degree of motivation for change. Unlike a strict diet that forces you to empty your fridge and cupboards into the bin, smart low-carb eating includes many of your favourite foods such as pasta, grains and even potatoes. No food is completely off-limits. The plan can be started immediately or gradually adopted over time. It is a plan that you can live with for good.

Our approach also incorporates new research that helps explain why low-carb eating reduces weight. We take into account all the beneficial aspects of the carbohydrate-controlled plans that have come before. But more important, we include the key elements of calorie control; glycaemic index; unsaturated versus saturated fat; the nutritional benefits of whole, natural foods; and the flexibility to choose from each of the major food groups.

Another unique part of the smart low-carb approach is that it addresses food triggers. Regardless of how nutritious and/or low in carbohydrates a food may be, if it somehow triggers you to overeat, reaching a healthy weight and overall good health might be an endless struggle. We show you how to identify and manage potential food triggers so that you can achieve your weight-loss goals and reach optimal health.

WHAT'S A CARBOHYDRATE?

Eating smart does not mean avoiding carbohydrates altogether. We're not about to tell you that carbohydrates are evil. The fact is, you can't live without them. Carbohydrates are one of three basic macronutrients needed to sustain life (the other two are protein and fat). But eating too many carbohydrates – especially refined carbohydrates – can cause you to gain weight and can adversely affect your health. Numerous studies demonstrate the relationship of these less-healthy carbohydrates to type 2 diabetes, heart disease and some kinds of cancer. It's true that eating too much of any food can cause weight gain and increase disease risk, but there's more to the story when it comes to carbohydrates.

Carbohydrates encompass a broad range of sugars, starches and fibres. There are two general classes of carbs – refined and unrefined. Refined carbohydrates are essentially refined sugars and refined flours. Unrefined carbohydrates are the kind found in whole grains, beans, fruits and many vegetables. Generally speaking, refined carbohydrates are less healthy for our bodies, and unrefined carbohydrates are more healthy. Here's a list of foods classified as refined or unrefined carbohydrates.

Refined Carbohydrates

Table sugar	Maple syrup: golden syrup
Fizzy drinks	Sweetened yoghurt
Any ingredient ending in '-ol', such as sorbitol	Any ingredient ending in '-ose', such as dextrose

Unrefined Carbohydrates

Vegetables	Buckwheat
Beans	Quinoa

Peas	Tapioca
Milk	Natural yoghurt
Fruit	Fruit juice
Amaranth	Whole grains (wheat,
Arrowroot	oats, barley, rye)
Potatoes	Wholegrain breads,
Sweet potatoes	cereals and pastas

Unrefined carbohydrates are usually more healthy because they include two kinds of fibre, soluble and insoluble. Fibre is extremely important for weight management because it makes you feel full so you don't overeat, and it helps to slow down your body's absorption of carbohydrate foods. Good sources of soluble fibre include citrus fruits, apples, dried peas, beans, oatmeal and oat bran. It helps to stabilise blood sugar levels and may help reduce the risk of heart disease. Good sources of insoluble fibre are whole grains, wheat bran, broccoli, carrots, asparagus and pears. Combined with soluble fibre, insoluble fibre helps maintain good bowel function. Because these fibre-rich foods are so important to a satisfying weight-loss plan, we've included a wide variety of them in this book.

CARB METABOLISM: THE GLYCAEMIC INDEX

If you want to lose weight and keep it off, it's important to know how various foods will affect your energy levels and your waistline. Here's how it works: all carbohydrates, including the lactose in milk, the starch in bread and the sucrose in table sugar, are eventually converted by your body into glucose (blood sugar), which is our primary source of energy. One hundred per cent of the carbohydrate you eat turns into glucose, but only 58 per cent of the protein and about 10 per cent of the fat you eat is converted to glucose. For this reason, carbohydrate-containing foods are often regarded as energy foods. It also takes your body longer to convert protein into glucose, and still longer to convert fat into glucose. Carbohydrates take a fraction of the time. That's why people with diabetes carry sugar pills or drink orange juice if they begin to feel weak. That's also why if you are feeling hungry and pop a mint or sweet into your mouth, the hunger quickly disappears for a while. You are raising your blood sugar (glucose).

Now it gets really interesting. Although all carbohydrates are converted to glucose and raise your blood sugar, not all are converted at the same rate. In the early 1980s, researchers began to study this phenomenon. You might think that all refined carbohydrate foods raise blood sugar quickly and all unrefined carbohydrate foods raise it more slowly. However, researchers demonstrated that this isn't always the case. They developed a number system called the glycaemic index (GI), which ranks carbohydrate-containing foods according to how quickly they raise your blood sugar within a 2- to 3-hour period after eating. The glycaemic index goes from 1 to 100, with the highest ranking of 100 assigned to pure glucose. The higher the

(continued on page 6)

the science behind low-carb success

I Did It!

Jeanne Bennett

Jeanne had a bicycle accident that led to years of medical problems and weight gain. None of the diets she tried worked very well, until she started reducing her intake of sugar and flour. Then she lost 20 kg/3 st 2 lb and has kept it off for 4 years and counting.

before

'I was always thin and healthy. I could eat anything I wanted without ever gaining weight. That was my life up to the age of 30. Then a bicycle accident marked the beginning of several physical and medical problems. I also had two children and was a stay-at-home mum.

'After recovering from the accident, I sent my second child off to school, and I was ready to return to the workplace. When I started assembling my wardrobe, I realised that I had gained almost 22 kg/3½ st! My life was loaded with stress and constant change

Weight lost: 20 kg/3 st 2 lb
Time kept off: 4 years
Weight-loss strategies: reduced carbohydrate intake, ate smaller portions
Weight-maintenance strategies: avoids foods containing sugar, eats whole grains instead of refined, does aerobic and strength-training exercises 3 times a week

the science behind low-carb success

around this time. I completed my master's degree in speech/language pathology, went through a divorce, remarried, moved to a different town and started a new job. Food was the only constant in my life! It was my comfort – and most likely my downfall because I usually ate quick, unhealthy meals on the run.

'My weight-loss efforts were always thwarted by medical problems, too. I was diabetic, had high cholesterol, could not get a good night's sleep, and suffered with arthritic pain. By the time I reached my fifties, I was desperate. As my doctor put it, "You have dodged a lot of bullets!". I was motivated to do more than dodge bullets. But I had no idea how to help myself. I only knew that all of the diets, sleep aids and pain relievers that I tried were merely temporary bandages on the symptoms rather than a cure for the underlying problems.

'I had managed to lose about 10 pounds on my own when my doctor referred me to a dietitian to develop a sound eating plan. That was when I really began to lose weight and keep it off. During my very first visit, the dietitian carefully listened to me, took a complete health and diet history, and gave me a plan of action. First, we had to know what I was eating every day. I soon realised that I had been eating way too much food

(about 2,500 calories a day) and far too many foods high in white sugar, white flour and other refined carbohydrates. Best of all, I learned that even though several physical and medical problems had resulted in my present health profile, I could take control. I could become healthy and I could lose weight.

'Over the next few months, I avoided eating foods high in refined sugar and refined flour. Instead, I began to eat more vegetables, lots of lean protein foods like fish, chicken, lean cuts of beef and pork, beans and some fresh fruit. My quality of life changed dramatically. I lost another 16 kg/2½ st in 4 months and my blood sugar levels normalised, my cholesterol came down, my arthritis pain was gone and I got more sleep. I was so much happier! I had accomplished a significant lifestyle change – not a diet, but a way of eating and living that was right for me.

'Now I'm in my late fifties and I no longer feel like I am "dodging bullets". It's more like I have been armed with understanding and the tools that I need to live a more healthy life. I watch my carbohydrate intake, eat the foods that are healthy for my body and exercise three times a week. I know I still have progress to make. But I'm much more motivated now that I've found a plan that works.'

GI, the quicker the food breaks down and increases blood sugar after you eat it. The lower the GI, the more gradually the food is absorbed and the more slowly it raises your blood sugar. Foods ranked 55 or below are considered low GI because they only cause a little blip in blood sugar. Foods ranked 56 and over are considered high GI because they can spike your blood sugar or send it soaring.

As a rule of thumb, choose more low-GI foods to help you lose weight. But don't avoid all high-GI foods. For instance, oatmeal has a 'high' GI of 59, but its soluble fibre makes it a healthy food, so there's no reason to avoid it. Likewise, a chocolate bar has a 'low' GI of 49, but that doesn't mean you should load up on chocolate – the extra calories and saturated fat will sabotage your weight-loss efforts.

To tell whether a high-GI or low-GI food is a healthy choice, take into account the other nutrients in the food. For example, wholemeal bread and white bread have similar GIs. But wholemeal bread is the healthier choice because it contains extra fibre and other important nutrients that white bread lacks. By the same token, brown rice is more nutritious than white, and wholewheat pasta is more healthy than white pasta. Surprisingly, potato crisps have a somewhat low GI, but they're not the healthiest snack choice due to their high calorie and low nutrient content. Peanuts or a plum would make a more nutritious snack.

Smart-Carb Insider Tip
STAY FOCUSED

Keep your eye on the big picture. When you can, look at your eating plan for the week. Will you be going out to eat? Do you have a special luncheon to attend? A reception of some sort? Will you be travelling? Decide when you will be able to make smart choices and when you're likely to throw caution to the wind. Some foods may be more important than others to your enjoyment of life. For instance, if you have planned to have lunch with friends, avoid carbohydrates that morning and indulge in that deep-pan pizza you dream about come lunchtime. Or if there's a cake you simply must have for dessert one night, plan on eating just a salad, protein and vegetables for that evening's dinner. Then enjoy your dessert. These occasional indulgences are crucial to maintaining a smart eating plan.

If you *do* choose to eat a high-GI food, try combining it with a low-GI food in the same meal or combining it with foods higher in protein or fat. This will slow down the rate at which the high-GI food raises your blood sugar. For instance, high-GI porridge could be balanced with a topping of low-GI milk and/or nuts. Again, no foods should be completely avoided. Variety, balance and moderation are the keys to a smart eating plan. Occasional indulgences are important, too.

Here's a snapshot of low-GI and high-GI foods. See 'The Glycaemic Index' on page 8 for a more detailed ranking of foods and their GI scores.

Low-GI Foods

Breads: pumpernickel

Cereals: rice bran, unsweetened high-fibre (all bran) cereals

Grains: easy-cook rice, barley, bulgar wheat, buckwheat

Pasta: angel hair, linguine and other thin strands; bean thread noodles (cellophane noodles); wholewheat spaghetti

Protein foods: beans, eggs, milk, unsweetened soya milk, unsweetened peanut butter

Vegetables: all, except those listed as high GI (page 9)

Fruits: cherries, grapes, apples, peaches, pears, plums, strawberries, oranges, grapefruit, dried apricots

Snacks: cheese, nuts, olives

Miscellaneous: low-fat yoghurt, foods sweetened with sucralose (Splenda), saccharin, fructose or aspartame

High-GI Foods

Breads: wholemeal bread, corn bread, baked goods made with white flour

Cereals: porridge oats, most dry cereals

Grains: cornmeal (polenta) and most corn products, most white rice and rice products, millet, couscous

Pasta: all thick shapes such as macaroni, penne and rigatoni

Vegetables: parsnips, potatoes, pumpkin, sweetcorn, beetroot

Fruits: watermelon, cantaloupe, raisins, pineapple, very ripe banana

Snacks: tortilla chips, corn chips, pretzels, rice cakes

Alcohol: all beer, all spirits and wine, except red wine

Miscellaneous: foods sweetened with a lot of sugar, honey, molasses, corn syrup, glucose or dextrose

KEEP INSULIN IN CHECK

So what's the real problem with eating lots of high-GI foods? A little hormone called insulin, which is good in moderation, but not in excess. Whenever carbohydrate foods are broken down into glucose in your body, glucose stimulates the release of insulin by the pancreas. The function of insulin is to grab the glucose and deliver it to your body's cells. Then your cells convert the glucose to energy or store the glucose as fat if there is already more than enough glucose to meet current energy requirements.

More important, though, are your insulin levels. When your blood sugar soars, so does your insulin. Eating high-GI foods causes your insulin levels to go up or 'spike', which researchers say may increase your risk of diabetes, heart disease and possibly cancer. Your body has a very precise means of regulating how much sugar stays in your bloodstream and how much gets into your cells. If you eat excessive amounts of quickly absorbed carbohydrates, you upset your body's precise balance of blood sugar, which puts you at risk of these diseases.

(continued on page 10)

THE GLYCAEMIC INDEX

Choosing foods with a low glycaemic index (GI) can help you lose weight. That's because low-GI foods are slowly digested and help prevent the spikes in blood sugar that can cause food cravings and lead to weight gain. Low-GI foods have a ranking of 55 or lower. High-GI foods have a ranking of 56 or higher. If you choose a high-GI food, try to combine it with a low-GI food or a food that is high in protein or fat. This will slow the absorption of the high-GI food and prevent your blood sugar from rising rapidly. Foods printed in green are high-GI foods that you need not avoid; these foods, such as watermelon, contain important nutrients as well as carbohydrates. Foods printed in red are low-GI foods that are best eaten sparingly; these foods, such as crisps, are high in fat or calories – and don't offer much else nutritionally. See page 3 for more details on the glycaemic index.

Food	GI	Food	GI	Food	GI
Baked Goods		**Cereals**		**Pastas**	
French bread	95	Puffed rice	88	Brown rice pasta	92
Waffle	76	Corn flakes	84	Gnocchi	68
Bread roll	73	Puffed wheat	74	Tinned macaroni	64
Bagel	72	Shredded wheat	69	and cheese	
Melba toast	70	Quick-cooking oats	66	Rice vermicelli	58
White bread	70	Porridge (rolled) oats	59	Durum wheat	55
Corn tortilla	70	Oat bran	55	spaghetti	
Wholemeal bread	69	All-Bran	42	Cheese tortellini	50
Taco shell	68	**Grains**		Linguine	46
Croissant	67	Instant rice	91	White spaghetti	41
Thin stoneground wheat	67	Millet	71	Meat-filled ravioli	39
cracker		White rice	68	Wholewheat spaghetti	37
100 per cent whole rye	65	Cornmeal	68	Vermicelli	35
bread		Couscous	65	Fettuccine	32
Rye crispbread	65	Brown rice	55	Bean thread noodles	26
Bran muffin	60	Buckwheat	54	**Legumes**	
Digestive biscuit	59	Bulgar wheat	48	Broad beans	79
Wholewheat pitta bread	57	Easy-cook (parboiled)	47	Tinned kidney	52
Oatcake	55	rice		beans	
Pumpernickel bread	41	Pearl barley	26	Tinned baked beans	48

Food	GI	Food	GI	Food	GI
Tinned borlotti beans	45	Mango	55	Beetroot	64
Black-eyed beans	42	Banana	53	Boiled new potato	62
Tinned chickpeas	42	Kiwifruit	52	Fresh sweetcorn	59
Dried chickpeas	33	Grapefruit juice	48	Sweet potato	54
Yellow split peas	32	Pineapple juice	46	Yam	51
Tinned butterbeans	31	Orange	43	Carrot	49
Green lentils	30	Grapes	43	Peas	48
Dried kidney beans	27	Apple juice	41	Tomato	38
Red lentils	26	Apple	36	**Snacks and Misc**	
Soya beans	18	Pear	36	Pretzel	83
Dairy and Ice Creams		Strawberries	32	Rice cake	82
Ice cream	61	Dried apricots	31	Tortilla chips	74
Sweetened		Peach	28	Corn chips	72
fruit yoghurt	33	Grapefruit	25	Table sugar	65
Skimmed milk	32	Plum	24	(sucrose)	
Whole milk	27	Cherries	22	Popcorn	55
Artificially sweetened,	14	**Vegetables**		Crisps	54
fruit-flavoured		Parsnip	97	Chocolate	49
yoghurt		Baked potato	85	Chocolate-covered	32
Fruits		Instant mashed	83	peanuts	
Watermelon	72	potato		Soya milk	31
Pineapple	66	French fries	75	Peanuts	14
Cantaloupe melon	65	Pumpkin	75		
Raisins	64	Swede	72		
Orange juice	57	Fresh mashed potato	70		

NOTE: Vegetables not appearing in this table (e.g. mushrooms, fennel, spinach, salad leaves) are all low-GI foods.
SOURCE: 'International Table of Glycemic Index', as it appears in *American Journal of Clinical Nutrition* and *The Glucose Revolution* by Thomas Wolever, MD, PhD

the science behind low-carb success

By eating less of the quickly absorbed carbohydrates, keeping moderate amounts of lean proteins and healthy fats in your diet, and getting a reasonable amount of physical activity, you set the stage for safe and effective weight loss. These strategies form the basis of the smart low-carb approach in this book. Put the emphasis on unrefined carbohydrate foods, and you will get more fibre, vitamins and minerals to help slow the absorption of carbohydrates into your bloodstream. Slow, gradual absorption will prevent your body from producing excess insulin and prevent sudden or excessive drops in blood sugar. As a result, you experience less hunger and are less likely to get sudden urges for sweets or extra portions.

We've talked to hundreds of people who found that this type of eating satisfaction is what really helped them to keep the weight off and stay healthy. Janet Lasky lost more than 70 kg/11 st and has kept it off for 8 years. 'I feel wonderful now!' she explains. 'My doctor discontinued my blood pressure medication; my blood sugars are within normal range despite my being diagnosed with diabetes years ago; and unlike earlier readings, my cholesterol now stays well within healthy limits. What I like best about this approach is that I don't ever feel deprived or like I am on a diet.'

Alice Cooper adopted the smart low-carb approach, lost 13 kg/2 st, and has kept it off for 4 years. '"Happy" does not describe how I feel these days,' she says. 'I don't have nearly as many cravings. My desire for foods has changed.'

WHY DOES LOW-CARB WORK?

As in so many areas of nutrition, some controversy surrounds the low-carb approach. Most health professionals agree that this eating strategy results in sustainable weight loss, but the reasons why are hotly contested. To the person who loses weight, keeps it off, and stays healthy in the long run, it may not matter what the reason is. Invariably, though, once you begin shedding pounds, an inquisitive relative, friend or colleague is going to ask why you think it works.

Proponents of the low-carb approach usually base their reasoning upon a comparison between how the body metabolises carbohydrates and how it breaks down proteins and fats, as explained above. Simply put, eating too many carbohydrate grams may increase insulin to such a high level in overweight people that more glucose becomes available to the cells than the body needs for energy. The excess glucose gets turned into fat. Consequently, blood sugar goes down because the glucose is going into the body's cells as fat. And when your blood sugar begins to drop, you feel hungry. If, like many people, you consume a lot of refined carbohydrates such as fizzy drinks and chocolate – or even crisps and biscuits – you are feeding a vicious cycle in your body that never really satisfies your hunger because you get only short-term relief. Plus, most refined carbohydrate foods are low in fibre. As mentioned earlier, eating fibre-rich foods gives you a sense of

SUGAR ADDICTION: IS IT POSSIBLE?

Science hasn't found that sugar is addictive in the way that nicotine or even alcohol can be. However, many people claim to be addicted to sugar (and carbohydrates). Here's some support for the theory. Sugar and alcohol do have something in common. They both release a brain chemical called serotonin, which makes you feel calm and relaxed. In our frenzied world, who wouldn't want to eat more of something that relieves stress? It's extremely interesting, too, that there is frequently alcoholism in the families of people who claim to be addicted to sugar. A study done in the Addiction Program at the Royal Ottawa Hospital in Ontario, Canada, even found a distinct subgroup of alcohol-dependent subjects who craved carbohydrates during sobriety.

Here's another possible explanation: when refined carbohydrates raise your blood sugar levels, these carbohydrates can stimulate the release of feel-good brain chemicals called endorphins. As with serotonin, it's natural for the body to want more and more endorphins to continue that good feeling. These explanations of sugar addiction are far from clear. The point is that some researchers believe that psychological processes are at the heart of both food cravings and addiction.

Recent research suggests that there may be a genetic explanation for your sweet tooth. Using data from the Human Genome Project, two separate research teams identified a gene that appears to regulate a sweet receptor on the nerves in your taste buds. Decreasing this gene's activity may help people control cravings for sweets.

What can you do today to stop cravings? Try replacing sugary foods or refined-carbohydrate foods with higher-protein foods for a few days. You may experience some fatigue early on, like many of the people we talked to who tried this trick. They described this temporary fatigue as sugar withdrawal. If you stick with the protein foods for more than a week, you may find, like they did, that you can break your sugar 'addiction'.

fullness. On the other hand, eating low-fibre simple carbohydrate foods leaves you feeling constantly hungry. This cycle may help to explain why sugar seems to have an addictive quality and how carbohydrate-rich meals may lead to excess weight.

As much sense as this explanation may make to you, sceptics of reduced-carbohydrate plans claim that this is not the whole story. They agree that reducing carbohydrates reduces insulin levels; however, they argue that the only reason low-carb eating works is that it diminishes hunger for some people, and they eat less. They remind us that the extra protein and fats in these diets also help satisfy hunger longer. The bottom line, according to sceptics, is that people lose weight on low-carb diets not because carbohydrates are reduced, but because total calories are reduced, even though protein and fat are increased.

(continued on page 14)

the science behind low-carb success

I D★id It!

Lindsay Dooley

Lindsay had been overweight for as long as she could remember. After adopting a low-carbohydrate diet in her teens, she became active in sport and went down four dress sizes.

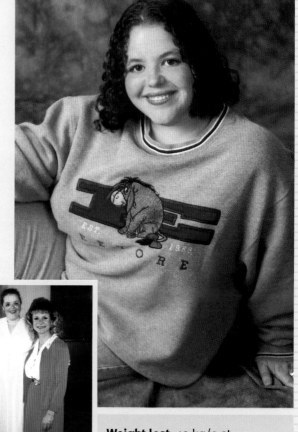

before

'From the time I started school, I was always called chunky. When I reached puberty at around the age of 13, I mysteriously gained 13 kg/ 2 st. It was a mystery because I didn't change the types or amounts of foods I was eating, nor the amount of exercise I was doing. I just gained weight. My mother tried her best to help me shed the excess pounds. She put me on a low-fat diet that limited my intake to 20 fat grams a day. When that approach failed, she took me to a doctor. He told her not to worry about my size (a women's 22!) and to stop focusing on diets. He warned her that she could cause me to

Weight lost: 19 kg/3 st
Time kept off: 4 years
Weight-loss strategies: avoided refined carbohydrates and trigger foods, strength-trained, played volleyball
Weight-maintenance strategies: controls carbohydrate intake, swims, stays active

have an eating disorder. For the next year, I went back to eating whatever I wanted to. I can remember having tremendous cravings for pasta with butter and salt. I rarely, if ever, ate sweets because I had been diagnosed with hypoglycaemia (abnormal blood sugar) when I was 4 years old. My mum told me that when I was a toddler, she could give me an ice cream cone and I would be sound asleep in less than half an hour. To this day, sugar sends me straight to sleep – usually for a 10-hour stint!

'Between the ages of 14 and 15, I gained another 22 kg/3½ st. Yes, 35 kg/5½ st in just 2 years! You can imagine what that did to my self-esteem at that critical time in my life. I became extremely depressed. Sometimes I sought solace in front of the television with any kind of food. Sometimes I would be so upset that I'd go without eating for 1 or 2 days. My depression worsened and my waistline spread as my mother searched for a doctor who could understand the weight problem.

'Finally, a doctor gave me antidepressants, which made me feel better, and identified that I had insulin resistance and several trigger foods. He advised me to eat a lower-carbohydrate diet and avoid my trigger foods, including wheat, milk, beef and eggs. Within 2 weeks of this new eating plan, I lost 3 kg/8 lb and immediately began feeling better. After avoiding my trigger foods for 3 months, I was able to reintroduce beef and milk into my diet every 4 days. (If I eat beef 2 days in a row, I have terrible insomnia.) I admit, the plan was somewhat difficult to follow at first. But that's only because it was different from what I was used to. I soon began to adore vegetables in salads and stir-fries. Any time I had a food craving or felt deprived, I reminded myself about how much better I was feeling by not eating those foods. I also realised that if I ate the foods that weren't right for my body, I would be depriving myself of feeling and looking my best. I steadily lost about 13 kg/2 st more and felt better and better. My energy was so great that I joined the volleyball team at school.

'I am leaving school this year. I can't wait to choose my dress for the leaving party – especially since it will be at least four sizes smaller than the size I once wore!'

There's no doubt that total calories and portion control are key factors in any long-term weight-loss plan. Here's some very basic weight-loss science: ½ kg / 1 lb of fat equals 3,500 calories. For every 3,500 calories you cut out of your diet or burn off through physical activity, you will lose ½ kg / 1 lb. Seems simple. But if you've ever tried a rapid weight-loss diet, you know there's more to it than that. Cutting too many calories too quickly makes your body go into starvation mode, and then your body hangs on to every calorie and bit of stored fat it can. That's why rapid weight-loss diets don't work. People regain weight on them.

A few studies provide insight into why 'calories in versus calories out' may oversimplify the route to successful weight loss – especially with regard to carbohydrates. Researchers at the Albert Einstein College of Medicine in New York looked at caloric intake of overweight teenagers following a low-carbohydrate plan compared to that of teens on a low-fat plan over a period of 12 weeks. Although the teenagers on the low-carb plan ate an average of 600 calories more per day than the other teens, they lost an average of 5 kg / 11 lb more. The teens on the low-fat plan ate fewer calories but lost an average of only 4.5 kg / 10 lb, while those on the low-carb plan ate more calories and lost around 9 kg / 20 lb. This study suggests that calories are not the only deciding factor in weight loss.

Another study found that a low-carb diet may lead to more sustainable weight loss and better health in the long run. Researchers at the University of Illinois compared the widely recommended United States Department of Agriculture (USDA) diet (high carbohydrate) to a lower-carbohydrate diet that is very similar to the one recommended in this book. Interestingly, both diets had the same number of calories. In the study, 24 midlife women above ideal weight ate 1,700 calories a day for 10 weeks. One group ate according to the

HIDDEN ROADBLOCK to weight loss

ALCOHOL

Carbohydrates, such as the grains in beer and whisky and the fruit in wine, form the basis of most alcoholic beverages. Alcohol supplies mostly empty calories and it can cause peaks in blood sugar levels. So it could be holding you back from losing the weight you'd like to lose. Surprisingly, the morning after having a drink with dinner, the scales may show that you have lost up to a pound. But within a day or two, most people regain the weight – and sometimes extra. If you drink alcohol, try slowly decreasing the amount to see if a little less alcohol might help you lose a little more weight. Or choose drinks lower in carbohydrates. A 25 ml (⅙ gill) measure of spirits has only trace carbs; a glass of red wine has about 1 gram of carbs; and a 300 ml/½ pint glass of beer has 12 grams of carbs. Always choose diet mixers to go with spirits.

standard food pyramid (55 per cent carbohydrates, 15 per cent protein and 30 per cent fat). The other group ate a lower-carbohydrate, higher-protein diet (40 per cent carbohydrates, 30 per cent protein and 30 per cent fat). After 10 weeks, the women in both groups lost about 7.2 kg/ 16 lb. But the women on the lower-carbohydrate diet had a more healthy weight loss. They lost about 5.4 kg/12 lb of body fat and just over ½ kg/1 lb of muscle mass. Those who followed the high-carb diet lost only 4.5 kg/10 lb of body fat and a surprising 1.3 kg/3 lb of much-needed muscle mass. Muscle mass is important because once you lose it, your body is less able to burn calories. The women on the low-carb diet lost very little muscle mass compared to the women on the high-carb diet. This means that the low-carb, high-protein diet was almost twice as effective for long-term weight loss because the women who followed this diet were more efficient at burning calories. The women on the low-carb diet also had increased levels of beneficial thyroid hormones at the end of the study, suggesting that their metabolisms went up – another plus for burning calories. One more bonus for the low-carb diet: the women following this plan experienced a sharp reduction in triglycerides (fat in the blood) and a slight increase in high-density lipoprotein (HDL, the beneficial type of cholesterol), which improved their overall heart health.

These studies coincide with our clinical observations of hundreds of low-carb clients over the years. Norma Gates was steadily gaining 4.5 kg/10 lb a year for over a decade. She cut back on refined sugar and refined flour – all junk food – lost 19 kg/3 st, and has kept it off for 3½ years so far. 'Within a few weeks of eating fewer refined carbs, I felt like I had broken my carbohydrate addiction. The food cravings finally subsided,' she says. 'I no longer put my head on the kitchen table right after dinner or make my way to lie on the couch, and I have new-found pleasures in life besides just food.'

HOW IT CAME TO THIS

There's no doubt that eating lower-carbohydrate foods – and especially reducing refined carbohydrates – can help you lose weight and stay healthy. Maybe this phenomenon can be explained simply. Perhaps our bodies are just not used to metabolising so many *refined* carbohydrate foods.

For example, the consumption of sugar in the UK has increased dramatically in the last two centuries. In the 1820s each person consumed 2 teaspoons a day; today the average woman consumes 17 teaspoons of sugar each day, while the average man eats 23 teaspoons, or more than 30 kg/67 lb of sugar each year. It comes from table sugar, confectionery and preserves, cakes, biscuits and puddings, and from soft drinks. The Dietary and Nutritional Survey of British adults found that the average UK citizen drinks 310 cans of soft drinks each year – and each can contains 4 teaspoons of sugar.

How much should we be eating? Experts recommend that people who eat the average 2,000-calorie daily diet get no more than 10 teaspoons of added sugar a day. But the average person is consuming about 20 teaspoons of added sugar every day – twice the recommended amount.

This liberal consumption would be of no concern if sugar had a nutrient value similar to that of vegetables, protein foods or other nutrient-dense foods. The problem is that sugar is not endowed with significant amounts of any nutrients. It provides you with only empty calories. The following chart shows just how many foods are loaded with teaspoon upon teaspoon of refined sugars. Don't forget that many low-fat foods are sky-high in sugar because sugar is often added to these foods to replace the flavour lost when fat is removed. Over-consumption of these low-fat products helps to explain why low-fat dieting is not necessarily the answer for everyone.

Food	Sugar (tsp)
Brownie, 75–100 g/2½–3½ oz	10
Ice cream, 100 g/3½ oz (not fat-free, with milk sugars)	10
Cheesecake, plain, 115 g/4 oz	9
Thick chocolate shake, 300 ml/½ pint	9
Cola, regular, sweetened, 330 ml/11½ fl oz	7
Chocolate bar, 60 g/2 oz	7
Currant bun	7
Baked beans, 200 g/7 oz	7

Food	Sugar (tsp)
Pie, fruit, double crust, 115 g/4 oz	7
Iced cup cake	6
Doughnut, yeast	6
Iced tea, sweetened, 330 ml/11½ fl oz	6
Chocolate chip cookies, 2 medium	5
Muffin, American-style	5
Tinned fruit, in heavy syrup, 100 g/3½ oz	4
Dry cereal, frosted, 30 g/1 oz	4
Fizzy lemonade, 300 ml/½ pint	4
Chocolate milk, 240 ml/8 fl oz	3
Gingernut biscuits, 4 medium	3
Pop Tart, frosted	3
Jam, 1 level tablespoon	3
Digestive biscuit, 1	2
Tinned fruit, in natural juice, 100 g/3½ oz	2
Orange squash, diluted, 240 ml/8 fl oz	1
Fish finger, 1	1
Bread, 1 slice	0
Tinned fruit, packed in water, 100 g/3½ oz	0
Oatmeal, plain, 170 g/6 oz	0

Increased consumption of refined wheat products such as bread, breakfast cereals, cakes and biscuits is also of some concern, because refined wheat lacks fibre and has a high glycaemic index. For instance, white bread comes in many shapes, but most have a high GI of 70 to 95, and are quickly turned into glucose and quickly raise your blood sugar.

Today's high consumption of sugar and wheat sheds some light on the continually rising obesity rates in the western world. The number of overweight or obese adults, teenagers and children has been steadily increasing for 30 years, concurrently with increased consumption of refined-carbohydrate foods like fizzy pop, white bread, biscuits and cakes. Experts predict that 25 per cent of UK adults will be obese by 2010.

If, like many others, you eat a lot of foods containing white flour or added sugars, you may have found one of the keys to lasting weight loss: eat fewer refined-carbohydrate foods. Instead, eat more unrefined-carbohydrate foods like whole grains, beans, vegetables and fruits; more lean protein foods; and some healthy fats and oils. Yes, fats. Don't be scared off by them. Dietary fats may not be as bad for you as you think. In 1998, researchers from the Harvard School of Public Health concluded that dietary fat does not appear to be the primary cause of the prevalence of excess body fat in western society and that a reduction in fat will not solve the problem. The fact is, fats make up most of the structure of the body's cell membranes. They play a vital role in the process of cellular communication. Certain fats and oils also contain essential fatty acids that are important for the body's formation of eicosanoids,

which regulate blood pressure, assist in blood clotting, help regulate body temperature, control pain and inflammation, and manufacture hormone-like substances. The fatty acids are called essential because all but two cannot be made in our bodies. We have to get them from the foods we eat.

If you want to lose weight, it's important to include enough fat in your diet. See page 25 for more details on the healthy fats that help to promote weight loss and peak physical condition.

COUNTERING THE LOW-CARB CONCERNS

Research and clinical observations have convinced us that a smart low-carb eating plan can help you lose weight and prevent disease. But you may still have some concerns. Here are the answers to the health questions that have been raised by doctors, nutritionists and sceptics of lower-carbohydrate diets.

Q: Does restricting carbohydrates reduce energy and cause fatigue?

A: Not likely. Only two out of several hundred people we spoke to complained about fatigue after the first few days of changing their diets. Some people experience fatigue during the first 1 to 3 days. This may be the result of withdrawal from refined sugar, refined wheat or other foods that the body may have been accustomed to digesting frequently. Yes, energy production is the main function of carbohydrates. However, you will get plenty of energy from the carbohydrates you do include on this plan as well as from the proteins and fats. Fatigue and energy loss are often signs of low blood sugar, and the smart low-carb approach keeps your blood sugar levels stable.

Q: Will eating more protein and fewer carbohydrates damage my kidneys?

A: Probably not. If you've never had a kidney problem, you probably don't need to worry about the warnings that eating more protein and fewer carbohydrates will wear out your kidneys. There is no research confirming this potential danger – even in people who consume three times the recommended amount of protein. Do pay attention to the warning if you already have kidney disease. A higher protein intake may be dangerous if your kidneys are not functioning properly. If you're unsure whether your kidneys are healthy, consult your doctor before changing your diet.

Q: Won't eating more fat raise my cholesterol and triglycerides and increase my risk of heart disease?

A: Quite the opposite. We have all been brainwashed into believing that eating foods with any type of fat will cause elevated cholesterol in everyone who eats them. However, saturated fat is the real culprit in increased heart disease risk. We've talked to several people who regularly ate foods high in mono- and polyunsaturated fats while reducing their carbohydrate intake – and their total

cholesterol has actually come down. Most people who eat fewer carbohydrates find that their triglyceride levels go down and their good HDL cholesterol goes up.

Here's a possible explanation: fat is stored in our bodies in the form of triglycerides. It's known that excess insulin causes excess triglycerides. A high carbohydrate intake requires lots of insulin to metabolise the extra carbohydrates. As the insulin goes up, so do triglycerides. Likewise, as insulin levels come down on a reduced-carbohydrate plan, so do triglycerides. The bottom line is that a reduced-carbohydrate eating plan may help reduce your risk of heart disease because it brings down your insulin levels and your triglycerides. Just to be sure, the smart low-carb approach in this book recommends limiting saturated fat and instead focusing on foods such as oils, nuts, and olives that are rich in healthy fats.

Q: Will everyone's blood lipids respond the same way to reducing carbohydrates and increasing protein and fat?

A: Most likely. Almost everyone who has followed the smart low-carb eating plan has witnessed dramatic reductions in triglycerides and significant increases in good HDL cholesterol. Of course, everyone is a little different. There may be a very small percentage of the population whose lipid levels respond negatively to the moderate increase in dietary fat that accompanies this reduced-carbohydrate plan. If you're concerned that this may be you, talk to your doctor before you begin, then ask him or her to check your blood fats 8 weeks later.

Q: Will eating more protein increase my risk of heart disease?

A: On the contrary – the research says otherwise. A study at the Harvard School of Public Health looked at 80,082 women aged 34 to 59 without any previous indication of heart disease. When all other risk factors for heart disease were controlled for, and irrespective of whether the women were on high- or low-fat diets, the results showed that both animal and vegetable proteins contributed to lower risk of heart disease. Researchers concluded that replacing refined carbohydrates with protein may reduce heart-disease risk.

Q: Can a reduced-carbohydrate/higher-protein plan lead to osteoporosis?

A: This is one warning we may need to heed. Increased protein makes the blood more acidic. The body responds by releasing calcium from the bones in an effort to bring the pH to a more alkaline level. However, if you eat lots of vegetables, you will minimise this problem because vegetables make the body more alkaline. Keep in mind that too little protein (which may be the case for people following a low-fat diet) can also be harmful to the skeleton. To safeguard against osteoporosis risk, the eating plans in this book set an upper limit on protein intake and boost vegetable consumption considerably.

Q: Does the plan in this book contain all the nutrients I need to protect my bones?

A: Yes. These eating plans are high in calcium-rich foods like cheese, dark green leafy vegetables, almonds, Brazil nuts, salmon, sardines and calcium-fortified soya products.

We also recommend that you eat a wide variety of foods and take a daily multivitamin. There are many other nutrients that play a role in bone health, including magnesium, vitamin D, vitamin C, vitamin K, zinc, boron, lysine, potassium and silicon. Hormonal balance and physical activity are important factors, too. If you're in doubt, ask your doctor whether a supplement is right for you.

Q: I have heard that you can eat more meat on a reduced-carbohydrate plan. I am concerned about eating more meat than I am used to eating because I've also heard that there is a link between meat and cancer. Is this true?

A: We have read similar studies! Just keep this motto in mind: moderation in all things. Scientists still do not fully understand all of the causes of cancer. Some of the facts we have are that 1) toxins that might cause cancer are stored in fat; 2) nitrates and nitrites, usually found in smoked, cured or pickled meats or fish, can form cancer-causing nitrosamines; 3) blackened or charred meats, fish or poultry contain substances known to cause cancer; 4) there may be oestrogens in the fat portions of meat that may raise oestrogen levels in the body and contribute to oestrogen-dominance-type cancers.

These are all valid concerns. However, we recommend several steps to minimise their impact. Eating lots of vegetables and some fruits will supply important antioxidants that help protect us from cancer. Also, remember that the body has a wonderful built-in detoxification system in the liver. Eating a wide variety of whole foods, as this plan encourages, will supply nutrients that support liver function. Cruciferous vegetables such as broccoli, cauliflower, brussels sprouts, kale, cabbage and others are particularly helpful. Bear in mind, too, that this book recommends eating more protein, but not necessarily more meat. If you prefer not to get your protein from meat, there are plenty of recipes and suggestions in this book for getting protein from beans, nuts and other non-animal sources. See also the cancer-reducing cooking tips on page 56.

Q: Is my breath going to smell funny on this diet, and should I expect to be constipated?

A: No. The ketone breath associated with low-carbohydrate diets is not a problem on this plan because the carbohydrates are not as restricted. This book advocates a smart lower-carbohydrate approach of avoiding refined carbohydrates, but not the severe carbohydrate restriction that triggers ketosis. The liberal use of high-fibre vegetables in our plan as well as high-fibre whole grains and fruits will ensure that you are not constipated. On the contrary, most people have found that the extra fibre improves regularity. It also reduces hunger because it makes them feel more full.

7 steps to smart weight loss

Are you a bread eater? Pasta lover? Ice cream binger? Crazy about sweets? Chocoholic? Cereal muncher? Beer guzzler? Dessert person? If so, there's good news. You don't need to eliminate these foods to lose weight. However, it may help to choose a different type of bread, a different type of pasta or a different type of cereal.

Losing weight is really a matter of making smart choices. What follows are seven choices that you can make to start shedding weight today. Together, these seven choices or steps make up the basis of the smart low-carbohydrate approach. You'll also find several detailed menu plans that put these steps into practice in your everyday life.

Whichever path you choose, the general steps or the detailed menu plans, remember the cardinal rule of successful weight loss: stick with it! The eating approach and recipes in this book include many of your favourite foods, because it's nearly impossible to stick with a plan that doesn't include them. Who wants to go through life without enjoying it? That's the whole purpose of losing weight in the first place. So enjoy your favourite foods. Enjoy the fabulous recipes in this book. And read on to see how you can make great-tasting food work for you instead of against you.

STEP 1: EAT MORE WHOLE GRAINS

Take a minute to think about the grain foods you typically eat, such as cereals, bread, rolls, biscuits and crackers, muffins, bagels, pasta and rice. If any of these foods are mostly white in colour or contain white flour, try replacing them with wholegrain foods. Today's supermarkets are full of wholegrain cereals, wholegrain breads, wholewheat pitta breads, wholewheat pasta, wholemeal flour and brown rice. These wholegrain foods have a more complex taste and texture than refined foods – and many people end up liking them better. If you bake at home, replace plain white flour with wholemeal flour, which makes excellent breads and cakes.

Make the switch. The switch to whole grains is one of the most important you can make for weight loss. The main reason: refined grains are so prevalent in the average diet that switching to whole grains will affect the majority of your food choices.

Gene Newman discovered this principle as his waistline expanded throughout his thirties. In addition to reducing his total carbohydrate intake, switching to whole grains helped Gene lose 19 kg/3 st. He has kept it off for 15 years. One reason is that replacing refined grain products with wholegrain products instantly boosts your fibre intake, which satisfies your hunger longer so you don't overeat. Fibre-rich foods come packed with vitamins, minerals and other nutrients that strengthen your immune system so you can ward off illness and also help reduce heart disease risk.

Read labels. When buying breads, cereals, pasta and other grain-based foods, look for the words 'wholegrain', 'wholewheat' or 'wholemeal' on the label. At least one whole grain should appear first on the ingredient list, indicating that it is the largest ingredient in the food. Some examples of whole, unrefined grains include

whole wheat, wholemeal flour, brown rice, rye, oats, pot barley, corn, quinoa, buckwheat and wholewheat couscous. Limit foods that contain refined wheat flour. See page 68 for more tips on buying and cooking with wholegrain foods.

Look for low-GI grains. Foods with a low glycaemic index (GI) can help you lose weight. They won't raise your blood sugar as quickly as foods with a high glycaemic index and may keep you satisfied longer. To step up your weight loss, put the emphasis on wholegrains with a low glycaemic index. For instance, a slice of wholegrain pumpernickel bread has a lower glycaemic index than most other breads. Surprisingly, pumpernickel has a lower glycaemic index than 100 per cent wholemeal bread. Oats are another good choice among whole grains because they are high in fibre.

Whenever you do eat a food with a higher GI, try to include some protein and fat in the same meal. For instance, if you must eat white bread, try eating it with peanut butter. The protein and fat in the peanut butter will lower the GI of the entire meal. See 'The Glycaemic Index' on page 8 for a list of low-GI foods.

Reduce your total intake of starches. Switching from refined grain foods like white bread, white pasta and white rice to low-GI whole grains should help you lose weight and stay satisfied. If you make these changes and still want to lose more weight, try reducing the total servings of starches in your diet, including unrefined grains, rice, pasta and beans. Aim to eat no more than four servings of starches per day. See page 38 to see what counts as a serving.

Count starchy vegetables as starches. Although they might not be grains, some starchy vegetables and plant foods really belong in the same food category because of their high starch content. These include sweetcorn, potatoes, sweet potatoes, broad beans, black-eyed beans, lentils and other dried or tinned beans. When monitoring your carbohydrate intake, count one serving of these foods as a serving of starch. There's no need to omit or even limit starchy vegetables, because they supply key nutrients, particularly fibre. However, when eating starchy vegetables, you may want to reduce your intake of bread, cereal, crackers or other grains to compensate.

Make smart restaurant choices. Most restaurant menus offer only refined grain foods. If that's the case, try to keep the portions minimal. For instance, have an open sandwich instead of a sandwich with two slices of bread. Or go for a salad instead of a sandwich. If the meal comes with a side dish of noodles or pasta, ask for a second vegetable instead. When ordering breakfast, choose an egg dish such as an omelette and skip the toast. And if the waiter brings a bread basket to your table, resist temptation by asking that it either be left in the kitchen or placed at the other end of the table. Order a glass of tomato juice and sip it while others are nibbling bread. You will reap the wonderful benefits of the phyto-nutrient lycopene rather than taking in the nutrient-poor starch of refined grains.

STEP 2: EAT MORE VEGETABLES AND FRUIT

We've known all along that they're good for us, but now science can explain why vegetables and fruit help prevent cancer, heart disease and numerous other maladies. A University of California scientist reviewed 156 studies on the relationship between eating fruit and vegetables and

HIDDEN ROADBLOCK to weight loss

OVEREATING

Portion control is a key component of any weight-loss plan. Many of us simply eat too much! Carbohydrates are often the most overeaten type of food, so keep an eye on serving sizes. If you feel you have a good grip on how much you eat but you are still not losing weight, try omitting one or two servings of the carbohydrate-containing foods in your diet for several days. This should help you start losing again. As always, if you have a medical condition or are taking any medication, check with your doctor before adjusting the carbohydrates to an extremely low level.

cancer risk and found that more than 80 per cent of those studies supported the cancer-protective effect of beta-carotene-rich foods. Experts say that all of us would reduce our cancer risk by 20 per cent just by increasing fruit and vegetable intake to 5 servings a day.

Eating more fruit and vegetables may reduce your risk of stroke, too. In 1999, the *Journal of the American Medical Association* looked at data from two large studies that followed 75,596 women for 14 years and 38,683 men for 8 years. The incidence of stroke was directly related to the number of servings of fruit and vegetables consumed by these women and men. The addition of just one daily serving of fruit or vegetable decreased stroke risk by 6 per cent. The produce with the most protective effects includes cruciferous vegetables such as cabbage, broccoli, cauliflower, kale, spring greens and brussels sprouts; dark green, leafy vegetables such as spinach; citrus fruits; and other vitamin C-rich fruit and vegetables such as strawberries and peppers.

If you're concerned about osteoporosis, vegetables may be just what you need. According to Katherine Tucker, PhD, associate professor of nutritional epidemiology at Tufts University in Boston, 'Fruits and vegetables are associated with bone mineral density and may help protect against osteoporosis'. With all these health benefits, including reduced risk of cancer, stroke and osteoporosis, it makes sense to trade in a serving of pasta or rice for a serving of vegetables.

Get fresh or get frozen. Choose a wide variety of fresh or frozen vegetables. Tinned vegetables work too – especially tinned tomato products. Avoid frozen vegetables with a breadcrumb coating or sauce; these tend to be high in carbohydrates, sodium and hydrogenated fats.

Eat mostly fresh, low-carb, low-GI vegetables. All green vegetables, such as cabbage, broccoli, asparagus, leafy greens such as spinach, lettuce and watercress, celery and cucumbers are smart choices for low-carb eating. So are mushrooms, radishes and cauliflower. These vegetables are low in carbs and have a low glycaemic index (they don't send your blood sugar soaring); these are the ones you should eat most often.

But don't completely eliminate higher-carb, higher-GI vegetables such as potatoes – especially if they help you stick with the low-carb approach in the long run. Many high-carb or high-GI vegetables provide important nutrients. These include beetroot, carrots, onions, peas, pumpkin and sweet potatoes. Bear in mind, too, that you'll probably eat most of your vegetables with a meal that also contains protein and fat, which will lower the overall glycaemic index of the meal. Low-GI choices are more crucial when you eat the vegetable by itself as a snack. For instance, if you like to snack on raw carrots, dip them in cottage cheese dip or tahini, or eat a few nuts at the same time. Each of these accompaniments will lower the overall glycaemic index.

Strive for five to nine. Needless to say, most people currently fall short of the recommended number of servings of fruit and vegetables. We should be getting at least five – and preferably nine – servings a day, but at the close of the 1990s, most of us were getting little more than three. It's not as hard as it might seem to get five a day. A 180 ml/6 fl oz glass of orange juice at breakfast counts as one. A bowl of salad at lunch makes two. Have some celery or carrot sticks for a snack, a vegetable side dish with dinner, and some fruit with dessert and you're there. Toss more vegetables into the next casserole that you make. Choose vegetable juice instead of other soft drinks. Even a small handful of dried fruit such as raisins or apricots counts as a serving of fruit. Try to get five to six servings of vegetables and two to three servings of fruit each day. Check out some of the recipes in this book to see other easy ways of incorporating fruit and vegetables into your meals. To get the most nutrients and health benefits, eat a wide variety of richly coloured fruit and vegetables.

STEP 3: FOCUS ON LEAN PROTEINS AND HEALTHY FATS

Some of the popular low-carb diets suggest eating as much protein and fat as you want, as long as you keep carbohydrates low. This may not be a healthy approach for everyone. Numerous studies show that diets high in saturated fat (the kind found in butter,

HIDDEN CARBS IN SEAFOOD

Generally, fish is a healthy choice. But some types of seafood are higher in carbs than others. Here's a ranking of fresh and prepared fish and shellfish to help you make smart choices.

SEAFOOD	CARB (G)
Breaded, fried scampi, 12	20
Prawn cocktail, 115 g/4 oz	20
Rollmop herrings, 100 g/3½ oz	16
Cod in batter, 100 g/3½ oz	14
Tuna salad (with celery, pickle, onion, egg and mayonnaise), 240 g/8 oz	7
Crab sticks, 3	5
Scallops, 115 g/4 oz	4
Fish finger, 1	4
Clams, raw, each	1
Lobster meat, 100 g/3½ oz	0.4
Crabmeat, 60 g/2 oz	0.4
Prawns, cooked, 100 g/3½ oz	0

cheese and fattier cuts of meat) can lead to heart disease. The key to smart low-carb eating is to replace refined carbs with moderate portions of lean protein foods and unsaturated fats. That means choosing mostly poultry, fish, seafood, eggs, some lean cuts of red meat, reduced-fat cheeses, nuts, liquid cooking oils and maybe a few soya foods such as tofu.

Go for lean cuts of meat. Red meat is rich in iron, zinc and B vitamins and adds variety to your diet. There's no need to swear off it, but try to limit red meats to two or three meals per week. Lean cuts are the smartest choice. If beef is on your menu or shopping list, choose fillet, sirloin or topside. For lamb, choose leg (whole or steaks), loin chops, fillet or shanks. When choosing pork, look for tenderloin/fillet, leg, loin or lean chops, lean ham or gammon. If you eat veal, any cut except commercially ground will be fairly lean. Game meats such as venison, hare, rabbit and ostrich are quite lean as well.

Buy the best minced beef. Extra-lean minced beef is the best choice for health. Try mixing it with ground turkey breast for juicy hamburgers, meatballs or chilli. If you're a beef purist, ask the butcher to mince sirloin steak.

Make it natural. If you eat cold meats, try to use those without added cereal products. Use only a minimal amount of smoked and cured meats such as ham, bacon and frankfurter sausages. If you eat these foods, try to have a tomato product at the same meal. It may help protect you from the possible cancer-causing effects of the nitrates and nitrites.

Choose poultry wisely. Most poultry is lean if you avoid the skin. Chicken breasts and legs make good choices. Read the labels when buying minced turkey or chicken. Minced turkey breast has the least fat; some minced turkey is sold as 'low-fat' and labelled with its fat content, typically 3 per cent. Packages labelled simply 'minced turkey' include the greatest

proportion of fat, which helps keep the minced meat moist.

Take another look at eggs. Most health experts have put eggs back on the menu as a good source of protein. Eggs contain important nutrients in both the yolk and the white. If you're a fan, eat up to six eggs a week.

Eat more fish. Fish is a terrific source of important healthy fats. Our bodies require two types of dietary fats: omega-6 and omega-3 fatty acids. Research shows that these fats help protect your heart. And they can only be obtained from food because our bodies do not make them. Omega-3 fatty acids are abundant in salmon, tuna, mackerel, herring, sardines, trout and halibut. To boost your heart health, try to eat some type of fish at least twice a week. When you can, choose fresh fish – the flavour beats frozen and tinned hands down. But tinned tuna and salmon also count as fish meals. If you stock frozen seafood, look for varieties without breadcrumbs or batter.

Go nuts. If you don't like fish, look to walnuts and flaxseed (linseed) for omega-3 fatty acids. Nuts, seeds, nut butters and nut oils also contain omega-6 fatty acids. Data from a long-term, large-scale research project in the US called the Nurses' Health Study showed that both of these fats can help reduce blood cholesterol levels, blood pressure and heart disease risk. That's why these essential fatty acids are referred to as healthy fats. The beneficial amount of nuts consumed in the Nurses' Health Study was 145–200 g/ 5–7 oz per week – which translates to a little less than 30 g/1 oz of nuts a day. Finally, a snack food that has health benefits!

Focus on unsaturated fats. Most unsaturated fats come from plant foods rather than animal foods. Both monounsaturated and polyunsaturated fats are considered healthy fats. Both kinds of unsaturated fat are liquid at room temperature as well as in your body. For this reason, they keep cell membranes flexible and fluid. They regulate blood cholesterol and reduce heart disease risk by helping to lower 'bad' LDL cholesterol and maintain 'good' HDL cholesterol. Use mostly liquid oils such as olive oil and rapeseed (sometimes known as canola) oil for cooking and salads. See page 61 for more tips on using liquid oils.

The less saturated fat, the better. Saturated fats – the fats that clog your arteries – are solid at room temperature. Saturated fat is found mostly in animal fats such as butter, full-fat dairy products, meats and poultry skin. Try to limit saturated fat to no more than two servings a day (about 2 rashers of bacon or 2 tablespoons of cream cheese). Less is even better.

Avoid hydrogenated fats. Food manufacturers do amazing things to once-healthy liquid oils. They transform them into solid fats. These trans fatty acids (trans fats) are made by heating liquid oils to very high temperatures for 6 to 8 hours, then chemically introducing hydrogen molecules. This results in hydrogenated fats that are less expensive, less perishable and more spreadable than natural fats. A good thing for food manufacturers but not for your body, because hydrogenated oils act more like saturated fat in your body; they tend to raise your blood cholesterol and increase heart disease risk. Hydrogenated or partially hydrogenated fats are found in most commercially made biscuits, pastries, crisps,

WHAT'S A SERVING OF NUTS?

A 30-g/1-oz serving of nuts each day can help reduce your risk of heart attack. See below to find out how many nuts this equals. Notice that nuts with fewer calories have more carbohydrates. To get the best balance in low-calorie, low-carb nuts, go for unsalted peanuts, pistachios or pine nuts.

Nuts	Cal	Carb (g)
Chestnuts, 3½	70	15
Cashews, 18	163	9
Pistachios, 47	160	8
Peanuts, 20	166	6
Pine nuts, 155	160	5
Almonds, 22	170	5
Hazelnuts, 12	183	5
Walnut halves, 14	185	4
Brazil nuts, 8	190	4
Pecan halves, 15	201	4
Macadamias, 12	200	4

THE BIG FIVE

Sugar is added to everything from frozen ready meals to commercial salad dressings. But most foods with added sugar are more obvious – such as biscuits, doughnuts and fizzy drinks. Here's where the majority of the added sugars in the our diets come from.

Table sugar, confectionery and preserves	29%
Cereal products (including cakes, biscuits and puddings)	23%
Soft drinks	17%
Milk and milk products	13%
Fruit and fruit products	8%

chocolates, crackers and breads. They're also the key ingredient in margarine and the oils used for frying foods in fast-food restaurants. If you can avoid these foods, you will be close to omitting all trans fats from your diet and decreasing your risk of heart disease.

Dip in the tub. If you use margarine instead of butter, buy it in a tub instead of a block. Tub margarine contains less than half the amount of trans fatty acids that solid margarine has. Better yet, look for tubs labelled 'low-fat spread with olive oil'.

Choose a better butter. If you use butter, limit saturated fat by choosing one of the newer brands that contain half the saturated fat and half the calories of regular butter. These taste great on toast, muffins

and vegetables. You can use them in baking, too, but reduce the amount of liquid in the recipe to compensate for the added water in half-fat butter. For instance, in muffins or pancakes, reduce the amount of milk or juice by about 60 ml/2 fl oz.

STEP 4: GO EASY ON ADDED SUGARS

Sweetness, one of the four basic flavours, is tasted right at the tip of your tongue. That helps to explain why both children and adults often prefer sweet-tasting foods to other basic flavours such as bitter, sour or salty. These other flavours are tasted on the sides or at the back of your tongue.

If sugar only had some valuable nutrients, eating it would not be much of a problem. Alas, sugar does not contain significant amounts of any nutrients and supplies merely empty carbohydrates to your diet. And it can really wreak havoc on your cravings for food. Here's how to tame your sugar intake so that you can reach your weight-loss goals.

Start with small steps. Take your time and go at your own pace. Whatever amount of sugar you can eliminate now is a move in a positive direction. Take a look at the list of refined carbohydrates found on page 2. Whenever you can, eat less of these foods. Howard Lee Whitehorne used to drink about 2½ litres/4 pints of sweetened cola every day. He was shocked when he learned that he was consuming

70 teaspoons of sugar each day from this beverage alone. Howard decided to eliminate just 120 ml/4 fl oz per day for 3 weeks. This one move helped him to lose just over 6 kg/1 st.

Norma Gates started each day with two slices of cinnamon raisin toast, had a mid-morning can of cola, ate dessert with lunch and supper, and snacked on biscuits, sweets or a sweetened drink before bed. Norma switched to mini bagels with bacon (pre-cooked) instead of cinnamon toast at breakfast, and in the evening she snacked on peanut butter. Norma made a few other changes and within 8 months she had lost nearly 19 kg/3 st. She has kept the weight off for 3½ years.

Try making one simple switch at a time. If you usually drink fizzy drinks, switch to water, tea, coffee or another unsweetened beverage. After a few weeks, try making another switch.

Beware of low-fat labels. Many low-fat foods contain added sugar to make up for the flavour lost when fat is taken out. Scan down to the 'sugars' line (immediately after the 'carbohydrate' line) on the nutrition information panel. Divide the grams of sugar by 4 and you will see how many teaspoons of sugar you'll get in each serving of the food. For instance, if the label says 'Sugars: 12 grams', divide 12 by 4 and you'll know that each serving contains a full 3 teaspoons of sugar. If you like to read ingredient lists instead, watch out for any of the following: sugar, brown

sugar, invert sugar, partially inverted sugar syrup, corn sweetener, corn syrup, high-fructose corn syrup, honey, fruit juice concentrate, molasses, sucrose, dextrose, fructose, maltose and lactose. Each of these simple sugars bumps up the carbohydrate content of the food.

Keep tabs on milk. To your body, the lactose in milk is a simple sugar very similar to table sugar. Of course, milk contains other important nutrients like calcium, vitamin D, niacin, riboflavin and vitamin A, so you shouldn't avoid milk altogether. But to limit milk's naturally occurring sugar, try to drink no more than 240 ml/8 fl oz of milk and eat no more than 230 g/8 oz of yoghurt a day. Choose reduced-fat dairy products whenever you can; they are not significantly higher in carbohydrates than whole-milk products but are much lower in fat. These are general guidelines. If you end up eating more dairy foods one day, try to balance your intake by eating fewer the next day. To keep up your intake of bone-strengthening calcium, eat more calcium-rich foods like dried figs, kale and calcium-fortified orange juice and soya milk. If you don't regularly eat these foods, you may want to take 500 milligrams of calcium as a daily supplement.

Eat mostly low-GI fruit. Fruit is generally good for you, but the fructose in fruit is a simple sugar, and your body metabolises this type of sugar much like table sugar. However, since it comes

HOW TO KICK A SUGAR CRAVING

If you have strong, persistent sugar cravings, take a tip from the low-carb pros. Place just a few granules of sugar on the tip of your little finger. Tap them into a tall glass of cool water. Drink all of the water. In a few minutes, the sugar craving should disappear.

packaged with a treasury of fibre and nutrients, aim to eat two or three servings of fruit a day. For weight loss, try to keep your fruit intake to no more than three servings a day. Eat low-GI fruit whenever you can. The glycaemic index is especially important with fruit because some fruits cause only a steady rise in blood sugar, while others send your blood sugar soaring. For instance, a less ripe banana raises blood sugar more gently than a ripe banana because the starch in the fruit has not yet 'ripened' or converted into sugar. Likewise, an apple has a more mild effect on blood sugar than apple juice. That's because apple juice lacks the fibre contained in the pulp and peel of the whole apple. For more low-GI fruit options, see page 9.

If you eat fruit with a high glycaemic index, remember the principle of balance. Eating a high-GI fruit with some nuts will help to balance out the overall GI of the meal. Many of the people we spoke to also found that fruit works best when eaten in the earlier part of the day. And one study supports the notion. Researchers at the University of Surrey found that our body's cells may be more receptive to the insulin rush of simple carbohydrates in the morning rather than later in the day or evening. So you may want to try eating most of your carbs in the morning, especially fruit. Focus on fresh or frozen unsweetened fruit rather than tinned fruit packed in syrup.

Avoid artificial sweeteners. Many of the people we spoke to had a love-hate relationship with artificial sweeteners. They liked the fact that they could get the sweetness of real sugar, without the calories or carbohydrates, but they said that eating artificial sweeteners did not reduce their cravings for sweet foods and often made them crave sweets even more. If you use artificial sweeteners, try to use less whenever you can and gradually reduce the amount you use. Try Splenda; this is the brand name for sucralose, an alternative sweetener that is made from cane sugar but has no carbohydrates. See page 57 for more information on using alternative sweeteners.

STEP 5: EAT REASONABLE PORTION SIZES

When it comes to food, size does matter. The difference between a standard 90 g/ 3 oz serving of pasta and the amount you

7 steps to smart weight loss

actually put on your plate could turn a good-for-you meal into a fattening one. Jeanne Bennett took a hard look at her diet and found that her portion sizes were out of control. She had gone through her twenties eating whatever she wanted without gaining weight. Then, as happens with many people, Jeanne hit her thirties, had two children, and started gaining weight. 'I soon realised that I had been eating way too much food (about 2,500 calories a day) and far too many foods high in white sugar, white flour and other refined carbohydrates.' Jeanne started eating sensible portions, cut back on sugar and flour, and lost 20 kg/3 st 2 lb.

If you need to, at least early on in your weight-loss plan, measure out your food a few times to get used to how a standard serving size looks on the plate. See page 38 for a list of standard serving sizes. Or use the following visual cues:

- 230 g/8 oz = closed fist
- 115 g/4 oz = tennis ball
- 2 tablespoons = ping-pong ball
- 1 teaspoon = top of thumb (from tip to joint)
- 90 g/3 oz of cooked meat, poultry, or fish = pack of cards
- 30 g/1 oz of cheese = top of thumb (from tip to joint)

Once you get used to dishing out standard serving sizes, you'll be able to do without the scales.

STEP 6: IDENTIFY YOUR TRIGGER FOODS

Some of the foods you eat may be secretly sabotaging your weight-loss efforts. Ask yourself if there are any foods that you feel you can't possibly live without. If you answer yes, make a list of those foods. There is a strong possibility that these are your 'trigger' or 'addictive' foods. They may actually be preventing you from reaching your weight-loss goals. According to experts, when people eat a trigger food, their bodies produce more endorphins. These are the same feel-good brain chemicals released when you have sex or a massage, experience runner's high or enjoy a good belly laugh. The problem may be that people need to eat more and more of their trigger foods to raise their endorphins to the same level. As a result, people feel like they can never get enough of certain foods and they overeat, leading to weight gain.

Look at what you eat. To identify your trigger foods, write down everything you eat and drink for a few days. Or take a look back at what you've eaten over the past few days and jot down those foods. Then, tick off your favourite foods on the list. There's a good chance that your trigger foods are lurking among your favourite foods. To narrow down potential trigger foods, group together the foods that belong to a particular food category such as sugary foods (fizzy drinks, biscuits, cakes and ice cream), refined starchy foods (bagels, white bread, white rice and white pasta), and snack foods (crisps, tortilla chips and pretzels). Bear in mind that the foods that you eat every day or numerous times daily are most suspect. For many people, refined carbohydrates like sugar and wheat products turn out to be their trigger foods because they are so prevalent in our diets. This is another reason why it's so important to eat a wide variety of foods and avoid eating the same food every day.

Once you identify your potential trigger foods, answer the following questions about them:

- Have I ever eaten this food in place of a meal?
- Do I eat this food even when I'm not really hungry?
- Do I get physiological cravings for this food?
- Is this a comfort food?
- Have I ever tried to give up this food before?
- If so, did I begin eating this food again?

If you answered 'yes' to these questions, particularly the last two, then you have found your trigger foods. These foods may be responsible for sabotaging your past attempts at losing weight. To be successful at losing weight, these foods should be carefully managed in your overall diet. You may not need to totally eliminate pasta, ice cream, lager, or whatever your 'addictive'

foods might be. But minimising or completely avoiding these foods for at least 3 weeks may really facilitate your weight-loss progress. If you feel very addicted to a particular food, such as sugar, you may need to avoid it for up to 3 months before trying to re-introduce it back into your diet.

Wean yourself away. Start by eating less of your trigger foods. If you love biscuits, set out just one or two instead of your usual portion. Then put the biscuits away to avoid being tempted to eat more. As you eat the biscuits in front of you, savour every bite so that you really enjoy the experience. If you're someone with good self-control, you may find that you can enjoy your trigger foods now and then in moderate portions.

Or go cold turkey. Some people told us it was easier to avoid their trigger foods completely. Joan Lawson swore off her trigger foods and lost 36 kg/5 st 10 lb in 18 months. She has kept the weight off for 6 years. If you think you won't be able to resist overeating your trigger foods, remove them from your house, desk, car, handbag or anywhere else they may be stashed. If the food isn't there, you'll be less tempted to eat it. When making a shopping list, avoid writing down any of your trigger foods. Keeping them out of sight is a giant first step towards avoiding them entirely.

Plan ahead for tempting situations. Some advance planning can help you avoid the most common times when people get into trouble with 'addictive' foods.

DRINK MORE WATER

It's extremely important to drink plenty of water every day. The smart low-carb approach to weight loss includes lots of fibre-rich foods like whole grains, vegetables and fruit. Water helps the fibre in these foods to do its cholesterol-reducing work, which ultimately helps to reduce your heart disease risk. Water also helps to flush out waste products that come from eating protein. And it can prevent fatigue. In fact, dehydration-related fatigue is the underlying cause of food cravings for many people trying to lose weight. The next time you feel hungry, reach for a drink of water instead of food. It may keep you focused so you eat less.

Aim to drink about ½ fl oz/15 ml of water per pound of body weight every day. For example, if you weigh 150 lb (10 st 10 lb), you should drink 75 fl oz (3¾ pints)/2¼ litres a day. Here's the maths: 0.5 fl oz × 150 lb = 75 fl oz, or about 9 cups (8 fl oz per cup). Pure water is best. But green tea, plain or flavoured soda water, or flavoured sparkling water without artificial sweeteners will do at a pinch.

- For many people, the first 15 minutes after getting home from work is an especially vulnerable time. If you usually come home hungry, plan to eat a healthy snack or appetiser as soon you walk in the door. This snack will take the edge off your hunger and may help prevent you from overeating at dinner, too. Stock fruit, nuts or other non-trigger foods especially for this snack time. See the recipes beginning on page 105 for other ideas.
- If you work at home, bear in mind that most people get hungry between 3 and 6 pm. It's wise to eat a healthy snack during these vulnerable hours.
- Plan ahead when eating out, going to parties, or attending other social events that involve food. Alcohol, fizzy drinks, bread, sweets and other common trigger foods are bound to be offered there. Before you head out, eat a handful of nuts, a piece of fruit or another non-trigger food, or take these foods with you.
- Whenever you eat, try not to do anything else at the same time. Avoid eating while watching TV, reading, talking on the phone or even standing up. These other activities distract you from what and how much you're eating. Instead, take the time to sit down and really enjoy your food.

Stay focused on your weight-loss goals. Avoiding your trigger foods takes commitment and time – and yes, you may feel a little crabby at first. Just bear in mind that breaking your 'addiction' to these foods can help your weight-loss

(continued on page 36)

I D★id It!

Alice Cooper

Alice was overweight and overcome with lightheadedness. Avoiding her trigger foods resolved her lightheadedness and helped her to lose 13 kg/2 st.

before

'It wasn't until I visited my doctor for help with another problem that the answer to my dieting failures became clear. I had been feeling lightheaded, so I visited the doctor to find out why.

'In the doctor's surgery, I tipped the scales at 86 kg/ 13½ st. My doctor's comment, 'You were supposed to *lose* weight,' only added to my frustration.

'It's not like I wasn't trying. For months, I went through one diet plan after another with absolutely no success. Why did these plans work for everyone else but not for me?

'To help explain the lightheadedness, my doctor and I agreed that I should have some tests done. While waiting for the

Weight lost: 13 kg/2 st
Time kept off: 4 years
Weight-loss strategies: avoided trigger foods, especially sugar and other refined carbohydrates

Weight-maintenance strategies: avoids trigger foods, eats protein with each meal, eats more vegetables, walks and rides an exercise bicycle three times a week

results, I decided to stop eating foods that I suspected were contributing to my light-headedness. I avoided eating any sugar, flour, wheat, white rice, potatoes and anything made from these foods. Amazingly, within a week, I was no longer lightheaded. My health problem was resolved. But the best news: I was lighter! Finally, I had begun to lose weight just by avoiding my "trigger foods".

'I must admit, avoiding these foods was not easy at first. It took me a while to get into the habit of reading food labels while shopping. At times, it felt like there was nothing I could eat. But I had hope because I was losing weight. For the first time in my life, I felt I understood which foods caused me to gain weight. I was optimistic that I would be able to maintain the weight loss this time. Within a few months, my new eating habits became a way of life. I had more energy and I even started exercising more. My only frustration was that I couldn't convince others to change their diets. It makes me wonder if certain foods are addictive like cigarettes.

'I have been following my new eating plan for 4 years. My weight has come down from 86 kg/13½ st to 75 kg/11½ st. I fit comfortably into a size 14 and my desire for foods has changed. I don't have nearly as many cravings. "Happy" does not describe how I feel these days. I can't find a word in the English language to describe my feelings. I only wish I could box up this remedy and give it to everyone I know.'

efforts tremendously. Plus, many people have told us that once their trigger foods were gone, they didn't miss them at all. 'My desire for foods has changed,' says Alice Cooper, who avoided her trigger foods, lost 13 kg/2 st, and has kept it off for 4 years. 'I don't have nearly as many food cravings. For the first time in my life, I feel like I understand which foods cause me to gain weight.'

Manage your trigger foods. Once you have broken the 'addictive' behaviour, you may be able to eat your trigger foods in moderation. These occasional indulgences may actually help you to be more successful at losing weight and keeping it off in the long run. Experiment with eating your trigger foods now and then to see what works for you. If you fall back into old eating habits, avoid your trigger foods completely.

STEP 7: KEEP MOVING!

Every day, scientists discover more and more about the health benefits of physical activity. It burns calories, improves your cardiovascular health and tones up your muscles. Strong muscles are particularly important for weight loss because strong muscles help you burn calories, which helps you lose more weight – and keep it off. It doesn't take much exercise to start seeing health benefits. Just 2 hours of walking per week can reduce your risk of heart disease by more than 50 per cent.

Smart-Carb Insider Tip
MAKE PLANNED-OVERS

Always pretend you have at least one extra guest for dinner and make extra 'planned-overs'. Store the additional servings of the main course so that they're ready to grab on the way out of the door the next morning. Some leftover dinners, such as quiche, may even become the next morning's breakfast. Invest in some single-serving storage containers and an insulated lunch bag to make lunchtime easy. This habit saves loads of preparation time, sidesteps difficult choices and provides healthy foods that are ready when you are.

Physical activity often makes people feel more motivated to make wise food choices, too. The key to sticking with it is to make exercise fun. It shouldn't be a chore.

Start slowly. If you are a true couch potato, there's no need to get outside right now and start running. Begin with a walk around the block. Then work up to walking this distance a few times a week. Then maybe increase the distance and jog it instead of walking. You get the idea.

Take every opportunity. Even small bursts of activity can add up to a big health payoff. Use the stairs more often. Grab a basket at the supermarket instead of a trolley. Visit your colleagues instead of sending e-mails. Park your car slightly farther away from your destination and walk the rest of the way. Or do more household chores instead of delegating them. An 86-kg/13½-st person can burn over 150 calories in 20 minutes just by mowing grass. In fact, three 20-minute periods of exercise burn the same number of calories as one continuous 1-hour workout.

Do what you like. For more sustained periods of exercise, choose activities that are fun so you'll actually look forward to them. Do you like dancing, skating, swimming, playing tennis or volleyball, riding a bike? Almost any activity that makes you breathe heavily or that works your muscles will help you to lose weight.

Switch it up. When you can, do activities that afford different kinds of exercise. Strength-training or weight-bearing exercise such as lifting weights helps prevent osteoporosis and age-related injuries. Aerobic activities support the cardiovascular system. Getting a mix of both types of activity gives you the most benefits for weight loss and long-term health.

Stick with it. Try to plan some type of activity every day. It doesn't matter whether you go for a walk, do some gardening, mow the grass, play tennis, take a bike ride, scrub the kitchen floor or go to the gym. Just keep moving! Twenty to 30 minutes of activity a day may spell the difference between weight-loss success and failure. If your schedule is tight, pencil in your exercise time so you won't skip it.

HELP! I'M NOT LOSING WEIGHT!

If you follow the general recommendations in the seven steps above, you should notice significant weight loss. Exactly how much weight loss depends upon how *closely* you follow each step as well as your particular genetic makeup and lifestyle.

Perhaps you'll lose a few pounds, but want to lose even more. If that's the case, you may need to lower your total carbohydrate intake, possibly by eating even fewer whole grains if necessary. Or you may need to reduce your portion sizes of proteins and fats. Remember that calories do count.

Take stock. Look again at the sources of carbohydrates in your diet. You may need to reduce the amount of each carbohydrate-rich food that you eat, especially breads, cereals, flours, grains and added sugars. Instead of these carb-rich foods, eat more lean protein foods. For example, if you miss out one serving of cereal, two slices of bread and a potato in your daily diet, you will drop your carbohydrates by at least 60 g/2 oz and cut about 320 calories – every day. Instead of these foods, eat an extra 60–90 g/2–3 oz of lean protein such as cooked skinless poultry, fish or lean meat, and for a snack, 2 tablespoons of peanut butter stuffed into some celery stalks. Extra servings of lower-carbohydrate vegetables such as broccoli and courgettes can also fill in any gaps. For a snapshot of what this smart low-carb approach looks

WHAT'S A SERVING?

Most of us have become accustomed to eating more than we should. The average takeaway bagel is at least twice as big as it should be. Even the average supermarket potato is bigger than what experts recommend. Here's a guide to smart low-carb serving sizes. Use these to keep track of how much you're eating.

Vegetable: 75 g/2½ oz raw, chopped, or cooked; 180 ml/6 fl oz vegetable juice; 90 g/3 oz raw, leafy greens

Starch: 1 slice wholemeal bread; ½ wholewheat bagel or muffin; 60 g/2 oz cooked wholegrain cereal, pasta, brown rice or other whole grain; 90 g/3 oz cooked beans, sweetcorn, potatoes, rice or sweet potatoes

Nuts: 30 g/1 oz nuts without shell; 30 g/1 oz unsweetened peanut butter

Protein: 30 g/1 oz cooked lean beef, pork, lamb, skinless poultry, fish or shellfish; 30 g/1 oz hard cheese (preferably reduced-fat); 1 egg

Fat, unsaturated: 1 teaspoon ghee (clarified butter); 1 teaspoon oil (such as olive, rapeseed, walnut or flaxseed oil); 1 teaspoon regular mayonnaise; 1 tablespoon low-fat mayonnaise; 1 tablespoon oil-and-vinegar dressing; 5 large olives; ⅛ medium avocado

Fat, saturated: 1 teaspoon butter; 1 slice bacon; 1 tablespoon double cream; 2 tablespoons soured cream; 1 tablespoon cream cheese; 2 tablespoons shredded unsweetened coconut

Fruit: 1 small to medium piece; 145 g/5 oz whole strawberries or melon cubes; 115 g/4 oz tinned or cut fruit; 180 ml/6 fl oz fruit juice; 40 g/1¼ oz dried fruit

Milk: 240 ml/8 fl oz skimmed milk; 230 g/8 oz fat-free or low-fat unsweetened yoghurt; 115 g/4 oz low-fat ricotta cheese or cottage cheese; 180 ml/6 fl oz unsweetened soya milk

like, see the 'Smart Low-Carb Food Pyramid' on page 42.

Be patient. How true the often-used saying is: you didn't gain it overnight, so don't expect to lose it that quickly. Losing ½ to 1 kg/1 to 2 lb a week is safe, effective and significant weight loss. If you are losing that much, hang on in there. In just 2 months, you could be around 7 kg/ 16 lb slimmer! Remember that truly successful weight loss is measured not by how many pounds you lose, but by how long you keep the weight off and how healthy you are. If you've lost 4.5 kg/10 lb so far, just keeping that weight from coming back is a big accomplishment. You will most likely have increased energy and reduced risk of cardiovascular disease, diabetes, cancer, gallstones and other conditions. So relax. Enjoy eating well and feeling great. Your body will find the weight that is most healthy for you.

PICK YOUR OWN WEIGHT-LOSS PLAN

Some people do better with detailed plans than with general recommendations. If that's you, pick one of the six detailed plans on page 40. Each one shows you what to eat – and how much – each day. The plans include a careful balance of foods containing carbohydrates, proteins and fats. Follow one of these plans, and you should automatically lose weight and keep your carbohydrate and calorie intake at a healthy level. Whichever plan you choose, keep in mind the seven general recommendations discussed earlier.

Determine your current calorie intake. Each of the plans on page 40 is based on choosing the daily calorie and carbohydrate intake levels that are right for you. If you have no idea of your current calorie intake, here's an easy way to find it. Step one is to decide how active you are. **Sedentary** means that you have a job or lifestyle that involves mostly sitting, standing or light walking. You exercise once a week or less. **Active** means that your job or lifestyle requires more activity than light walking

(such as full-time housecleaning or construction work), or you get 45 to 60 minutes of aerobic exercise 3 times a week. **Very active** means that you get aerobic exercise for at least 45 to 60 minutes 4 or more times a week.

Choose the description that best fits your current lifestyle, then find your activity factor from the table below.

IF YOU ARE A . . .	YOUR ACTIVITY FACTOR IS . . .
Sedentary woman	12
Sedentary man	14
Active woman	15
Active man	17
Very active woman	18
Very active man	20

Multiply your activity factor by your current weight in pounds. The resulting number is the approximate number of calories you currently need to maintain your weight. The maths looks like this:

activity factor $\times$ weight in pounds = current calorie needs

Here's an example for an active woman who weighs 77 kg/12 st 2 lb (170 lb): $15 \times 170 = 2,550$ calories a day.

Pick a new calorie level. Rather than choosing a goal weight, simply reduce your current calorie intake by 500 to 1,000 calories a day. This will lead to safe, effective weight loss of ½ to 1 kg/1 to 2 lb per week. For instance, if you currently take in 2,300 to 2,500 calories a day, try reducing

SIX WEIGHT-LOSS PLANS FOR EVERY NEED

Here are six smart low-carb weight-loss plans to fit your needs – even if those needs change along the way. Simply choose the calorie and carbohydrate levels that are right for you, then eat from the food groups listed below. To choose your calorie and carbohydrate levels, see pages 39 and 41. Most people will start to lose weight following one of the 180-gram plans.

180 grams

CALORIES	1,500–1,800			1,800–2,200			2,200–2,500		
Food Group	Serv	Cal	Carb (g)	Serv	Cal	Carb (g)	Serv	Cal	Carb (g)
Protein	8	440	0	11	665	0	13	815	0
Fat	5	225	0	6	270	0	8	360	0
Nuts	0.5	100	2	1	200	4	1.5	300	6
Veggies	5	125	25	6	150	30	5	125	25
Starch	6	480	90	6	480	90	6	480	90
Fruit	3	180	45	3	180	45	3	180	45
Milk	1	90	12	1	90	12	1	90	12
Totals		**1,640**	**174**		**2,035**	**181**		**2,350**	**178**

125 grams

CALORIES	1,500–1,800			1,800–2,200			2,200–2,500		
Food Group	Serv	Cal	Carb (g)	Serv	Cal	Carb (g)	Serv	Cal	Carb (g)
Protein	9	495	0	14	890	0	17	1,075	0
Fat	6	270	0	8	360	0	10	450	0
Nuts	1	200	4	1	200	4	1	200	4
Veggies	5	125	25	5	125	25	5	125	25
Starch	4	320	60	4	320	60	4	320	60
Fruit	2	120	30	2	120	30	2	120	30
Milk	0.5	45	6	0.5	45	6	0.5	45	6
Totals		**1,575**	**125**		**2,060**	**125**		**2,335**	**125**

your daily intake to 1,800 to 2,000 calories. This will be your new daily calorie level. (Remember that as you lose weight or increase physical activity, you will need to recalculate your activity factor and daily calorie needs.)

Determine your current carbohydrate intake. Carbohydrates in the average diet supply 50 to 60 per cent of total calories. If you calculated your current calorie intake with the formula on page 39, check the table below to find out the approximate grams of carbohydrates in your diet. You might be surprised by how many grams of carbohydrate you actually eat now. This table is based upon 55 per cent of the calories from carbohydrate – the average percentage consumed by most people. If your diet is more heavily weighted in carbohydrates, the figures may be on the low side.

DAILY CALORIES	CARBS (G)
1,800	248
2,000	275
2,400	330
2,800	385
3,000	413
3,500	481
4,000	550

Choose a new carbohydrate level. Most people who now consume a high-carbohydrate, low-fat diet (the standard weight-loss diet) will likely lose weight by cutting back on carbohydrates and

replacing them with protein and fats. That means following the seven general recommendations discussed earlier or keeping your carbohydrate intake to about 180 grams a day. Some people may need to reduce carbohydrates further to approximately 125 grams a day. Both plans – 180 and 125 grams of carbohydrate a day – appear on the opposite page. As with any dietary change, if you are pregnant or breastfeeding, or if you have a kidney problem, check with your doctor before starting any of these plans.

Try the 180-gram plan first. To get started straight away, try the 180-gram plan for about a week. If you don't notice a change in your weight, stick with the same plan for another week, but reduce your protein and fat servings. If you still don't see a change, move down to the 125-gram plan. Bear in mind that losing ½ to 1 kg/1 to 2 lb per week is great progress.

Eat from all the food groups. Once you pick the calorie and carbohydrate levels that are right for you, simply eat the daily number of servings of food listed under that plan. For example, if you follow the 180-gram plan at 1,800 to 2,200 calories, you should eat 11 servings of protein foods, 6 servings of fats, 1 serving of nuts, 6 servings of starches, 3 servings of fruit and 1 serving of milk-based foods.

Keep saturated fat to a minimum. Notice that on each plan, as the servings of carbohydrate foods (such as starch, fruit,

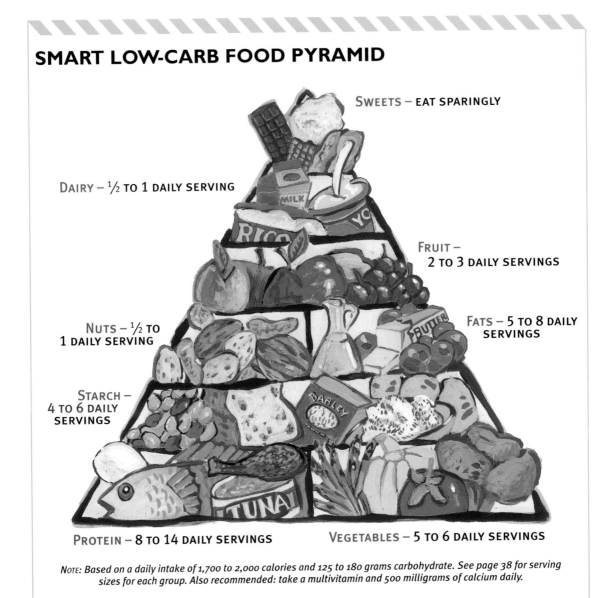

SMART LOW-CARB FOOD PYRAMID

SWEETS – EAT SPARINGLY

DAIRY – ½ TO 1 DAILY SERVING

FRUIT – 2 TO 3 DAILY SERVINGS

NUTS – ½ TO 1 DAILY SERVING

FATS – 5 TO 8 DAILY SERVINGS

STARCH – 4 TO 6 DAILY SERVINGS

PROTEIN – 8 TO 14 DAILY SERVINGS

VEGETABLES – 5 TO 6 DAILY SERVINGS

NOTE: *Based on a daily intake of 1,700 to 2,000 calories and 125 to 180 grams carbohydrate. See page 38 for serving sizes for each group. Also recommended: take a multivitamin and 500 milligrams of calcium daily.*

and milk) go down, the servings of protein foods and fat foods go up. Be sure to choose the healthiest protein and fat foods you can find. For protein, that means fish, eggs, poultry and occasionally lean cuts of beef, pork and lamb. For fats, focus on mono- and polyunsaturated fats such as olive oil, rapeseed oil, nut oils and avocados, instead of butter and bacon. These healthier choices will help minimise your intake of saturated fat, thereby helping to prevent heart disease. Try to eat no more than two servings of saturated fat a day. Less is even better. To see what counts as a serving, turn to page 38.

Keep in mind the carb content of the food groups. Fats and protein foods have no carbohydrate, but the other food groups contain varying amounts of carbohydrate. Generally, one serving of vegetables contains 5 grams; one serving of milk contains 12 grams; and one serving of starch or fruit contains 15 grams of carbs. Because these food groups all contain carbohydrate, you can make substitutions here and there.

Substitute other foods if you need to. If there are certain foods unavailable to you on a particular day, or if you don't fancy eating them, you can substitute foods from other food groups. See the suggested substitutions below. The numbers of carbohydrate grams are roughly equivalent.

FOOD GROUP	SUGGESTED SUBSTITUTION
Starch, 1 serving	Milk, ½ serving + Fruit, ½ serving
Milk, 1 serving	Starch, 1 serving
Fruit, ½ serving	Milk, ½ serving + Vegetable, 1 serving
Nuts, 1 serving	Vegetable, 1 serving + Fat, 2 servings
Vegetable, 1 serving	Fruit, ½ serving

Treat yourself. Once you start eating the smart low-carb way and enjoying the delicious recipes in this book, chances are that you won't miss some of the foods you once considered special treats. The rich-tasting Chocolate Hazelnut Flourless Cake on page 338 would satisfy almost anyone's food cravings. However, if there are favourite foods that you know you miss – don't go without them for too long. Treat yourself to that special food or meal once a week. Maybe you like a certain ethnic dish that you know is loaded with carbohydrates; perhaps you look forward to a doughnut or ice cream. Go ahead. Enjoy it guilt-free. Then get right back on track at the very next meal. The key is not to deny yourself for too long. If you really have a yen for something high in carbohydrates, eat it. Try to keep the portion small; take your time consuming it and avoid doing anything else at the same time you are eating this favourite food. Before you start eating it, remind yourself of your weight-loss goals. Then dig in and fully savour the food. Stop eating as soon as you are satisfied. You may be surprised to find that a few mouthfuls of your favourite food are sufficient to overcome your urge.

7 DAYS TO A SLIMMER YOU

Here's where you can see what smart low-carb eating really looks like. We took the best recipes from the book (and a few other common foods) and organised them into a variety of great-tasting, balanced meals. Each daily menu includes three main meals and two snacks. Just one look and you'll see that losing weight does not mean depriving yourself.

Each of these menus contains approximately 125 grams of carbohydrate per day (the 125-gram plan outlined on page 40). To choose the calorie level that's right for you, see page 39.

Drinks aren't included here. They're up to you. Remember that water, black tea or coffee, and herbal tea are all calorie-free and carbohydrate-free.

These meals offer a great starting place for weight loss. Adjust the foods to fit your personal likes and dislikes. And once you start eating the smart low-carb way, experiment by creating your own delicious menus.

Day 1

Menu	CALORIE LEVELS		
	1,500–1,800	**1,800–2,200**	**2,200–2,500**
BREAKFAST			
Fried Eggs with Vinegar (page 85)	1 serving	1 serving	1 serving
Skimmed milk	120 ml/4 fl oz	120 ml/4 fl oz	120 ml/4 fl oz
Apple juice	120 ml/4 fl oz	120 ml/4 fl oz	120 ml/4 fl oz
Wholemeal bread	1 slice	1 slice	1 slice
Butter	1 tsp	1 tsp	2 tsp
SNACK			
Nectarine or pear	1	1	1
Cottage cheese	—	—	115 g/4 oz
LUNCH			
Grilled boneless, skinless chicken breast	115 g/4 oz	145 g/5 oz	170 g/6 oz
brushed with Italian dressing	1 tsp	1 tbsp	1 tbsp
Red leaf lettuce	90 g/3 oz	90 g/3 oz	90 g/3 oz
Carrots, grated	45 g/1½ oz	45 g/1½ oz	45 g/1½ oz
Cucumber, sliced	75 g/2½ oz	75 g/2½ oz	75 g/2½ oz
Italian dressing	2 tsp	2 tbsp	2 tbsp
SNACK			
Walnuts	30 g/1 oz	30 g/1 oz	30 g/1 oz
DINNER			
Topside of Beef Marinated in	115 g/4 oz	145 g/5 oz	170 g/6 oz
Soy Sauce with Mustard (page 205)			
Spanish-Style French Beans (page 322)	1 serving	1 serving	1 serving
Couscous	90 g/3 oz	90 g/3 oz	90 g/3 oz
SNACK			
Orange-Walnut Biscotti (page 333)	2	2	2
TOTAL CALORIES (APPROX)	**1,660**	**1,900**	**2,260**
TOTAL CARBS (G)	**125**	**125**	**125**

Day 2

MENU	CALORIE LEVELS		
	1,500–1,800	**1,800–2,200**	**2,200–2,500**
BREAKFAST			
Cherry Porridge (page 104)	1 serving	1 serving	1 serving
Skimmed milk	120 ml/4 fl oz	120 ml/4 fl oz	120 ml/4 fl oz
Turkey sausage	30 g/1 oz	30 g/1 oz	30 g/1 oz
SNACK			
Apple	1	1	1
LUNCH			
Tuna	90 g/3 oz	115 g/4 oz	145 g/5 oz
Celery, chopped	30 g/1 oz	30 g/1 oz	30 g/1 oz
Onion, chopped	30 g/1 oz	30 g/1 oz	30 g/1 oz
Mayonnaise, reduced-fat	2 tbsp	30 g/1 oz	30 g/1 oz
Green olives	10 small	10 small	10 small
Green leaf lettuce, torn	60 g/2 oz	60 g/2 oz	60 g/2 oz
Sourdough bread	1 slice	1 slice	1 slice
SNACK			
Pecans	30 g/1 oz	30 g/1 oz	45 g/1½ oz
DINNER			
Pork Chops Baked with Cabbage and Cream (page 286)	1 serving	1 serving	1½ servings
Steamed butternut squash or marrow	60 g/2 oz	60 g/2 oz	60 g/2 oz
SNACK			
Pumpernickel bread	1 slice	1 slice	½ slice
Edam cheese, reduced-fat	30 g/1 oz	60 g/2 oz	60 g/2 oz
Butter	1 tsp	2 tsp	2 tsp
TOTAL CALORIES (APPROX)	**1,690**	**1,980**	**2,260**
TOTAL CARBS (G)	**126**	**126**	**126**

Day 3

MENU	CALORIE LEVELS		
	1,500–1,800	**1,800–2,200**	**2,200–2,500**
BREAKFAST			
Scrambled egg	1	2	2
Orange juice	120 ml/4 fl oz	120 ml/4 fl oz	120 ml/4 fl oz
Rye toast	1 slice	1 slice	1 slice
Butter	1 tsp	2 tsp	2 tsp
Skimmed milk	120 ml/4 fl oz	120 ml/4 fl oz	120 ml/4 fl oz
SNACK			
Kiwifruit	1	1	1
LUNCH			
Salad of lentils, cooked	90 g/3 oz	90 g/3 oz	90 g/3 oz
Turkey breast, cooked and cubed	90 g/3 oz	115 g/4 oz	145 g/5 oz
Carrots, sliced	90 g/3 oz	90 g/3 oz	90 g/3 oz
Peppers, chopped	60 g/2 oz	60 g/2 oz	60 g/2 oz
Peas, cooked	45 g/1½ oz	45 g/1½ oz	90 g/3 oz
Olive oil	2 tsp	1 tbsp	4 tsp
Cheddar cheese	15 g/½ oz	15 g/½ oz	30 g/1 oz
SNACK			
Brazil nuts	30 g/1 oz	30 g/1 oz	30 g/1 oz
DINNER			
Stir-Fried Chicken and Broccoli (page 264)	1 serving (chicken) 115 g/4 oz	1 serving 145 g/5 oz	1 serving 200 g/7 oz
SNACK			
Pecan Muffins (page 99)	1	1	1
Butter	1 tsp	2 tsp	2 tsp
TOTAL CALORIES	**1,590**	**1,960**	**2,240**
TOTAL CARBS (G)	**122**	**122**	**122**

Day 4

MENU

MENU	CALORIE LEVELS		
	1,500–1,800	1,800–2,200	2,200–2,500
BREAKFAST			
Pecan Muffins (page 99)	1	1	1
Cottage cheese	2 tbsp	6 tbsp	6 tbsp
Peach	1	1	1
Skimmed milk	120 ml/4 fl oz	120 ml/4 fl oz	120 ml/4 fl oz
SNACK			
Grapefruit	½	½	½
LUNCH			
Sandwich of rice cakes topped with (15 g/½ oz carbohydrate per rice cake)	2	2	2
Sardines, boneless, skinless	115 g/4 oz	145 g/5 oz	170 g/6 oz
Cream cheese	2 tbsp	2 tbsp	3 tbsp
Tomato	2 slices	2 slices	2 slices
Courgette, sticks	60 g/2 oz	60 g/2 oz	60 g/2 oz
SNACK			
Almonds	30 g/1 oz	30 g/1 oz	30 g/1 oz
DINNER			
Lamb chop, baked with	115 g/4 oz	145 g/5 oz	200 g/7 oz
garlic powder	⅛ tsp	⅛ tsp	¼ tsp
Mint leaves, chopped	2 tsp	1 tbsp	1 tbsp
Barley, cooked	100 g/3½ oz	100 g/3½ oz	100 g/3½ oz
Stewed tomatoes	170 g/6 oz	170 g/6 oz	170 g/6 oz
French beans, sautéed in	100 g/3½ oz	100 g/3½ oz	100 g/3½ oz
olive oil	2 tsp	3 tsp	4 tsp
SNACK			
Wholemeal bread	1 slice	1 slice	1 slice
Butter	1 tsp	2 tsp	2 tsp
Chicken, sliced	30 g/1 oz	60 g/2 oz	60 g/2 oz
TOTAL CALORIES (APPROX)	**1,700**	**1,950**	**2,210**
TOTAL CARBS (G)	**122**	**122**	**122**

Day 5

MENU	CALORIE LEVELS		
	1,500–1,800	1,800–2,200	2,200–2,500
BREAKFAST			
Sweet potato, cooked and topped	90 g/3 oz	90 g/3 oz	90 g/3 oz
with walnut oil	½ tsp	1 tsp	1 tsp
Walnuts, chopped	30 g/1 oz	30 g/1 oz	30 g/1 oz
Coconut, shredded	1 tbsp	2 tbsp	2 tbsp
Pineapple, crushed	60 g/2 oz	60 g/2 oz	60 g/2 oz
Chicken breast, cooked	—	60 g/2 oz	90 g/3 oz
Skimmed milk	120 ml/4 fl oz	120 ml/4 fl oz	120 ml/4 fl oz
SNACK			
Pear	½	½	½
LUNCH			
Salad of spinach	115 g/4 oz	115 g/4 oz	115 g/4 oz
Chickpeas	90 g/3 oz	90 g/3 oz	90 g/3 oz
Egg, hard-boiled	1	2	2
Ham, boiled, lean	—	—	60 g/2 oz
Artichoke hearts	75 g/2½ oz	75 g/2½ oz	75 g/2½ oz
Olive oil	2 tsp	3 tsp	5 tsp
Lemon juice	1 tbsp	1 tbsp	1½ tbsp
Wholewheat pitta bread	½	½	½
SNACK			
Double Gloucester cheese	60 g/2 oz	60 g/2 oz	60 g/2 oz
DINNER			
Breaded Baked Cod with Tartar Sauce (page 234)	1 serving	1 serving	1½ servings
Red cabbage, sautéed in	45 g/1½ oz	45 g/1½ oz	45 g/1½ oz
sesame oil	1 tsp	1 tsp	1 tsp
Courgette, steamed	75 g/2½ oz	75 g/2½ oz	75 g/2½ oz
Butter	1 tsp	1 tsp	1 tsp
Cantaloupe Sorbet (page 349)	1 serving	1 serving	1 serving
SNACK			
Popcorn, air-popped	60 g/2 oz	60 g/2 oz	30 g/1 oz
Butter	1 tsp	2 tsp	2 tsp
Double Gloucester cheese	60 g/2 oz	60 g/2 oz	60 g/2 oz
TOTAL CALORIES (APPROX)	**1,680**	**2,000**	**2,330**
TOTAL CARBS (G)	**120**	**120**	**120**

Day 6

MENU	CALORIE LEVELS		
	1,500–1,800	**1,800–2,200**	**2,200–2,500**
BREAKFAST			
Cottage cheese	60 g/2 oz	115 g/4 oz	170 g/6 oz
Blueberries	115 g/4 oz	115 g/4 oz	115 g/4 oz
Cinnamon	Pinch	Pinch	Pinch
Bacon, organic, nitrate-free, cooked	1 rasher	2 rashers	2 rashers
SNACK			
Grapes, red	15 small	15 small	15 small
LUNCH			
Hamburger, lean	115 g/4 oz	145 g/5 oz	170 g/6 oz
Hamburger bun, wholemeal	½	½	½
Leaf lettuce	1 leaf	1 leaf	1 leaf
Tomato	1 slice	1 slice	1 slice
Onion, sliced	1 slice	1 slice	1 slice
Mustard	1 tsp	1 tsp	1 tsp
Mayonnaise	2 tsp	3 tsp	3 tsp
Chips	10 small	10 small	10 small
Olives, green	—	5 small	10 small
SNACK			
Hazelnuts	30 g/1 oz	30 g/1 oz	30 g/1 oz
Cheddar, reduced-fat	—	45 g/1½ oz	45 g/1½ oz
DINNER			
Mushroom and Kasha Soup (page 136)	1 serving	1 serving	1 serving
Turkey breast, cooked	115 g/4 oz	145 g/5 oz	200 g/7 oz
Carrots, baby, cooked	60 g/2 oz	60 g/2 oz	60 g/2 oz
Peas, cooked	45 g/1½ oz	45 g/1½ oz	45 g/1½ oz
Olive oil	1 tsp	2 tsp	2 tsp
SNACK			
Peanut Butter Cookies (page 330)	1 cookie	1 cookie	1 cookie
Skimmed milk	120 ml/4 fl oz	120 ml/4 fl oz	120 ml/4 fl oz
TOTAL CALORIES (APPROX)	**1,570**	**1,890**	**2,230**
TOTAL CARBS (G)	**125**	**125**	**125**

Day 7

MENU	CALORIE LEVELS		
	1,500–1,800	**1,800–2,200**	**2,200–2,500**
BREAKFAST			
Bran cereal, flaked	20 g/³/₄ oz	20 g/³/₄ oz	20 g/³/₄ oz
Skimmed milk	120 ml/4 fl oz	120 ml/4 fl oz	120 ml/4 fl oz
Banana	½	½	½
Cottage cheese	115 g/4 oz	115 g/4 oz	115 g/4 oz
SNACK			
Cherries, large	10	10	10
Protein bar (16 g protein, 2 g carb)	—	³/₄ bar	³/₄ bar
LUNCH			
Sausage, Egg and Vegetable Casserole (page 284)	1 serving	1 serving	2 servings
Spinach, steamed	115 g/4 oz	115 g/4 oz	115 g/4 oz
Wholemeal bread	1 slice	1 slice	1 slice
SNACK			
Almonds	30 g/1 oz	30 g/1 oz	30 g/1 oz
Edam cheese, reduced-fat	—	60 g/2 oz	60 g/2 oz
DINNER			
Scallops in Tarragon Cream (page 259)	1 serving	1 serving	1 serving
Asparagus, steamed	115 g/4 oz	115 g/4 oz	115 g/4 oz
Tomato, grilled	1 large	1 large	—
Brown rice, cooked	90 g/3 oz	90 g/3 oz	90 g/3 oz
Butter	—	1 tsp	1 tsp
SNACK			
Gingerbread Cake with Peach Whipped Cream (page 334)	1 serving	1 serving	1 serving
TOTAL CALORIES (APPROX)	**1,630**	**2,050**	**2,450**
TOTAL CARBS (G)	**131**	**131**	**134**

mastering carbs
in and out of the kitchen

All of the world's weight-loss science and action plans are useless if they fail to include the most important element of success: great-tasting food. In fact, there's no sense following any eating plan that doesn't include foods that you like to eat.

That's why favourite foods, delicious recipes and occasional indulgences are built into this book.

Here's where you'll learn the ins and outs of stocking a smart low-carb store cupboard, how to cut carbohydrates in your favourite recipes and how to plan family-pleasing meals.

You'll also find tips on using alternatives to plain white flour, the best alternatives to sugar and how to read food labels to decipher the carb content. The following tips cover all of the principles of smart low-carb cooking.

USE YOUR NOODLE WHEN COOKING MEATS

Eating wisely means reducing your intake of refined carbohydrates and not going overboard on saturated fats. Translation: use oil instead of butter, use reduced-fat cheese and choose fish, poultry or lean cuts of meat whenever you can. See page 26 for the best choices of lean meats. Here's how to get the most flavour from meats while reducing any potential health risks.

Dry off your meats for better browning. Browning involves quickly cooking meats over high heat until the surface is browned. This cooking method seals in moisture and creates intense flavour, especially in leaner cuts. Before browning beef, pork, poultry and even fish, pat the food dry to remove excess surface moisture. The dry surface helps

(continued on page 56)

STOCKING THE SMART LOW-CARB KITCHEN

Keep the items below to hand and you'll minimise last-minute shopping. Here is everything you need to whip up delicious low-carbohydrate meals – a big plus on busy nights when less-healthy takeaway options might tempt you. Some of the refrigerator items like parsley and lemons may not last as long as other foods, but they have so many uses and are so inexpensive, it's wise to consider them staples. In addition to the foods below, be sure to stock the foods that your family likes best – even some of the higher-carbohydrate ones. If eating high-carbohydrate foods now and then helps you stick to your overall eating plan, then it's worth keeping them around. Smart tip: make several photocopies of this list and put them up on your fridge or keep them in a drawer. Each one is a ready-made shopping list that you can tailor to your needs before heading to the shops.

COOL, DRY PLACE
Bananas
Garlic
Marrow
Melon (cantaloupe, honeydew, watermelon)
Onions
Oranges
Plums
Sweet potatoes

REFRIGERATOR
Butter (preferably half-fat)
Cheese (Cheddar, mozzarella,
   Parmesan, Double Gloucester, cream
   cheese – preferably light)
Eggs
Milk (semi-skimmed)
Orange juice
Apple juice
Crème fraîche (reduced-fat)
Yoghurt (low-fat natural)
Apples
Aubergine
Broccoli

Cabbage (green or red)
Carrots
Cauliflower
Celery
Courgettes
Cucumbers
Fresh greens
Grapefruit
Grapes
Lemons
Mushrooms
Parsley
Peppers
Raisins
Spring onions
Nuts (walnuts, pecans, almonds, hazelnuts,
   pine nuts, pistachios, macadamia nuts)
Seeds (sunflower, sesame)

FREEZER
Tortillas (corn and wholewheat)
Wholemeal bread
Frozen fruit (no sugar added)
Broccoli

French beans
Peas
Prawns
Salmon
Spinach
Sweetcorn
Veggie burgers
Bacon (lean)
Beef (lean minced, fillet, various steaks)
Chicken (skinless, boneless breasts and
  jointed pieces)
Lamb (minced, chops)
Pork (chops, tenderloin/fillet)
Sausage (pork or turkey)
Turkey (escalopes, minced breast)

STORE CUPBOARD
Dried apricots
Dried mushrooms
Stock cubes or bouillon powder
Tinned clams
Tinned fish (tuna, salmon, sardines,
  anchovies, trout fillets)
Tinned fruit in fruit juice
Bottled mild green chillis
Tinned tomatoes (whole, chopped,
  passata/sieved tomatoes, juice)
Dried or tinned beans (black-eyed, borlotti,
  butterbeans, cannellini, haricot, pinto, red
  kidney, chickpeas, brown lentils)
Oats
Oat flour
Soya flour
Wholewheat couscous
Wholewheat flour

Wholewheat pasta
Wholemeal flour
Brown rice
Pearl barley
Quinoa
Hot-pepper sauce
Tomato-based pasta sauce
Mayonnaise (reduced-fat)
Mustard
Pesto
Salt
Vinegar (cider, white wine, red wine,
  balsamic)
Soy sauce
Worcestershire sauce
Brown sugar (or brown sugar substitute)
Splenda
All-fruit spread (various flavours)
Maple syrup (low-sugar if possible)
Peanuts, unsalted (and other nuts)
Peanut butter, natural
  (and other natural nut butters)
Rapeseed oil
Olive oil
Sesame oil
Olives
Roasted peppers (bottled)
Tea, herbal teas
Unsweetened cocoa powder
Unsweetened desiccated coconut
Wholegrain crackers

the heat of the pan or flame to brown the food and caramelise its natural sugars, the key to creating flavour. If the surface of the meat is wet, the food will steam rather than brown and release some of its flavours into the air.

Avoid HCAs. Scientists have found that when meat is cooked at high temperatures, as in pan frying, grilling or barbecuing, it can form potentially carcinogenic compounds called heterocyclic amines (HCAs). That doesn't mean you should stop grilling food: it's a good way to cook without using extra fat. The vegetables and fruits in your diet contain numerous phytonutrients that help protect you from these potentially cancer-causing compounds. Here are some other ways to reduce HCAs.

- **Trim the fat.** The fat in meat contributes to the formation of HCAs. Cooking with lean cuts can reduce your cancer risk considerably. It's wise to trim any visible fat before cooking. Save the more fat-laden cuts for special occasions or for when you want to treat yourself.

- **Marinate.** According to the American Institute for Cancer Research, marinating meats can reduce the formation of cancer-causing substances by as much as 92 to 99 per cent. See the recipe for Topside of Beef Marinated in Soy Sauce and Mustard on page 205. Even bottled salad dressing or stir-fry sauce works well as a marinade.

- **Lower the heat.** Experts recommend using lower-heat cooking methods such as roasting, braising, baking, microwaving, stir-frying, steaming and stewing.

- **Microwave first.** Before placing meats under the grill or in the pan, microwave them to get rid of some of the fat that could contribute to HCAs. Microwave burgers for 1 to 2 minutes and steaks for 2 to 3 minutes, then pour off the liquid.

- **Use aluminium foil on the grill.** Place a piece of foil on the grill and poke holes in it. This will minimise the fumes that carry HCAs back into the meat.

- **Mix minced beef with beans.** When making burgers, meat loaf, meatballs or chilli, combine the minced beef with mashed black-eyed beans, borlotti beans or kidney beans. This will help reduce the fat that contributes to HCAs and boost your intake of fibre – and research shows that eating fibre-rich foods may lower your risk of colon cancer. Instead of beans, you could also use cooked grains such as rice or quinoa.

- **Flip burgers often.** Under the grill or in a pan, turning burgers frequently reduces HCAs, kills bacteria, speeds cooking and makes burgers more moist.

- **Eat veggies and fruits, too.** Don't forget the cancer-preventive importance of phytonutrients in vegetables and fruits. For instance, eating cooked tomato products will increase your intake of lycopene, a phytonutrient that helps fight several types of cancer. No wonder beef-and-tomato dishes like spaghetti bolognese and chilli con carne have been around so long.

SWAP SWEETS WHEN YOU CAN

Sugar crops up in so many foods, it's nearly impossible to avoid. Fortunately, when you're the one choosing the food or adding the sweetener, you're in control. Here are some alternatives to popular sweeteners and a few words of caution about using artificial sweeteners. The natural alternatives discussed below either have fewer calories, a lower glycaemic index or the benefit of additional nutrients that are lacking in table sugar. In some cases, these alternatives will help prevent the cravings caused by eating excess sugary foods.

Use fruit spread. Unlike jam, which is loaded with sugar and/or glucose syrup, fruit spread is sweetened only with concentrated fruit juice (usually grape or apple). If you swop it for jam, you'll save around 7 grams of carbohydrate in every 50 g/1¾ oz you use. Try fruit spread on bread and muffins, or use it instead of sugar to sweeten your breakfast porridge, as well as desserts like fruit pies and compotes. It can even replace sugar in some cake recipes: see the recipe for Pecan Muffins (page 99).

Look for low-sugar or sugar-free syrup. Instead of pure maple syrup, look for low-sugar or sugar-free alternatives (sometimes labelled pancake syrup). You'll save 14 grams of carbohydrate in every 2 tablespoons.

Try brown sugar. When it comes to replacing sugar, the bottom line is that nothing tastes or performs quite the same way in cooking. However, you can reduce your carbohydrate intake by using brown sugar instead of white sugar. Brown sugar is a mixture of white sugar and molasses, which gives it a slightly lower carbohydrate content than that of white sugar. If you swap brown for white, you'll save between 1 and 7 grams of carbohydrate in every 100 g/3½ oz you use – it also gives a richer flavour. Many of the cakes and desserts in this book use light brown sugar. Bear in mind that brown sugar is still a refined sugar and is not the lowest-carbohydrate sweetener.

Don't be fooled by fructose. You might be wondering if fructose is an option. Fructose is a simple sugar that occurs naturally in fruits, and can also be refined from corn. Sometimes used as a sweetener, fructose may be found in soft drinks, sweets and baked goods. It is not the best choice as a sugar alternative, not only because it is a refined sugar, but also because its effect upon our health is questionable. The potential negative impact of fructose upon the body's levels of cholesterol and triglycerides, platelet clumping in the blood, and status of chromium and

(continued on page 60)

I Did It!

Amanda Di Pietro

A lifetime of weight problems didn't keep Amanda from finding a successful approach. She identified her trigger foods and found an eating plan that works.

before

'My weight has always been like a yo-yo. I've had a weight problem since I was a child. With diligence, I managed to keep it in check throughout most of my life – until I became pregnant. I've had three pregnancies and gained more weight with each one. In 1970, after my youngest son was born, I was suddenly more than 13 kg/2 st overweight. I adopted a low-carbohydrate eating plan and it helped me lose all the weight. I stuck with the plan and kept the weight off for almost 20 years. Then in 1989, a number of changes in my life brought my stress levels to their limits. I sent my last child off to university, moved from my home of 20 years,

Weight lost: 13.6 kg/2 st 2 lb
Time kept off: 2 years
Weight-loss strategies: avoided trigger foods, reduced carbohydrates, did Pilates or Jazzercise most days of the week

Weight-maintenance strategies: avoids trigger foods and refined carbohydrates, exercises several days a week, maintains good self-esteem

relocated and started my own business – all within the span of three weeks. For comfort, I turned to my favourite foods like potatoes, anything containing sugar and any kind of bread. My health paid the price, as did my waistline – once again! That year, I gained 22 kg/3½ st.

'Because I was having various health problems, I decided to see a homeopathic doctor. He diagnosed me with a sluggish thyroid and suspected that I had several trigger foods that were causing me to gain weight. I immediately went on a diet that avoided my trigger foods. This diet was simple – it rotated a variety of foods in and out of my menus every week. I could not believe the difference it made! My cravings for sugar and other refined carbohydrates disappeared. I learned to listen to my body for hunger signals rather than just resort to food whenever I thought I needed it. Best of all, I started to lose weight again and keep it off.

'I am amazed that eating sugar can cause me to crave food all of the time, even when I am full. I now realise that sugar was behind my mood swings, too. Dairy foods are another trigger food for me. Whenever I eat them, my stomach gets bloated and my head gets congested. I'm so glad I know these things now. I never realised how food can regulate not only my weight, but also my health and mental well-being.

'Now I choose lean protein foods like chicken breasts, lean pork chops and pork tenderloin, lots of fish and occasionally fillet steak. I also limit my carbohydrates to only whole grains, starchy vegetables and beans. For treats, I snack on fresh fruit. I am also more diligent about my exercise routine. I do Pilates (simple body conditioning) four times a week and attend Jazzercise classes three times a week.

'My new eating and exercise plan has made me more successful in every aspect of my life – particularly the weight-loss aspect! I have more energy and I'm not nearly as depressed (for some reason, sugar depresses me). Everything in my life just looks better. I am more able to stay focused on my weight now that I've found out what works. I also know that reaching my goal weight is as important for my self-esteem as it is for my health and longevity.'

copper in the body has made some experts suspicious.

Have a taste of Splenda. You may have seen Splenda, a newly available type of sweetener, in a box next to the sugar on your supermarket's shelves. It's another good option among alternative sweeteners. The key ingredient in Splenda is sucralose, a sugar substitute processed from real sugar that has been modified so that it isn't absorbed by the body. Sucralose was first discovered in 1976. More than 20 years and 100 studies later, the safety of sucralose has been endorsed by 25 countries. Sucralose is calorie-free, does not affect blood sugar levels, does not promote tooth decay and maintains its sweetness across a broad range of temperatures.

Splenda, the commercial form of sucralose, is a real breakthrough for low-calorie, low-carbohydrate cooking. It measures spoon for spoon like sugar; it performs almost like sugar in recipes; and when used in moderate amounts, it doesn't have the cloying aftertaste associated with artificial sweeteners. Splenda is especially useful in baking, but bear in mind that it doesn't caramelise like sugar. If you're reducing your sugar intake, one option is to split the difference and use half sugar and half Splenda. You'll still get the caramelising and browning properties of sugar, but fewer calories and carbohydrates. See the recipes for Strawberry Cream Cake (page 336), Double Chocolate Custard (page 341) or Cantaloupe Sorbet (page 349). As with any alternative sweetener (or any sweetener for that matter), don't go overboard with Splenda. Moderation and variety are key.

Be cautious of artificial sweeteners. Aspartame and saccharin are two options you may have considered. Of the two, aspartame is generally considered safer and more palatable. That's the sweetener found in Canderel and NutraSweet brands.

HIDDEN ROADBLOCK to weight loss

UNDEREATING

That's right, it's possible that you're not eating enough! Consuming too few calories signals your metabolism to slow down in order to protect your body from what it thinks might be an oncoming famine. Also, if you're not eating enough, chances are that your body is not getting enough of the nutrients that it needs to efficiently metabolise carbohydrates, proteins and fats. If you are following one of the specific plans in this book, you will be getting adequate calories – unless you are very active or extremely overweight. If that's you, try eating more protein foods and slightly more fat, rather than more carbohydrates. Bear in mind that no one should consume fewer than 1,200 calories a day, especially without medical supervision. Going too low puts your body into starvation mode, which slows down your metabolism so much that you may not be able to lose any weight.

Though most scientists disagree, some scientists suspect that aspartame may cause brain damage that leads to memory loss, so be cautious. As for saccharin, some research on animals shows that, in very high doses, it may lead to cancer. But many scientists consider it safe for humans at the levels found in food.

Keep an eye out for sugar substitutes in processed foods. Sucralose, saccharin, aspartame and acesulfame-K are artificial sweeteners that don't supply any calories. They're often used in diet drinks and other diet foods. Sugar substitutes are sometimes called nutritive sweeteners because they do contain some calories. However, their energy values (calories) are lower than that of sugar because these carbohydrates are slowly and incompletely absorbed. Thus they have a lower glycaemic index than sugar, too. Sugar substitutes often crop up in products labelled 'sugar-free' or 'no added sugar'. You can usually spot a sugar substitute because the name ends in '-ol', as in mannitol, xylitol and sorbitol. Two other sugar substitutes are isomalt and hydrogenated starch hydrolysate.

Use sugar-free products sparingly. Several world health organisations consider sugar substitutes to be safe for human consumption. The drawback of sugar substitutes is that these less-digestible carbohydrates pull water into the intestine. This can result in diarrhoea if you eat too much. Also, bacteria in the colon ferment this kind of carbohydrate, which can cause flatulence or wind. Use caution. One half-stick of sugar-free chewing gum is enough to cause some people discomfort!

Know what the labels mean. Nutritional labelling in Great Britain is subject to the Food Labelling Regulations, 1996, which sets out guidelines for certain nutrition claims on food labelling and advertising; similar but separate legislation exists in Northern Ireland. Bear the following in mind when making low-carb choices.

Sugar-free: may contain sugar substitutes, and should contain less than 0.2 grams of sugar per 100g

No added sugar or low sugar: although no sugar may be added during processing, the food may be sweetened with concentrated fruit juice or an artificial sweetener

Reduced sugar: should have at least 25% less sugar than the standard version of the product

CHOOSE THE BEST OILS

Most liquid oils are a more healthy choice than saturated or solid fats such as butter or white cooking fat. Various types of oil are used throughout this book. The big two are olive oil and rapeseed oil. Nut oils such as walnut oil are suggested in a few recipes for their tremendous flavour. But other oils can be substituted in most cases. Here's the low-down on several types of oils. All contain 125 calories, 14 grams of

(continued on page 64)

mastering carbs in and out of the kitchen

SMART LOW-CARB SUBSTITUTIONS

Keeping carbs in check doesn't mean eliminating your favourite food groups. A simple switch within the same group may be all it takes. You can dodge nearly 40 grams of carbohydrate by snacking on a handful of popcorn instead of a handful of crackers. Or skip 25 grams by opting for wholemeal bread instead of a bagel. Try these substitutions in the kitchen and when you eat out.

INSTEAD OF . . .	TRY . . .	CARBS SAVED (G). . .
Breads, Pasta and Flour		
Bagel, plain (10 cm/4 in)	Bread, wholemeal (1 slice)	25
Bread, white (1 slice)	Bread, wholemeal (1 small slice)	2.3
Flour, plain or wholemeal (40 g/1¼ oz)	Flour, soya (40 g/1¼ oz)	14
	Flour, oat (40 g/1¼ oz)	12
French toast (1 slice)	Omelette, ham and cheese (2 eggs)	12
Lasagne pasta (60 g/2 oz dry)	Aubergine or courgette slices (115 g/4 oz)	35
Tortilla, flour	Tortilla, corn (15 cm/6 in)	6
Pancakes, from mix (two 15 cm/6 in)	Eggs, large (2)	56
Desserts, Sweets and Dairy Foods		
Cake, sponge, with vanilla icing (1 slice)	Cheesecake (1 slice)	18
Ice cream (1 scoop/115 g/4 oz)	Jelly, low-sugar (115 g/4 oz), with whipped cream (2 tbsp)	14
Milk, chocolate (240 ml/8 fl oz)	Milkshake, chocolate, high-protein, low-carb (240 ml/8 fl oz)	26
Milk, skimmed (240 ml/8 fl oz)	Milk, soya, unsweetened (240 ml/8 fl oz)	9
Pie, apple (1 slice)	Pie, pumpkin (1 slice)	10
Sugar, granulated (8 tbsp/100 g/3½ oz)	Splenda (4 tbsp)	48
Sugar, granulated (4 tbsp/60 g/2 oz)	All-fruit spread (4 tbsp/60 g/2 oz)	9
Rice pudding, tinned (200 g/7 oz)	Fruit bar (75 g/2½ oz)	13
Yoghurt, with fruit (230 g/8 oz)	Yoghurt, low-fat natural (230 g/8 oz)	30
Fruits		
Apple	Celery (1 stick)	18
Banana	Kiwifruit	10
Blueberries, fresh (75 g/2½ oz)	Strawberries, fresh (75 g/2½ oz)	5

INSTEAD OF ...	TRY ...	CARBS SAVED (G)...
Honeydew melon (¼ medium)	Grapefruit (½ medium)	13
Apricots, dried (5)	Grapes, large seedless (15)	3
Pineapple chunks in syrup (100 g/3½ oz)	Pineapple chunks in juice (100 g/3½ oz)	4

Main Dishes, Sauces and Soups

Steak pie (1 serving)	Hamburger (1), no bun	40
Linguine with cream and clam sauce (1 serving)	Spaghetti with tomato sauce (1 serving)	31
Pasta salad, seafood (170 g/6 oz)	Tuna mayonnaise (170 g/6 oz)	3
Sandwich, chicken, fast food	Hamburger, in bun, fast food	8
Soup, tomato, tinned (240 ml/8 fl oz)	Gazpacho soup (240 ml/8 fl oz)	12
Mayonnaise, regular (1 tbsp)	Mayonnaise, reduced-fat (1 tbsp)	1
Blue cheese dressing (2 tbsp)	Oil and vinegar (1 tbsp each)	4
Vinaigrette, bottled (2 tbsp)	Oil and vinegar (1 tbsp each)	2

Snacks and Beverages

Juice, grapefruit (240 ml/8 fl oz)	Juice, tomato (240 ml/8 fl oz)	12
Cola (350 ml/12 fl oz)	Diet cola, sparkling water (350 ml/12 fl oz)	38
Cashews (60 g/2 oz)	Brazil nuts (60 g/2 oz)	9
Ritz crackers (10)	Popcorn, air-popped (2 handfuls/20 g/¾ oz)	35
Fig rolls (2)	Gingernut biscuits (2)	20
Digestive biscuits (3)	Oatcakes (2)	2
Fruit pastilles (10)	Apricots, dried (5)	5

Vegetables and Side Dishes

Carrot (1)	Celery (1 stick)	5
Onions, chopped (60 g/2 oz)	Spring onions, chopped (60 g/2 oz)	3
Potato, baked (1 medium)	Corn-on-the-cob (1 medium)	34
Potatoes, mashed (170 g/6 oz)	Turnips, mashed (230 g/8 oz)	26
Baked beans in tomato sauce (200 g/7 oz tin)	Frozen peas (80 g/3 oz)	21
Potato salad (115 g/4 oz)	Cauliflower salad (115 g/4 oz)	11
Coleslaw salad (115 g/4 oz)	Tomato salad (115 g/4 oz)	7

fat and 0 grams of carbohydrate per table-spoon, so choose the ones you like best.

Olive oil. One of the best oils for healthy cooking, olive oil is high in heart-healthy monounsaturated fats and holds up fairly well to heat. Use it for dressings, sauces, marinades, sautéing, stir-frying – and even baking. There are three main categories of olive oil: extra-virgin, virgin and ordinary or 'pure'. *Extra-virgin olive oil* must be extracted from the first cold pressing of the olives. It usually has a dark green or deep golden colour and a bold flavour – sometimes the label will de-scribe it as fruity, peppery or 'mild'. Its flavour shows up best in uncooked dishes such as dressings, marinades and sauces. Or add it at the end of cooking to boost the flavour of pasta or vegetables, for ex-ample. *Virgin olive oil* is also cold-pressed (i.e. extracted without heating) and is usually paler in colour and gentler in flavour than extra virgin. This is a good all-purpose choice for sautéing and cooking. *Pure olive oil* is heat-treated to ex-tract more oil, then refined; it has a less noticeable olive flavour. If you have never used olive oil in your cooking, this type is probably the best to start with. Use it for sautéing, stir-frying or baking; it stands up well to high temperatures. Many people keep a large bottle of virgin olive oil and smaller bottles of extra-virgin olive oil from different regions for special uses. Store olive oil away from heat and light to keep it at its best – up to 1 year. The refrigerator is a good place. Don't

worry if the oil becomes cloudy or solidi-fies: its translucence will return when the oil reaches room temperature.

Rapeseed oil. This type of oil (known as canola oil in the US) is usually consid-ered a monounsaturated fat, although it has about 20 per cent less monounsatu-rated fat than olive oil. Rapeseed oil is nearly flavourless, so it won't interfere with other flavours in a dish. It's a good all-purpose oil for cooking and baking.

Vegetable oil. Most vegetable oils in the UK are made mainly from rapeseed, but vegetable oil may be blended from vegetables, nuts and seeds. Use vegetable oil for cooking, baking, dressings, mari-nades and sauces.

Groundnut (peanut) oil. This has a delicate flavour (nothing like peanut butter!) and is a good choice for cooking at high temperatures, especially for stir-fries.

Safflower and sunflower oils. These light-tasting oils do not solidify when chilled, so they're great for salad dressings, mayonnaise and dips. They can also be used for baking. Safflower oil is also an excellent choice for sautéing and pan frying because of its high smoke point (232°C/450°F).

Nut oils. Pure nut oils have a fragrant, nutty flavour achieved by grinding whole nuts or big pieces of nuts, roasting the ground nuts and only lightly filtering the oil. These oils make a good choice for both flavour and heart-healthy mono- and polyunsaturated fats. Remember that price equals flavour. Avoid the less-expensive nut oils, which are often a very mild-tasting mixture of mascerated nuts and vegetable oil. Pure walnut, almond and hazelnut oils are good types to try if you're new to nut oils. *Almond oil* is fairly mild-tasting and holds up to heat fairly well. It's a good choice for dressings, light sautéing or baking. Try almond oil in muffins or on green beans with almonds. *Walnut oil* has a delicate toasted walnut flavour that is destroyed by cooking, so use walnut oil for dressings, dips or adding to hot dishes just before serving. See the recipe for Asparagus with Orange-Walnut Vinaigrette (page 307). *Hazelnut oil* is high in monounsaturated fats and has a delicious flavour. It is best kept for dressings and marinades, but it can withstand the heat of sautéing, so it can also be used in hot dishes. As with all nut oils, a little goes a long way (another reason why they're slightly higher in price).

Nut oils are more prone to rancidity than vegetable oils, so buy only small quantities and keep them in a cool, dark place, where they will last for up to a year, if you're lucky.

EAT BEANS – THEY'RE EASY AND FILLING

Beans are one kind of starch you can't complain about getting bored with. There are more than 100 different varieties. Beans provide all the protein, carbohydrate, fats, vitamins and minerals needed for plants to grow and mature. That's why they're so nutrient rich and healthy for us to eat. It's true that beans are not overly low in carbohydrates, but they are one of the best sources of fibre, which gives them a low glycaemic index. Numerous studies have demonstrated the cardiovascular benefits of eating beans.

Use tinned beans for convenience. Tinned beans are already soaked and cooked, so they are ready to use. Keep several varieties in your store cupboard. Add tinned beans to salads and pasta dishes, or mash them to make dips. For instance, see the recipe for Cannellini Beans with Cheese and Basil (page 114). To reduce the sodium content of tinned beans, drain and rinse them before using. Rinsing until all the bubbles disappear removes up to 40 per cent of the sodium as well as some of the wind-producing oligosaccharides. One drained tin (420 g/14½ oz) yields about (230 g/8 oz) of beans.

FOOD LABELS FOR THE CARB-SAVVY

The 'Nutrition Information' label has made great strides in clarifying nutrition information on food products; most manufacturers now follow labelling guidelines in a helpful and consistent manner. However, the details of carbohydrate content can still be confusing. Here are some tips to make things clearer.

1. Check the serving size. Nutrition information is based on 100 g/3½ oz of the product, but bear in mind that sometimes a typical serving will be more than 100 g (a small tub of yoghurt is 150 g/5 oz), sometimes less (a bowl of cornflakes weighs about 30 g/1 oz).

2. Think about extras. Packaged products sometimes need eggs or milk to finish preparation or to serve. Some nutrition information labels include 'as served' figures.

3. Avoid calorie confusion. The first figure you will see is for energy, expressed as kilojoules (kJ) and kilocalories (kcal). The kJ figure looks high, but don't worry – most dietary calorie counts are based on the kcal figure.

4. Focus on the carbohydrate figures. These are the most important figures to look at when you're watching carb intake. The carbohydrate figure includes the amount of sugars and starch present. Specific figures for sugars and starch may be listed underneath. Choose foods that will balance out your overall carbohydrate intake for the day or week.

5. Convert grams of sugar to teaspoons. Teaspoons of sugar are easier to visualise than grams. To convert grams to teaspoons, simply divide the number of grams by 4. For instance, if the label lists 8 grams of sugar, dividing by 4 tells you that the product contains 2 teaspoons of sugar per serving. Bear in mind that the total recommended amount of sugar intake per day is less than 10 teaspoons. Choose foods with the least sugar when you can.

6. Strive for fibre. Eat foods with the most fibre when you can. Fibre helps to make you feel full so that you don't overeat. Fibre also helps to slow the absorption of sugar in carbohydrate-containing foods. Try to get 25 to 35 grams of fibre a day.

7. Go high-pro. Look for foods that are high in protein, especially breads and other starchy foods. Depending upon your calorie intake and weight-loss goals, you should get approximately 75 to 150 grams of protein a day.

Use dried beans for more flavour.
Some recipes, such as soup, taste remarkably better made with dried beans. That's because as the beans cook, they release their delicious flavours into the soup (some of the flavour of tinned beans goes down the drain with the liquid). Many of the soup recipes in the book use dried beans instead of

tinned. Don't be scared to use dried beans. They only need to be soaked before cooking. Here's what you need to know.

Soak dried beans the quick way. First, spread the dried beans on a clean surface and pick out any pebbles, debris or mis-shapen beans. Put the sorted beans in a colander and rinse them, then transfer to a large saucepan (big enough to hold at least twice the volume of the beans). Cover with cold water and soak overnight, then drain and rinse. Or to soak dried beans the quick way, add 2.4 litres/4 pints of hot water for each 455 g/1 lb of beans. Bring to the boil over medium-high heat, then boil for 2 to 3 minutes. Remove from the heat, cover and leave to soak for 1 to 4 hours. Drain off the soaking water and rinse the beans. At this point, the beans are ready for cooking as directed in most recipes. Or if you want to cook 455 g/1 lb of soaked beans for another purpose, put them in a large (3–4 litre/5–7 pint) saucepan and add 1.5 litres/2½ pints hot water, 2 table-spoons oil and 2 teaspoons salt. Simmer over medium heat for 1 to 2 hours, or until tender but not mushy. Avoid overcooking beans that will be used in salads or casseroles; they should remain somewhat firm. 455 g/1 lb of dried beans makes 910 g–1.3 kg/2–3 lb of cooked beans.

A few more tips: if you have hard water, shorten cooking time by adding bi-carbonate of soda to the cooking water; use ⅛ to ¼ teaspoon for each 455 g/1 lb of beans. Also, don't add acidic ingredients such as tomatoes or vinegar until the end of cooking time because acidic ingredients will slow down the cooking of beans. Keep dried beans in a cool, dry place in airtight glass or metal containers. If you have left-over cooked or tinned beans, drain them and freeze them for up to 6 months. Thaw before using.

GIVE SOYA A TRY

Soya beans are one of the most nutrient-dense beans available. Numerous studies show that soya protein helps to lower blood cholesterol levels and may help reduce the risk of osteoporosis and some forms of cancer. The easiest way to get these benefits is to include some soya milk, tofu and soya flour in your kitchen.

Sample soya milk. Soya milk is made from soya beans that have been soaked and squeezed to release their liquid. One big advantage of soya milk is that it's lower in carbohydrates than cow's milk because it does not contain lactose. Its protein content is about the same as that of cow's milk. And most brands are fortified with calcium, vitamin D and vitamin B_{12} so that the milk is nutritionally similar to cow's milk. Soya milk can replace cow's milk in cereal, shakes or smoothies, sauces, baking and for almost any recipe. The best-tasting varieties are often sold in the refrigerated dairy section at the supermarket. Try a few brands to see which you like best. Read labels care-fully. Some brands of soya milk are sweet-ened with malt, rice syrup or other sweeteners. The carbohydrate content can range from 2 to 13 grams for a 240 ml/ 8 fl oz glass. Buy unsweetened soya milk for the fewest carbs. If you buy a brand sold in a long-life container, it can be stored for several months in a cool, dry place. Once opened, all soya milk will keep in the fridge for 5 to 7 days. You can buy powdered soya milk, too. Store it in the refrigerator in a sealed container for up to 6 months. Once rehydrated with water, it will also last for up to 7 days in the refrigerator.

Try tofu. No doubt you've heard about the possibilities for tofu in the kitchen. If you eat meat, there's no reason to replace meat with tofu. But you might want to use tofu in other ways for the health benefits associated with soya protein. Firm tofu can be cut into cubes, browned and tossed into a stir-fry. Or it can be cut into thick slabs and marinated, then grilled, baked or pan-fried. You can also buy ready-marinated tofu that's ready to eat straight from the pack or tossed into salads or stir-fries. Soft tofu and silken tofu have a more custard-like texture than firm tofu. Soft tofu can be pureed as the basis for dips, sauces and puddings.

Keep a small bag of soya flour in stock. Lower in carbohydrates than wheat flour, soya flour is a smart addition to your shopping list. The regular roasted variety (not defatted) is the best-tasting one with the fewest carbohydrates. Soya flour is excellent for dredging and sautéing foods such as fish fillets or chicken because it browns beautifully and quickly. That's an easy switch from wheat flour. In baking,

things get a little trickier. It's best to replace no more than one-quarter of the wheat flour (or other flour) called for in a baking recipe with soya flour. Baked goods made with soya flour tend to brown more quickly and have a more grainy texture. In certain cases, the effect is desirable. For instance, a little bit of soya flour makes wonderfully crisp, browned waffles. You can add soya flour to muffins and pancakes, too. If the food is browning too quickly, reduce the oven temperature or shorten the baking time. Bear in mind that soya flour doesn't work as well with delicate cakes. Soya flour has a higher fat content than most refined flours, so store it tightly wrapped in the fridge or freezer to prevent rancidity. It also packs down during storage. Before measuring, stir or sift it.

Experiment with soya mince. Dried soya mince is easy to use and stores well; it needs to be rehydrated by adding boiling water. It can be bland, but a dash or two of soy sauce will lift its flavour. Use soya mince instead of beef in dishes such as spaghetti bolognese or chilli con carne, or as a bread substitute for stuffing when serving poultry. See the recipe for Roast Chicken with Vegetable and Soya Stuffing (page 186). Look for soya mince in health food shops and supermarkets.

GO WHOLE GRAIN

Here they are again: whole grains. We can't recommend them enough. They offer more nutritional benefits than refined grains and they can help you lose weight. Refined grains, on the other hand, may actually sabotage your weight-loss plans. Take a look at a few of the nutrients lost when wholemeal flour is refined into plain white flour:

Bran	100%
Manganese	86%
Vitamin E	86%
Magnesium	85%
Vitamin B$_6$	72%
Copper	68%
Chromium	40%

Similar nutrients are lost when other grains such as rice are refined. For healthy weight loss, fibre is the most crucial nutrient retained in whole grains. Fibre helps you to feel full so you're not tempted to overeat, and it can reduce your risk of heart disease. Here are some tips on using fibre- and vitamin-rich whole grains.

Switch to wholewheat pasta. Swap white pasta for wholewheat pasta one for one and you'll get more fibre, a lower glycaemic index and – believe it or not – more flavour! Wholewheat pasta has a more complex, nutty taste than refined white pasta. Use wholewheat pasta in any of your favourite recipes. Most supermarkets carry both strand and shaped wholewheat pastas such as spaghetti, linguine and penne. Look for them next to the refined white pastas. Wholewheat couscous is another type of higher-fibre tiny pasta that can be used in place of regular couscous. It's excellent for making grain salads and pilafs. See the recipe for Couscous Salad with Lime-Cumin Dressing (page 324).

Don't settle for boring white rice. Here's another simple trade-in. Use brown rice instead of white. Brown rice is higher in fibre and vitamins than white rice, and it has a more chewy texture and nutty flavour. Both short- and long-grain varieties work well in casseroles and as simple side dishes. For example, see the recipe for Brown Rice Pilaf with Hazelnuts (page 328). Many supermarkets also carry wholegrain rice mixes that include various types of wild rice and brown rice. The taste of these rice mixes beats plain white rice hands down. Of course, white rice has its place – alongside a stir-fry, for instance. If you must choose white rice, go for parboiled (easy-cook or boil-in-the-bag) rice instead of regular white rice. It has been soaked and steamed for about 10 minutes and then dried; the nutrients in the bran are made to 'stick' to the starches, and it has a lower glycaemic index.

Reach for wholegrain bread. Good choices here include 100 per cent wholemeal bread and 100 per cent rye bread. Read the label to make sure that at least the first flour used is a wholegrain flour, such as whole rye, whole wheat or whole oat flour. Look for thinly sliced wholemeal bread – it's a simple way to reduce carbohydrates slice for slice.

Coat foods with wholewheat breadcrumbs. For breading fish or chicken, use wholewheat breadcrumbs instead of regular breadcrumbs. To make 60 g/2 oz of fresh wholewheat breadcrumbs, place two slices of wholemeal bread in a food processor and process until fine crumbs form. Use immediately or freeze to use another time. For a taste of how good wholewheat breadcrumbs can be, see the recipe for Breaded Baked Cod with Tartar Sauce (page 234).

Use wholegrain flours when you can. If you bake, try mixing in some wholegrain flour along with the plain flour. You can even use wholegrain flours for thickening sauces and dredging meats. (See page 68 for tips on using soya flour.) Here's what you need to know about using the most popular wholegrain flours.

- **Wholemeal flour.** If you bake bread, strong wholemeal (whole wheat) flour can be substituted for white bread flour. Look for 100% stoneground wholemeal flour for the best texture and flavour. In most soda bread and scone recipes (which do not use yeast), you can replace the plain flour with wholemeal plain flour. For most other uses in the kitchen, substitute plain or self-raising wholemeal flour for white flour: as a thickener; for coating meats, poultry and fish; and in baking. For delicate baked goods like cakes, use a combination of wholemeal flour and oat flour to create a lighter texture. For instance, to replace 145 g/ 5 oz plain flour, use 75 g/2½ oz wholemeal flour and 75 g/2½ oz oat flour. See the recipe for Strawberry Cream Cake (page 336) for a good example of how well these flours work together. You can also achieve a lighter texture from wholemeal flour by sifting it a few times before using. Because wholemeal flour soaks up more liquid than refined white flour, you might need to add a few tablespoons of liquid to your recipe or use a few tablespoons less wholemeal flour than the recipe calls for.

- **Oat flour.** Made from whole oats, oat flour has a lower carbohydrate content and a lower glycaemic index than plain white flour. It's a great substitute for wheat and has a slightly sweet taste. It's important to sift oat flour before using it because it clumps easily. When replacing plain white flour in a recipe, use a few tablespoons less oat flour than is called for. If you can't find oat flour at your supermarket or health food shop, you can make it at home by running whole rolled oats (porridge oats) through your food processor until finely ground.

- **Kamut® flour.** Pronounced ka-MOOT, this flour is an ancient relative of modern common wheat. It has a higher amino acid and mineral content than common wheat. The gluten content in kamut makes it easy to substitute for white flour in your recipes. The taste is richer and nuttier – with more protein and fibre – than that of plain flour.

■ **Buckwheat flour.** Buckwheat is not related to wheat, but is the seed of a plant related to rhubarb. Technically, buckwheat is not even a grain. Buckwheat is widely used in Russia and Poland, where the roasted seeds are known as kasha; it is also grown in Brittany, and the flour is used in France to make savoury pancakes or galettes. Buckwheat flour is gluten-free and unsuitable for breadmaking unless mixed with another cereal. It works well in pancakes (blinis), dumplings and pastas such as soba noodles (buckwheat noodles).

■ **Amaranth flour.** This flour makes an excellent addition to wholemeal and soya flours for baking. It tenderises the final product somewhat and adds a pleasant nutty flavour. For recipes containing more than one type of flour, substitute 145 g/5 oz of amaranth flour for 145 g/5 oz plain flour. Look for it in health food shops and Caribbean food shops.

■ **Quinoa flour.** Considered a complete protein, quinoa flour contains all of the essential amino acids. It's also lower in carbohydrates than most of the other flours. However, quinoa lacks gluten, the substance that gives flours elasticity. Rather than use it alone, only replace up to 50 per cent of the flour in a recipe to allow for adequate gluten. When mixed with buckwheat flour, cornmeal and some plain flour, quinoa flour makes excellent pancakes.

Store wholegrain flours in the fridge. To best preserve the flavours of wholegrain flours, store them tightly wrapped in the refrigerator. For longer storage, keep them in the freezer. Be sure to bring the flour to room temperature before using (unless it's for a pie or scone dough that calls for chilled ingredients).

Sift before using. Most baked goods made with wholegrain flours will be a little heavier than those made with white flour. But you can still get a fairly light product if you sift the flour two or three times to incorporate some air. If you don't have a sifter, whisk the flour after you put it in a bowl.

Work quickly but gently. Here's another tip to ensure light-tasting wholegrain baked goods. Preheat the oven and prepare the pans first. This will reduce the amount of time that the wholegrain flour has to sit in the bowl and absorb moisture. Avoid letting batters sit. Also, avoid over-mixing the batter for pancakes and muffins. The more you mix, the heavier the result is likely to be.

Add extra liquid. Wholegrain flours *love* liquid. The extra fibre in them soaks it up readily. For baking, this means that you'll probably need to add a little extra oil or liquid to the recipe to prevent dryness.

GET A LITTLE NUTTY

The ancient Romans often served nuts with or after dessert. Take a tip from the ancients and reap a wealth of health benefits by including nuts in your daily diet. Most are relatively high in fat, but even a small serving can pack in the protein, iron and other important vitamins and minerals. (See 'What's a Serving of Nuts?' on page 27 to see how much.) Here are some surprising nut facts:

- 30 g/1 oz of almonds (20 to 25 almonds) contains as much calcium as 60 ml/2 fl oz milk. The same amount also supplies 35 per cent of the RDA of vitamin E, plus trace amounts of magnesium, zinc, phosphorus, fibre and folic acid.
- Pecans contain 65 to 70 per cent oil. Most of this oil is the same kind of heart-healthy monounsaturated fat found in olive oil.
- Walnuts are the oldest tree food, dating back to 7000 BC, and were traded throughout the Mediterranean. It takes 6 to 8 years for trees to yield a crop, but then the tree continues to bear nuts for nearly a century.
- Pine nuts have the highest protein content of any nut. Measure for measure, pine nuts contain approximately the same amount of protein as beef.
- Cashews are in the same botanical family as poison ivy, poison oak, poison sumac and mangoes. All of these plants contain volatile substances that can irritate the skin and, because the shells of cashews contain an irritant, they are never sold in the shell.

Cashews have a higher carbohydrate content than most other nuts.

Choose the freshest nuts for the most flavour. Autumn and winter are generally considered nut season. But nuts are available all year round. If you buy fresh nuts in bulk, get them from a shop with a high turnover. Shelled nuts can become rancid fairly quickly because of their high fat content. For the freshest nuts, buy them in the shell. Avoid any that feel light for their size or have holes or splits in the shell. These are probably past their prime.

Keep them in a cool, dark place. Nuts (and seeds) will generally last about a month at room temperature. They will last longer and taste fresher when stored in a cool, dry place away from light (or in the refrigerator). If you have a large stockpile of nuts, keep them in the freezer in airtight containers, where they will last for up to a year.

Bring out the flavour. Toasting nuts enhances their flavour. To toast nuts, place them in a dry heavy frying pan over medium heat and stir frequently until lightly coloured and fragrant. This should only take 2 to 3 minutes. If your oven is already on, place the nuts on a baking tray and toast at 180°C/350°F/gas 4 for 3 to 5 minutes.

Add nuts to almost any dish. Nuts are incredibly versatile. They can be eaten alone as a snack or added to almost any dish – both savoury and sweet. Sprinkle nuts on wholegrain cereal or yoghurt, into bread or biscuit dough, into casseroles, on pasta or over desserts. Pasta dishes and casseroles are typically made with high-GI ingredients. To lower the glycaemic index, add nuts. Pine nuts are terrific with pasta or couscous. Pecans, walnuts and almonds work well with casseroles, vegetables and rice dishes. Nuts even work with meats. See the recipe for Meat Loaf with Walnuts (page 212).

Stock up on nut butters. If you like peanut butter, try the unsweetened variety, also called natural peanut butter. Unsweetened peanut butter is made without hydrogenated fats, sugar or other flavouring agents. It has a more peanutty taste and a lower glycaemic index than most commercial varieties, so it won't raise your blood sugar as rapidly.

Give other nut butters a try, too. Cashew butter is exceptionally rich-tasting and delicious on toast with fruit spread. Creamy macadamia nut butter makes a great sandwich spread. And almond butter is fantastic in sauces. You can use almost any nut butter to make a dip or sauce. See the recipe for Crudités with Spicy Peanut Dipping Sauce (page 118). Tahini (sesame seed butter) is another good choice for making dips and sauces. These nut butters are sold in most health food shops and some supermarkets.

FLAVOUR UP!

The cardinal rule of any successful eating plan is this: don't settle for bland-tasting food! Sometimes all a dish needs is a little something. Here are a few last-minute additions to help perk up the flavour of your food.

Toss in some herbs. The volatile oils in herbs are teeming with aromas. When using dried herbs, add them early on in the cooking so they have time to release flavour. Crush them before using to release even more flavour. More delicate fresh herbs such as basil and parsley are best added towards the end of cooking.

Sprinkle on sweet spices. To enhance sweetness without adding calories or carbohydrates, use sweet spices – especially in baking. A sprinkle of cinnamon, nutmeg, cloves or allspice might be all you need to make your biscuits, pancakes or scones sing with flavour. See, for example, the recipe for Gingerbread Cake with Peach Whipped Cream (page 334).

Add a bit of acidity. Acidic foods can help balance out the taste of a dish or add a last-minute shot of flavour. A squeeze of lemon, lime or orange juice adds fresh flavour to everything from chicken and fish to pasta and vegetables. Or use freshly grated zest to bring out more flavour in baked goods like biscuits and muffins. Vinegars add bright flavours too. Splash flavoured vinegars such as raspberry onto salads, vegetable side dishes and beans.

Look to a salty flavour. Ditch the salt cellar. Save on sodium by using other condiments like soy sauce (reduced-sodium if possible), mustard and Worcestershire sauce.

INSTANT PROTEIN

If you like to get your protein in a powder or a bar, here are some things to bear in mind about both.

Protein bars. The carbohydrate content of a protein bar can be as low as 1.5 grams per bar or as high as 44 grams. The caloric range is 190 to 340 calories per bar. Read labels carefully to keep track of what you're eating. Not all protein bars are fortified with vitamins and minerals. Some bars are really just sweets in disguise, while others may be a suitable meal replacement on occasion.

Protein powders and shakes. These include a variety of products marketed mostly to bodybuilders. The protein sources are usually egg (albumin), soya or milk (whey) and less frequently, rice or vegetable protein. As with the bars, carbohydrate contents vary widely. Pure protein powder contains from only a trace to about 3 grams of carbohydrate per serving. Flavoured varieties are often sweetened with fructose and may contain up to 22 grams of carbohydrate per serving. The shakes make a good snack or occasional meal replacement. The powders can be sprinkled into recipes such as smoothies, muffins or casseroles. See the recipe for Strawberry Protein Shake on page 124. Both powders and shakes are easiest to find in a health food shop, but some large supermarkets carry them, too. They are very economical compared to meat. Generally, the ready-to-drink versions cost a little more than the powders.

Unlock the flavour of dried food. Dried foods are concentrated sources of wow-that-tastes-good flavour. A handful of chopped sun-dried tomatoes can really deepen the taste of pizza, pasta and salads. Or add rehydrated dried mushrooms to rice dishes, soups or casseroles. Dried porcini mushrooms are especially good. If you're making muffins, breads or a dessert sauce, try dried fruit. When heated with almost any type of liquid, the rich, sweet flavour of dried apricots, dates, figs and raisins blossoms beautifully.

Kick it up! Nothing perks up a dish like hot sauce. Salsa, hot-pepper sauce, or even dried chilli flakes may be just the thing to boost the flavour of a dish.

BRIGHTEN UP BREAKFAST

Let's get specific and talk about smart choices you can make at each meal throughout the day. Many of the people we talked to said that they skip breakfast or eat the same thing every morning. Neither approach is the best way to start the day. The key to a healthy diet is variety. And breakfast time may be the best time to eat carbohydrates. One study shows that our bodies are more receptive to the insulin rush of carb-rich foods in the morning. Keep breakfast time fresh with some of these ideas.

Switch to wholegrain starches. If you're married to your morning cereal, try a wholegrain or high-fibre version such as All-Bran, oat bran cereal or porridge, whole rolled wheat or rye, kasha (roasted buckwheat), or unsweetened puffed grains such as brown rice, corn or whole wheat. Top with cow's milk or soya milk and some fruit such as blueberries or strawberries. Or try a few wholegrain crackers, a wholewheat tortilla, or wholemeal toast spread with cream cheese, almond butter or macadamia nut butter.

Get creative with eggs. This excellent source of protein can be scrambled, hard-boiled, poached, fried or made into an omelette, frittata or even egg mayonnaise in a wholemeal bread sandwich for breakfast. Add leftover vegetables, meats and some reduced-fat cheese to eggs to make a quick omelette or frittata. Leftover quiche, hot or cold, also makes an excellent breakfast dish.

Find new uses for cottage cheese. Cottage cheese can be mixed with a teaspoon of all-fruit spread, cut-up whole fruit and a sprinkle of cinnamon for breakfast. Or try it with some chopped vegetables or a chopped hard-boiled egg.

Think different. Pressed for time? Remember that breakfast doesn't have to be as you've always known it. Be daring. Who says you can't reheat leftovers from supper or have a bowl of soup? In Japan, it is customary to start the day with a bowl of warming soup. And don't forget beans. Baked beans are a terrific source of protein and make an excellent accompaniment to eggs. Or try some seasoned lentils or kidney, pinto or cannellini beans.

Enjoy a Good Lunch

For most of us, lunch is a grab-and-go meal. Fortunately, plenty of satisfying low-carb lunches are out there. You just need to know where to look.

Make a salad out of almost anything. With so many varieties of greens and prepared salads readily available in today's supermarkets and fast food restaurants, there's no reason to get bored with salad. Try all different kinds. Mix cut-up, raw vegetables with cooked ones. For instance, the contrast of raw, leafy vegetables with hot, cooked cauliflower or sugar snap peas tastes fantastic. For protein, add chunks or slices of meat, poultry, fish, hard-boiled eggs, shellfish or some chickpeas or other beans to a salad. Get creative with toppings like Parmesan cheese or other grated cheeses, real bacon bits, olives, sunflower seeds or croutons.

Make a wrap with lettuce. Soft lettuce leaves make excellent sandwich wrappers. Top a large lettuce leaf with tuna, egg, chicken, turkey, prawns or crabmeat and roll it into a neat package. Fasten with wooden cocktail sticks or toothpicks to take with you.

Switch to spinach. Try using spinach instead of lettuce now and then. Spinach is packed with vitamin A, folate and magnesium. And it contains some vitamin C, calcium, potassium, fibre and important B

EATING OUT LOW-CARB

Reducing your carbohydrate intake doesn't mean settling for boring restaurant meals. In fact, most restaurant main dishes focus on protein rather than carbohydrates, so it shouldn't be too hard to choose a great-tasting, low-carb meal. Just keep your eyes open for menu terms that may indicate extra carbohydrates and ask whether foods are prepared with flour, breadcrumbs or sugar. For example, meats, poultry or fish may be dredged in flour, or a dish may include a gravy or sauce not specified on the menu. Here are a few menu terms that may indicate extra carbohydrate content:

- à la mode
- barbecued
- breaded
- creamed
- crispy
- honey-baked
- loaf
- parmigiana
- pie
- stuffed
- crust
- fruited
- glazed
- gravy
- stuffing
- sweet and sour
- tetrazzini

When ordering, don't be bashful. Ask questions. Many restaurants are willing to make something special or to substitute a serving of vegetables or small salad for a potato, rice, pasta or other starchy dish. If you have bread with the meal, remember that an average-size bread roll is the equivalent of two servings of starch. It's unlikely that you'll be able to get wholemeal bread or pasta or brown rice in some restaurants. But if you eat out only occasionally, it won't hinder your weight loss or adversely affect your health to enjoy the refined versions of these foods now and then.

vitamins. Whenever you make a sandwich, try using spinach instead of lettuce. Having salad? Make it a spinach salad. Baby spinach comes prewashed in bags and ready to eat.

Have a real sandwich. If you like sandwiches at lunchtime, just remember to use wholemeal or whole rye bread, wholewheat pittas or wholewheat tortillas for wraps. You could also make an open sandwich with just one slice of bread to reduce your carb intake. Top with a lettuce leaf instead of another slice of bread. See the sandwich recipes beginning on page 145.

Have eggs for lunch. If you haven't had eggs for breakfast, an omelette can be very satisfying at lunchtime. Include some finely chopped vegetables and cheese, meat, poultry or fish.

Make extra servings. One of the easiest ways to plan for lunch is to make extra servings of dinner the night before. Pack an extra serving in a microwaveable container and keep it refrigerated until lunchtime. You can also add leftover chicken, turkey, beef, pork or fish to a shop-bought salad. Whenever you have time in the kitchen, make one of your favourite casseroles or soups, then freeze individual portions in microwaveable containers. With these frozen assets, you'll never be at a loss for smart lunch solutions.

SIMPLE DINNER IDEAS

Dinner is by far the easiest low-carb meal to plan because most dinner menus have some type of protein food at the centre, a serving or two of vegetables and relatively few carbohydrates. This book includes more than 100 main-dish recipes that serve as excellent examples. Here are a few things to bear in mind when planning dinner.

Get balance. Try to include at least one protein food, one to two vegetables (cooked or raw) and a starch if you have not already eaten much from these food groups earlier in the day.

Vary your protein source. Eating the same food again and again may hinder or even halt your weight loss. To avoid flavour fatigue and trigger foods (which could wreak havoc on your weight-loss plans), rotate different sources of protein in and out of your diet every few days. If you can, make enough food to have the leftovers the next day for lunch. Below are 4 days of menus that help explain this principle of variety.

- **Day One** (lunch and supper): beef, lamb, cod or haddock
- **Day Two** (lunch and supper): chicken, tuna or mackerel
- **Day Three** (lunch and supper): pork, prawns, crab, lobster, flounder, halibut, sole or turbot
- **Day Four** (lunch and supper): turkey, salmon, trout or sea bass

MAKE SNACKS A HEALTHY HABIT

Here's some great news for weight watchers: snacks are good for you! In fact, you should eat or drink something every 2 to 4 hours to avoid setting yourself up for a starvation-binge scenario. If you're used to having breakfast, lunch and dinner every day, fill in the gaps with smart snack choices. Here are a few simple ideas for keeping carbs low. See the recipes beginning on page 105, too.

Snack on nuts. Nutritious, filling and a source of protein and monounsaturated fats, nuts make a perfectly healthy snack. It takes a few minutes after eating nuts to feel satisfied, so eat them slowly. Allow yourself at least 10 minutes before reaching for something else.

Stuff some celery. Spread with a little peanut butter or seasoned cream cheese, celery sticks make an easy, satisfying and quite portable snack.

Try a little fruit. Fruit is a natural at snacktime. Try to combine it with nuts to lessen its effect on your blood sugar. For instance, have a banana or apple with some peanut butter. Or munch on raisins and peanuts.

Go with crackers. Wholegrain crackers with nut butter or reduced-fat cheese make a satisfying, low-carbohydrate nibble that you can enjoy anytime.

About the Recipes in This Book

All of the basic principles of smart low-carb cooking have been discussed above. To see these principles in action, turn to the recipe section and try a recipe that takes your fancy. How about Pecan Muffins (page 99), Pesto Chicken Sandwich with Roasted Peppers (page 156) or Chocolate-Almond Meringue Biscuits (page 331)? All 200 recipes are quick to make and most of them use easy-to-find ingredients. Here are a few general notes about the recipes to bear in mind.

Nutrition notes. Every recipe in this book comes with a complete nutrition analysis that was calculated with Dietplan5 – Forestfield Software. When a recipe offers an alternative ingredient, only the first ingredient has been used for analysis. Optional ingredients have not been included in the analysis. Each nutrition analysis includes energy (expressed as calories and kilojoules), protein, carbohydrate (including total sugars), fat (including saturated fat), fibre and sodium. The figures have been rounded down or up to the nearest whole number. As with any food you eat, use these nutrition facts to make smart choices and eat a balanced diet overall.

Some recipes are higher in carbohydrates. Most of the 200 recipes in this book are low to moderate in carbohydrates. You may notice that some recipes are higher in carbs than you might expect (30 grams or more per serving). Don't worry. In most cases, these recipes have a low glycaemic index. For instance, oats are fairly high in carbs, but their relatively low glycaemic index makes them a healthy food. Other higher-carb recipes are intended as splurge foods to be eaten occasionally as an indulgence. These high-carb treats are important to sticking with a reduced-carb plan in the long run. If you're eating about 180 grams of carbohydrate a day (the amount recommended for most people), one dish with 30 or 40 grams of carbohydrate can easily be fitted into a day's worth of meals. Either way, don't get too hung up on just counting carbohydrates. Balancing both low-carbohydrate foods and low-glycaemic index foods is the real cornerstone of smart low-carb eating.

Some recipes are higher in fat. Don't be alarmed if you see that some of these recipes are higher in fat than you might expect (20 grams or more). These recipes are still good for you. We've just been conditioned to believe that all fat is bad. But in fact, several types of fat are essential for your body's long-term health. These mono- and polyunsaturated fats are the types used most often in the higher-fat recipes in this book. It's okay to eat a bit more of these now and then. Notice that saturated fat is kept to a minimum. See page 25 for more on healthy versus less-healthy fats.

Consider using the Diet Exchanges. To get balance by looking broadly at food groups, use the Diet Exchanges, too. Diet Exchanges make it easier to keep track of how much you are eating from each food group in the food pyramid (page 42). The basic food groups include milk (dairy products), vegetable, fruit, bread (starches), meat (protein foods) and fat. In the Diet Exchanges, the number in front of each food group shows how many servings from that group are provided by the recipe. You might notice that certain recipes contain no meat, yet have a number in front of the meat group. That's because all protein foods, including nuts and eggs, are counted here as meat (protein). If you're following one of the suggested plans in this book, the Diet Exchanges will help you to eat the right amount from each food group and reach your weight-loss goals.

Enjoy your food. No matter how you decide to implement the principles of smart low-carb eating, it's important to enjoy your food. When you try one of these recipes, or when you eat any food, take the time to really savour it. Many people say that when they slow down and enjoy their food, they are rewarded with an eating satisfaction that leaves them feeling less hungry later on.

FRIED EGGS WITH VINEGAR
232 calories, 0 g carbs

30 g/1 oz butter

8 large eggs

1 teaspoon salt

¼ teaspoon ground black pepper

⅛ teaspoon dried marjoram or basil

4 teaspoons red wine vinegar

**1 teaspoon chopped fresh parsley
(optional)**

Melt half of the butter in a large non-stick frying pan over medium-low heat. Add the eggs and sprinkle with the salt, pepper and marjoram or basil (work in batches if necessary). Cover and cook until the whites are set and the yolks are almost set, 3 to 5 minutes. (For steam-basted eggs, add 1 teaspoon water to the pan and cover with a lid.)

Remove to plates. Place the frying pan over low heat and add the remaining butter. Cook until the butter turns light brown, 1 to 2 minutes. Add the vinegar. Pour the vinegar mixture over the eggs. Sprinkle with the parsley (if using). Serve hot.

Makes 4 servings

Per serving: energy 232 cals/962 kJ; protein 15 g; carbohydrate 0 g (of which 0 g sugars); fat 19 g (of which 8 g saturates); fibre 0 g; sodium 224 mg

Diet Exchanges: 0 milk, 0 vegetable, 0 fruit, 0 bread, 2 meat, 2½ fat

Time-Savers

Cook the eggs 1 to 2 days ahead and keep them in the refrigerator in a covered container for a speedy breakfast or packed lunch. Reheat at 180°C/350°F/gas 4 for 8 to 10 minutes. Or serve at room temperature in a sandwich with cress and sliced cheese.

Baked Eggs with Cheese and Courgettes and Sesame Buttermilk Scones (page 101)

BAKED EGGS WITH CHEESE AND COURGETTES
285 calories, 2 g carbs

7 g/¼ oz butter

2 teaspoons olive oil

½ small onion, chopped

2 courgettes (340 g/12 oz), thinly
sliced

½ teaspoon dried basil

½ teaspoon salt

¼ teaspoon ground black pepper

30 g/1 oz sharp provolone or Jarlsberg
cheese, grated

8 large eggs

1 tablespoon double cream or chicken
stock

Preheat the oven to 180°C/350°F/gas 4.

Heat the butter and oil in a large non-stick frying pan over medium heat until the butter has melted. Add the onion, courgettes, basil, ¼ teaspoon of the salt and ⅛ teaspoon of the pepper. Cook, stirring occasionally, until crisp-tender, 5 to 8 minutes.

Spread the courgette mixture over the bottom of 4 individual, shallow ovenproof dishes (or use 1 large ovenproof dish). Sprinkle with half of the cheese and add the eggs (without breaking the yolks or stirring). Sprinkle with the remaining salt and pepper and the remaining cheese. Drizzle with the cream or stock. Cover with foil and bake until the whites are set and the yolks begin to thicken, about 15 minutes for individual dishes or 20 minutes for 1 large dish.

Makes 4 servings

Per serving: energy 285 cals/1183 kJ; protein 19 g; carbohydrate 2 g (of which 2 g sugars); fat 22 g (of which 9 g saturates); fibre 1 g; sodium 232 mg

Diet Exchanges: 0 milk, 1 vegetable, 0 fruit, 0 bread, 2 meat, 2½ fat

Time-Savers

Make extra servings of this dish and refrigerate in a covered container for up to 2 days. Reheat, covered, at 180°/350°F/gas 4 for 10 to 15 minutes.
For an on-the-go breakfast sandwich, tuck the eggs into a bread roll or between slices of bread.

PUFFY FRITTATA WITH HAM AND GREEN PEPPER

295 calories, 2 g carbs

30 g/1 oz butter

1 small onion, chopped

1 green pepper, chopped

½ teaspoon salt

½ teaspoon ground black pepper

8 slices (170 g/6 oz) ham, chopped

8 large eggs, at room temperature

4 tablespoons water

45 g/1½ oz Cheddar cheese, grated (optional)

Preheat the oven to 130°C/250°F/gas ½.

Melt half of the butter in a large non-stick frying pan over low heat. Add the onion, pepper, ¼ teaspoon of the salt and ¼ teaspoon of the pepper. Cook, stirring occasionally, until tender-crisp, 3 to 4 minutes. Stir in the ham and cook for 1 minute, stirring occasionally. Transfer to a plate.

Separate the eggs, placing the yolks in a medium-size bowl and the whites in a large bowl. Lightly beat the yolks with the water, the remaining ¼ teaspoon salt and the remaining ¼ teaspoon pepper. Beat the egg whites until they form stiff, but not dry, peaks. Fold the yolks into the whites.

Melt the remaining butter in the frying pan over low heat. Pour in the eggs and spread them evenly with a rubber spatula. Scatter the ham mixture and cheese (if using) over the top, cover and cook until the eggs are set, 25 to 30 minutes. Slide the frittata onto a plate and serve immediately (puffiness will subside in 5 to 7 minutes).

Makes 4 servings

Per serving: energy 295 cals/1226 kJ; protein 23 g; carbohydrate 2 g (of which 2 g sugars); fat 21 g (of which 9 g saturates); fibre 1 g; sodium 785 mg

Diet Exchanges: 0 milk, 1½ vegetable, 0 fruit, 0 bread, 3 meat, 2 fat

Time-Saver

Extra servings make wonderful sandwiches at room temperature or hot. Refrigerate the frittata for up to 2 days. To reheat: place the frittata on a baking tray coated with cooking spray, cover and bake at 180°C/350°F/gas 4 for about 10 minutes.

Puffy Frittata with Ham and Green Pepper

COURGETTE AND MUSHROOM FRITTATA

256 calories; 4 g carbs

30 g/1 oz butter

1 small onion, chopped

1 courgette (170 g/6 oz), thinly sliced

4 large mushrooms (115–145 g/ 4–5 oz), chopped

½ large red pepper, chopped

½ teaspoon salt

¼ teaspoon dried thyme

¼ teaspoon ground black pepper

8 large eggs, at room temperature

1½ tablespoons grated Parmesan cheese (optional)

Place the grill pan in the lowest position possible from the heat source and preheat the grill.

Melt half of the butter in a large non-stick frying pan over medium heat. Add the onion, courgette, mushrooms, red pepper, ¼ teaspoon of the salt, the thyme and ⅛ teaspoon of the pepper. Cook, stirring occasionally, until the vegetables are tender and no juices remain in the pan, 8 to 10 minutes.

In a large bowl, combine the eggs, the remaining ¼ teaspoon salt, the remaining ⅛ teaspoon pepper and the grated cheese (if using).

Melt the remaining butter in the frying pan over very low heat. Pour in the egg mixture. Cook, uncovered and without stirring, until only the top remains runny, 15 to 20 minutes. Place the frying pan under the grill and cook until the eggs are just set, about 2 minutes. Slide the frittata onto a large serving plate and serve hot, warm or at room temperature.

Makes 4 servings

Per serving: energy 256 cals/1065 kJ; protein 17 g; carbohydrate 4 g (of which 3 g sugars); fat 19.5 g (of which 8 g saturates); fibre 1 g; sodium 228 mg

Diet Exchanges: 0 milk, 1½ vegetable, 0 fruit, 0 bread, 1½ meat, 2½ fat

Time-Saver

Completely prepare the frittata up to 2 days ahead, cover and refrigerate. Reheat, covered, at 180°C/ 350°F/gas 4 until warm, about 10 minutes.

ASPARAGUS AND GOAT'S CHEESE OMELETTES
321 calories, 4 g carbs

- **285 g/10 oz asparagus spears, trimmed and cut into 1 cm/ ½ in lengths**
- **8 large eggs**
- **180 ml/6 fl oz skimmed milk**
- **4 tablespoons chopped fresh basil**
- **½ teaspoon salt**
- **½ teaspoon ground black pepper**
- **15 g/½ oz butter, cut into 4 equal pieces**
- **1 garlic clove, finely chopped**
- **90 g/3 oz goat's cheese, crumbled**

Preheat the oven to 130°C/250°F/gas ½. Coat a large baking tray with cooking spray.

Cook the asparagus in boiling water over high heat until tender-crisp, 2 to 5 minutes. Drain in a colander and pat dry on kitchen paper.

To make one omelette at a time: break 2 of the eggs into a small bowl. Add 3 tablespoons milk and lightly beat with a fork. Stir in 1 tablespoon of the basil, ⅛ teaspoon of the salt and ⅛ teaspoon of the pepper.

Melt 1 piece of the butter in a 20 cm/ 8 in non-stick frying pan over medium heat. Add a quarter of the garlic and cook until soft, 2 minutes. Stir in a quarter of the asparagus, then pour in the egg mixture. Cook until the eggs are almost set, 4 minutes, lifting the edge occasionally to let the raw eggs flow under.

Spoon 2 tablespoons of the goat's cheese along the centre. Fold the omelette in half, remove to the prepared baking tray and place in the oven to keep warm.

Prepare 3 more omelettes in the same fashion and serve hot.

Makes 4

Per serving: energy 321 cals/1335 kJ; protein 24 g; carbohydrate 4 g (of which 3.5 g sugars); fat 23.5 g (of which 10 g saturates); fibre 1 g; sodium 583 mg

Diet Exchanges: 0 milk, 1 vegetable, 0 fruit, 0 bread, 2½ meat, 2½ fat

▶Flavour Tip
Omelettes taste much better when made individually. If you make one large omelette, the eggs are bound to become overcooked and rubbery.

SCRAMBLED EGGS WITH SAUSAGE AND SPRING ONIONS

251 calories, 3 g carbs

145–170 g/5–6 oz turkey sausages, cut into bite-size pieces

8 large eggs

3 spring onions, thinly sliced

¼ teaspoon salt

¼ teaspoon ground black pepper

6 drops hot-pepper sauce

7 g/¼ oz butter

Warm a large non-stick frying pan over medium heat. Add the sausage and cook until heated through, 8 to 10 minutes.

Meanwhile, break the eggs into a bowl and beat lightly with a fork. Stir in the spring onions, salt, pepper and hot-pepper sauce.

Melt the butter in the frying pan with the sausage over medium-low heat. Pour in the eggs. Cook, stirring almost continually, until the eggs are set but still soft and creamy, 6 to 8 minutes. Serve hot.

Makes 4 servings

Per serving: energy 251 cals/1046 kJ; protein 20 g; carbohydrate 3 g (of which 0.5 g sugars); fat 18 g (of which 6 g saturates); fibre 0.5 g; sodium 657 mg

Diet Exchanges: 0 milk, ½ vegetable, 0 fruit, 0 bread, 3 meat, 2 fat

Time-Saver

Store the eggs in a covered container in the refrigerator for up to 2 days. To reheat: place in an ovenproof dish, cover with foil and reheat at 180°C/350°F/gas 4 for 5 minutes.

POACHED EGGS ON TOMATO-AUBERGINE BEDS
242 calories, 2 g carbs

1½ tablespoons distilled white vinegar

1 small aubergine (8 cm/3 in diameter), peeled and cut into 8 rounds (each 5 mm/¼ in thick)

1 tablespoon olive oil

½ teaspoon salt

½ teaspoon ground black pepper

2 tomatoes, cut into 8 slices (each 5 mm/¼ in thick)

¼ teaspoon garlic powder (optional)

4 slices (90 g/3 oz) ham, halved

8 large eggs

3 tablespoons chopped fresh basil (optional)

Preheat the oven to 220°C/425°F/gas 7. Fill a large, deep frying pan with hot water to within 2–3 cm/1 in from the top. Add enough of the vinegar to the water so it tastes faintly of vinegar. Bring to a simmer over medium heat.

Meanwhile, brush both sides of the aubergine slices with the oil and season with ¼ teaspoon of the salt and ¼ teaspoon of the pepper. Place on a baking tray in a single layer. Bake just until tender, 5 to 8 minutes. Remove to a platter or plates. Place 1 slice of tomato on top of each and season with ⅛ teaspoon of the salt, ⅛ teaspoon of the pepper and the garlic powder (if using). Top each with a slice of ham.

Break the eggs one at a time into a bowl, then slip them one at a time into the simmering water. Cook, uncovered, until the whites are set and the yolks are almost set, 3 to 5 minutes. Remove with a slotted spoon, drain well and place on top of the ham. Sprinkle all with the remaining salt and pepper and the basil (if using). Serve hot.

Makes 4 servings

Per serving: energy 242 cals/1008 kJ; protein 20 g; carbohydrate 2 g (of which 2 g sugars); fat 17 g (of which 5 g saturates); fibre 1 g; sodium 697 mg

Diet Exchanges: 0 milk, 2½ vegetable, 0 fruit, 0 bread, 2 meat, 2 fat

WHOLEMEAL CREPES WITH BANANA AND KIWIFRUIT

191 calories, 33 g carbs

CREPES

- **145 g/5 oz wholemeal plain flour**
- **¼ teaspoon salt**
- **1 egg**
- **280 ml/9 fl oz unsweetened soya milk or whole milk**
- **1½ teaspoons vanilla essence**
- **7 g/¼ oz butter**
- **1–2 tablespoons water**

FILLING

- **115 g/4 oz low-fat natural yoghurt**
- **1 banana, cut into 24 diagonal slices**
- **2 kiwifruit, peeled, cut in half lengthwise and sliced**
- **2 teaspoons lime juice (optional)**
- **½ teaspoon ground cinnamon**

To make the crepes: In a large bowl, combine the flour and salt.

In a small bowl, beat the egg, then stir in the milk and vanilla. Pour into the flour and mix well.

Melt a quarter of the butter in a 20 cm/ 8 in non-stick frying pan over medium heat. Pour 3 tablespoons of batter into the pan and tilt the pan to coat the bottom in a thin layer (if the batter seems too thick add 1 to 2 tablespoons water). Cook the first side until nicely browned, about 2 minutes. Using a spatula, turn the crepe and cook the second side for 1 to 2 minutes (the second side will look spotted). Slide the crepe onto a plate and cover with foil to keep warm. Continue making crepes in the same fashion, buttering the pan after every second crepe, until all the butter and batter are used.

To make the filling and assemble: Place a crepe on a serving plate, attractive side down, and spread with 1 tablespoon of yoghurt. Arrange 3 banana slices and a quarter of a kiwifruit in strips one-third of the way from one edge. Sprinkle with ¼ teaspoon of the lime juice and a pinch of the cinnamon and roll up. Continue assembling the remaining crepes.

Makes 4 servings (8 crepes)

Per serving: energy 191 cals/807 kJ; protein 8.5 g; carbohydrate 33 g (of which 9.5 g sugars); fat 4 g (of which 1.5 g saturates); fibre 4 g; sodium 207 mg

Diet Exchanges: ½ milk, 0 vegetable, 1 fruit, 1 bread, 0 meat, 1 fat

Time-Saver

To make these ahead, cook the crepes, stack and cover with foil and refrigerate or freeze. Thaw if frozen, then reheat the foil-wrapped stack on a baking tray at 180°C/350°F/gas 4 until the crepes are warm and pliable, 5 to 8 minutes, or in a frying pan on the hob. Assemble as directed.

Wholemeal Crepes with Banana and Kiwifruit

Wholemeal Pancakes with Berry Cream Syrup

WHOLEMEAL PANCAKES WITH BERRY CREAM SYRUP

268 calories, 30 g carbs

PANCAKES

- **100 g/3½ oz wholemeal plain flour**
- **60 g/2 oz buckwheat flour**
- **1½ teaspoons baking powder**
- **½ teaspoon bicarbonate of soda**
- **⅛ teaspoon salt**
- **240 ml/8 fl oz buttermilk**
- **1 large egg, at room temperature, separated**
- **3 tablespoons + 2 teaspoons melted butter**
- **2 tablespoons Splenda**

SYRUP

- **4 tablespoons raspberry fruit spread**
- **2 tablespoons double cream**
- **3–4 teaspoons orange or apple juice (optional)**

To make the pancakes: In a large bowl, combine the wholemeal flour, buckwheat flour, baking powder, bicarbonate of soda and salt.

In a measuring jug, mix the buttermilk, egg yolk, 3 tablespoons butter and the Splenda. Stir into the flour mixture until well-combined. In a small bowl, beat the egg white until it forms stiff, but not dry, peaks. Fold into the batter. (The batter will be light but not fluid.)

Heat a non-stick frying pan or griddle over medium-low heat and add 1 teaspoon of the remaining melted butter. For each pancake, spoon 3 tablespoons of the batter into the frying pan, making 4 cakes at a time, each about 10 cm/4 in in diameter. Cook the first side until the edges begin to look dry, about 3 minutes. Flip the pancakes and cook the second side for 2 to 3 minutes. Continue making pancakes in the same manner until all the butter and batter are used. Serve hot with the syrup.

To make the syrup: In a small bowl, combine the fruit spread, cream and enough juice (if using) to make a syrup. (Without the juice, the topping will have the consistency of a spread.)

Makes 4 servings (8 pancakes)

Per serving: energy 268 cals/1123 kJ; protein 7 g; carbohydrate 30 g (of which 14 g sugars); fat 14 g (of which 8 g saturates); fibre 2 g; sodium 362 mg

Diet Exchanges: ½ milk, 0 vegetable, 0 fruit, 1½ bread, 0 meat, 2½ fat

▶Flavour Tip

For an elegant blueberry variation on this dish, fold 60 g/2 oz blueberries into the finished batter and prepare as above. Serve with low-sugar pancake syrup, fresh blueberries and a dollop of whipped cream.

KAMUT CREPES WITH COTTAGE CHEESE AND FRUIT
216 calories, 27 g carbs

CREPES

60 g/2 oz Kamut flour

2 tablespoons wholemeal plain flour

1 tablespoon unflavoured protein powder

⅛ teaspoon salt

80 ml/3 fl oz apple juice

120 ml/4 fl oz + 1–2 tablespoons water

1 large egg, lightly beaten

15 g/½ oz butter, melted

FILLING

200 g/7 oz reduced fat cottage cheese or ricotta cheese, at room temperature

2 pears (285 g/10 oz), at room temperature, peeled and thinly sliced

4 tablespoons low-calorie maple syrup

To make the crepes: In a large bowl, stir together the Kamut flour and wholemeal flour, protein powder and salt.

In a small bowl, whisk together the apple juice, water, egg and half of the butter. Whisk into the flour mixture to make a smooth batter.

Spread half of the remaining butter in a non-stick frying pan over medium heat. Pour 3 tablespoons of batter into the pan and tilt the pan to coat the bottom in a thin layer (if the batter seems too thick, add 1 to 2 tablespoons of water). Cook the first side until lightly browned, about 1 minute. Using a spatula, turn and cook the second side for 30 to 60 seconds (the second side will look spotted). Slide the crepe onto a plate and cover with foil to keep warm. Continue making crepes in the same fashion, buttering the pan after every second crepe, until all the butter and batter are used.

To make the filling and assemble: Place a crepe on a plate, attractive side down. Arrange the cottage cheese or ricotta cheese and pear in a line one-third of the way from one edge and roll up. Fill the remaining crepes in the same manner. Serve drizzled with syrup.

Makes 4 servings (8 crepes)

Per serving: energy 216 cals/898 kJ; protein 6 g; carbohydrate 27 g (of which 7 g sugars); fat 8 g (of which 4 g saturates); fibre 3 g; sodium 360 mg

Diet Exchanges: 0 milk, 0 vegetable, ½ fruit, 1 bread, 1 meat, 1 fat

▶Flavour Tip

Crepes cooked in butter brown beautifully. If you substitute cooking spray, increase the heat to medium-high and the crepes will brown moderately well.

PECAN MUFFINS
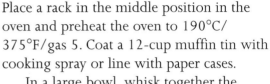
225 calories, 19 g carbs

- **200 g/7 oz wholemeal plain flour**
- **60 g/2 oz soya flour**
- **2½ teaspoons baking powder**
- **½ teaspoon salt**
- **½ teaspoon ground nutmeg**
- **60 g/2 oz toasted pecans, chopped**
- **120 ml/4 fl oz vegetable oil**
- **115 g/4 oz apricot or peach fruit spread**
- **2 large eggs, lightly beaten**
- **1½ teaspoons vanilla essence**
- **2 tablespoons Splenda**

Place a rack in the middle position in the oven and preheat the oven to 190°C/375°F/gas 5. Coat a 12-cup muffin tin with cooking spray or line with paper cases.

In a large bowl, whisk together the wholemeal flour, soya flour, baking powder, salt, nutmeg and pecans.

In a small bowl, combine the oil, fruit spread, eggs, vanilla and Splenda. Add to the flour mixture and stir just until the dry ingredients are moistened.

Spoon into the prepared muffin cups until ¾ full. Bake until a toothpick inserted in the centre of a muffin comes out clean, 12 to 14 minutes. Serve warm.

Makes 12 muffins

Per serving: energy 225 cals/936 kJ; protein 5 g; carbohydrate 19 g (of which 12 g sugars); fat 10 g (of which 2 g saturates); fibre 1 g; sodium 689 mg

Diet Exchanges: 0 milk, 0 vegetable, 0 fruit, 1 bread, ½ meat, 2½ fat

Time-Saver

Make a double batch and cut preparation time in half. To store: let the muffins cool, then wrap them individually and place in a resealable bag. Keep for up to 2 days in the refrigerator or 2 months in the freezer. Thaw the muffins at room temperature and reheat on a baking tray at 180°/350°F/gas 4 for 5 to 10 minutes.

eggs and breakfast foods

RAISIN SPICE QUICK BREAD
185 calories, 31 g carbs

145 g/5 oz wholemeal plain flour

145 g/5 oz oat flour

2 teaspoons baking powder

1½ teaspoons allspice

½ teaspoon cinnamon

½ teaspoon salt

1 large egg, at room temperature

240 ml/8 fl oz semi-skimmed milk

45 g/1½ oz brown sugar

30 g/1 oz butter, melted

1 teaspoon vanilla essence

90 g/3 oz raisins

Preheat the oven to 180°C/350°F/gas 4. Oil a 20 × 10 cm/8 × 4 in loaf tin.

In a large bowl, combine the wholemeal flour, oat flour, baking powder, allspice, cinnamon and salt.

In a medium bowl, lightly beat the egg with the milk, sugar, butter and vanilla. Pour into the flour mixture and stir until just combined. Fold in the raisins.

Pour the batter into the prepared tin and smooth the top.

Bake until a toothpick inserted into the middle comes out clean, 45 to 50 minutes. Cool in the tin on a rack for 10 minutes. Turn out onto rack to cool. Serve warm or at room temperature in thick slices.

Makes 1 loaf (10 slices)

Per slice: energy 185 cals/781 kJ; protein 5 g; carbohydrate 31 g (of which 13 g sugars); fat 5 g (of which 2 g saturates); fibre 2.5 g; sodium 243 mg

Diet Exchanges: 0 milk, 0 vegetable, ½ fruit, 1½ bread, 0 meat, ½ fat

Time-Savers

This bread stores well and is excellent for lunch. Let the loaf cool, then wrap it in clingfilm and place it in a resealable bag. Keep at room temperature for up to 3 days. Reheat at 180°C/350°F/gas 4. For a special treat, spread bread slices with apricot fruit spread and rewarm them topped with a knob of butter.
If you prefer muffins instead of a whole loaf, pour the batter into a 12-cup muffin tin coated with cooking spray and bake for 20 minutes.

SESAME BUTTERMILK SCONES *(photo on page 86)*
204 calories, 18 g carbs

- **170 g/6 oz + 2 tablespoons wholemeal plain flour**
- **75 g/2½ oz soya flour**
- **2½ teaspoons baking powder**
- **½ teaspoon bicarbonate of soda**
- **½ teaspoon salt**
- **1 tablespoon toasted sesame seeds**
- **90 g/3 oz cold butter, cut in pieces**
- **180 ml/6 fl oz cold buttermilk**

Place a rack in the middle position in the oven and preheat the oven to 220°C/425°F/gas 7.

In a large bowl, combine 170 g/6 oz of the wholemeal flour, the soya flour, baking powder, bicarbonate of soda, salt and sesame seeds. Using a pastry blender or fork, cut the butter into the flour mixture until the mixture looks like coarse bread-crumbs.

Using a fork, stir the buttermilk into the flour mixture just until the dry ingredients are moistened and form a rough mound. Dust a work surface with the remaining 2 tablespoons wholemeal flour and turn out the dough. Press together (the dough will be moist) and knead gently about 5 or 6 times.

Using a floured rolling pin, roll out the dough to form a 2 cm/¾ in-thick circle. Using a 6 cm/2½ in-diameter cutter, cut out circles and place 2–3 cm/1 in apart on an ungreased baking tray. Pinch together the scraps, reroll and cut out additional scones.

Bake until the bottoms are golden and the tops lightly coloured, 11 to 13 minutes. Serve hot, warm or at room temperature.

Makes 8 scones

Per serving: energy 204 cals/851 kJ; protein 7 g; carbohydrate 18 g (of which 3 g sugars); fat 12 g (of which 7 g saturates); fibre 3 g; sodium 275 mg

Diet Exchanges: ½ milk, 0 vegetable, 0 fruit, 1 bread, 0 meat, 1½ fat

Time-Savers

Toast the sesame seeds in a small baking dish in the oven while it preheats.

To save preparation time, make a double batch of these scones and freeze for later. Let the scones cool, wrap them individually in clingfilm and place in a resealable bag. Keep at room temperature for up to 2 days or in the freezer for up to 2 months. Reheat on a baking tray at 180°C/350°F/gas 4 for 5 to 10 minutes.

PORRIDGE WITH RICOTTA, FRUIT AND NUTS
209 calories, 32 g carbs

450 ml/15 fl oz apple juice

450 ml/15 fl oz water

200 g/7 oz rolled oats

⅛ teaspoon salt

½ teaspoon ground cinnamon

60 g/2 oz ricotta cheese

1 large peach or plum (115 g/4 oz), chopped

2 tablespoons sunflower seeds or toasted almonds, chopped

Combine the juice, water, oats and salt in a medium saucepan. Bring to the boil over medium heat. Reduce the heat to low. Cook, uncovered, until thick and creamy, stirring occasionally, 3 to 5 minutes.

Spoon into bowls and sprinkle with the cinnamon. Top with the ricotta, peach or plum and nuts or seeds. Serve hot.

Makes 6 servings

Per serving: energy 209 cals/882 kJ; protein 6 g; carbohydrate 32 g (of which 10 g sugars); fat 7 g (of which 2 g saturates); fibre 3 g; sodium 37 mg

Diet Exchanges: 0 milk, 0 vegetable, 1 fruit, 1 bread, ½ meat, ½ fat

▶Flavour Tips
For a chewier texture, bring the juice, water and salt to the boil, then stir in the oats.
For sweeter porridge, drizzle each serving with 1 to 2 teaspoons low-calorie maple syrup.

CREAMY QUINOA
360 calories, 39 g carbs

600 ml/1 pint semi-skimmed milk

⅛ teaspoon salt

170 g/6 oz quinoa, thoroughly rinsed until the water runs clear

60 g/2 oz chopped dried figs or dates

30 g/1 oz butter (optional)

⅛ teaspoon ground cardamom

2 tablespoons Splenda

30 g/1 oz toasted walnuts, chopped

Combine the milk and salt in a saucepan and bring to the boil. Stir in the quinoa and reduce the heat to low. Cover and cook until all the liquid has evaporated and the grains are tender-crunchy, about 15 minutes. Stir in the figs or dates, butter (if using), cardamom and Splenda.

Remove from the heat. Sprinkle each serving with walnuts. Serve hot.

Makes 4 servings

Per serving: energy 360 cals/1497 kJ; protein 14 g; carbohydrate 39 g (of which 17 g sugars); fat 11 g (of which 3 g saturates); fibre 3 g; sodium 155 mg

Diet Exchanges: 1 milk, 0 vegetable, ½ fruit, 2 bread, 0 meat, 1½ fat

Smart-Carb Insider Tip
WHY NOT EGGS?

Always have eggs in the refrigerator. They are a great source of protein and B vitamins, low in saturated fat and have less than 1 gram of carbohydrate each. Hard boil half a dozen at a time for quick breakfasts or snacks on the run. Or shell two or three of them, place in a resealable bag with some mayonnaise, mustard, onion powder and pepper, then seal and 'squish' to desired consistency. Cut off a corner of the bag and squeeze out the egg mayonnaise onto a lettuce leaf and roll up into a sandwich; or squeeze the mixture into a cucumber, courgette or celery boat for an instant lunch. Other ideas: reheat some leftover veggies, beat some eggs, pour them over the veggies and pop into the microwave or heat in a frying pan for a satisfying vegetable-egg scramble.

Cherry Porridge

203 calories, 42 g carbs

- **500 ml/18 fl oz water**
- **300 ml/10 fl oz apple juice**
- **¼ teaspoon salt**
- **170 g/6 oz instant oat cereal or rolled oats**
- **4 teaspoons cherry fruit spread**
- **⅛ teaspoon ground nutmeg**
- **⅛ teaspoon ground cardamom or cinnamon**
- **1½ tablespoons chopped hazelnuts (optional)**

Combine the water, juice and salt in a saucepan and bring to the boil over medium heat. Stir in the oats and reduce the heat to low. Cook, uncovered, until thick, stirring occasionally, 2 to 6 minutes. Remove from the heat and stir in the fruit spread.

Spoon into bowls and sprinkle with the nutmeg, cardamom and hazelnuts (if using). Serve hot.

Makes 4 servings

Per serving: energy 203 cals/844 kJ; protein 3 g; carbohydrate 42 g (of which 9 g sugars); fat 1 g (of which 0 g saturates); fibre 5 g; sodium 159 mg

Diet Exchanges: 0 milk, 0 vegetable, 1 fruit, 2 bread, 0 meat, 0 fat

snacks, appetisers & beverages

CHEESE, APPLE AND NUT BUTTER ROLL-UPS 106

SOFT YOGHURT CHEESE WITH OLIVES 107

SOFT YOGHURT CHEESE 107

COURGETTE CHIPS 108

ROASTED MIXED NUTS 109

CURRIED EGGS WITH HORSERADISH AND SPRING ONIONS 110

CRACKED WHEAT SALAD WITH SPINACH 111

AVOCADO WITH BLACK BEAN SALAD 113

CANNELLINI BEANS WITH CHEESE AND BASIL 114

CHICORY WITH AUBERGINE, OLIVES AND PINE NUTS .117

CRUDITÉS WITH SPICY PEANUT DIPPING SAUCE 118

MINI AUBERGINE PIZZAS 119

PRAWNS IN MUSTARD-HORSERADISH SAUCE 120

COURGETTE-STUFFED MUSHROOMS 122

ICED ORANGE-COCONUT DRINK 123

HOT APPLE JUICE WITH GINGER 124

STRAWBERRY PROTEIN SHAKE 124

BUTTERMILK FRUIT SHAKE 125

MINT-INFUSED DARJEELING TEA 125

PEACH-PEAR SMOOTHIE 126

CHEESE, APPLE AND NUT BUTTER ROLL-UPS
152 calories, 3 g carbs

4 thin slices (115 g/4 oz) Jarlsberg or Double Gloucester cheese, at room temperature

½ large apple (90 g/3 oz), thinly sliced

1 tablespoon macadamia nut butter or 2 teaspoons unsweetened peanut butter

Place the cheese on a cutting board. Arrange the apple slices in a horizontal row 2–3 cm/ 1 in from a narrow end of each cheese slice, drizzle or spread with the nut butter and roll up. Secure with toothpicks.

Makes 4 servings

Per serving: energy 152 cals/631 kJ; protein 8 g; carbohydrate 3 g (of which 3 g sugars); fat 12 g (of which 7 g saturates); fibre 0.6 g; sodium 193 mg

Diet Exchanges: 0 milk, 0 vegetable, ½ fruit, 0 bread, 1 meat, 1 fat

Time-Saver

Make this easy snack whenever you have a few minutes. It keeps in the refrigerator or at room temperature for 2 to 3 hours. If making ahead, be sure to completely cover the apple slices with nut butter to keep them from browning.

HIDDEN ROADBLOCK to weight loss
NOT ENOUGH FAT

Believe it or not, a lack of fat in your daily diet may slow down your weight-loss efforts. Fats make up the basic structure of our cell membranes and are needed for several vital functions. Fats also satisfy our hunger. If you don't eat enough fats, you may end up overeating other foods to make up for what's missing. If you think that eating fat is not conducive to weight loss, consider this: in 1998, several teams of researchers studied the impact of all macronutrients on the development of obesity. Keeping calorie intake constant, they found that there is no data to substantiate the theory that fat promotes the development of obesity more than any other macronutrient. Of course, this doesn't mean it's OK to gorge yourself on butter, steaks and bacon. Just be sure to choose a variety of healthy fats every day, like those found in nuts, seeds, olives, avocados, salmon and vegetable oils. By the same token, try to minimise the saturated fats and trans fats found in butter, margarine, lard and processed snack foods such as crackers.

SOFT YOGHURT CHEESE WITH OLIVES
114 calories, 3 g carbs

230 g/8 oz Soft Yoghurt Cheese (below)

2 tablespoons olive oil

½–¾ teaspoon flaxseed (linseed) oil (optional)

10 pitted black kalamata or green Spanish olives (45 g/1½ oz), chopped

¼ teaspoon salt

⅛ teaspoon ground black pepper

15 celery sticks, cut into 8–10 cm/ 3–4 in pieces

Place the yoghurt cheese in a large bowl and gradually stir in the olive oil. Stir in the flax-seed oil (if using), olives, salt and pepper.

Serve straight away or chill for 1 hour or up to 5 days. Use as a dip with the celery.

Makes 4 servings

Per serving: energy 114 cals/477 kJ; protein 8 g; carbohydrate 3 g (of which 3 g sugars); fat 8 g (of which 1.5 g saturates); fibre 2 g; sodium 685 mg

Diet Exchanges: ½ milk, 1 vegetable, 0 fruit, 0 bread, 0 meat, 1½ fat

SOFT YOGHURT CHEESE
26 calories, 1 g carbs

625 g/1 lb 6 oz low-fat natural yoghurt

Rinse a 35–40 cm/14–16 in length of muslin in cold water and wring out. Fold in half and line a large colander, leaving overhanging sides. Spoon the yoghurt into the colander, place over a larger bowl, cover with clingfilm and refrigerate for 10 to 12 hours or overnight. Discard the liquid in the bowl.

Lift the muslin by the sides and turn the cheese into a clean bowl. Use immediately or refrigerate for up to 5 days.

Makes 230 g/8 oz

Per 2 tablespoons: energy 26 cals/110 kJ; protein 4 g; carbohydrate 1 g (of which 1 g sugars); fat 1 g (of which 0.5 g saturates); fibre 0 g; sodium 126 mg

Diet Exchanges: ½ milk, 0 vegetable, 0 fruit, 0 bread, 0 meat, 0 fat

▶Flavour Tips

To make a salad dressing, mix the yoghurt cheese with 1 tablespoon prepared mustard, 1 teaspoon lemon juice or vinegar, 2 tablespoons oil and 2 to 4 tablespoons unsweetened soya milk to make it pourable.

COURGETTE CHIPS
55 calories, 3 g carbs

**2–3 large courgettes
(680–800 g/1½–1¾ lb)**

1 tablespoon olive oil

¼ teaspoon salt

¼ teaspoon garlic powder (optional)

Preheat the oven to 200°C/400°F/gas 6. Coat 2 baking trays with cooking spray.

Thinly slice the courgettes on the diagonal, about 3 mm/⅛ in thick. Place the slices in a large bowl and toss well with the oil, salt and garlic powder (if using). Arrange in a single layer on the baking trays.

Bake, turning often, for 25 minutes. Reduce the oven temperature to 150°C/300°F/gas 2 and bake until splotchy brown and crisp, 10 to 15 minutes. Remove to kitchen paper and let cool. These will keep at room temperature, uncovered, for several hours.

Makes 4 servings

Per serving: energy 55 cals/227 kJ; protein 3 g; carbohydrate 3 g (of which 3 g sugars); fat 3 g (of which 0.5 g saturates); fibre 1.5 g; sodium 147 mg

Diet Exchanges: 0 milk, 1 vegetable, 0 fruit, 0 bread, 0 meat, 1 fat

Smart-Carb Insider Tip
STOCK SNACKS

Keep a few low-carbohydrate snacks in your kitchen, desk, car or bag. Nuts and cheeses are really satisfying; pine nuts, in particular, are high in protein and very filling. Keep a jar of nut butter or a tub of cream cheese to hand to spread on sticks of celery for a snack. Or snack on mozzarella or other cheeses.

Roasted Mixed Nuts
207 calories, 2 g carbs

- **115 g/4 oz mixed unsalted pecans, walnuts and macadamia nuts**
- **1½ tablespoons apple, grape or other fruit juice**
- **½ teaspoon celery salt and/or curry powder**

Preheat the oven to 180°C/350°F/gas 4.

In a small bowl, combine the nuts, juice, celery salt and/or curry powder. Toss to coat and spread in a single layer on a baking tray. Roast until light golden, 4 to 6 minutes. Let cool before serving. These will keep at room temperature, uncovered, for several days.

Makes 4 servings

Per serving: energy 207 cals/855 kJ; protein 3 g; carbohydrate 2 g (of which 1.5 g sugars); fat 21 g (of which 2 g saturates); fibre 1.5 g; sodium 181 mg

Diet Exchanges: 0 milk, 0 vegetable, 0 fruit, ½ bread, ½ meat, 3½ fat

▶Flavour Tip

If humid weather makes the nuts soft, reheat them at 180°C/350°F/gas 4 for 1 to 2 minutes.

snacks, appetisers and beverages

CURRIED EGGS WITH HORSERADISH AND SPRING ONIONS

203 calories, 1 g carbs

4 large eggs

2 tablespoons mayonnaise

1 teaspoon Dijon mustard

1 teaspoon prepared horseradish

1 tablespoon finely chopped spring onions

¼ teaspoon salt

⅛ teaspoon ground black pepper

⅛ teaspoon paprika (optional)

Place the eggs in a single layer in a saucepan and cover with cold water by 2–3 cm/1 in. Cover the pan and bring to the boil over high heat. As soon as the water begins to boil, remove the pan from the heat and let it sit, covered, for 15 minutes. Drain, then run cold water over the eggs. Let them sit in the water until completely cooled. To remove the shells, gently tap the eggs all over on a hard surface, roll the eggs between your hands, then peel away the shells.

Cut the eggs in half lengthwise and place the yolks in a small mixing bowl. Mash, adding the mayonnaise and mustard, until a smooth paste forms. Stir in the horseradish, spring onions, salt and pepper. Using a teaspoon, stuff the egg cavities with the yolk mixture and sprinkle with paprika (if using). Serve at room temperature or chilled.

Makes 4 servings

Per serving: energy 203 cals/839 kJ; protein 8 g; carbohydrate 1 g (of which 0.5 g sugars); fat 19 g (of which 4 g saturates); fibre 0 g; sodium 304 mg

Diet Exchanges: 0 milk, 0 vegetable, 0 fruit, 0 bread, 1 meat, 2 fat

Time-Savers

Make these eggs ahead and keep them in a covered container in the refrigerator for up to 24 hours. To keep them from sliding around, serve on a bed of tossed salad or spinach leaves. If you have leftovers, chop the eggs and roll up in lettuce leaves for a sandwich.

CRACKED WHEAT SALAD WITH SPINACH

144 calories, 24 g carbs

170 g/6 oz cracked wheat (bulgar)

350 ml/12 fl oz boiling water

2 tablespoons olive oil

2 tablespoons lemon juice

1 large tomato, chopped

6 spring onions, finely sliced

30 g/1 oz fresh parsley and/or mint, chopped

¾ teaspoon salt

¼ teaspoon ground black pepper

Pinch of garlic powder

Pinch of ground cumin (optional)

12–18 spinach leaves

Combine the cracked wheat and boiling water in a large bowl, cover and let stand until the wheat is tender, 20 to 30 minutes. Drain off any unabsorbed water.

Add the oil and lemon juice and toss to mix. Stir in the tomato, spring onions, parsley and/or mint, salt, pepper, garlic powder and cumin (if using). Chill for 1 to 2 hours.

Place the spinach leaves on 6 plates and spoon the salad on top.

Makes 6 servings

Per serving: energy 144 cals/606 kJ; protein 3 g; carbohydrate 24 g (of which 1.5 g sugars); fat 5 g (of which 1 g saturates); fibre 1 g; sodium 239 mg

Diet Exchanges: 0 milk, ½ vegetable, 0 fruit, 1 bread, 0 meat, 1 fat

▶Flavour Tips

Replace 180 ml/6 fl oz of the water with 180 ml/ 6 fl oz hot vegetable stock. You can also add 75 g/ 2½ oz chopped cucumber to the salad. To eat this as an appetiser or sandwich, roll up 1 to 2 tablespoons in very large spinach or lettuce leaves, folding in the ends as you roll. This salad keeps in the refrigerator for up to 4 days.

Avocado with Black Bean Salad

AVOCADO WITH BLACK BEAN SALAD
263 calories, 20 g carbs

**About 1 tablespoon lime juice
    or white wine vinegar**

1½ tablespoons olive oil

**1 tin (about 420 g/14½ oz) black
    beans, drained**

¼ green pepper, finely chopped

1 garlic clove, finely chopped

½ teaspoon salt

⅛ teaspoon ground black pepper

⅛ teaspoon chilli powder (optional)

**1½ teaspoons chopped fresh
    coriander**

1 avocado (230 g/8 oz), quartered

Place the lime juice or vinegar in a large bowl and gradually whisk in the oil. Stir in the beans, green pepper, garlic, salt, black pepper and chilli powder (if using). Taste and add more lime juice or vinegar if you like. Stir in the coriander.

Place the avocado, cavities up, on 4 plates. Spoon the bean mixture into the cavities so it overflows onto the plate.

Makes 4 servings

Per serving: energy 263 cals/1098 kJ; protein 10 g; carbohydrate 20 g (of which 2 g sugars); fat 16 g (of which 3 g saturates); fibre 6 g; sodium 253 mg

Diet Exchanges: 0 milk, 0 vegetable, ½ fruit, 1 bread, ½ meat, 2½ fat

Time-Saver

Make the bean salad up to 5 days ahead and store it in the refrigerator. Cut the avocado just before serving to minimize the darkening that occurs when avocado is exposed to air.

CANNELLINI BEANS WITH CHEESE AND BASIL

108 calories, 12 g carbs

- **1½ tins (about 425 g/15 oz each) cannellini or other white beans, drained, 80 ml/3 fl oz liquid reserved**
- **1 tablespoon olive oil**
- **½ teaspoon salt**
- **¼ teaspoon garlic powder**
- **⅛ teaspoon ground black pepper**
- **1½ tablespoons chopped fresh basil**
- **3 tablespoons grated Parmesan or pecorino cheese**

Preheat the oven to 220°C/425°F/gas 7.

Place the beans and reserved liquid in a large mixing bowl and partially mash the beans against the side of the bowl with a wooden spoon. Stir in the oil, salt, garlic powder and pepper. Mix in the basil. Place in a small shallow ovenproof dish and sprinkle with the cheese. Bake until bubbling, 15 to 20 minutes. Serve hot or warm.

Makes 6 servings

Per serving: energy 108 cals/454 kJ; protein 7 g; carbohydrate 12 g (of which 1 g sugars); fat 4 g (of which 1 g saturates); fibre 4 g; sodium 578 mg

Diet Exchanges: 0 milk, 0 vegetable, 0 fruit, ½ bread, ½ meat, ½ fat

Time-Saver

Make this dish whenever you have a minute and store it covered in the refrigerator for up to 4 days. Reheat, covered, at 180°C/350°F/gas 4 for about 20 minutes.

Cannellini Beans with Cheese and Basil

Chicory with Aubergine, Olives and Pine Nuts

CHICORY WITH AUBERGINE, OLIVES AND PINE NUTS

41 calories, 2 g carbs

- **1 small aubergine (230 g/8 oz)**
- **1½ teaspoons walnut or olive oil**
- **3 kalamata or other purple olives, chopped**
- **2 teaspoons toasted pine nuts**
- **¼ teaspoon lemon juice (optional)**
- **¼ teaspoon salt**
- **¼ teaspoon ground black pepper**
- **12 chicory leaves**
- **1 teaspoon chopped fresh parsley (optional)**

Preheat the oven to 220°C/425°F/gas 7.

Pierce the aubergine in 4 or 5 places with a fork and place in a baking tin. Roast until completely soft, 20 to 30 minutes, turning once or twice. Remove from the oven and let cool.

Cut the aubergine in half lengthwise and scrape out the pulp, discarding the stem and skin. Finely chop the aubergine and place it in a medium mixing bowl. Gradually add the oil, stirring vigorously, until the aubergine absorbs it. Stir in the olives, pine nuts, lemon juice (if using), salt and pepper.

Spoon the aubergine onto the wide end of the chicory leaves and sprinkle with parsley (if using).

Makes 4 servings

Per serving: energy 41 cals/170 kJ; protein 1 g; carbohydrate 2 g (of which 1 g sugars); fat 3.5 g (of which 0.5 g saturates); fibre 1.5 g; sodium 215 mg

Diet Exchanges: 0 milk, 2 vegetable, 0 fruit, 0 bread, 0 meat, ½ fat

Time-Savers

Roast the aubergine up to 4 days ahead of time and store in a covered container in the refrigerator. Pour off any accumulated liquid before completing the recipe. Or mix the chopped aubergine with the olives, pine nuts and seasoning and store in the refrigerator for up to 3 days.
You can also use the filling to roll inside thin slices of turkey or ham for a snack or lunch.

CRUDITÉS WITH SPICY PEANUT DIPPING SAUCE

84 calories, 4 g carbs

90 g/3 oz unsweetened peanut butter

1–2 small hot chilli peppers (20–30 g/ ¾–1 oz), seeded and chopped (wear plastic gloves when handling)

2 small garlic cloves, finely chopped

About 3 tablespoons mango nectar or apple juice

4 tablespoons lime juice

2 tablespoons soy sauce

¼ teaspoon salt

230 g/8 oz assorted raw vegetables

In a blender, combine the peanut butter, chilli peppers, garlic, nectar or juice, lime juice, soy sauce and salt. Process until a thick and smooth sauce forms, adding a little more nectar or juice as needed. Serve as a dip with the vegetables.

Makes 8 servings

Per serving: energy 84 cals/348 kJ; protein 3 g; carbohydrate 4 g (of which 3 g sugars); fat 6 g (of which 1 g saturates); fibre 1 g; sodium 338 mg

Diet Exchanges: 0 milk, ½ vegetable, 0 fruit, 0 bread, ½ meat, 1 fat

Time-Saver

Make a double batch of the sauce and use some as a sandwich spread, some as a salad dressing. It's also delicious with apple slices, crisp wholewheat pitta chips or drizzled over grilled prawns or plaice. Store in the refrigerator in a covered container for up to 5 days.

MINI AUBERGINE PIZZAS
95 calories, 7 g carbs

1 aubergine (8 cm/3 in diameter), peeled and cut into 4 slices 1 cm/½ in thick

4 teaspoons olive oil

½ teaspoon salt

⅛ teaspoon ground black pepper

1 large ripe tomato, cut into 4 slices

½ teaspoon dried oregano

¼ teaspoon dried basil

½ teaspoon garlic powder

75 g/2½ oz smoked or regular mozzarella, finely chopped

Preheat the oven to 220°C/425°F/gas 7.

Brush both sides of the aubergine with the oil and season with the salt and pepper. Arrange on a baking tray and bake until browned and almost tender, 6 to 8 minutes, turning once.

Place a tomato slice on each aubergine slice and season with the oregano, basil and garlic powder. Top with the cheese and bake until the cheese melts, 3 to 5 minutes. Serve hot.

Makes 4 servings

Per serving: energy 95 cals/396 kJ; protein 3 g; carbohydrate 7 g (of which 6.5 g sugars); fat 6 g (of which 2 g saturates); fibre 3 g; sodium 257 mg

Diet Exchanges: 0 milk, 2 vegetable, 0 fruit, 0 bread, ½ meat, 1 fat

▶Flavour Tip

You can replace the aubergine with wholewheat mini pitta breads, each split to make 2 pizzas.

PRAWNS IN MUSTARD-HORSERADISH SAUCE
124 calories, 1 g carbs

PRAWNS

1 thin lemon slice

Salt to taste

**20 large fresh, uncooked prawns
(455 g/1 lb), cleaned and deveined**

MUSTARD-HORSERADISH SAUCE

4 teaspoons lemon juice

4 teaspoons Dijon mustard

2½ tablespoons olive oil

1 tablespoon prepared horseradish

2 teaspoons soured cream

¼ teaspoon salt

⅛ teaspoon ground black pepper

**2 teaspoons finely chopped
spring onions**

To cook the prawns: In a saucepan, combine 1.5 litres/2½ pints of water, the lemon slice and salt to taste. Bring to the boil over high heat. Reduce the heat and cook for 5 minutes. Add the prawns to the lemon water and cook until they are opaque and pink, 2 to 3 minutes. Drain, and discard the lemon slice.

To make the sauce: Mix the lemon juice and mustard in a large bowl. Gradually whisk in the oil to make a slightly thickened sauce. Stir in the horseradish, sour cream, salt and pepper.

Add the prawns to the sauce and toss to coat. Sprinkle with the spring onions. Serve immediately, at room temperature or chilled.

Makes 4 servings

Per serving: energy 124 cals/514 kJ; protein 10 g; carbohydrate 1 g (of which 1 g sugars); fat 9 g (of which 1.5 g saturates); fibre 0 g; sodium 1028 mg

Diet Exchanges: 0 milk, 0 vegetable, 0 fruit, 0 bread, 1 meat, 1½ fat

Time-Saver

Make this recipe 1 day ahead and refrigerate in a covered container.

Prawns in Mustard-Horseradish Sauce

COURGETTE-STUFFED MUSHROOMS
91 calories, 2 g carbs

1 tablespoon olive oil

1 small onion, finely chopped

1 celery stick, finely chopped

1 small courgette (90–115 g/3–4 oz), finely chopped

1 large garlic clove, finely chopped

12 large mushrooms (400–455 g/ 14 oz–1 lb), stems removed and reserved

2 teaspoons vinegar

½ teaspoon dried thyme

½ teaspoon dried oregano

½ teaspoon paprika (optional)

30 g/1 oz grated Parmesan cheese

¾ teaspoon salt

⅛ teaspoon ground black pepper

3 tablespoons dry sherry or water

Preheat the oven to 230°C/450°F/gas 8.

Heat the oil in a large non-stick frying pan over low heat. Add the onion, celery, courgette and garlic. Finely chop the mushroom stems and add to the frying pan. Cook until the mushrooms are tender, 3 to 5 minutes, stirring occasionally. Stir in the vinegar, thyme and oregano. Cover and cook, stirring occasionally until the celery is crisp-tender, 10 to 15 minutes. Remove to a small bowl and stir in the paprika (if using). Let cool.

Stir in 3 tablespoons of the Parmesan and the salt and pepper. With a teaspoon, fill the mushroom caps, mounding the mixture and firming it slightly with your fingers. Coat an ovenproof dish with cooking spray. Arrange the caps in the dish in a single layer and sprinkle with the remaining 1 tablespoon cheese. Pour the sherry or water evenly around the bottom of the dish. Cover and bake for 5 minutes. Uncover and bake until sizzling, 5 to 7 minutes more. Serve hot.

Makes 4 servings

Per serving: energy 91 cals/378 kJ; protein 4 g; carbohydrate 2 g (of which 1.5 g sugars); fat 6 g (of which 2 g saturates); fibre 2 g; sodium 446 mg

Diet Exchanges: 0 milk, 1½ vegetable, 0 fruit, 0 bread, ½ meat, 1 fat

Time-Savers

To cut down on last-minute preparation, make the stuffing up to 3 days ahead and store it covered in the refrigerator. Or prepare the entire recipe up to 2 days ahead and store in the refrigerator. To reheat: bring the stuffed mushrooms to room temperature, then sprinkle with the cheese and bake at 230°C/450°F/gas 8 for 10 to 12 minutes.

Iced Orange-Coconut Drink
196 calories, 12 g carbs

450 ml/15 fl oz orange juice

240 ml/8 fl oz unsweetened soya milk

90 g/3 oz unsweetened grated coconut

Combine half of the orange juice, soya milk and coconut in a blender and process until the mixture is smooth, 2 to 3 minutes. Repeat with the remaining ingredients. Serve over ice. Store extra servings in the refrigerator for up to 12 hours.

Makes 4 servings

Per serving: energy 196 cals/812 kJ; protein 4 g; carbohydrate 12 g (of which 12 g sugars); fat 15 g (of which 12 g saturates); fibre 3 g; sodium 37 mg

Diet Exchanges: 0 milk, 0 vegetable, 1 fruit, 0 bread, meat, 1½ fat

▶Flavour Tip

Use pineapple juice in place of 240 ml/8 fl oz of the orange juice.

snacks, appetisers and beverages

124

HOT APPLE JUICE WITH GINGER
95 calories, 25 g carbs

1 litre/1¾ pints apple juice

4 thin slices fresh ginger, unpeeled

¼ teaspoon ground cinnamon

⅛ teaspoon ground nutmeg or cloves (optional)

Combine the juice and ginger in a medium saucepan and bring to a simmer over medium heat. Pour into mugs, placing 1 piece of the ginger in each mug. Sprinkle with the cinnamon and nutmeg or cloves (if using).

Makes 4 servings

Per serving: energy 95 cals/410 kJ; protein 0 g; carbohydrate 25 g (of which 25 g sugars); fat 0 g (of which 0 g saturates); fibre 3 g; sodium 5 mg

Diet Exchanges: 0 milk, 0 vegetable, 2 fruit, 0 bread, 0 meat, 0 fat

Time-Saver

Instead of using the hob, heat the mixture in a microwave oven on medium power until hot, 2 to 3 minutes. This hot drink travels well in an insulated bottle.

STRAWBERRY PROTEIN SHAKE
96 calories, 20 g carbs

16 large frozen unsweetened straw-berries (350 g/12 oz), quartered

230 g/8 oz low-fat natural yoghurt

450 ml/15 fl oz cold orange juice or 350 ml/12 fl oz orange juice plus 120 ml/4 fl oz sparkling water

1½ teaspoons vanilla essence

4 tablespoons unflavoured protein powder

Combine half of the berries, yoghurt, orange juice, vanilla and protein powder in a blender and process until the mixture is smooth, thick and creamy, 1 to 2 minutes.

Repeat with the remaining ingredients. Serve cold.

Makes 4 servings

Per serving: energy 96 cals/407 kJ; protein 4 g; carbohydrate 20 g (of which 20 g sugars); fat 1 g (of which 0.5 g saturates); fibre 1 g; sodium 64 mg

Diet Exchanges: ½ milk, 0 vegetable, 1 fruit, 0 bread, ½ meat, fat

▶Flavour Tips

Substitute pear, peach or mango nectar for the orange juice. Replace the strawberries with blueberries.

BUTTERMILK FRUIT SHAKE *(photo on page 146)*
69 calories, 9 g carbs

250 g/9 oz frozen unsweetened blueberries or sliced strawberries

450 ml/15 fl oz buttermilk

I teaspoon vanilla essence

60–120 ml/2–4 fl oz apple juice (optional)

Combine half of the berries, buttermilk and vanilla in a blender and process until smooth. Mix in half the apple juice (if using) to sweeten. Repeat with the remaining ingredients. Serve cold.

Makes 4 servings

Per serving: energy 69 cals/290 kJ; protein 4 g; carbohydrate 9 g (of which 9 g sugars); fat 2 g (of which 1 g saturates); fibre 1 g; sodium 66 mg

Diet Exchanges: ½ milk, 0 vegetable, ½ fruit, 0 bread, 0 meat, 0 fat

BEVERAGE FOR SLIMMERS

Sweetened colas and fruit drinks are among the top sources of sugar and calories in the average diet. Flavoured teas make a delicious low-calorie alternative with less sugar. You can infuse regular tea with ginger, lemon, chopped mint or spices such as cinnamon.

MINT-INFUSED DARJEELING TEA
2 calories, 0 g carbs

I litre/1¾ pints water

**3–4 tablespoons coarsely chopped fresh mint or
I tablespoon dried mint**

3 Darjeeling tea bags

Boil the water in a saucepan and add the mint and tea bags. Remove from the heat, cover and steep for 3 to 5 minutes. Strain into mugs.

Makes 4 servings

Per serving: energy 2 cals/0 kJ; protein 0 g; carbohydrate 0 g (of which 0 g sugars); fat 0 g (of which 0 g saturates); fibre 0 g; sodium 0 mg

Diet Exchanges: 0 milk, 0 vegetable, 0 fruit, 0 bread, 0 meat, 0 fat

snacks, appetisers and beverages

PEACH-PEAR SMOOTHIE
114 calories, 24 g carbs

240 ml/8 fl oz cold peach or mango nectar

2 pears, peeled and chopped

240 ml/8 fl oz semi-skimmed milk or unsweetened soya milk

⅛ teaspoon ground nutmeg

Combine half of the nectar, pears and milk in a blender and process until very smooth. Pour into glasses and sprinkle with half of the nutmeg. Repeat with the remaining ingredients. Serve cold. Store extra servings in a covered container in the refrigerator for up to 2 days.

Makes 4 servings

Per serving: energy 114 cals/473 kJ; protein 3 g; carbohydrate 24 g (of which 20 g sugars); fat 2 g (of which 1 g saturates); fibre 2 g; sodium 35 mg

Diet Exchanges: ½ milk, 0 vegetable, 1½ fruit, 0 bread, 0 meat, 0 fat

▶Flavour Tip

Replace the peach nectar with 230 g/8 oz tinned peaches in water (drained) and substitute soda water for all or part of the milk. Serve over ice cubes with a sprig of mint.

soups & sandwiches

WHITE BEAN SOUP WITH SAUSAGE 128

HEARTY COUNTRY VEGETABLE SOUP 130

CREAMY BROCCOLI SOUP WITH CHICKEN 131

CHICKEN GUMBO 133

LAMB AND BARLEY SOUP 134

MUSHROOM AND KASHA SOUP 136

LENTIL SOUP WITH CAULIFLOWER AND YOGHURT 137

CLAM CHOWDER WITH GREENS 139

ITALIAN BEAN SOUP WITH CHARD AND MUSHROOMS 140

CHILLED MELON SOUP WITH BASIL 141

CHILLED CUCUMBER, SPRING ONION AND YOGHURT SOUP 142

MEXICAN-STYLE COURGETTE SOUP 144

ROAST BEEF SANDWICH WITH MUSTARD-HORSERADISH MAYONNAISE 145

TURKEY SANDWICH WITH JARLSBERG AND APPLE 147

BECKY'S TROPICAL CHICKEN SALAD IN LETTUCE WRAPS 150

SMOKED SALMON AND CREAM CHEESE ON RYE CRISPBREAD 151

HAM AND SOFT YOGHURT CHEESE ON RYE CRISPBREAD 152

TWO-CHEESE PITTA MELT 153

BACON-MUSHROOM MELT 154

PESTO CHICKEN SANDWICH WITH ROASTED PEPPERS 156

CHICKPEA PANCAKES WITH SPICY VEGETABLES 158

CRISP TORTILLA WITH AVOCADO, BEANS AND CHEESE 159

TUNA SALAD IN LETTUCE WRAPS 160

WHITE BEAN SOUP WITH SAUSAGE
231 calories, 21 g carbs

1 tablespoon + 1 teaspoon olive oil

230 g/8 oz fresh Italian sausage, cut into 2–3 cm/1 in pieces

½ large onion, chopped

3 celery sticks, chopped

230 g/8 oz green or red cabbage, chopped

230 g/8 oz dried white beans, soaked overnight and drained

1.7–2.2 litres/2¾–3¾ pints chicken stock

1 tin (400 g/14 oz) chopped tomatoes

1 teaspoon dried mixed herbs

1 large bay leaf

¼ teaspoon ground black pepper

Heat 1 teaspoon of the oil in a large saucepan over medium-low heat. Add the sausage and cook, stirring occasionally, just until cooked through, about 5 minutes. Remove to a plate, cover and refrigerate.

Pour the remaining 1 tablespoon oil into the same pan over medium heat and stir in the onion, celery and cabbage. Cook, stirring occasionally, until the vegetables begin to soften, 8 to 10 minutes.

Add the beans, 1.7 litres/2¾ pints of the stock and the tomatoes to the pan. Bring to the boil and immediately lower the heat, skimming off any froth that comes to the top. Stir in the herbs and bay leaf. Partially cover and cook until the beans are tender, 1¼ to 1½ hours depending on the beans, adding more stock if the soup becomes too thick. Stir in the sausage and pepper; simmer for 2 minutes. Discard the bay leaf before serving.

Makes 8 servings

Per serving: energy 231 cals/968 kJ; protein 12 g; carbohydrate 21 g (of which 4 g sugars); fat 12 g (of which 4 g saturates); fibre 3 g; sodium 520 mg

Diet Exchanges: 0 milk, 1½ vegetable, 0 fruit, ½ bread, 1 meat, 2 fat

Time-Saver

Make this soup ahead and store it in a covered container in the refrigerator for up to 5 days or in the freezer for up to 2 months. To reheat, thaw the soup in the refrigerator overnight, then cook it in a saucepan over low heat until heated through.

White Bean Soup with Sausage

HEARTY COUNTRY VEGETABLE SOUP
120 calories, 14 g carbs

- **3 tablespoons olive oil**
- **½ large onion, thinly sliced**
- **3 celery sticks, thinly sliced**
- **1 small head (455 g/1 lb) green cabbage, coarsely chopped**
- **2 carrots, sliced into 1 cm/½ in-thick rounds**
- **2 garlic cloves, finely chopped**
- **115 g/4 oz dried white beans, soaked overnight and drained**
- **1–1.5 litres/1¾–2½ pints vegetable stock**
- **½ teaspoon dried thyme**
- **½ teaspoon dried savory or sage**
- **230 g/8 oz French beans, cut into 1 cm/½ in lengths**
- **1 courgette (170 g/6 oz), coarsely chopped**
- **½ teaspoon ground black pepper**
- **2–3 tablespoons chopped fresh basil or dill (optional)**

Heat the oil in a large saucepan over medium-low heat. Stir in the onion, celery, cabbage, carrots and garlic. Cover the pan and cook, stirring occasionally, until the vegetables soften, 12 to 15 minutes. Add the white beans and 1 litre/1¾ pints of the stock; bring to the boil. Reduce the heat to medium-low and stir in the thyme and savory or sage. Cover and cook until the beans are almost tender, 1 to 1½ hours, adding stock if the soup becomes too thick.

Stir in the green beans and courgette. Partially cover and cook until the beans are tender, 20 to 30 minutes. Season with the pepper and basil or dill (if using). Divide among bowls.

Makes 8 servings

Per serving: energy 120 cals/503 kJ; protein 6 g; carbohydrate 14 g (of which 5 g sugars); fat 5 g (of which 1 g saturates); fibre 4 g; sodium 289 mg

Diet Exchanges: 0 milk, 2 vegetable, 0 fruit, ½ bread, 0 meat, 1 fat

▶Flavour Tips
Substitute fennel for all or part of the celery. You can also add 115 g/4 oz chopped tomatoes with the white beans. For a nice touch, serve the soup sprinkled with grated Parmesan cheese or a drizzle of extra-virgin olive oil.

CREAMY BROCCOLI SOUP WITH CHICKEN
96 calories, 6 g carbs

30 g/1 oz butter

1 onion, thinly sliced

1 garlic clove, sliced (optional)

3 tablespoons wholemeal flour

1.3 litres/2¼ pints chicken stock

685 g/1½ lb broccoli, cut into florets, stems peeled and thinly sliced

¾ teaspoon dried sage

1 bay leaf

¼ teaspoon ground black pepper

230 g/8 oz boneless, skinless chicken breasts, cut into chunks

80 ml/3 fl oz single cream

Melt the butter in a large saucepan over low heat. Stir in the onion and garlic (if using). Cover and cook until the onion is almost translucent, 8 to 10 minutes, stirring occasionally. Stir in the flour and cook, stirring frequently, for 1 minute. Gradually stir in the stock, bring the soup to a simmer over medium heat and add the broccoli, sage and bay leaf. Cook until the broccoli is tender, 10 to 15 minutes.

Discard the bay leaf. Reserve 115 g/4 oz broccoli florets if desired. Ladle the soup into a blender, process until smooth and return to the pan. Add the pepper, chicken and single cream. Cook just until the chicken is no longer pink, 3 to 4 minutes, stirring once or twice. Top each serving with the reserved broccoli florets (if using).

Makes 6 servings

Per serving: energy 96 cals/400 kJ; protein 8 g; carbohydrate 6 g (of which 2 g sugars); fat 5 g (of which 3 g saturates); fibre 2 g; sodium 215 mg

Diet Exchanges: 0 milk, 1½ vegetable, 0 fruit, ½ bread, 1 meat, 1 fat

Time-Saver

Make this soup ahead of time and store it in a covered container in the refrigerator for up to 4 days or freeze it for up to 2 months. To reheat, thaw the soup in the refrigerator overnight, then cook it in a saucepan over low heat until heated through.

Chicken Gumbo

CHICKEN GUMBO
187 calories, 12 g carbs

- **3 tablespoons vegetable oil**
- **I small onion, chopped**
- **3 celery sticks, chopped**
- **I large green pepper, chopped**
- **I garlic clove, finely chopped**
- **½ teaspoon ground black pepper**
- **3½ tablespoons wholemeal flour**
- **1–1.5 litres/1¾–2½ pints chicken stock**
- **170 g/6 oz chopped tomatoes**
- **115 g/4 oz boneless smoked ham, cut into 1 cm/½ in pieces**
- **3 skinless chicken thighs (340 g/ 12 oz)**
- **I teaspoon dried thyme**
- **I bay leaf**
- **⅛ teaspoon chilli powder**
- **I tablespoon chopped fresh parsley**

Heat the oil in a large saucepan over medium heat and add the onion, celery, pepper, garlic and black pepper. Cover and cook just until the vegetables begin to soften, 5 to 6 minutes. Stir in the flour and cook, stirring frequently, for 3 minutes. Gradually stir in 1 litre/1¾ pints of the stock and bring it to a simmer.

Add the tomatoes, ham, chicken, thyme, bay leaf and chilli powder. Partially cover and cook until the chicken is tender, 25 to 35 minutes, adding the remaining stock as necessary if the gumbo is too thick. Remove from the heat, transfer the chicken to a plate and let cool slightly. Cut into bite-size pieces, discarding the bones, and return to the pan. Reheat briefly and stir in the parsley. Remove the bay leaf before serving.

Makes 6 servings

Per serving: energy 187 cals/783 kJ; protein 15 g; carbohydrate 12 g (of which 2 g sugars); fat 9 g (of which 2 g saturates); fibre 2 g; sodium 647 mg

Diet Exchanges: 0 milk, 1 vegetable, 0 fruit, ½ bread, 2 meat, 2 fat

▶Flavour Tips
Substitute Polish sausage for the ham. Add 285 g/ 10 oz frozen okra along with the chicken.

LAMB AND BARLEY SOUP
176 calories, 15 g carbs

- **I tablespoon olive oil**
- **455 g/I lb lean lamb, cut into bite-size pieces**
- **I small onion, chopped**
- **2 carrots, chopped**
- **4 celery sticks, chopped**
- **I garlic clove, finely chopped**
- **1.7 litres/2¾ pints chicken stock**
- **2 tablespoons tomato puree (optional)**
- **130 g/4½ oz barley**
- **¾ teaspoon dried rosemary, crumbled**
- **½ teaspoon dried oregano**
- **½ teaspoon ground black pepper**

Heat the oil in a large saucepan over low heat. Add the lamb and cook, stirring frequently, until browned all over, 3 to 5 minutes. Remove to a plate. Stir the onion, carrots, celery and garlic into the pan. Cover and cook, stirring occasionally, until the vegetables begin to soften, about 10 minutes.

Return the lamb to the pan and add the stock. Bring to a simmer and add the tomato puree (if using), barley, rosemary, oregano and pepper. Partially cover and cook until the barley is tender-chewy, 45 to 55 minutes. Skim fat from the surface of the soup if necessary.

Makes 8 servings

Per serving: energy 176 cals/739 kJ; protein 14 g; carbohydrate 15 g (of which 2 g sugars); fat 7 g (of which 3 g saturates); fibre 1 g; sodium 332 mg

Diet Exchanges: 0 milk, 1 vegetable, 0 fruit, 1 bread, 2 meat, 1 fat

▶Flavour Tips

In place of the 4 celery sticks, use 2 celery sticks and ½ fennel bulb. Stir in 2 tablespoons of chopped parsley before serving. You can also replace the lamb with small pieces of stewing beef.

Lamb and Barley Soup

MUSHROOM AND KASHA SOUP
109 calories, 12 g carbs

90 g/3 oz kasha (roasted buckwheat)

2 tablespoons olive oil

570 g/1¼ lb mushrooms, coarsely chopped

½ onion, finely chopped

1 carrot, finely chopped

1½ celery sticks, finely chopped

½ red pepper, finely chopped

½ teaspoon ground black pepper

1 litre/1¾ pints chicken or vegetable stock

1 teaspoon dried dill or thyme

1 bay leaf

Toast the kasha in a large saucepan over medium heat, stirring, for 2 to 3 minutes. Remove to a bowl.

Heat the oil in the same pan over medium-low heat. Stir in the mushrooms, onion, carrot, celery, red pepper and black pepper. Cover and cook, stirring occasionally, for 8 to 10 minutes. Stir in the kasha and stock. Bring to a simmer and add the dill or thyme and the bay leaf. Partially cover and cook until the kasha is tender, about 10 minutes. Remove the bay leaf before serving.

Makes 6 servings

Per serving: energy 109 cals/453 kJ; protein 5 g; carbohydrate 12 g (of which 2 g sugars); fat 7 g (of which 1 g saturates); fibre 3 g; sodium 575 mg

Diet Exchanges: 0 milk, 1½ vegetable, 0 fruit, ½ bread, 0 meat, 1 fat

▶Flavour Tips
Serve sprinkled with chopped spring onions.
For a vegetarian stew, cook with only 240 ml/8 fl oz vegetable stock.

LENTIL SOUP WITH CAULIFLOWER AND YOGHURT
159 calories, 21 g carbs

- 1½ tablespoons olive oil
- 1½ carrots, finely chopped
- 1 onion, finely chopped
- 1½ celery sticks, finely chopped
- 1 garlic clove, finely chopped
- 90 g/3 oz tinned chopped tomatoes
- 250 g/9 oz lentils, rinsed and drained
- 1.7–1.9 litres/2¾–3¼ pints vegetable stock
- 1 bay leaf
- ½ head (455 g/1 lb) cauliflower, cut into bite-size florets
- 2–3 tablespoons lemon juice
- ½ teaspoon ground black pepper
- 115 g/4 oz low-fat natural yoghurt

Heat the oil in a large saucepan over medium heat. Stir in the carrots, onion, celery and garlic. Cover and cook until the onion begins to turn translucent, 5 minutes. Stir in the tomatoes, lentils and 1.5 litres/2½ pints of the stock. Bring to the boil and immediately reduce the heat.

Skim off any froth that comes to the top and stir in the bay leaf. Cover and cook until the lentils are tender, 40 to 45 minutes, adding stock as needed.

Stir in the cauliflower. Partially cover and cook until the cauliflower is tender, 5 to 8 minutes. Stir in the lemon juice and the pepper. Serve garnished with the yoghurt. Discard the bay leaf.

Makes 8 servings

Per serving: energy 159 cals/672 kJ; protein 12 g; carbohydrate 21 g (of which 5 g sugars); fat 3.5 g (of which 1 g saturates); fibre 4 g; sodium 392 mg

Diet Exchanges: 0 milk, 2 vegetable, 0 fruit, ½ bread, 0 meat, 1 fat

▶Flavour Tips

If you don't like cauliflower, you can omit it. To make a thicker soup, puree 350 ml/12 fl oz of the soup (mostly lentils) in a blender, then stir the puree back into the soup. Add ½ teaspoon curry powder.

Clam Chowder with Greens

CLAM CHOWDER WITH GREENS
238 calories, 11 g carbs

- **115 g/4 oz lean bacon, chopped**
- **1 tablespoon vegetable oil**
- **1 onion, finely chopped**
- **1 garlic clove, finely chopped**
- **340 g/12 oz greens, coarse stems removed and discarded, leaves chopped**
- **850 ml/1½ pints chicken stock**
- **2 tins (280 g/10 oz each) baby clams, juice reserved**
- **240 ml/8 fl oz single cream**
- **2–2½ tablespoons potato flour (see Flavour Tip)**
- **¼ teaspoon ground black pepper**

Cook the bacon in a large saucepan over medium-low heat until crisp. Drain on a kitchen paper-lined plate. Add the oil to the pan, then add the onion and garlic. Cook, stirring occasionally, until the onion is translucent, 8 to 10 minutes.

Add the greens and cook for 2 minutes. Stir in the stock and the reserved clam juice. Bring to a simmer over medium heat and cook for 10 minutes. Stir in the cream and heat through. Sprinkle 2 tablespoons potato flour over the soup and stir in. Add the remaining ½ tablespoon flour for a thicker soup if desired. Stir in the pepper and clams and cook for 1 to 2 minutes. Sprinkle the bacon over each serving.

Makes 6 servings

Per serving: energy 238 cals/991 kJ; protein 20 g; carbohydrate 11 g (of which 5 g sugars); fat 13 g (of which 6 g saturates); fibre 3 g; sodium 771 mg

Diet Exchanges: 0 milk, 1 vegetable, 0 fruit, ½ bread, ½ meat, 2 fat

▶ Flavour Tip

Potato flour is used as the thickener in this recipe to lend the characteristic flavour of potatoes without as many carbohydrates. Look for it in the baking aisle of supermarkets or health food shops. Or you can use 1½ tablespoons cornflour mixed with 2 tablespoons water instead.

ITALIAN BEAN SOUP WITH CHARD AND MUSHROOMS

133 calories, 17 g carbs

2 tablespoons olive oil

½ bunch (170 g/6 oz) chard, chopped

230 g/8 oz mushrooms, chopped

1½ large red or green peppers, chopped

1 garlic clove, finely chopped

230 g/8 oz dried white beans, soaked overnight and drained

1.3 litres/2¼ pints vegetable stock

¾ teaspoon dried rosemary, crumbled

½ teaspoon dried sage

6 spring onions, thinly sliced

½ teaspoon ground black pepper

Heat the oil in a large saucepan over medium heat. Stir in the chard, mushrooms, peppers and garlic. Cover and cook until the vegetables soften, 6 to 8 minutes, stirring occasionally.

Add the beans and stock, bring to the boil and immediately reduce the heat. Skim off any froth that comes to the top and stir in the rosemary and the sage. Cover and cook until the beans are tender, 1 to 1½ hours.

Stir in the spring onions and the black pepper. Cook for 2 to 3 minutes.

Makes 8 servings

Per serving: energy 133 cals/560 kJ; protein 9 g; carbohydrate 17 g (of which 2 g sugars); fat 4 g (of which 1 g saturates); fibre 3.5 g; sodium 307 mg

Diet Exchanges: 0 milk, 2 vegetable, 0 fruit, ½ bread, 0 meat, ½ fat

Time-Saver

Make this soup ahead for a quick one-dish meal. Store in a tightly covered container in the refrigerator for up to 5 days or in the freezer for up to 2 months. To reheat, thaw the soup in the refrigerator overnight, then cook it in a saucepan over low heat until heated through.

CHILLED MELON SOUP WITH BASIL
70 calories, 15 g carbs

¾ large honeydew (2 kg/4½ lb) or other melon, cubed

2–3 tablespoons lime juice

2–3 tablespoons dry sherry or grape juice

½ teaspoon salt

1½ tablespoons soured cream (optional)

4 tablespoons chopped fresh basil

Place half of the melon, 1 tablespoon of the lime juice and 1 tablespoon of the sherry or grape juice in a blender. Process until very smooth, about 1 minute. Add the salt and up to ½ tablespoon more lime juice or sherry if desired. Repeat with the remaining ingredients, combine the batches in a bowl and refrigerate until chilled, at least 1 hour.

Top each serving with a dollop of sour cream (if using) and sprinkle with the basil.

Makes 6 servings

Per serving: energy 70 cals/285 kJ; protein 1 g; carbohydrate 15 g (of which 15 g sugars); fat 0 g (of which 0 g saturates); fibre 1 g; sodium 233 mg

Diet Exchanges: 0 milk, 0 vegetable, 1 fruit, 0 bread, 0 meat, 0 fat

▶Flavour Tip

The flavour and colour of melon soup is best within the first few hours. If you refrigerate the soup for more than 18 hours, refresh it with a little lime juice or sherry before serving.

CHILLED CUCUMBER, SPRING ONION AND YOGHURT SOUP
166 calories, 10 g carbs

- **1 kg/2¼ lb low-fat natural yoghurt**
- **80 ml/3 fl oz olive oil**
- **2 tablespoons balsamic vinegar**
- **4 tablespoons cold water**
- **2–3 cucumbers (340 g/12 oz), peeled, seeded and chopped**
- **3 spring onions, finely chopped**
- **½ teaspoon salt**
- **¼ teaspoon ground black pepper**
- **2 tablespoons toasted walnuts (optional)**
- **1½ teaspoons chopped fresh dill**

Preheat the oven to 180°C/350°F/gas 4.

Place the yoghurt in a large bowl and gradually whisk in the oil. Whisk in the vinegar and enough of the cold water to make a somewhat thick mixture. Stir in half of the cucumbers, the spring onions, salt and pepper. Puree in a blender or food processor. Transfer back into the bowl and stir in the remaining cucumbers. Refrigerate until well chilled, at least 1 hour.

Serve the chilled soup sprinkled with the walnuts (if using) and the dill.

Makes 6 servings

Per serving: energy 166 cals/688 kJ; protein 7 g; carbohydrate 10 g (of which 10 g sugars); fat 11 g (of which 2 g saturates); fibre 0.5 g; sodium 266 mg

Diet Exchanges: 1 milk, ½ vegetable, 0 fruit, 0 bread, 0 meat, 3 fat

▶Flavour Tip

Just before serving, lightly sprinkle with ground cumin.

Chilled Cucumber, Spring Onion and Yoghurt Soup

MEXICAN-STYLE COURGETTE SOUP
63 calories, 5 g carbs

- **20 g/¾ oz butter**
- **½ large onion, thinly sliced**
- **4 courgettes (685 g/1½ lb), chopped**
- **2 garlic cloves, finely chopped**
- **½ large red pepper, chopped**
- **60 g/2 oz drained, chopped tinned tomatoes**
- **1 litre/1¾ pints chicken stock**
- **½ teaspoon ground black pepper**
- **½ teaspoon dried oregano**
- **¼ teaspoon ground cumin**
- **1½ tablespoons cornmeal**

Melt the butter in a large saucepan over medium heat. Stir in the onion, courgettes, garlic and red pepper. Cook, stirring occasionally, until excess liquid from the courgettes has evaporated, 8 to 10 minutes. Stir in the tomatoes and stock. Reduce the heat to low and stir in the black pepper, oregano and cumin. Cook the soup, uncovered, until the vegetables are tender, about 10 minutes.

Stir in the cornmeal and cook until thickened slightly, 5 minutes.

Makes 6 servings

Per serving: energy 63 cals/262 kJ; protein 3 g; carbohydrate 5 g (of which 4 g sugars); fat 3 g (of which 2 g saturates); fibre 2 g; sodium 271 mg

Diet Exchanges: 0 milk, 1 vegetable, 0 fruit, ½ bread, 0 meat, ½ fat

▶Flavour Tips

Cook 3 rashers of bacon in the saucepan until crisp. Drain on a kitchen paper-lined plate. Use 1½ tablespoons of the dripping in place of the butter to cook the vegetables. Crumble the bacon over each serving. For a thinner soup, omit the cornmeal.

ROAST BEEF SANDWICH WITH MUSTARD-HORSERADISH MAYONNAISE

441 calories, 26 g carbs

- **3 tablespoons mayonnaise**
- **2 teaspoons Dijon mustard**
- **2 teaspoons prepared horseradish**
- **8 slices wholemeal bread**
- **12 spinach or lettuce leaves**
- **½ cucumber (90 g/3 oz total), peeled and thinly sliced**
- **12 slices roast beef (340 g/12 oz)**
- **½ teaspoon salt**
- **¼ teaspoon ground black pepper**

In a small bowl, combine the mayonnaise, mustard and horseradish. Spread over the bread and cover 4 of the slices with the spinach or lettuce. Arrange the cucumber and beef over the spinach or lettuce. Season with the salt and pepper. Top with the remaining bread and cut in half.

Makes 4 servings

Per serving: energy 441 cals/1849 kJ; protein 31 g; carbohydrate 26 g (of which 2 g sugars); fat 24 g (of which 4 g saturates); fibre 4 g; sodium 845 mg

Diet Exchanges: 0 milk, ½ vegetable, 0 fruit, 1½ bread, 3 meat, 1½ fat

▶Flavour Tips

Substitute chicken or turkey for the beef. You could also eliminate the bread. Instead, spread the meat with the mayonnaise, top with the cucumber and wrap in the spinach or lettuce leaves.

Turkey Sandwich with Jarlsberg and Apple with Buttermilk Fruit Shake (page 125)

TURKEY SANDWICH WITH JARLSBERG AND APPLE

404 calories, 30 g carbs

3 tablespoons macadamia or other nut butter

8 slices wholemeal bread, lightly toasted

4 slices (115 g/4 oz) Jarlsberg cheese

8 slices (230 g/8 oz) cooked turkey breast

¼ teaspoon salt

⅛ teaspoon ground black pepper (optional)

1 small apple (115 g/4 oz), thinly sliced

½ bunch watercress sprigs or 4 large lettuce leaves

Spread the nut butter over the bread. Arrange the cheese on 4 slices, top with the turkey and season with the salt and pepper (if using). Top with the apple, watercress or lettuce and the remaining bread. Cut in half.

Makes 4 servings

Per serving: energy 404 cals/1696 kJ; protein 32 g; carbohydrate 30 g (of which 5 g sugars); fat 18 g (of which 7 g saturates); fibre 5 g; sodium 937 mg

Diet Exchanges: 0 milk, 0 vegetable, ½ fruit, 2 bread, 3 meat, 1½ fat

Time-Saver

This sandwich can be assembled ahead and refrigerated for up to 3 hours.

soups and sandwiches

I Did It!

Becky Cleveland

For most of her life, Becky's mother was overweight and led a sedentary lifestyle, which later contributed to numerous medical problems. Becky was determined not to let that happen to herself. After a slew of diet and exercise plans failed, Becky went on a reduced-carbohydrate diet, discovered the joys of cycling and lost 28.6 kg/4½ st.

before

'I was very slender when I met my husband. However, I started to gain weight immediately after the wedding – maybe it was all that wedding cake! Five years later, when our first child was born, I stayed at home and had little time for exercise. I also enjoyed preparing lots of dishes using pasta, and making treats like chocolate chip cookies. I now know that these were loaded with refined carbohydrates. My weight continued to climb. After I gave birth to our second child, I gained 19 kg/3 st and

Weight lost: 28.6 kg/4½ st
Time kept off: 3 years
Weight-loss strategies: lower-carbohydrate diet, exercise, drank lots of water
Weight-maintenance strategies: avoids refined carbohydrates, moderates total carbohydrates, stays active

soups and sandwiches

weighed in at just over 77 kg/12 st. I tried nearly every diet plan out there. Some of them worked for a short time, but then I regained all the weight I had lost – plus more.

'When our kids were a little older I was able to exercise more, but I never had a formal programme. It was when I tipped the scales at nearly 95 kg/15 st that I decided to hire a personal trainer. He developed a customised exercise and diet plan and helped me stick to it. I strengthened my muscles and toned up. I managed to lose 13 kg/2 st, but I regained 4.6 kg/10 lb. Looking back, I think I rationalised that the more I exercised, the more I could eat!

'My real motivation for weight loss came when my mother was told that her sedentary lifestyle and excess weight were severely affecting her health. She became disabled to the point where she was restricted to a wheelchair and bed. I was determined not to let that happen to me if there was any way I could prevent it.

'Gloria, a friend of mine who is a nutritionist, convinced me to make an appointment with her. She reassured me that the reduced-carbohydrate plan she had in mind would be easy to follow and I would not feel hungry. Gloria and I met on a weekly basis. I have to admit, it was hard adjusting to eating fewer carbohydrates the first week. Then it became easier because I understood why I needed to change my food choices. Gloria taught me how little nutritional value refined carbohydrates had and how important normal insulin levels

were for good health. It wasn't long before I began to enjoy the wholegrain substitutes. These dietary changes brought my weight down from about 86 kg/13½ st to 68 kg/10 st 4 lb. I was so happy to be able to get into size 12/14 jeans and size 10/12 dresses. At one time I was wearing a size 22!

'Once my diet improved, I was able to step up the exercise too. Mostly I walked and rode my bike. My son, Adam, who had lost 54 kg/8½ st, motivated me further by buying me a new bike. The long bike rides we took were great stress reducers. Now I also swim and do water aerobics for 2 hours 3 days a week.

'These days, the reduced-carbohydrate approach is second nature to me. My family eats out often, but I know to stay away from the huge servings of pasta and breadcrumb-coated foods. I order my salad right away so I'm not tempted to eat the bread and other appetisers. Sure, there are times when I eat foods not on my plan. But I get back on track straight away instead of waiting until Monday to start choosing foods wisely again.

'I only wish I had listened to an older friend of mine 30 years ago when she told me that I was too young to weigh as much as I did. Losing weight has given me such a wonderful new perspective on life. I have just turned 50. And I have more energy and am in better shape physically and mentally than I can ever recall. I even get more compliments today than when I was younger!'

(continued)

I Did It! (cont.)

BECKY'S TROPICAL CHICKEN SALAD IN LETTUCE WRAPS

360 calories, 20 g carbs

- **1 container (170 g/6 oz) low-fat piña colada or coconut yoghurt**
- **60 g/2 oz reduced-fat mayonnaise**
- **1 tin (230 g/8 oz) crushed pineapple, drained**
- **½ teaspoon mixed dried herbs**
- **¼ teaspoon salt**
- **455 g/1 lb boneless, skinless, cooked chicken breasts, chopped**
- **115 g/4 oz red or white seedless grapes (about 16), halved**
- **1 small celery stick, chopped**
- **1 small apple, chopped (optional)**
- **60 g/2 oz flaked almonds, toasted**
- **2 tablespoons chopped chives or spring onions (optional)**
- **8 large lettuce leaves**

In a large bowl, combine the yoghurt, mayonnaise, pineapple, poultry seasoning and salt. Stir in the chicken, grapes, celery, apple (if using), almonds and chives or spring onions (if using). Divide the salad among the lettuce leaves and roll up to enclose.

Makes 4 servings

Per serving: energy 360 cals/1508 kJ; protein 30 g; carbohydrate 20 g (of which 20 g sugars); fat 18 g (of which 3 g saturates); fibre 2 g; sodium 295 mg

Diet Exchanges: 0 milk, 0 vegetable, 1 fruit, 0 bread, 6 meat, 2½ fat

SMOKED SALMON AND CREAM CHEESE ON RYE CRISPBREAD
356 calories, 24 g carbs

115 g/4 oz light cream cheese

2 teaspoons capers, drained

2½ tablespoons finely chopped red onion

2 tablespoons chopped walnuts

8 slices rye crispbread

8 slices (230 g/8 oz) smoked salmon

¼ teaspoon ground black pepper

In a small bowl, mix together the cream cheese, capers, onion and walnuts. Spread the mixture over the crispbread. Fold the salmon to fit on top of the cream cheese and sprinkle with the pepper.

Makes 4 servings

Per serving: energy 356 cals/1490 kJ; protein 20 g; carbohydrate 24 g (of which 1.5 g sugars); fat 20 g (of which 9 g saturates); fibre 2.5 g; sodium 1458 mg

Diet Exchanges: 0 milk, 0 vegetable, 0 fruit, 1 bread, 1 meat, 2½ fat

▶Flavour Tips
Use flavoured yoghurt cheese (see recipe for Soft Yoghurt Cheese on page 107) instead of the cream cheese. Substitute other smoked fish, such as trout, or tuna for the salmon, or top with skinless, boneless sardines. Add ½ teaspoon dried dill to the cheese mixture.

Time-Savers
Make the cream cheese mixture ahead and store it in a covered container in the refrigerator for up to 3 days. You can also store the assembled sandwiches in the refrigerator for up to 4 hours.

HAM AND SOFT YOGHURT CHEESE ON RYE CRISPBREAD
325 calories, 26 g carbs

230 g/8 oz Soft Yoghurt Cheese (page 107)

1 tablespoon Dijon mustard

2 teaspoons chopped fresh dill

¼ teaspoon salt

⅛ teaspoon ground black pepper

8 slices rye crispbread

75 g/2½ oz radishes or beansprouts

2 tomatoes, cut into 8 slices

16 thin slices (340 g/12 oz) ham

In a small bowl, mix together the yoghurt cheese, mustard, dill, salt and pepper. Spread over the crispbread and cover with the radishes or beansprouts. Arrange the tomatoes on top. Fold the ham to fit over the tomatoes.

Makes 4 servings

Per serving: energy 325 cals/1365 kJ; protein 26 g; carbohydrate 26 g (of which 4 g sugars); fat 14 g (of which 7 g saturates); fibre 3 g; sodium 1534 mg

Diet Exchanges: ½ milk, 1 vegetable, 0 fruit, 1 bread, 2 meat, 0 fat

Time-Saver

Make the flavoured cheese ahead and store it in a covered container in the refrigerator for up to 5 days.

HIDDEN ROADBLOCK to weight loss

ARTIFICIAL SWEETENERS

Many of the people we talked to said that artificial sweeteners have kept them from losing weight. These sweeteners appear to stimulate the desire for real sweets and other foods containing sugar. There is even some preliminary research suggesting that aspartame may increase insulin levels like glucose does. And extra insulin means extra fat storage. Luckily, there are healthy alternatives for those who crave something sweet. See page 57 for sugar substitutes that do not have negative health effects.

TWO-CHEESE PITTA MELT
221 calories, 24 g carbs

- **4 mini wholewheat pittas, split**
- **4 teaspoons Dijon mustard**
- **4 thin slices (90–115 g/3–4 oz) mozzarella cheese**
- **4 thin slices (90–115 g/3–4 oz) Jarlsberg**
- **115 g/4 oz red or green cabbage, shredded**
- **½ teaspoon dried oregano**
- **½ teaspoon garlic powder (optional)**
- **¼ teaspoon salt**
- **¼ teaspoon ground black pepper**

Preheat the oven to 200°C/400°F/gas 6.

Spread the inside of the pittas with the mustard and arrange the sliced mozzarella and Jarlsberg inside.

In a bowl, toss the cabbage, oregano, garlic powder (if using), salt and pepper. Stuff into the pittas. Arrange on a baking sheet and bake until the cheese melts and the edges of the pittas are crisp, 12 to 15 minutes.

Makes 4 servings

Per serving: energy 221 cals/929 kJ; protein 11 g; carbohydrate 24 g (of which 3 g sugars); fat 10 g (of which 6 g saturates); fibre 1.5 g; sodium 639 mg

Diet Exchanges: 0 milk, ½ vegetable, 0 fruit, 1 bread, 1½ meat, 1½ fat

▶Flavour Tips
Replace one of the cheeses with feta or goat's cheese. Substitute cooked broccoli for the cabbage.

BACON-MUSHROOM MELT
405 calories, 14 g carbs

8 rashers lean bacon, halved

4 slices wholemeal bread, toasted

2 tablespoons mayonnaise

4 mushrooms (115 g/4 oz), thinly
   sliced

⅛ teaspoon salt

¼ teaspoon ground black pepper

4 slices tomato

145 g/5 oz Port Salut cheese, sliced

145 g/5 oz alfalfa or beansprouts
   (optional)

Place a grill pan in the lowest position possible from the heat source and preheat the grill.

Arrange the bacon in a large frying pan and cook over low heat until crisp, turning occasionally, 5 to 8 minutes. Drain on a kitchen paper-lined plate.

Spread the bread with the mayonnaise and place on a baking tray. Top with the mushrooms and season with the salt and pepper. Arrange the tomato over the mushrooms. Cover with slices of cheese and top with the bacon.

Grill until the cheese melts. Top with the alfalfa or beansprouts (if using).

Makes 4 servings

Per serving: energy 405 cals/1689 kJ; protein 23 g; carbohydrate 14 g (of which 1 g sugars); fat 30 g (of which 11 g saturates); fibre 2 g; sodium 1451 mg

Diet Exchanges: 0 milk, 1 vegetable, 0 fruit, ½ bread, 2 meat, 3½ fat

▶Flavour Tip

Substitute sliced turkey, chicken, ham, or tuna or salmon for the bacon.

Bacon-Mushroom Melt

PESTO CHICKEN SANDWICH WITH ROASTED PEPPERS

425 calories, 45 g carbs

**4 wholewheat tortillas
(15 cm/6 in diameter)**

4 tablespoons pesto sauce

**230 g/8 oz sliced cooked chicken
breasts, warmed**

¼ teaspoon salt

¼ teaspoon ground black pepper

**2 roasted red peppers (60 g/2 oz),
drained and halved**

**4 thin slices (90–115 g/3–4 oz)
mozzarella cheese**

4 Cos lettuce leaves

Preheat the oven to 180°C/350°F/gas 4.

Arrange the tortillas on a baking tray.
Spread the pesto evenly over each. Arrange
the chicken in a row down the centre of
each tortilla and sprinkle with the salt and
black pepper. Top with the roasted peppers
and mozzarella.

Bake just until heated through and the
cheese melts. Top with the lettuce, roll into
a cylinder and serve.

Makes 4 servings

Per serving: energy 425 cals/1785 kJ; protein 22 g;
carbohydrate 45 g (of which 4 g sugars); fat 19 g (of
which 4 g saturates); fibre 2 g; sodium 572 mg

Diet Exchanges: 0 milk, ½ vegetable, 0 fruit,
1½ bread, 3 meat, 2½ fat

Smart-Carb Insider Tip

DON'T GO NO-CARB

Carbohydrates are a key element in any
healthy diet. But it's important to choose the
right ones. Beans, for instance, are higher in
carbs than many other foods, but they're also
high in fibre and other beneficial nutrients, so
there's no reason to avoid them altogether.
Also, onions and carrots are slightly higher in
carbohydrates than other vegetables. But that
doesn't mean you have to substitute onion
powder for real onions in your cooking. Doing
so would only save you about 1 gram of carbohydrate for an equivalent amount used – and
you would sacrifice a lot of delicious flavour! Be
smart when making low-carb choices. It's just
not practical to eliminate carbohydrates entirely.

Pesto Chicken Sandwich with Roasted Peppers

CHICKPEA PANCAKES WITH SPICY VEGETABLES
127 calories, 16 g carbs

- **145 g/5 oz chickpea flour (gram flour)**
- **180 ml/6 fl oz + 1–2 tablespoons cold water**
- **3 tablespoons olive oil**
- **1 egg**
- **¼ teaspoon salt**
- **¼ teaspoon ground black pepper**
- **½ small onion, finely chopped**
- **1 courgette (170 g/6 oz), finely chopped**
- **2 large cauliflower florets (170 g/6 oz), finely chopped**
- **1 teaspoon finely chopped fresh ginger**
- **⅛ teaspoon ground cumin**
- **⅛ teaspoon dried chilli flakes**
- **2 tablespoons tomato sauce**
- **1 spring onion, thinly sliced**

Generously coat a 20 cm/8 in non-stick frying pan with cooking spray and heat over medium heat. Place the flour in a bowl and gradually whisk in 180 ml/6 fl oz cold water to make a smooth batter the consistency of thin cream (add more water if needed). Whisk in 2 tablespoons of the oil, the egg, ⅛ teaspoon of the salt and ⅛ teaspoon of the pepper.

Pour 3 tablespoons batter into the frying pan and quickly tilt the pan to coat the bottom with a thin layer of batter. Cook the first side until nicely browned, about 1 minute. Turn the pancake and cook the second side for 30 to 45 seconds (it will look spotted). Slide the pancake onto a plate and cook the rest in the same fashion. Cover with foil to keep warm.

Heat the remaining 1 tablespoon oil in another frying pan over medium heat. Stir in the onion, courgette, cauliflower, ginger, cumin and chilli flakes. Cover and cook, stirring occasionally, for 3 minutes. Stir in the tomato sauce, cover and cook until the vegetables are tender and the liquid has evaporated, 10 to 15 minutes. Stir in the spring onion, the remaining ⅛ teaspoon salt and the remaining ⅛ teaspoon pepper.

Arrange a pancake, attractive side down, on a plate and spoon the vegetables in a line one-third of the way from one edge and roll up. Assemble the remaining pancakes in the same manner.

Makes 8

Per 2 pancakes: energy 127 cals/531 kJ; protein 4 g; carbohydrate 16 g (of which 1 g sugars); fat 6 g (of which 1 g saturates); fibre 3 g; sodium 105 mg

Diet Exchanges: 0 milk, 1 vegetable, 0 fruit, 1 bread, ½ meat, 2 fat

CRISP TORTILLA WITH AVOCADO, BEANS AND CHEESE
371 calories, 41 g carbs

- **4 corn tortillas (15 cm/6 in diameter)**
- **1 tin (420 g/14½ oz) borlotti, pinto or black-eyed beans, drained, with 2 tablespoons liquid reserved**
- **¼ teaspoon salt**
- **¼ teaspoon onion powder**
- **¼ teaspoon garlic powder**
- **1 avocado, thinly sliced**
- **1 jalapeño chilli, seeded and chopped (wear plastic gloves when handling)**
- **115 g/4 oz Cheddar or Double Gloucester cheese, grated**

Preheat the oven to 180°C/350°F/gas 4.

Arrange the tortillas on a baking tray in a single layer. Bake, turning occasionally, until golden and crisp, 18 to 20 minutes.

Meanwhile, in a small saucepan over low heat, combine the beans, reserved liquid, ⅛ teaspoon of the salt, the onion powder and the garlic powder. Cook until hot, 2 to 3 minutes.

Arrange the avocado slices over the tortillas. Season with the remaining ⅛ teaspoon salt and top with the jalapeño chilli. Spoon the beans over the top and cover with the cheese. Bake until the cheese melts, 5 to 8 minutes.

Makes 4 servings

Per serving: energy 371 cals/1557 kJ; protein 18 g; carbohydrate 41 g (of which 5 g sugars); fat 16 g (of which 7 g saturates); fibre 8 g; sodium 940 mg

Diet Exchanges: 0 milk, ½ vegetable, 0 fruit, 1½ bread, 1½ meat, 3 fat

►Flavour Tips

Use bottled or tinned jalapeño or other chillies instead of fresh. You could also mash the avocado and spread it over the tortilla instead of slicing.

For a soft taco, heat the tortillas just long enough to soften them, then fill and roll without baking.

TUNA SALAD IN LETTUCE WRAPS
150 calories, 1 g carbs

2 tins (170 g/6 oz each) water-packed tuna, drained

4 tablespoons mayonnaise

1 teaspoon Dijon mustard

1 tablespoon lemon juice

2 tablespoons finely chopped red pepper or celery

2 teaspoons capers, drained

2 spring onions, thinly sliced

¼ teaspoon salt

⅛ teaspoon ground black pepper

8 large lettuce leaves

In a bowl, flake the tuna with a fork. Stir in the mayonnaise, mustard and lemon juice. Stir in the pepper or celery, capers, spring onions, salt and pepper. Arrange the lettuce on a work surface with the rib end closest to you and the 'cup' facing up. Spoon the tuna mixture onto the leaf near the rib end and roll to enclose.

Makes 4 servings

Per serving: energy 150 cals/624 kJ; protein 10 g; carbohydrate 1 g (of which 1 g sugars); fat 12 g (of which 2 g saturates); fibre 0.5 g; sodium 213 mg

Diet Exchanges: 0 milk, ½ vegetable, 0 fruit, 0 bread, 3½ meat, 2 fat

▶Flavour Tips

Substitute tinned or cooked salmon or boneless, skinless sardines for the tuna. Add 1 chopped hard-boiled egg and ½ teaspoon dried dill to the salad.
You can also add 3 or 4 thin slices of apple or a slice of Jarlsberg or mozzarella cheese to the wrap.

chicken & turkey main dishes

CHICKEN BREASTS WITH ROASTED PEPPERS AND THYME 162

CHICKEN BREASTS IN SHERRY SAUCE WITH GRAPES AND CUCUMBERS 163

CHICKEN BREASTS WITH MOZZARELLA, PEPPERS AND OLIVES 165

CHICKEN SCALLOPINI WITH SAGE AND CAPERS 166

CHICKEN THIGHS WITH LEMON-PEPPER SAUCE 168

ROASTED CHICKEN BREASTS WITH LEMON AND MUSTARD 169

CURRIED CHICKEN WITH COCONUT 171

LYNNE'S ON-THE-GO CHICKEN 174

GRILLED ORANGE-ROSEMARY CHICKEN 175

SAUTÉED CHICKEN WITH SHALLOTS AND WHITE WINE 176

GINGER-SOY CHICKEN WINGS 178

PAN-FRIED CHICKEN WITH PEPPERY CREAM SAUCE 179

ITALIAN CHICKEN 180

CHICKEN TETRAZZINI 182

GRILLED LEMON-THYME CHICKEN THIGHS .183

GRILLED MARINATED CHICKEN KEBABS 184

CHICKEN DRUMSTICKS ROASTED WITH HERBS 185

ROAST CHICKEN WITH VEGETABLE AND SOYA STUFFING 186

GRILLED CHICKEN DIAVOLO 187

GRILLED CHICKEN WITH MANGO SALSA 188

TURKEY ESCALOPES WITH HAM AND PROVOLONE 191

TURKEY DRUMSTICK CURRY 192

ROAST TURKEY BREAST WITH HERB RUB AND PAN JUICES 193

TURKEY LOAF 194

TURKEY BURGERS STUFFED WITH CHILLIES AND CHEESE 196

BREADED TURKEY ESCALOPES WITH OREGANO AND LEMON 198

CHICKEN BREASTS WITH ROASTED PEPPERS AND THYME
286 calories, 9 g carbs

4 boneless, skinless chicken breasts (170 g/6 oz each)

½ teaspoon salt

¼ teaspoon ground black pepper

2 tablespoons lemon juice

40 g/1¼ oz soya flour

2 tablespoons olive oil

60 g/2 oz roasted red peppers, chopped

1½ teaspoons fresh thyme leaves or ½ teaspoon dried

Arrange the chicken on a plate and season with the salt and black pepper. Drizzle with 1 tablespoon of the lemon juice. Coat with the flour.

Heat 1 tablespoon of the oil in a large non-stick frying pan over medium heat. Add the chicken and cook until the first side is golden brown, 2 to 3 minutes. Turn and brown the other side, 2 to 3 minutes. Reduce the heat to low and cook until the chicken juices run clear and a meat thermometer registers 75°C/170°F, 12 to 15 minutes. Remove to a serving dish.

Add the remaining tablespoon of oil to the pan and stir in the red peppers, thyme and the remaining 1 tablespoon lemon juice. Heat for 30 to 60 seconds, stirring. Spoon over the chicken.

Makes 4 servings

Per serving: energy 286 cals/1202 kJ; protein 38 g; carbohydrate 9 g (of which 1 g sugars); fat 11 g (of which 3 g saturates); fibre 1 g; sodium 366 mg

Diet Exchanges: 0 milk, ½ vegetable, 0 fruit, 0 bread, 6 meat, 1½ fat

Time-Saver

Make these easy chicken breasts ahead for a future dinner or lunch. They can be refrigerated for up to 2 days. To reheat, arrange in a baking dish and bake at 170°C/325°F/gas 3 until heated through, 10 to 15 minutes. Drizzle with a little oil and lemon juice to replace lost moisture.

CHICKEN BREASTS IN SHERRY SAUCE WITH GRAPES AND CUCUMBERS

303 calories, 6 g carbs

- **4 boneless, skinless chicken breasts (170 g/6 oz each)**
- **½ teaspoon salt**
- **¼ teaspoon ground black pepper**
- **15 g/½ oz butter**
- **115 g/4 oz red or green seedless grapes, halved**
- **1 cucumber (170 g/6 oz), peeled, seeded and finely chopped**
- **4 tablespoons dry sherry or chicken stock**
- **80 ml/3 fl oz single cream**
- **1 teaspoon chopped fresh dill or ¼ teaspoon dried**

Season the chicken with ¼ teaspoon of the salt and the pepper. Melt the butter in a large non-stick frying pan over medium-low heat. Add the chicken and cook, turning once or twice, until the juices run clear and a meat thermometer registers 75°C/170°F, 12 to 15 minutes.

Remove to a serving dish and cover with foil to keep warm. Stir the grapes and cucumber into the pan and cook for 1 minute. Add the sherry or stock and cream. Increase the heat to high and cook until thick enough to lightly coat the chicken, 3 to 4 minutes. Add the dill and the remaining ¼ teaspoon salt. Pour over the chicken.

Makes 4 servings

Per serving: energy 303 cals/1271 kJ; protein 38 g; carbohydrate 6 g (of which 6 g sugars); fat 12 g (of which 6 g saturates); fibre 1 g; sodium 406 mg

Diet Exchanges: 0 milk, ½ vegetable, ½ fruit, 0 bread, 5½ meat, 1½ fat

Time-Saver

To halve grapes easily, line them up in the 'gutter' of a cutting board and slice the whole row with a long knife.

Chicken Breasts with Mozzarella, Peppers and Olives

CHICKEN BREASTS WITH MOZZARELLA, PEPPERS AND OLIVES
428 calories, 1 g carbs

- **4 boneless, skinless chicken breasts (170 g/6 oz each)**
- **1 tablespoon fresh basil or ½ teaspoon dried**
- **4 slices (170 g/6 oz) smoked or regular mozzarella cheese, each 5 mm/ ¼ in thick**
- **½ teaspoon salt**
- **¼ teaspoon ground black pepper**
- **2 tablespoons olive oil**
- **1 large green and/or red pepper, cut into thin strips**
- **80 ml/3 fl oz dry white wine or chicken stock**
- **90 g/3 oz pitted black olives, quartered lengthwise**

Preheat the oven to 180°C/350°F/gas 4.

Make an 8 cm/3 in-long horizontal pocket in each chicken piece (cut through the thicker edge to 1 cm/½ in from the opposite edge). Sprinkle the basil over the cheese. Slip a cheese slice into each pocket, folding it to fit if necessary. Close the edges and secure with toothpicks. Season with ¼ teaspoon of the salt and the pepper.

Heat the oil in a large ovenproof frying pan over medium-low heat. Stir in the pepper and season with the remaining ¼ teaspoon salt. Cook, stirring occasionally, until lightly browned and starting to wilt, 4 to 5 minutes. Push the pepper to the edge of the pan and add the chicken. Cook until lightly browned, 2 to 3 minutes. Turn and arrange the pepper around the chicken. Add the wine or stock and the olives.

Bake, uncovered, until the chicken juices run clear and a meat thermometer registers 75°C/170°F, 12 to 15 minutes, turning once or twice.

Using a slotted spoon, remove the chicken to plates and top with the peppers and olives. There should be about 2 tablespoons of juices in the pan. If more, put the frying pan over medium heat and cook until the liquid is reduced, 1 to 3 minutes. Spoon over the chicken.

Makes 4 servings

Per serving: energy 428 cals/1786 kJ; protein 46 g; carbohydrate 1 g (of which 1 g sugars); fat 25 g (of which 10 g saturates); fibre 1 g; sodium 1435 mg

Diet Exchanges: 0 milk, ½ vegetable, 0 fruit, 0 bread, 7 meat, 3½ fat

Time-Saver

Prepare extra portions of these stuffed breasts for a quick lunch or supper. Store in a covered container in the refrigerator for up to 2 days. To reheat, arrange the chicken in a baking dish, cover and bake at 180°C/350°F/gas 4 until heated through, 10 to 15 minutes. Drizzle with a little olive oil to replace lost moisture.

CHICKEN SCALLOPINI WITH SAGE AND CAPERS

400 calories, 12 g carbs

80 ml/3 fl oz chicken stock

4 tablespoons dry white wine or chicken stock

1 tablespoon drained capers

4 boneless, skinless chicken breasts (170 g/6 oz each), pounded to 5 mm/¼ in thick

½ teaspoon salt

¼ teaspoon ground black pepper

¾ teaspoon dried sage

3 tablespoons wholemeal flour

4 teaspoons olive oil

1 teaspoon cornflour

2 teaspoons cold water

20 g/¾ oz cold butter, cut in small pieces

2 teaspoons chopped fresh parsley (optional)

In a small bowl, combine the stock, wine (if using) and capers.

Season the chicken with the salt, pepper and sage. Lightly coat with the flour, patting off the excess. Heat a large non-stick frying pan over high heat and add 2 teaspoons of the olive oil. Add 2 pieces of the chicken and cook until browned, 2 to 3 minutes. Reduce the heat to medium and turn the chicken. Cook until the chicken is no longer pink and the juices run clear, about 2 minutes. Remove to a plate and cover with foil to keep warm.

Add the remaining 2 teaspoons olive oil and cook the remaining chicken in the same fashion. Remove to the plate.

In a small cup, combine the cornflour and water. Pour the caper mixture into the pan and heat over medium heat. Bring to a simmer and whisk in the cornflour mixture. Cook, whisking until thickened, about 15 seconds. Whisk in the butter and spoon the sauce over the chicken. Sprinkle with the parsley (if using).

Makes 4 servings

Per serving: energy 400 cals/1674 kJ; protein 39 g; carbohydrate 12 g (of which 0 g sugars); fat 21 g (of which 6 g saturates); fibre 1 g; sodium 495 mg

Diet Exchanges: 0 milk, 0 vegetable, 0 fruit, ½ bread, 5½ meat, 2 fat

Time-Saver

Make these scallopini ahead or store the leftovers in a covered container in the refrigerator for up to 2 days. To reheat, arrange the scallopini in a baking dish, cover and bake at 180°C/350°F/gas 4 until heated through, about 15 minutes. Drizzle with a little olive oil to replace lost moisture.

Chicken Scallopini with Sage and Capers

CHICKEN THIGHS WITH LEMON-PEPPER SAUCE

198 calories, 1 g carbs

Juice of half a lemon

1 tablespoon Worcestershire sauce

2 teaspoons olive oil

1½ teaspoons Dijon mustard

¼ teaspoon ground black pepper

⅛ teaspoon dried chilli flakes

3–4 tablespoons water

**4 skinless chicken thighs
(200 g/7 oz each)**

4 tablespoons chicken stock

Preheat the oven to 190°C/375°F/gas 5.

In a small bowl, mix the lemon juice, Worcestershire sauce, oil, mustard, black pepper, chilli flakes and 2 tablespoons of the water.

Place the chicken in an ovenproof frying pan and pour the mustard mixture evenly over the top. Bake until the juices run clear and a meat thermometer registers 80°C/180°F, 25 minutes, adding 1 to 2 tablespoons water if necessary to keep the chicken moist. Remove the chicken to a plate and keep warm.

Add the stock to the pan and cook over medium heat until slightly reduced and thickened, 2 to 4 minutes. Spoon over the chicken.

Makes 4 servings

Per serving: energy 198 cals/834 kJ; protein 31 g; carbohydrate 1 g (of which 1 g sugars); fat 8 g (of which 2 g saturates); fibre 0 g; sodium 197 mg

Diet Exchanges: 0 milk, 0 vegetable, 0 fruit, 0 bread, 2 meat, 1 fat

Time-Savers

Make the mustard sauce up to 3 days ahead and store it in a covered container in the refrigerator. Or store the fully prepared chicken in a covered container in the refrigerator for up to 2 days. To reheat, arrange the chicken in an ovenproof dish, cover and bake at 180°C/350°F/gas 4 until heated through, about 15 minutes.

ROASTED CHICKEN BREASTS WITH LEMON AND MUSTARD

248 calories, 6 g carbs

4 teaspoons Dijon mustard

Juice of half a lemon

1 large egg

½ teaspoon Worcestershire sauce

2 teaspoons olive oil

¼ teaspoon salt

¼ teaspoon ground black pepper

8 tablespoons cornmeal

4 boneless, skinless chicken breasts (170 g/6 oz each)

Place the oven rack in the top position and preheat the oven to 230°C/450°F/gas 8.

In a small bowl, mix 2 teaspoons of the mustard and the lemon juice.

In another small bowl, lightly beat the egg and stir in the Worcestershire sauce, oil, salt, pepper and remaining 2 teaspoons mustard. Dip the chicken into the egg mixture. Press each piece into the cornmeal and turn to coat both sides. Place on a plate in one layer and refrigerate, uncovered, for 10 to 60 minutes to help the cornmeal mixture stick.

Coat a baking tray with cooking spray and preheat it on the upper rack of the oven for 5 minutes. Arrange the chicken breasts, thickest side down, on the tray and cook until golden brown, 8 to 10 minutes. Turn and cook until the juices run clear and a meat thermometer registers 75°C/170°F, 4 to 5 minutes. Drizzle with the lemon-mustard sauce.

Makes 4 servings

Per serving: energy 248 cals/1044 kJ; protein 38 g; carbohydrate 6 g (of which 0 g sugars); fat 8 g (of which 2 g saturates); fibre 1 g; sodium 321 mg

Diet Exchanges: 0 milk, 0 vegetable, 0 fruit, ½ bread, 6 meat, 1 fat

▶Flavour Tips

Use 5 tablespoons cornmeal with 3 tablespoons grated Parmesan or pecorino cheese. Add 1 teaspoon Dijon mustard to the egg mixture and serve the chicken with lemon wedges instead of the lemon-mustard sauce.

Curried Chicken with Coconut

CURRIED CHICKEN WITH COCONUT
320 calories, 13 g carbs

2 teaspoons groundnut (peanut) oil or walnut oil

7 g/¼ oz butter

½ large onion, chopped

2 garlic cloves, finely chopped

1 fennel bulb (230 g/8 oz) or 2 celery sticks, chopped

½ large green or red pepper, chopped

4 boneless, skinless chicken breasts (170 g/6 oz each), cut into 3 cm/ 1 in cubes

½ teaspoon salt

¼ teaspoon ground black pepper

1 tablespoon curry powder

170 g/6 oz tinned chopped tomatoes

120 ml/4 fl oz chicken stock

3 tablespoons chopped peanuts

3 tablespoons grated unsweetened coconut

Heat the oil and butter in a saucepan over medium heat until the butter is melted. Stir in the onion, garlic, fennel or celery and red or green pepper. Cover and cook just until translucent, stirring occasionally, 8 to 10 minutes.

Stir in the chicken, salt and black pepper. Cook, stirring frequently, until the chicken has lost most of the pink colour, 3 to 5 minutes. Sprinkle with the curry powder and cook for 30 seconds, stirring. Add the tomatoes and stock and bring to a simmer. Cover, reduce the heat to medium-low and cook until the chicken is tender, about 30 minutes.

Serve with the nuts and coconut for sprinkling on top.

Makes 4 servings

Per serving: energy 320 cals/1331 kJ; protein 41 g; carbohydrate 13 g (of which 4 g sugars); fat 10 g (of which 3 g saturates); fibre 3 g; sodium 480 mg

Diet Exchanges: 0 milk, 1 vegetable, 0 fruit, ½ bread, 5½ meat, 1½ fat

▶Flavour Tips
Substitute turkey for the chicken.
For a spicier dish, add ½ small chopped hot chilli pepper or chilli powder. You can also toast the coconut.

I Did It!

Lynne Peters

After she moved to a different part of the country, Lynne's diet went steadily downhill. Eventually, she joined a 12-step weight-loss programme and lost a few excess pounds. But it wasn't until she lowered her carbohydrate intake that Lynne's dress size shrank dramatically and her energy levels soared.

before

'In my thirties, I consistently gained weight for 5 years before I could admit that it was a problem for me. I had an endless list of excuses for not dealing with the extra pounds. Stress, turning 40, hormonal changes, quitting smoking, relocating to a new house, exercising less often, depression . . . the list went on and on. Although there was some truth in all of these reasons, I knew that they were just excuses.

'I wasn't always overweight.

Weight lost: 13.6 kg/2 st 2lb
Time kept off: 3 years
Weight-loss strategies: followed low-carbohydrate diet, ate three meals and two snacks a day, maintained support from a structured programme
Weight-maintenance strategies: follows low-carbohydrate diet, eats three meals and two snacks a day, maintains support from a structured programme, exercises regularly

Throughout my twenties, I was 20 to 30 pounds *underweight* because I hardly ate and I exercised obsessively. In my thirties, I reached a normal weight for the first time in my life. Around that time, I began selling food for a living and – big surprise – eating a lot more. I got to know the best chefs in town and thoroughly enjoyed duplicating their recipes in my own kitchen. Whenever I noticed my clothes getting tight, I would immediately eat less or eat liquid meals. While I enjoyed a normal weight, I was absolutely clueless about what I was consuming in the way of calories and the nutritional balance of my overall diet.

'Then a job transfer took me to a different part of the country and I began to eat what most people call comfort foods. My new diet consisted of fried foods in breadcrumbs or batter that were high in fat and starchy foods that were high in carbohydrates.

'I ate fried chicken, fried fish and fried prawns. Ham, bacon and sausage became favourites. I ate tons of pasta and mashed potatoes with gravy. And I loved eating cheese or anything with cheese sauce. I adopted a couch potato lifestyle, too. In no time, I was 22 kg/3½ st overweight. It seemed that no matter what I did, the pounds kept adding up. At that time, my highest weight put me into a tight extra-large size.

'During the worst of it, I would wake up in the middle of the night and be unable to go back to sleep unless I ate. That's when I admitted true defeat and turned to a 12-step programme for help.

'When I started the programme I was encouraged to cut sugar out of my diet and eat three balanced meals a day. I contacted a nutritionist who gave me a food plan that included three meals and two snacks for a total of 1,700 calories a day. In 3 or 4 months, I lost 7.7 kg/1 st 3 lb and could fit into a size 14. But the drawback was that I had daily slumps in my energy level – in both the afternoon and the early evening. I know now that refined carbohydrates were probably to blame.

'Because my energy was so low then, I decided to get a second opinion from another nutritionist. She suggested that I omit refined flour products and sugar from my diet as well as reduce my overall carbohydrate intake. I began eating mostly low-carbohydrate foods like lean meats, fish and beans, and eating lots of vegetables. I also avoided anything made with sugar or wheat.

'The difference is amazing. On this reduced-carbohydrate plan, it seems like my energy is boundless. Best of all, I am a size 12 and love it! I'm more active now, too. I do strength training for my legs and abs three times a week at the gym and I attend aerobics classes about three times a week. I have such a busy, enjoyable life these days and my spirit feels alive thanks to eating the foods that are right for my body.'

(continued)

I Did It! (cont.)

LYNNE'S ON-THE-GO CHICKEN
390 calories, 13 g carbs

455 g/1 lb boneless, skinless chicken pieces

450 ml/15 fl oz tomato-based pasta sauce

115 g/4 oz Jarlsberg cheese, grated

170 g/6 oz Parmesan cheese, grated

230–285 g/8–10 oz fresh young spinach or chopped spinach leaves

240 ml/8 fl oz water

1 teaspoon dried mixed herbs

¼ teaspoon salt

Coat a large, deep frying pan or saucepan with cooking spray and heat over medium heat. Add the chicken and cook, turning occasionally, until lightly browned, about 5 minutes. Add the pasta sauce, Jarlsberg and Parmesan. Cook, stirring, until the cheese melts. Add the spinach, water, herbs and salt. Cook for 15 minutes. Serve immediately.

Makes 4 servings

Per serving: energy 390 cals/1662 kJ; protein 40 g; carbohydrate 13 g (of which 4 g sugars); fat 19 g (of which 8 g saturates); fibre 3 g; sodium 823 mg

Diet Exchanges: 0 milk, 0 vegetable, 0 fruit, 1 bread, 5 meat, 3 fat

▶Flavour Tips
Serve this with brown rice or wholewheat pasta. For an alternative presentation, cook the chicken without the cheese. At the end of cooking, sprinkle the cheese over the entire dish and grill until melted, about 2 minutes.

GRILLED ORANGE-ROSEMARY CHICKEN

315 calories, 6 g carbs

- 1 **large orange**
- 1 **tablespoon olive oil**
- 2 **tablespoons finely chopped fresh rosemary or 1½ teaspoons dried**
- 1 **teaspoon salt**
- ½ **teaspoon dried chilli flakes**
- 1.6 kg/3½ lb **skinless chicken pieces**

Grate the zest from the orange into a large, shallow dish. Squeeze the juice into the dish. Stir in the oil, rosemary, salt and chilli flakes. Add the chicken and toss to coat evenly. Cover and refrigerate for at least 24 hours or up to 3 days.

Coat a grill rack with cooking spray. Preheat the grill. Arrange the chicken on the rack and cook until nicely browned, turning frequently, until the juices run clear and a meat thermometer registers 75°C/170°F for breasts and 80°C/180°F for other parts.

Makes 4 servings

Per serving: energy 315 cals/1310 kJ; protein 49 g; carbohydrate 6 g (of which 1 g sugars); fat 12 g (of which 3 g saturates); fibre 1 g; sodium 689 mg

Diet Exchanges: 0 milk, 0 vegetable, ½ fruit, 0 bread, 6½ meat, 1½ fat

▶## Flavour Tips

Rub the chicken with a halved garlic clove before marinating. Use chicken breasts only. When chilled, this chicken travels well for a packed lunch.

HIDDEN ROADBLOCK to weight loss

PRESCRIPTION MEDICATIONS

Some medications may hinder weight loss – or even cause you to gain weight. These especially include steroids, birth control pills and some anti-depressant drugs. One teenager we spoke to gained 26 kg/4 st in 1 month when she started on an anti-depressant. If you are on any medications, read the instructions or check with your doctor or pharmacist about any weight-gain side-effects. Don't stop taking your medication. But do discuss possible alternatives with your health care provider.

SAUTÉED CHICKEN WITH SHALLOTS AND WHITE WINE
300 calories, 3 g carbs

1.6 kg/3½ lb skinless chicken pieces

¾ teaspoon salt

¾ teaspoon dried thyme

¼ teaspoon ground black pepper

1 teaspoon olive oil

1 large shallot (75 g/2½ oz), sliced

1 large garlic clove, finely chopped

2 small tomatoes (115 g/4 oz), coarsely chopped

3 tablespoons dry white wine

7 g/¼ oz cold butter, cut into 2–3 pieces

2 teaspoons chopped parsley

Season the chicken with ½ teaspoon of the salt, the thyme and ⅛ teaspoon of the pepper. Heat the oil in a large non-stick frying pan over medium-high heat. Add the chicken, thickest side down, and cook until golden, about 5 minutes. Turn and cook until golden, 3 to 4 minutes.

Reduce the heat to very low, pour off the fat and arrange the shallot, garlic and tomatoes around the chicken. Cook for 1 minute. Add the wine or stock, cover and cook until the breast juices run clear and a meat thermometer registers 75°C/170°F, 12 to 15 minutes. Remove the breasts to a dish and cover loosely with foil to keep warm. Cook the remaining chicken, uncovered, until the juices run clear and a meat thermometer registers 80°C/180°F, 8 to 10 minutes. Remove to the dish and cover.

There should be about 6 tablespoons of liquid left in the pan. If there's more, boil it down over high heat or, if there's less, stir in water, wine or stock to bring it to 6 tablespoons. Bring to a boil over medium heat and stir in the butter, parsley, the remaining ¼ teaspoon salt and the remaining ⅛ teaspoon pepper. Pour over the chicken.

Makes 4 servings

Per serving: energy 300 cals/1248 kJ; protein 44 g; carbohydrate 3 g (of which 2 g sugars); fat 11 g (of which 3 g saturates); fibre 1 g; sodium 500 mg

Diet Exchanges: 0 milk, ½ vegetable, 0 fruit, 0 bread, 6 meat, 3 fat

Time-Saver

Make this dish ahead and refrigerate it in a covered container for up to 1 day or freeze it for up to 2 months. To reheat, thaw the chicken in the refrigerator overnight, then bake it in a covered ovenproof dish at 190°C/375°F/gas 5 until heated through, about 10 minutes. Drizzle with a little olive oil to replace lost moisture.

Sautéed Chicken with Shallots and White Wine

GINGER-SOY CHICKEN WINGS

328 calories, 1 g carbs

3 tablespoons soy sauce

1 teaspoon ground ginger

½ teaspoon garlic powder

½ teaspoon ground black pepper

1.6 kg/3½ lb chicken wings, first wing tip trimmed

2 tablespoons reduced-fat mayonnaise

2 tablespoons low-fat natural yoghurt

2 tablespoons chopped fresh basil

1 teaspoon lime juice

In a large bowl, mix the soy sauce, ginger, garlic powder and pepper. Add the chicken and toss to coat. Cover and refrigerate for up to 24 hours.

Place the oven rack in the top position and preheat the oven to 230°C/450°F/gas 8.

Coat a large rimmed baking tray with cooking spray and preheat in the oven for 5 minutes. Arrange the chicken on the baking tray, leaving at least 1 cm/½ in between

each piece. Cook, turning once or twice, until the chicken is browned, the juices run clear, and a meat thermometer registers 80°C/180°F, 20 to 25 minutes.

In a small bowl, combine the mayonnaise, yoghurt, basil and lime juice. Serve with the chicken wings.

Makes 6 servings

Per serving: energy 328 cals/1381 kJ; protein 34 g; carbohydrate 1 g (of which 1 g sugars); fat 16 g (of which 3 g saturates); fibre 0 g; sodium 172 mg

Diet Exchanges: 0 milk, 0 vegetable, 0 fruit, 0 bread, 3 meat, 1 fat

Time-Saver

Make the wings and sauce ahead and refrigerate them separately in covered containers for up to 2 days. To reheat, place the wings on a baking tray and bake at 200°C/400°F/gas 6 until heated through, about 5 minutes. Serve with the sauce.

PAN-FRIED CHICKEN WITH PEPPERY CREAM SAUCE
450 calories, 21 g carbs

450 ml/15 fl oz buttermilk

3 large garlic cloves, crushed

½ teaspoon dried thyme

½ teaspoon dried marjoram

¾ teaspoon salt

½ teaspoon ground black pepper

1 bay leaf

⅛ teaspoon dried chilli flakes (optional)

1.6 kg/3½ lb skinless chicken pieces, legs separated from thighs and breasts cut into 2 pieces

4 tablespoons vegetable oil

75 g/2½ oz + 2 teaspoons wholemeal flour

75 g/2½ oz soya flour

240 ml/8 fl oz single cream

Pour the buttermilk into a resealable bag or an ovenproof dish large enough to hold the chicken in one layer. Stir in the garlic, thyme, marjoram, ¼ teaspoon of the salt, ¼ teaspoon of the black pepper, the bay leaf and the chilli flakes (if using). Add the chicken pieces and turn to coat. Cover or seal and refrigerate for up to 24 hours.

Heat the oil in a large, heavy frying pan over medium-low heat and preheat the oven to 130°C/250°F/gas ½. Cover a baking tray with a double layer of kitchen paper.

In a large, shallow bowl, combine 75 g/2½ oz of the wholemeal flour, the soya flour and ¼ teaspoon of the salt. Remove the chicken from the marinade and dredge in the flour mixture. Place on a large dish or baking tray. Discard the marinade.

When the oil is hot, add the chicken in batches and cook until deep brown on the first side, 6 to 8 minutes. Turn the pieces, cover the pan loosely with foil and cook until the chicken is golden, the juices run clear and a meat thermometer registers 75°C/170°F for breasts and 80°C/180°F for other parts, 10 to 15 minutes for wings, 15 minutes for breasts and 20 minutes for thighs and drumsticks. Remove to the lined baking tray and keep warm in the oven.

Using a slotted spoon, remove most of the loose browned bits from the pan. Stir the remaining 2 teaspoons wholemeal flour into the oil left in the pan. Cook and stir for 1 minute. Gradually whisk in the cream and cook, stirring, until thickened, 2 to 3 minutes. Season with the remaining ¼ teaspoon salt and remaining ¼ teaspoon pepper. Serve the sauce with the chicken.

Makes 6 servings

Per serving: energy 450 cals/1885 kJ; protein 37 g; carbohydrate 21 g (of which 6 g sugars); fat 25 g (of which 9 g saturates); fibre 2 g; sodium 259 mg

Diet Exchanges: 0 milk, 0 vegetable, 0 fruit, ½ bread, 5 meat, 3 fat

chicken and turkey main dishes

ITALIAN CHICKEN
307 calories, 12 g carbs

SAUCE

- **1 tablespoon olive oil**
- **2 garlic cloves, finely chopped**
- **285 g/10 oz tinned chopped tomatoes**
- **2 tablespoons tomato puree**
- **1 teaspoon dried oregano**
- **2 tablespoons coarsely chopped fresh basil**
- **¼ teaspoon salt**
- **⅛ teaspoon ground black pepper**

CHICKEN

- **4 slices wholemeal bread**
- **2 large eggs**
- **4 boneless, skinless chicken breasts (170 g/6 oz each), pounded to 5 mm/¼ in thickness**
- **¼ teaspoon salt**
- **½ teaspoon ground black pepper**
- **40 g/1¼ oz wholemeal or soya flour**
- **2 teaspoons olive oil**
- **170 g/6 oz low-fat mozzarella cheese, finely chopped**

To make the sauce: Heat the oil in a small saucepan over low heat. Stir in the garlic and cook, stirring frequently, for 30 seconds. Add the tomatoes, tomato puree, oregano and basil. Cook until thick and rich, 12 to 15 minutes, stirring occasionally. Season with the salt and pepper. Cover and keep warm.

To make the chicken: While the sauce is cooking, preheat the oven to 130°C/250°F/gas ½. Place the bread on a baking tray and bake until completely dry, 10 to 12 minutes. Let cool slightly. Transfer the bread to a food processor and grind to make about 60 g/2 oz crumbs. Remove to a large plate. In a shallow bowl, lightly beat the eggs with 2 tablespoons water. Season the chicken with the salt and pepper and coat with the flour. Dip into the egg mixture, then press into the crumbs to coat both sides.

Place the grill rack about 10 cm/4 in from the heat and preheat the grill.

Heat 1 teaspoon of the oil in a large frying pan over medium heat. Add 2 of the coated chicken breasts and cook until golden brown on the first side, 2 to 3 minutes. Turn and cook until no longer pink and the juices run clear, 2 to 3 minutes. Remove to a 33 × 23 cm/13 × 9 in oven-proof dish. Repeat with the remaining teaspoon of oil and remaining chicken. Top with the sauce and sprinkle with the cheese. Grill until the cheese melts, 1 to 2 minutes.

Makes 4 servings

Per serving: energy 307 cals/1286 kJ; protein 33 g; carbohydrate 12 g (of which 3 g sugars); fat 15 g (of which 6 g saturates); fibre 1 g; sodium 642 mg

Diet Exchanges: 0 milk, ½ vegetable, 0 fruit, 1 bread, 5 meat, 2 fat

chicken and turkey main dishes

Italian Chicken

Chicken Tetrazzini
483 calories, 25 g carbs

- **20 g/¾ oz butter**
- **130 g/4½ oz wholewheat penne or other short pasta**
- **500 ml/18 fl oz chicken stock**
- **4 tablespoons dry white wine or chicken stock**
- **1 bay leaf**
- **4 boneless, skinless chicken breasts (170 g/6 oz each), cut widthwise into 5 mm/¼ in-wide strips**
- **6–8 large mushrooms (230 g/8 oz), sliced**
- **120 ml/4 fl oz double cream**
- **2 tablespoons cornflour**
- **2½ tablespoons water**
- **¼ teaspoon ground black pepper**
- **170 g/6 oz Parmesan cheese, grated**

Place the oven rack in the top position and preheat the oven to 220°C/425°F/gas 7. Butter a 20 × 20 cm/8 × 8 in ovenproof dish with 7 g/¼ oz of the butter.

Cook the pasta according to the directions on the packet. Drain well and remove to a warm, large bowl.

Meanwhile, in a saucepan, combine 350 ml/12 fl oz of the stock, the wine and bay leaf. Bring to a simmer over medium heat. Add the chicken and cook just until cooked through, 8 minutes, stirring once.

Using a slotted spoon, remove the chicken to the pasta bowl. Add the mushrooms to the stock and cook until tender, 3 to 4 minutes. Remove the mushrooms to the pasta bowl. Discard the bay leaf.

Measure the stock left in the pan. If it is more than 350 ml/12 fl oz, boil it until reduced. If it is less than 350 ml/12 fl oz, add more stock. Add the cream and simmer for 1 minute. Increase the heat to medium-high and bring to the boil. In a cup, combine the cornflour and water. Whisk into the stock mixture and cook, whisking until thickened, 30 to 60 seconds. Season with the pepper and add to the pasta bowl. Toss to mix.

Pour into the prepared ovenproof dish. Sprinkle with the cheese and dot with the remaining butter, cut into small pieces. Bake on the top rack until light brown and bubbling, 15 to 20 minutes.

Makes 6 servings

Per serving: energy 483 cals/2021 kJ; protein 37 g; carbohydrate 25 g (of which 2 g sugars); fat 26 g (of which 15 g saturates); fibre 2 g; sodium 566 mg

Diet Exchanges: 0 milk, 0 vegetable, 0 fruit, 1 bread, 5 meat, 1½ fat

▶Flavour Tips
Use turkey, fish or seafood in place of the chicken. Add a fresh herb, such as chopped parsley or basil, or spring onions to the pasta mixture.

GRILLED LEMON-THYME CHICKEN THIGHS

209 calories, 1 g carbs

3 tablespoons lemon juice

1½ tablespoons brandy or chicken stock

1 tablespoon chopped fresh thyme or 1 teaspoon dried

1–2 teaspoons olive oil

¼ teaspoon ground black pepper

4 skinless chicken thighs (200 g/7 oz each)

½ teaspoon salt

In a large bowl, stir together the lemon juice, brandy or stock, thyme, oil and pepper. Add the chicken, turning to coat. Cover and refrigerate for up to 24 hours, mixing once or twice.

Place the grill rack in the lowest position possible from the heat source and preheat the grill.

Coat a grill pan with cooking spray.

Remove the chicken from the marinade, season with the salt and arrange, skin side up, in the pan. Cook until well-browned, 8 to 10 minutes. Turn and cook until the juices run clear and a meat thermometer registers 80°C/180°F, 8 to 10 minutes. (If the chicken is browning too much, finish cooking in the oven at 180°C/350°F/gas 4.)

Makes 4 servings

Per serving: energy 209 cals/881 kJ; protein 31 g; carbohydrate 1 g (of which 1 g sugars); fat 8 g (of which 2 g saturates); fibre 0 g; sodium 343 mg

Diet Exchanges: 0 milk, 0 vegetable, 0 fruit, 0 bread, 2 meat, 1 fat

Time-Savers

Make the chicken ahead and store it in a covered container in the refrigerator for up to 2 days. To reheat, place on a baking tray and bake at 180°C/350°F/ gas 4 until heated through, 8 to 10 minutes. You can use extra portions in salads or sandwiches. Dress the salad with oil and vinegar and add chopped crunchy raw vegetables, such as celery and radishes.

GRILLED MARINATED CHICKEN KEBABS

236 calories, 1 g carbs

- **4 tablespoons soy sauce**
- **4 teaspoons sesame oil**
- **1 tablespoon finely chopped fresh ginger**
- **2 teaspoons Japanese mirin or dry sherry (optional)**
- **¼–½ teaspoon hot-pepper sauce**
- **685 g/1½ lb boneless, skinless chicken breasts, cut into 4 cm/1½ in cubes**
- **1 courgette (170 g/6 oz), cut into 3 cm/1 in pieces**
- **4 large mushrooms (115 g/4 oz), quartered**

In a large bowl, mix together the soy sauce, sesame oil, ginger, mirin or sherry (if using) and hot-pepper sauce. Add the chicken, courgette and mushrooms and toss to coat. Cover and refrigerate for up to 2 hours.

Coat a grill rack with cooking spray. Preheat the grill.

Thread the chicken and vegetables onto skewers. Place on the grill rack and cook, turning occasionally, until browned and the chicken juices run clear, 12 to 15 minutes.

Makes 4 servings

Per serving: energy 236 cals/995 kJ; protein 39 g; carbohydrate 1 g (of which 1 g sugars); fat 9 g (of which 2 g saturates); fibre 1 g; sodium 125 mg

Diet Exchanges: 0 milk, ½ vegetable, 0 fruit, 0 bread, 5½ meat, 2 fat

Time-Savers

Make this dish ahead and store it in a covered container in the refrigerator for up to 2 days. To reheat, arrange the chicken and vegetables on a baking tray or in a shallow ovenproof dish and bake at 180°C/350°F/gas 4 until heated through, about 5 minutes.

The chicken also makes a great salad or sandwich filling when tossed with finely chopped celery and apple and dressed with mayonnaise or Soft Yoghurt Cheese (page 107).

CHICKEN DRUMSTICKS ROASTED WITH HERBS

315 calories, 3 g carbs

2 tablespoons wholemeal flour

1 teaspoon dried oregano

1 teaspoon dried thyme

**¾ teaspoon dried dill
    or dill seed**

**½ teaspoon dried savory or
    rosemary, crumbled**

½ teaspoon paprika

1 teaspoon onion powder

1 teaspoon salt

½ teaspoon ground black pepper

**8 skinless chicken drumsticks
    (about 145 g/5 oz each)**

1 tablespoon olive oil

Preheat the oven to 220°C/425°F/gas 7. Generously coat a baking tray with cooking spray.

In a bowl, mix together the flour, oregano, thyme, dill, savory or rosemary, paprika, onion powder, salt and pepper. Coat the chicken with the oil. Sprinkle with the herbed flour, toss to coat and press the flour onto the drumsticks.

Preheat the prepared baking tray for 5 minutes. Arrange the drumsticks on the tray, leaving at least 3 cm/1 in between each. Roast, turning occasionally, until the chicken is browned and crisp, the juices run clear, and a meat thermometer registers 80°C/180°F, 30 to 35 minutes.

Makes 4 servings

Per serving: energy 315 cals/1310 kJ; protein 29 g; carbohydrate 3 g (of which 0 g sugars); fat 9 g (of which 3 g saturates); fibre 1 g; sodium 600 mg

Diet Exchanges: 0 milk, 0 vegetable, 0 fruit, ½ bread, 4 meat, 1½ fat

▶Flavour Tips

Instead of using all wholemeal flour, combine 1 tablespoon soya flour and 1 tablespoon wholemeal flour. Use 4 whole legs or separate the thighs from the drumsticks. Serve with 240 ml/8 fl oz passata.

ROAST CHICKEN WITH VEGETABLE AND SOYA STUFFING

360 calories, 12 g carbs

- **100 g/3½ oz dried soya mince**
- **300 ml/10 fl oz boiling chicken stock or water**
- **2 tablespoons olive oil**
- **3 celery sticks, finely chopped**
- **½ small onion, finely chopped**
- **1 carrot, finely chopped**
- **½ large red pepper, finely chopped**
- **½ teaspoon dried thyme**
- **¼ teaspoon dried sage**
- **½ teaspoon salt**
- **¼ teaspoon ground black pepper**
- **½ teaspoon soy sauce**
- **1 orange**
- **1 whole chicken (about 1.8 kg/4 lb), rinsed and dried**
- **3 whole sprigs rosemary**

Preheat the oven to 200°C/400°F/gas 6.

Put the soya mince in a bowl, stir in the boiling stock or water and leave to stand.

Heat 1½ tablespoons of the oil in a saucepan over medium-low heat. Stir in the celery, onion, carrot and red pepper. Cover and cook until tender, stirring occasionally, about 10 minutes. Add the soya mince along with the thyme, sage, ¼ teaspoon of the salt and ⅛ teaspoon of the black pepper. Add 120 ml/4 fl oz water and the soy sauce and simmer for 10 minutes, stirring occasionally. Transfer to an ovenproof dish, cover and set aside.

Grate the zest from the orange into a small bowl. Cut the orange in half and place inside the chicken cavity. Finely chop 1 of the rosemary sprigs and add to the zest. Place the remaining 2 whole rosemary sprigs inside the chicken cavity. Stir the remaining ¼ teaspoon salt and ⅛ teaspoon pepper into the zest mixture. Carefully lift the skin from the chicken and place the zest mixture evenly underneath. Tie the ends of the legs together with string and rub the remaining ½ tablespoon oil all over the skin. Place on a rack in a roasting pan and cook for 1 hour.

At the end of the hour, place the soya stuffing in the oven and cook until heated through, the chicken juices run clear, and a meat thermometer registers 80°C/180°F (in the breast), about 15 minutes more. Let stand for 10 minutes before carving. Serve with the pan juices and stuffing. Remove chicken skin before eating.

Makes 4 servings

Per serving: energy 360 cals/1497 kJ; protein 44 g; carbohydrate 12 g (of which 2 g sugars); fat 13 g (of which 2 g saturates); fibre 2 g; sodium 565 mg

Diet Exchanges: 0 milk, 1 vegetable, ½ fruit, 0 bread, 7 meat, 3½ fat

GRILLED CHICKEN DIAVOLO
325 calories, 1 g carbs

- **1 tablespoon lemon juice**
- **1 tablespoon olive oil**
- **1 teaspoon salt**
- **¾ teaspoon ground black pepper**
- **¼–½ teaspoon chilli powder**
- **1.6–1.8 kg/3½–4 lb skinless chicken pieces, legs separated from thighs and breasts cut into 2 pieces**

Place the grill rack in the lowest position possible from the heat source and preheat the grill.

In a large bowl, combine the lemon juice, oil, salt, black pepper and chilli powder. Add the chicken and toss to coat.

Arrange the chicken, skin side up, on a grill pan. Cook, turning, until the chicken is browned, the juices run clear and a meat thermometer registers 75°C/170°F for breasts, 18 to 20 minutes, and 80°C/180°F for thighs and drumsticks, 26 to 30 minutes.

Makes 4 servings

Per serving: energy 325 cals/1364 kJ; protein 52 g; carbohydrate 1 g (of which 1 g sugars); fat 13 g (of which 4 g saturates); fibre 0 g; sodium 683 mg

Diet Exchanges: 0 milk, 0 vegetable, 0 fruit, 0 bread, 6 meat, 1 fat

▶ Flavour Tip

Add 1 teaspoon mixed dried herbs to the marinade, such as thyme, oregano, marjoram and rosemary.

Smart-Carb Insider Tip
DON'T GO FAT-FREE

We need fat in our diets – especially healthy fats like those found in olive oil, fish and nuts. Feel free to eat these foods whenever you can. But avoid anything that says 'hydrogenated', 'partially hydrogenated' or 'trans fat' – these terms are found on many processed food labels. Trans fats can be as harmful to your heart as saturated fat. To keep saturated fat low, use oil instead of butter when you can, choose mostly lean cuts of meat and trim visible excess fat. When possible, microwave meats on high for a minute to drain away excess fat before you start cooking.

GRILLED CHICKEN WITH MANGO SALSA
247 calories, 6 g carbs

- **1 mango (about 340 g/12 oz), peeled and finely chopped**
- **1 tablespoon lime juice**
- **1½ tablespoons orange juice**
- **¼ small onion, finely chopped**
- **¾ teaspoon salt**
- **5 or 6 drops hot-pepper sauce**
- **2 teaspoons chopped fresh coriander**
- **4 boneless, skinless chicken breasts (170 g/6 oz each)**
- **1 tablespoon vegetable oil**
- **½ teaspoon salt**
- **¼ teaspoon ground black pepper**

In a medium bowl, combine the mango, lime juice, orange juice, onion, salt and hot-pepper sauce. Stir in the coriander.

Coat a grill rack with cooking spray. Preheat the grill. Rub the chicken with the oil and season with the salt and pepper. Place on the rack and grill, turning once, until the juices run clear and a meat thermometer registers 75°C/170°F, 10 to 12 minutes.

Serve topped with the salsa.

Makes 4 servings

Per serving: energy 247 cals/1039 kJ; protein 37 g; carbohydrate 6 g (of which 6 g sugars); fat 8 g (of which 2 g saturates); fibre 1 g; sodium 367 mg

Diet Exchanges: 0 milk, ½ vegetable, ½ fruit, 0 bread, 5½ meat, 1 fat

▶Flavour Tips
Add finely chopped pineapple or papaya to the salsa. You can also cook the chicken in a ridged chargrilling pan. Refrigerate leftover chicken in a covered container for up to 2 days, then cut the chicken into strips and roll up with the salsa in wholewheat tortillas or large lettuce leaves.

Grilled Chicken with Mango Salsa

Turkey Escalopes with Ham and Provolone

TURKEY ESCALOPES WITH HAM AND PROVOLONE
276 calories, 1 g carbs

- **4 turkey escalopes (115 g/4 oz each)**
- **½ teaspoon salt**
- **¼ teaspoon ground black pepper**
- **40 g/1¼ oz soya flour**
- **1 tablespoon olive oil**
- **4 thin slices (90 g/3 oz) ham, sliced in half**
- **4 thin slices (115 g/4 oz) provolone cheese, sliced in half**
- **4 lemon wedges**

Season the turkey with the salt and pepper. Coat in the flour and pat off the excess.

Heat the oil in a large non-stick frying pan over high heat. Add the turkey and cook until browned on the first side, 2 to 3 minutes. Turn, reduce the heat to low, and layer the ham and cheese on top. Cover and cook until the turkey juices run clear and the cheese is melted, 2 to 3 minutes. Serve immediately, with the lemon wedges for squeezing.

Makes 4 servings

Per serving: energy 276 cals/1155 kJ; protein 38 g; carbohydrate 1 g (of which 1 g sugars); fat 14 g (of which 6 g saturates); fibre 1 g; sodium 710 mg

Diet Exchanges: 0 milk, 0 vegetable, 0 fruit, ½ bread, 5½ meat, 2½ fat

▶Flavour Tips

Substitute Jarlsberg or mozzarella cheese for the provolone and sprinkle the turkey with 1 tablespoon chopped fresh parsley or 1 teaspoon dried thyme. Serve with 2 tablespoons passata.
After adding the ham and cheese you can finish cooking the turkey under a hot grill.

TURKEY DRUMSTICK CURRY
297 calories, 17 g carbs

- **40 g/1¼ oz butter**
- **1 small onion, chopped**
- **1 large celery stick, thinly sliced**
- **4 turkey drumsticks
   (285–340 g/10–12 oz each)**
- **½ teaspoon salt**
- **½ teaspoon ground black pepper**
- **1 teaspoon finely chopped fresh
   ginger (optional)**
- **2–3 teaspoons curry powder**
- **2 tablespoons wholemeal flour**
- **240 ml/8 fl oz chicken stock**
- **1 bay leaf**
- **1 tart apple (200 g/7 oz),
   peeled and cut into chunks**
- **10 dried apricots (60 g/2 oz),
   quartered**

Preheat the oven to 170°C/325°F/gas 3.

Melt the butter in a flameproof casserole dish or deep ovenproof pan over low heat. Add the onion and celery. Cover and cook just until soft, about 5 minutes. Add the turkey and sprinkle with the salt, pepper, ginger (if using), curry powder to taste and flour. Turn the turkey to cook the curry powder and flour, 1 to 2 minutes.

Add the stock and bay leaf and bring to a simmer. Cover the pan, place in the oven and cook for 45 minutes, turning the turkey twice. Add the apple and apricots. Cover and cook until the turkey is fork tender, 30 to 45 minutes more. Remove bay leaf before serving.

Makes 4 servings

Per serving: energy 297 cals/1242 kJ; protein 28 g; carbohydrate 17 g (of which 10 g sugars); fat 13 g (of which 7 g saturates); fibre 3 g; sodium 593 mg

Diet Exchanges: 0 milk, ½ vegetable, 1 fruit, ½ bread, 5 meat, 1½ fat

Time-Saver

Make this curry ahead and keep it in a covered container in the refrigerator for up to 4 days. The flavour improves with age. To reheat, place it in a deep casserole dish, cover and bake at 170°C/325°F/gas 3 until heated through, 20 to 25 minutes. If the sauce is too thick, thin it with 60 ml/2 fl oz single cream, stock or water.

ROAST TURKEY BREAST WITH HERB RUB AND PAN JUICES

225 calories, 1 g carbs

- ¾ **teaspoon dried thyme**
- ¾ **teaspoon dried tarragon**
- ½ **teaspoon dried rosemary, crumbled**
- ½ **teaspoon garlic powder**
- ¾ **teaspoon onion powder**
- ¼ **teaspoon ground black pepper**
- **I teaspoon salt**
- **2 teaspoons olive oil or melted butter**
- **I whole turkey breast on the bone (2.75 kg/6 lb)**
- **120 ml/4 fl oz dry white wine or chicken stock**
- **120 ml/4 fl oz chicken stock**
- **I½ teaspoons cornflour (optional)**

Preheat the oven to 230°C/450°F/gas 8.

In a small bowl, mix together the thyme, tarragon, rosemary, garlic powder, onion powder, pepper and ¾ teaspoon of the salt. Rub the oil or butter over the turkey and sprinkle with the herb mixture, pressing it in lightly. Place in a roasting pan and in the oven, immediately reducing the heat to 180°C/350°F/gas 4.

Roast, basting occasionally with the fat in the pan, until a meat thermometer inserted in the thickest part registers 75°C/170°F, about 2½ hours. Remove to a dish, reserve the pan juices and let rest for 15 minutes before carving.

Pour the pan juices into a glass measuring jug. Discard the fat that rises to the top and pour the juices (about 2 tablespoons) back into the roasting pan. Add the wine and stock. Bring to a simmer, scraping up the browned bits that are stuck to the bottom of the pan. Boil for 3 minutes, adding any accumulated juices from the dish. (If you would like a thicker sauce, whisk the cornflour with 2 teaspoons cold water. Stir into the pan, cooking until slightly thickened, about 30 seconds.) Strain if desired and season with the remaining ¼ teaspoon salt.

Makes 12 servings

Per serving: energy 225 cals/945 kJ; protein 35 g; carbohydrate 1 g (of which 1 g sugars); fat 9 g (of which 3 g saturates); fibre 0 g; sodium 253 mg

Diet Exchanges: 0 milk, 0 vegetable, 0 fruit, 0 bread, 5 meat, ½ fat

Time-Saver

Extra portions of this turkey breast are wonderful warm or cold. Store the turkey and gravy in a covered container in the refrigerator for up to 3 days. To reheat, place turkey slices and enough sauce or stock just to cover in a frying pan. Cover and heat over very low heat just until heated through, 3 to 4 minutes, without letting the mixture bubble (which would toughen the meat).

TURKEY LOAF
248 calories, 8 g carbs

120 ml/4 fl oz chicken stock or water

45 g/1½ oz quinoa, rinsed until the water runs clear

1 large egg

1½ tablespoons Worcestershire sauce

1½ tablespoons tomato puree

1 tablespoon Dijon mustard

1 small garlic clove, finely chopped

½ teaspoon salt

½ teaspoon dried savory or dill

½ teaspoon ground allspice

¼ teaspoon ground black pepper

685 g/1½ lb turkey breast, minced

2 tablespoons grated Parmesan cheese

1 large shallot or 5 spring onions, white part only, finely chopped

In a small saucepan, bring the stock or water to the boil over medium heat. Stir in the quinoa. Reduce the heat to low, cover and cook until the liquid has evaporated and the quinoa is crunchy-tender, 12 to 15 minutes (if there is liquid left, drain it).

Preheat the oven to 190°C/375°F/gas 5. Coat a large ovenproof dish or baking tray with cooking spray.

In a large bowl, lightly beat the egg, Worcestershire sauce, tomato puree, mustard, garlic, salt, savory or dill, allspice and pepper. Stir in the turkey, Parmesan, shallot or spring onions and the quinoa. Using a fork, lightly but thoroughly combine the ingredients. Gently form into a loaf about 18 × 10 cm/7 × 4 in and place on the prepared dish or baking tray. Bake just until cooked through but still juicy, and a meat thermometer registers 73°C/165°F, 45 to 50 minutes.

Makes 4 servings

Per serving: energy 248 cals/1047 kJ; protein 43 g; carbohydrate 8 g (of which 2 g sugars); fat 5 g (of which 2 g saturates); fibre 0 g; sodium 368 mg

Diet Exchanges: 0 milk, 0 vegetable, 0 fruit, 1 bread, 5½ meat, 2 fat

▶Flavour Tips

For best results, mix the meat as little as possible; the texture of an overhandled loaf can become mealy.
To make a simple sauce, combine 60 g/2 oz low-fat natural yoghurt, 2 teaspoons lime juice and 1 teaspoon honey.

Turkey Loaf

TURKEY BURGERS STUFFED WITH CHILLIES AND CHEESE
315 calories, 1 g carbs

**1 large jalapeño chilli (30–45 g/
   1–1½ oz); wear plastic gloves
   when handling**

685 g/1½ lb lean minced turkey

**4 slices (20 g/¾ oz each) Cheddar or
   Double Gloucester cheese**

**4 pimento-stuffed green olives
   (30 g/1 oz), sliced**

¾ teaspoon salt

¼ teaspoon ground black pepper

1 tablespoon vegetable oil

Place the jalapeño chilli in a small, heavy frying pan. Cook over very low heat, turning frequently, until the skin has blistered and blackened slightly, 10 to 15 minutes. Remove from the pan and let cool. Peel off the skin and cut the chilli in half lengthwise, discarding the stem, seeds and ribs. Coarsely chop.

Divide the turkey into 8 pieces. Gently press or pat to make rounds about 10 cm/ 4 in diameter. Layer the cheese, chopped chilli and olives on the 4 patties. Top with the remaining 4 patties and pinch the edges together to seal. Season with the salt and pepper.

Heat the oil in a large non-stick frying pan over medium-high heat. Add the patties and cook until browned on the first side, 3 to 4 minutes. Flip and cook until browned, 2 to 3 minutes more. Reduce the heat to low and cook until the meat is no longer pink but still juicy, 6 to 8 minutes.

Makes 4 servings

Per serving: energy 315 cals/1315 kJ; protein 45 g; carbohydrate 1 g (of which 1 g sugars); fat 15 g (of which 6 g saturates); fibre 1 g; sodium 1213 mg

Diet Exchanges: 0 milk, ½ vegetable, 0 fruit, 0 bread, 6 meat, 3 fat

▶Flavour Tips

Replace the jalapeño with 2 to 3 tablespoons drained, chopped bottled green chillies. Or omit the chillies altogether and serve the burgers topped with a tablespoon of hot salsa.

Turkey Burgers Stuffed with Chillies and Cheese

BREADED TURKEY ESCALOPES WITH OREGANO AND LEMON

264 calories, 6 g carbs

4 turkey escalopes (145–170 g/ 5–6 oz each)

3 tablespoons lemon juice

2 tablespoons olive oil

2 tablespoons chopped parsley

1½ teaspoons sweet Hungarian paprika (optional)

1 teaspoon dried oregano

½ teaspoon ground black pepper

60 g/2 oz wholewheat breadcrumbs

2 large eggs

1 tablespoon water

½ teaspoon salt

40 g/1¼ oz wholemeal or soya flour

15 g/½ oz butter

4 lemon wedges

Drizzle the turkey with the lemon juice and 1 tablespoon of the oil, lightly rubbing to coat. Sprinkle both sides with the parsley, paprika (if using), oregano and pepper, lightly patting in the seasonings. Cover and refrigerate for 1 hour to 2 hours.

Spread the breadcrumbs on a large plate. In a shallow bowl, lightly beat the eggs with the water. Sprinkle the salt over the turkey and coat with the flour, patting lightly. Dip the turkey into the egg mixture, then press into the breadcrumbs to coat both sides.

Heat the butter and the remaining 1 tablespoon oil in a large non-stick frying pan over medium to medium-high heat. When the butter froths, add the turkey. Cook until browned on the first side, 2 to 3 minutes. Turn, reduce the heat to low and cook until the turkey juices run clear, 2 to 4 minutes. Serve with the lemon wedges.

Makes 4 servings

Per serving: energy 264 cals/1107 kJ; protein 35 g; carbohydrate 6 g (of which 0 g sugars); fat 11 g (of which 3 g saturates); fibre 1 g; sodium 341 mg

Diet Exchanges: 0 milk, 0 vegetable, 0 fruit, ½ bread, 6 meat, 3 fat

▶**Flavour Tip**

For the best flavour and texture when cooking breaded escalopes, allow the eggs to set before turning the escalopes.

beef, pork & lamb main dishes

PAN-FRIED STEAK WITH MUSHROOMS 200

ROAST BEEF WITH ONION PAN JUICES 201

GRILLED FILLET STEAK WITH MUSTARD SAUCE 203

FILLET STEAK WITH TOMATOES AND ROSEMARY 204

TOPSIDE OF BEEF MARINATED IN SOY SAUCE AND MUSTARD 205

BRAISED BEEF WITH TURNIPS 206

CUBAN-STYLE BEEF PICADILLO 208

SPICY MEATBALLS WITH COCONUT MILK 209

BEEF KEBABS WITH YOGHURT AND SPICES 211

MEAT LOAF WITH WALNUTS 212

ITALIAN-STYLE BEEF BURGERS 213

BOLOGNESE SAUCE FOR PASTA 214

PORK MEDALLIONS WITH LEMON-CAPER SAUCE AND DILL 215

PORK CHOPS WITH CIDER, WALNUTS AND PRUNES 216

PORK CHOPS IN MUSTARD-WINE SAUCE 218

GRILLED PORK STEAKS WITH SPICY LENTILS 219

ROAST PORK TENDERLOIN WITH SHERRY, CREAM AND ALMONDS 221

BARBECUED SPARERIBS 222

PORK STEW WITH CABBAGE 223

ROAST PORK LOIN WITH ORANGE JUICE AND WHITE WINE 224

PEPPERED VENISON FILLETS 225

LAMB WITH GARLIC AND MUSHROOMS 226

LAMB KEBABS WITH MUSHROOMS AND TOMATOES 227

LAMB CHOPS WITH OLIVES 229

LAMB BURGERS WITH TOMATOES AND FETA CHEESE 230

PAN-FRIED STEAK WITH MUSHROOMS

360 calories, 3 g carbs

**4 sirloin steaks (170 g/6 oz each),
2 cm/¾ in thick**

½ teaspoon salt

½ teaspoon ground black pepper

2 tablespoons olive oil

285 g/10 oz mushrooms, sliced

1 large garlic clove, finely chopped

**2 teaspoons finely chopped fresh
rosemary or ½ teaspoon dried
and crumbled**

**2 tablespoons soured cream
(optional)**

Season the steaks with ¼ teaspoon of the salt and ¼ teaspoon of the pepper. Heat 1 tablespoon of the oil in a large, heavy frying pan over high heat. Add the steaks and cook until deeply browned on the first side, 3 to 4 minutes. Turn cook until well-browned and a meat thermometer registers 70°C/160°F for medium, 5 to 7 minutes. Remove to a plate.

Pour off the excess fat and add the remaining 1 tablespoon oil to the pan. Reduce the heat to medium-low and add the mushrooms and garlic. Cook, stirring occasionally, until the juices start to flow, 2 to 4 minutes. Add the rosemary, the remaining ¼ teaspoon salt and the remaining ¼ teaspoon pepper. Cook until the mushrooms' juices have evaporated, 2 to 3 minutes more. Remove from the heat. Stir in the soured cream (if using) and beef juices that have accumulated on the plate. Serve the steaks with the mushrooms.

Makes 4 servings

Per serving: energy 360 cals/1497 kJ; protein 36 g; carbohydrate 3 g (of which 0 g sugars); fat 19 g (of which 3 g saturates); fibre 1 g; sodium 360 mg

Diet Exchanges: 0 milk, ½ vegetable, 0 fruit, 0 bread, 5 meat, 1 fat

▶Flavour Tips

Choose a heavy frying pan for this dish; its ability to hold heat will help create a good crust on the meat and melt the soured cream.

You can replace the rosemary with oregano or another dried herb. Or add 1 finely chopped spring onion to the mushrooms before serving.

If you prefer, grill the steak instead of pan-frying it; rub it with 1 to 2 teaspoons olive oil before cooking.

Roast Beef with Onion Pan Juices

340 calories, 3 g carbs

- **1 tablespoon olive oil**
- **1 tablespoon red wine vinegar or cider vinegar**
- **1 tablespoon Worcestershire sauce**
- **½ teaspoon dried thyme**
- **¼ teaspoon ground black pepper**
- **Pinch of ground cloves**
- **1 onion, thinly sliced**
- **1 bay leaf**
- **1.15 kg/2½ lb sirloin joint**
- **¼ teaspoon salt**
- **400 ml/14 fl oz beef stock**

In a large glass bowl, mix together the oil, vinegar, Worcestershire sauce, thyme, pepper and cloves. Stir in the onion and the bay leaf. Add the beef and turn to coat in the marinade. Cover and refrigerate for at least 5 hours or up to 24 hours, turning the beef once or twice.

Preheat the oven to 260°C/500°F/gas 10. Coat a 25 cm/10 in roasting tin or heavy ovenproof frying pan with cooking spray. Sprinkle the salt over the beef and place in the pan, fat side up. Roast for 5 minutes. Reduce the heat to 170°C/325°F/gas 3, add the marinade and onions and pour 350 ml/12 fl oz of the stock around the beef.

Cook until a meat thermometer registers 70°C/160°F for medium, 1¼ to 1½ hours, adding more stock if the liquid drops to less than 1 cm/½ in. Remove from the oven, discard the bay leaf and let rest for 15 minutes before carving.

Slice thinly and serve with the onion pan juices.

Makes 6 servings

Per serving: energy 340 cals/1414 kJ; protein 42 g; carbohydrate 3 g (of which 0 g sugars); fat 15 g (of which 5 g saturates); fibre 0 g; sodium 450 mg

Diet Exchanges: 0 milk, ½ vegetable, 0 fruit, 0 bread, 6½ meat, 2 fat

▶Flavour Tips

If you substitute a less expensive cut of beef, slice the roast as thinly as possible to avoid toughness. If you have leftovers, refrigerate them for up to 4 days. To reheat, dip thin slices in hot stock for a few seconds and serve immediately. Or serve the meat chilled as part of a main course salad.

Grilled Fillet Steak with Mustard Sauce

GRILLED FILLET STEAK WITH MUSTARD SAUCE
252 calories, 1 g carbs

3 tablespoons mayonnaise

1½ tablespoons soured cream or low-fat natural yoghurt

1 spring onion, finely chopped

1 teaspoon Dijon mustard

¾ teaspoon soy sauce

½ teaspoon ground black pepper

¼ teaspoon salt

685 g/1½ lb tail-end fillet steak, in 1 piece

In a small bowl, combine the mayonnaise, soured cream or yoghurt, spring onion, mustard, soy sauce, ¼ teaspoon of the pepper and ⅛ teaspoon of the salt. Cover and let sit at room temperature.

Meanwhile, coat a heavy, ridged char-grilling pan with cooking spray. Preheat the pan. Season the beef with the remaining ¼ teaspoon pepper and the remaining ⅛ teaspoon salt. Cook over medium-high heat, turning once, until a meat thermometer registers 70°C/160°F for medium, 11 to 13 minutes. Remove to a plate and let rest for 5 minutes.

Slice thinly and serve topped with the mustard sauce.

Makes 6 servings

Per serving: energy 252 cals/1048 kJ; protein 26 g; carbohydrate 1 g (of which 0 g sugars); fat 15 g (of which 4 g saturates); fibre 0 g; sodium 280 mg

Diet Exchanges: 0 milk, 0 vegetable, 0 fruit, 0 bread, 3½ meat, 3 fat

Time-Savers

Leftovers can be covered and refrigerated for up to 3 days. Add to grain and vegetable salads for a quick main dish. Or serve leftover slices of steak wrapped around slices of Jarlsberg cheese, cress and sliced tomatoes for a sandwich or snack.
The sauce can be made ahead and refrigerated for up to 3 days.

FILLET STEAKS WITH TOMATOES AND ROSEMARY
300 calories, 3 g carbs

2 teaspoons soy sauce

1½ teaspoons Dijon mustard

1½ teaspoons finely chopped fresh rosemary or ½ teaspoon dried and crumbled

⅛ teaspoon garlic powder

2 tomatoes (230 g/8 oz), finely chopped

2 teaspoons olive oil

4 fillet steaks (170 g/6 oz each), 4 cm/1½ in thick

¼ teaspoon salt

½ teaspoon ground black pepper

Preheat the oven to 200°C/400°F/gas 6.

In a bowl, combine the soy sauce, mustard, rosemary and garlic powder. Fold in the tomatoes.

Heat the oil in a large, heavy ovenproof frying pan over high heat. Season the beef with the salt and pepper. Place in the pan and deeply brown the first side, 4 to 5 minutes. Turn and brown the second side for 30 seconds. Place the pan in the oven and cook until a meat thermometer registers 63°C/145°F for medium rare, 12 to 14 minutes. Serve topped with the tomatoes.

Makes 4 servings

Per serving: energy 300 cals/1248 kJ; protein 35 g; carbohydrate 3 g (of which 0 g sugars); fat 13 g (of which 4 g saturates); fibre 1 g; sodium 415 mg

Diet Exchanges: 0 milk, ½ vegetable, 0 fruit, 0 bread, 5 meat, ½ fat

▶Flavour Tips

Grill the beef instead of pan-searing it; rub the meat with 1 to 2 teaspoons olive oil before cooking. Replace the beef with venison or ostrich fillets.

TOPSIDE OF BEEF MARINATED IN SOY SAUCE AND MUSTARD

305 calories, 1 g carbs

- **1 tablespoon mustard powder**
- **4 teaspoons soy sauce**
- **2 teaspoons red wine vinegar**
- **1 teaspoon onion powder**
- **¼ teaspoon garlic powder**
- **1 tablespoon olive oil**
- **1 beef topside joint (685 g/1½ lb), fat trimmed**
- **¼ teaspoon salt**
- **¼ teaspoon ground black pepper**

In a small bowl, combine the mustard and soy sauce to make a paste. Stir in the vinegar, onion powder and garlic powder. Whisk in the olive oil.

Using a very sharp knife, cut halfway down through the diameter of the beef, then open it out and place between 2 sheets of greaseproof paper. Pound with a meat mallet or rolling pin until the beef is about 3 cm/1 in thick. Place the beef in an oven-proof glass dish. Pour the mustard mixture over the beef and rub lightly to coat all over. Cover and refrigerate for 2 hours or up to 24 hours.

Remove from the refrigerator 15 minutes before cooking.

Place the grill rack 5 cm/2 in from the heat source and preheat the grill. Coat a grill pan with cooking spray.

Transfer the beef to the pan and sprinkle with the salt and pepper. Grill until the top is browned, 4 to 5 minutes. Turn and cook the second side until a meat thermometer registers 63°C/145°F for medium-rare, 3 to 4 minutes. Remove to a plate and let rest for 5 minutes.

Using a very sharp knife, slice very thinly on the diagonal and serve with the pan juices.

Makes 4 servings

Per serving: energy 305 cals/1269 kJ; protein 37 g; carbohydrate 1 g (of which 0 g sugars); fat 18 g (of which 5 g saturates); fibre 0 g; sodium 570 mg

Diet Exchanges: 0 milk, 0 vegetable, 0 fruit, 0 bread, 5 meat, 3 fat

Time-Saver

Refrigerate leftovers in a covered container for up to 3 days. Use them for superfast suppers and lunches. To reheat, slice the beef and dip into simmering beef stock until heated through, 30 to 60 seconds.

BRAISED BEEF WITH TURNIPS
254 calories, 18 g carbs

**8 pieces bone-in short ribs of beef
(170 g/6 oz each)**

½ teaspoon salt

½ teaspoon ground black pepper

1 tablespoon olive oil

1 onion, chopped

1 small carrot, grated

1 tablespoon wholemeal flour

400 ml/14 fl oz beef stock

1 tablespoon tomato puree

½ teaspoon dried thyme

1 bay leaf

**2 turnips (455 g/1 lb), peeled and cut
into 2–3 cm/1 in cubes**

Preheat the oven to 170°C/325°F/gas 3.

Season the beef with the salt and pepper. Heat the oil in a flameproof casserole dish over medium-high heat. Working in 2 batches, add the beef and cook until browned on all sides, turning often, 6 to 8 minutes. Remove to a plate.

Reduce the heat to medium-low and add the onion and carrot. Cover, and cook for 3 minutes, stirring occasionally. Stir in the flour and cook, stirring almost continuously, for 1 minute. Gradually stir in the stock to make a smooth sauce. Add the tomato puree, thyme and bay leaf. Return the beef, along with any juices on the plate, to the casserole. Bring to a simmer.

Cover, and place in the oven until almost tender, 1¾ to 2 hours. Stir in the turnips, cover and cook until both the turnips and the beef are tender, 20 to 30 minutes. Remove the beef and turnips to a plate. Skim the fat from the surface of the liquid. Discard the bay leaf. Return the beef and turnips to the casserole or a warmed serving dish.

Makes 4 servings

Per serving: energy 254 cals/1070 kJ; protein 27 g; carbohydrate 18 g (of which 13 g sugars); fat 9 g (of which 3 g saturates); fibre 7 g; sodium 451 mg

Diet Exchanges: 0 milk, ½ vegetable, 0 fruit, 0 bread, 7 meat, 2 fat

Time-Saver

Make ahead and store in a covered container in the refrigerator for up to 4 days or in the freezer for up to 2 months. To reheat, thaw in the refrigerator. Cook in a flameproof casserole dish over low heat for 2 to 3 minutes, then transfer to the oven at 170°C/325°F/gas 3 until heated through, 30 to 40 minutes.

Braised Beef with Turnips

CUBAN-STYLE BEEF PICADILLO
350 calories, 18 g carbs

685 g/1½ lb extra-lean minced beef

1 green pepper, finely chopped

4 spring onions, finely chopped

10 pimento-stuffed green olives, chopped

300 ml/10 fl oz passata

45 g/1½ oz raisins

2 tablespoons drained capers

3 garlic cloves, finely chopped

1½ teaspoons ground cumin

1 teaspoon dried oregano

2 tablespoons olive oil

¼ teaspoon salt

¼ teaspoon ground black pepper

In a large bowl, combine the beef, green pepper, spring onions, olives, passata, raisins, capers, garlic, cumin and oregano. Cover and set aside for 20 minutes.

Heat the oil in a large, deep frying pan over medium heat. Add the beef mixture and cook, breaking it up with a spoon, until the beef is no longer pink, 3 to 4 minutes. Season with the salt and black pepper and cook, stirring occasionally, until it starts to brown in the pan, 25 to 30 minutes.

Makes 4 servings

Per serving: energy 350 cals/1456 kJ; protein 36 g; carbohydrate 18 g (of which 6 g sugars); fat 16 g (of which 4 g saturates); fibre 4 g; sodium 900 mg

Diet Exchanges: 0 milk, 1½ vegetable, ½ fruit, 0 bread, 5 meat, 2½ fat

▶Flavour Tips

Serve in crisp taco shells or with cooked brown rice with salsa. You could also serve the mixture with warmed corn tortillas to make soft, rolled tacos.
Or make a casserole out of the cooked picadillo by mixing it with cooked brown rice or tortilla chips; top with 115–170 g/4–6 oz grated Cheddar or Double Gloucester cheese and bake at 190°C/375°F/gas 5 until the cheese melts, about 5 minutes.

SPICY MEATBALLS WITH COCONUT MILK
220 calories, 3 g carbs

685 g/1½ lb extra-lean minced beef

3 spring onions, finely chopped

1 large egg, lightly beaten

5 tablespoons + 120 ml/4 fl oz coconut milk

2 tablespoons soy sauce

1½ teaspoons ground cumin

¾ teaspoon ground coriander seed

½ teaspoon dried chilli flakes

Place the grill rack 10 cm/4 in from the heat source and preheat the grill. Coat a large grill pan with cooking spray.

In a large bowl, combine the beef, spring onions, egg, 5 tablespoons of the coconut milk, 1½ tablespoons of the soy sauce, the cumin, coriander and chilli flakes.

Gently form into 4 cm/1½ in-diameter meatballs and arrange on the prepared grill pan, at least 1 cm/½ in apart. Grill (without turning) just until browned on the top, no longer pink inside and the juices run clear. Remove to a serving dish and discard the fat drippings in the pan. Pour the remaining 120 ml/4 fl oz coconut milk into the pan and scrape up the browned bits, stirring until dissolved. Season with the remaining ½ tablespoon soy sauce and pour over the meatballs.

Makes 6 servings

Per serving: energy 220 cals/915 kJ; protein 22 g; carbohydrate 3 g (of which 1 g sugars); fat 10 g (of which 7 g saturates); fibre 1 g; sodium 370 mg

Diet Exchanges: 0 milk, 0 vegetable, 0 fruit, 0 bread, 4 meat, 2 fat

▶Flavour Tips

Spoon over a bed of wholewheat couscous, brown rice or buckwheat noodles (soba). Or tuck sliced meatballs into a sandwich. Sprinkle with 1 tablespoon chopped fresh coriander just before serving.

Beef Kebabs with Yoghurt and Spices

BEEF KEBABS WITH YOGHURT AND SPICES
350 calories, 14 g carbs

- **115 g/4 oz low-fat natural yoghurt**
- **1 tablespoon soy sauce**
- **1 tablespoon lemon juice**
- **1 teaspoon ground ginger**
- **1 teaspoon ground cumin**
- **¼ teaspoon ground black pepper**
- **685 g/1½ lb boneless beef sirloin, fat trimmed, cut into 4 cm/1½ in cubes**
- **2 small red and/or green peppers (170 g/6 oz), cut into 4 cm/1½ in squares**

In a large bowl, combine the yoghurt, soy sauce, lemon juice, ginger, cumin and black pepper. Add the beef, tossing to coat. Cover and refrigerate for 6 to 8 hours.

Coat a grill rack with cooking spray. Preheat the grill. Thread the beef onto skewers, alternating with the peppers. Place the skewers on the grill rack and cook, turning to brown all sides, until no longer pink and a meat thermometer registers 63°C/145°F for medium rare, 12 to 15 minutes.

Makes 4 servings

Per serving: energy 350 cals/1456 kJ; protein 31 g; carbohydrate 14 g (of which 3 g sugars); fat 19 g (of which 6 g saturates); fibre 4 g; sodium 690 mg

Diet Exchanges: 0 milk, 2 vegetable, 0 fruit, 0 bread, 4 meat, 3½ fat

Time-Savers

Make extra portions of this dish for a speedy supper or lunch later in the week. Store in a covered container in the refrigerator for up to 4 days. To re-heat, arrange on a baking tray or in a shallow baking dish and bake at 200°C/400°F/ gas 6 until heated through, about 5 minutes. Serve with a little steak sauce to replace lost moisture. To make sandwiches, tuck the beef into wholewheat pittas or roll into tortillas.

beef, pork and lamb main dishes

MEAT LOAF WITH WALNUTS

240 calories, 5 g carbs

1 large egg, lightly beaten

2 tablespoons Worcestershire sauce

4 tablespoons tomato puree

½ teaspoon dried thyme

½ teaspoon salt

½ teaspoon ground black pepper

½ onion, finely chopped

1 large garlic clove, finely chopped

45 g/1½ oz ground walnuts

685 g/1½ lb extra-lean minced beef

120 ml/4 fl oz passata

Preheat the oven to 190°C/375°F/gas 5.

In a large bowl, combine the egg, Worcestershire sauce, tomato puree, thyme, salt and pepper. Add the onion, garlic, walnuts and beef. Using a fork, gently combine the meat with the seasonings. Form into a loaf and place in a 23 × 13 × 8 cm/9 × 5 × 3 in loaf pan. Spread the passata evenly over the top. Bake until the juices run clear and a meat thermometer registers 70°C/160°F, 50 to 55 minutes. Pour off the fat in the tin and slice the loaf.

Makes 6 servings

Per serving: energy 240 cals/998 kJ; protein 24 g; carbohydrate 5 g (of which 1 g sugars); fat 10 g (of which 4 g saturates); fibre 1 g; sodium 410 mg

Diet Exchanges: 0 milk, 1 vegetable, 0 fruit, 0 bread, 4 meat, 1½ fat

Time-Savers

A rotary cheese grater is excellent for grinding nuts. Store leftover meat loaf in a covered container in the refrigerator for up to 3 days. To reheat, slice the meat loaf and arrange it in an ovenproof dish. Add a few tablespoons of stock, cover and bake at 180°C/350°F/gas 4 until heated through, 8 to 12 minutes.

ITALIAN-STYLE BEEF BURGERS
265 calories, 2 g carbs

685 g/1½ lb extra-lean minced beef

30 g/1 oz grated pecorino cheese

30 g/1 oz pine nuts, toasted and finely chopped

½ teaspoon salt

1 teaspoon dried oregano

¾ teaspoon garlic powder

¼ teaspoon ground black pepper

Place the grill rack about 5 cm/2 in from the heat source and preheat the grill.

Place the beef in a large bowl and break into pieces. Add the cheese, nuts, salt, oregano, garlic powder and pepper. Using a fork, gently combine the beef and seasonings. Divide the meat into 4 equal portions and gently form into burgers approximately 10 cm/4 in diameter and 2–3 cm/1 in thick.

Place on a grill pan and cook until the top is browned, 4 to 6 minutes. Turn and cook until done and a meat thermometer registers 70°C/160°F for medium, 4 to 6 minutes.

Makes 4 servings

Per serving: energy 265 cals/1102 kJ; protein 35 g; carbohydrate 2 g (of which 0 g sugars); fat 13 g (of which 6 g saturates); fibre 0 g; sodium 460 mg

Diet Exchanges: 0 milk, 0 vegetable, 0 fruit, 0 bread, 5 meat, 1½ fat

▶Flavour Tips

For burgers with the best texture, handle the meat as little as possible. You can pan-fry the burgers instead of grilling them. Top with a slice of mozzarella cheese during the last minute of cooking if desired. Serve with 240 ml/8 fl oz passata.

To make an easy meat sauce for wholewheat pasta, break the burgers into pieces and cook them in 700 ml/1¼ pints passata for 3 to 5 minutes.

BOLOGNESE SAUCE FOR PASTA

220 calories, 7 g carbs

2 tablespoons olive oil

1 celery stick, finely chopped

1 small carrot, finely chopped

1 small onion, finely chopped

2 garlic cloves, finely chopped

340 g/12 oz extra-lean minced beef

115 g/4 oz minced pork

180 ml/6 fl oz dry red wine or
    beef stock

240 ml/8 fl oz passata

240 ml/8 fl oz beef stock

2 tablespoons tomato puree

1 teaspoon dried oregano

½ teaspoon salt

¼ teaspoon ground black pepper

2 tablespoons chopped fresh basil or
    parsley (optional)

Heat the oil in a saucepan over medium-low heat. Stir in the celery, carrot, onion and garlic and cook until the celery and onion are soft, 4 to 6 minutes. Add the minced beef and minced pork, increase the heat to medium-high, and cook, stirring and breaking the meat up, until the meat is no longer pink, 3 to 5 minutes. Add the wine or stock and reduce the heat to medium so that the liquid simmers. Cook until reduced to about 80 ml/3 fl oz, 12 to 15 minutes.

Stir in the passata, stock, tomato puree and oregano. Partially cover and cook until thick, 40 to 45 minutes. Season with the salt, pepper and basil or parsley (if using).

Makes 6 servings

Per serving: energy 220 cals/915 kJ; protein 17 g; carbohydrate 7 g (of which 0 g sugars); fat 10 g (of which 3 g saturates); fibre 2 g; sodium 430 mg

Diet Exchanges: 0 milk, 2 vegetable, 0 fruit, 0 bread, 2 meat, 2 fat

▶ Flavour Tips

Replace the pork with chopped salami. Serve this wonderfully rich sauce with 60–90 g/2–3 oz of whole-wheat pasta per person, tossing half of it with the pasta and spooning the other half on top. Top each serving with grated Parmesan.

PORK MEDALLIONS WITH LEMON-CAPER SAUCE AND DILL
285 calories, 4 g carbs

- **685 g/1½ lb pork tenderloin, cut into 5 mm/¼ in thick slices**
- **¼ teaspoon salt**
- **½ teaspoon ground black pepper**
- **75 g/2½ oz soya flour**
- **1 tablespoon olive oil**
- **30 g/1 oz butter, cut into small pieces**
- **120 ml/4 fl oz chicken stock**
- **2 tablespoons lemon or lime juice**
- **1 tablespoon capers, drained**
- **1 tablespoon chopped fresh dill**

Season the pork with the salt and pepper. Coat with the flour, patting off the excess.

Heat 1½ teaspoons of the oil and 7 g/¼ oz of the butter in a large frying pan over medium heat. When the butter froths, add as much of the pork as will fit in the pan without crowding. Cook until browned on the first side, 1 to 2 minutes. Turn and cook the second side just until the juices run clear, 2 to 3 minutes. Remove to a plate. Use the remaining oil and another 7 g/¼ oz of the butter to cook the remaining pork in the same manner. Cover loosely with foil to keep warm.

Reduce the heat to medium and add the stock, lemon or lime juice and capers to the pan. Simmer the sauce until reduced to about 4 tablespoons, 3 to 4 minutes. Stir in the remaining butter and pour over the pork. Sprinkle with the dill.

Makes 4 servings

Per serving: energy 285 cals/1185 kJ; protein 26 g; carbohydrate 4 g (of which 0 g sugars); fat 17 g (of which 6 g saturates); fibre 2 g; sodium 450 mg

Diet Exchanges: 0 milk, 0 vegetable, 0 fruit, ½ bread, 4 meat, 3 fat

Time-Saver

Make a double batch for later use. Store in a covered container in the refrigerator for up to 3 days. To re-heat, arrange on a baking tray coated with cooking spray and top with slices of mozzarella cheese. Bake at 190°C/375°F/gas 5 until heated through and the cheese melts, 5 to 10 minutes.

PORK CHOPS WITH CIDER, WALNUTS AND PRUNES

290 calories, 10 g carbs

4 pork chops (170–230 g/6–8 oz each), 2 cm/¾ in thick

½ teaspoon salt

½ teaspoon dried sage

¼ teaspoon ground black pepper

I tablespoon walnut oil or olive oil

6 pitted prunes (60–90 g/2–3 oz), chopped

120 ml/4 fl oz apple juice

4 tablespoons cider or dry white wine

2 tablespoons chopped walnuts

Season the pork with the salt, sage and pepper. Heat the oil in a large frying pan over medium-high heat. Add the pork and cook until browned on the first side, 4 to 5 minutes. Hold the chops on the edges and cook the edges until browned if desired, 1 to 2 minutes. Turn and cook until the second side is browned, about 1 minute.

Reduce the heat to low and pour off any fat in the pan. Add the prunes, apple juice and cider or wine and cook until the juices run clear and a meat thermometer registers 68°C/155°F, turning once or twice, 12 to 15 minutes.

Remove the chops to plates and spoon the prunes on top. There should be about 2 tablespoons of juice left in the pan. If more, cook over low to medium heat until reduced. Spoon the juices over the pork and sprinkle with the walnuts.

Makes 4 servings

Per serving: energy 290 cals/1206 kJ; protein 24 g; carbohydrate 10 g (of which 1 g sugars); fat 19 g (of which 5 g saturates); fibre 1 g; sodium 360 mg

Diet Exchanges: 0 milk, 0 vegetable, 1 fruit, 0 bread, 3 meat, 2 fat

Time-Saver

Leftovers of these chops make for quick suppers and lunches. Store the leftovers in a covered container in the refrigerator for up to 3 days. To reheat, arrange in an ovenproof dish and drizzle with apple juice or cider to replace lost moisture. Cover and bake at 190°C/375°F/gas 5 until heated through, about 15 minutes.

Pork Chops with Cider, Walnuts and Prunes

PORK CHOPS IN MUSTARD-WINE SAUCE

375 calories, 5 g carbs

240 ml 8 fl oz apple juice

80 ml/3 fl oz Madeira, Marsala or port

1 tablespoon Dijon mustard

1 teaspoon dried thyme

1 teaspoon vegetable oil

4 pork chops (170–230 g/6–8 oz each), 2–3 cm/1 in thick

⅛ teaspoon ground black pepper

In a small bowl, mix the apple juice, wine, mustard and thyme.

Heat the oil in a large frying pan over medium-high heat. Add the pork and cook until browned on the first side, about 2 minutes. Turn and cook until browned on the second side, about 1 minute. Pour off any fat in the pan, reduce the heat to low and pour the apple juice mixture over the pork. Cook, turning once, until the juices run clear and a meat thermometer registers 70°C/160°F, 5 to 7 minutes.

There should be about 2 tablespoons of lightly thickened juices in the pan. If there is more, remove the pork to a dish and cook the pan juices over medium heat until reduced to 2 tablespoons, 5 to 7 minutes. Pour the juices over the chops and sprinkle with the pepper.

Makes 4 servings

Per serving: energy 375 cals/1560 kJ; protein 40 g; carbohydrate 5 g (of which 1 g sugars); fat 17 g (of which 5 g saturates); fibre 0 g; sodium 390 mg

Diet Exchanges: 0 milk, 0 vegetable, ½ fruit, 0 bread, 6 meat, 2½ fat

▶Flavour Tips

Stir 2 teaspoons finely chopped spring onions into the sauce before pouring over the chops.
Substitute a thick gammon steak for the pork chops.

GRILLED PORK STEAKS WITH SPICY LENTILS
517 calories, 22 g carbs

- **1 tablespoon olive oil**
- **½ onion, chopped**
- **1 small green pepper, chopped**
- **115 g/4 oz brown lentils, rinsed and drained**
- **300 ml/10 fl oz vegetable stock or chicken stock**
- **2 tablespoons raisins**
- **¼ teaspoon ground black pepper**
- **⅛ teaspoon chilli powder**
- **4 pork steaks (170 g/6 oz each), 2 cm/¾ in thick**
- **½ teaspoon paprika**
- **¼ teaspoon salt**

Heat 1 teaspoon of the oil in a saucepan over medium heat. Add the onion and green pepper and cook, stirring occasionally, for 4 minutes. Stir in the lentils. Add the stock and bring to a simmer. Cover and cook, without stirring, until the lentils are tender but still retain their shape, 35 to 40 minutes. Drain any excess liquid. Fold in the raisins, a pinch of the black pepper and the cayenne pepper. Cover and keep warm.

Place the grill rack 10 cm/4 in from the heat source and preheat the grill. Coat a grill pan with cooking spray. Rub the pork with the remaining 2 teaspoons oil and season with the paprika, salt and remaining black pepper. Arrange in the grill pan. Grill, turning once, until lightly browned and a meat thermometer registers 70°C/160°F for medium, 12 to 14 minutes. Arrange on a bed of lentils and serve hot.

Makes 4 servings

Per serving: energy 517 cals/2150 kJ; protein 62 g; carbohydrate 22 g (of which 10 g sugars); fat 19 g (of which 6 g saturates); fibre 8 g; sodium 479 mg

Diet Exchanges: 0 milk, 0 vegetable, ½ fruit, 1 bread, 8 meat, 2½ fat

▶Flavour Tips

Garnish with 1 tablespoon chopped parsley or fresh mint. Use currants or other dried fruit instead of the raisins. Substitute lamb chops.

Roast Pork Tenderloin with Sherry, Cream and Almonds

ROAST PORK TENDERLOIN WITH SHERRY, CREAM AND ALMONDS

350 calories, 4 g carbs

- **1 pork tenderloin/fillet (685–800 g/ 1½–1¾ lb)**
- **¾ teaspoon paprika**
- **½ teaspoon ground black pepper**
- **¼ teaspoon salt**
- **1 tablespoon wholemeal flour**
- **1 tablespoon olive oil**
- **2 large shallots or ¾ onion, sliced**
- **80 ml/3 fl oz dry sherry**
- **80 ml/3 fl oz + 1–2 tablespoons chicken stock**
- **4 tablespoons single cream**
- **30 g/1 oz sliced almonds or 24 whole almonds, toasted**

Preheat the oven to 180°C/350°F/gas 4.

Season the pork with the paprika, pepper and salt. Coat with the flour.

Heat the oil in a heavy roasting pan or a heavy ovenproof frying pan over medium heat. Add the pork and cook until lightly browned on all sides, 4 to 5 minutes. Scatter the shallots or onion in the pan and cook, stirring once or twice, for 1 minute. Pour the sherry and 80 ml/3 fl oz of the stock around the meat.

Roast, turning once or twice, until the juices run clear and a meat thermometer registers 68°C/155°F for medium, 25 to 30 minutes. If the pan juices appear to be less than 3 to 4 tablespoons, add 1 to 2 tablespoons more stock.

Remove to a dish and let rest for 10 minutes. Place the pan of juices over medium-low heat and stir in the cream. Cook until slightly thickened, 1 to 2 minutes, stirring once or twice. Slice the pork on a slight diagonal and sprinkle with the almonds. Serve the cream sauce on the side.

Makes 4 servings

Per serving: energy 350 cals/1456 kJ; protein 39 g; carbohydrate 4 g (of which 1 g sugars); fat 15 g (of which 5 g saturates); fibre 1 g; sodium 307 mg

Diet Exchanges: 0 milk, 0 vegetable, 0 fruit, ½ bread, 4½ meat, 1½ fat

BARBECUED SPARERIBS
315 calories, 5 g carbs

350 ml/12 fl oz tomato juice

80 ml/3 fl oz apple juice

2 tablespoons Worcestershire sauce

1½ tablespoons cider vinegar

2 teaspoons Dijon mustard

¾ teaspoon ground black pepper

½ teaspoon chilli powder

¼ teaspoon salt

¼ teaspoon garlic powder

8 boneless spareribs (100 g/3½ oz each), fat trimmed

Preheat the oven to 180°C/350°F/gas 4.

In a roasting pan or ovenproof dish, combine the tomato juice, apple juice, Worcestershire sauce, vinegar, mustard, pepper, chilli powder, salt and garlic powder. Add the pork and coat completely.

Cover with foil and bake, turning once, until very tender, 1¾ to 2 hours. If the sauce thickens too much, thin it with a little hot water.

Makes 6 servings

Per serving: energy 315 cals/1310 kJ; protein 30 g; carbohydrate 5 g (of which 1 g sugars); fat 18 g (of which 6 g saturates); fibre 0 g; sodium 450 mg

Diet Exchanges: 0 milk, ½ vegetable, 0 fruit, 0 bread, 4½ meat, 1 fat

Time-Saver

These flavourful ribs can be made ahead of time. Store them in a covered container in the refrigerator for up to 4 days or in the freezer for up to 2 months. To reheat, thaw the ribs in the refrigerator overnight, then arrange them in a shallow ovenproof dish. Add a small amount of water and bake at 170°C/325°F/gas 3 until heated through, about 20 minutes.

PORK STEW WITH CABBAGE
379 calories, 16 g carbs

685 g/1½ lb boneless pork, cut into 4 cm/1½ in cubes

½ teaspoon ground black pepper

2 tablespoons olive oil

1 small onion, chopped

1 garlic clove, finely chopped

1½ tablespoons red wine or cider vinegar

1 tablespoon wholemeal flour

400 ml/14 fl oz beef stock

1 tin (400 g/14 oz) chopped tomatoes

1 teaspoon dried thyme

1 teaspoon dried oregano

1 bay leaf

½ head green cabbage (285 g/10 oz), cored and cut into 2–3 cm/1 in pieces

Preheat the oven to 180°C/350°F/gas 4.

Season the pork with the pepper. Heat 1½ tablespoons of the oil in a heavy oven-proof pan over medium-high heat. Working in batches, add the pork and cook until browned on all sides, 5 to 6 minutes, removing the pieces to a plate when they are done.

Reduce the heat to medium and add the remaining ½ tablespoon oil. Stir in the onion and garlic. Cover and cook, stirring occasionally, until the vegetables begin to soften, about 5 minutes. Stir in the wine or vinegar, return the meat to the pan and stir in the flour. Cook, stirring frequently, for 1 minute. Add the stock, tomatoes, thyme, oregano and bay leaf. Bring to a simmer, cover the pan and transfer to the oven. Bake for 1 hour.

Stir in the cabbage and bake for another 20 to 30 minutes or until the pork is tender. Discard the bay leaf before serving.

Makes 4 servings

Per serving: energy 379 cals/1576 kJ; protein 45 g; carbohydrate 16 g (of which 2 g sugars); fat 18 g (of which 5 g saturates); fibre 0 g; sodium 624 mg

Diet Exchanges: 0 milk, 3 vegetable, 0 fruit, 0 bread, 5 meat, 2½ fat

▶Flavour Tips

Sprinkle with ½ teaspoon caraway seeds or 2 teaspoons chopped fresh dill when serving.
Use lamb instead of pork. Use tomato juice or passata instead of chopped tomatoes.

Roast Pork Loin with Orange Juice and White Wine

339 calories, 7 g carbs

- ¾ **teaspoon paprika**
- ¾ **teaspoon garlic powder**
- ½ **teaspoon onion powder**
- ½ **teaspoon dried oregano**
- ½ **teaspoon salt**
- ¼ **teaspoon ground black pepper**
- 1.15–1.25 kg/2½–2¾ **lb loin of pork on the bone, trimmed of visible fat**
- 180 ml/6 fl oz **orange juice**
- 180 ml/6 fl oz **white wine**

Preheat the oven to 230°C/450°F/gas 8.

In a small bowl, combine the paprika, garlic powder, onion powder, oregano, salt and pepper. Pat over the top of the pork and place in a small, heavy roasting pan or heavy ovenproof frying pan.

Roast for 10 minutes. Reduce the heat to 170°C/325°F/gas 3 and pour the orange juice and wine around the pork (not over). Roast until the juices run clear and a meat thermometer registers 70°C/160°F for medium, 1 to 1¼ hours.

Remove from the oven and let rest in the pan for 15 minutes. There should be about 80 ml/3 fl oz juices left in the pan. If there is more, remove the pork to a dish and cook over medium-low heat until the juices are reduced to 80 ml/3 fl oz. Slice the pork and spoon the pan juices over the top.

Makes 4 servings

Per serving: energy 339 cals/1410 kJ; protein 40 g; carbohydrate 7 g (of which 6 g sugars); fat 15 g (of which 5 g saturates); fibre 0 g; sodium 624 mg

Diet Exchanges: 0 milk, 0 vegetable, ½ fruit, 0 bread, 5½ meat, 2½ fat

beef, pork and lamb main dishes

Peppered Venison Fillets

330 calories, 7 g carbs

- **7 g/¼ oz butter, softened**
- **1 tablespoon wholemeal flour**
- **8 venison loin medallions (90 g/3 oz each), 2–3 cm/1 in thick**
- **1½ teaspoons ground black pepper**
- **¼ teaspoon salt**
- **2–3 tablespoons vegetable oil or walnut oil**
- **400 ml/14 fl oz beef or mushroom stock**
- **2 tablespoons plum or redcurrant fruit spread, at room temperature (optional)**

In a small bowl, cream the butter and flour to make a paste.

Season the venison with the pepper and the salt. Heat 1 tablespoon of the oil in a large, heavy frying pan over medium-high heat. Slip in as much venison as will fit without crowding. Cook until browned on the first side, 3 to 4 minutes. Turn, reduce the heat to medium, and cook until a meat thermometer registers 63°C/145°F for medium-rare, 3 to 4 minutes, turning once. If necessary to prevent sticking, add up to ½ tablespoon additional oil during cooking.

Remove to a dish. Cook the remaining venison with the remaining oil and remove to the dish. Cover with foil to keep warm.

Reduce the heat to low and add the stock (it should boil from the heat of the pan). Using a wooden spoon, scrape up the browned bits stuck to the bottom. Whisk in the butter-flour paste to make a smooth sauce and cook until slightly thickened, 30 to 60 seconds (if too thin, cook 1 to 2 minutes more). Whisk in the fruit spread (if using). Serve over the venison.

Makes 4 servings

Per serving: energy 330 cals/1372 kJ; protein 43 g; carbohydrate 7 g (of which 1 g sugars); fat 14 g (of which 3 g saturates); fibre 0 g; sodium 570 mg

Diet Exchanges: 0 milk, 0 vegetable, 0 fruit, ½ bread, 5½ meat, 2 fat

Flavour Tip

Use beef fillet instead of venison.

LAMB WITH GARLIC AND MUSHROOMS
301 calories, 5 g carbs

685 g/1½ lb lean lamb, cubed

½ teaspoon salt

½ teaspoon ground black pepper

2 tablespoons olive oil

570 g/1¼ lb mushrooms, sliced

4 cloves garlic, finely chopped

¼ teaspoon dried chilli flakes

**240 ml/8 fl oz red wine
   (or beef stock)**

400 ml/14 fl oz beef stock

3 tablespoons soured cream

**1 tablespoon chopped fresh parsley
   (optional)**

Season the lamb with the salt and pepper. Heat the oil in a large ovenproof frying pan over medium-high heat. Add the lamb and cook, stirring frequently, until lightly browned, 2 to 3 minutes. Stir in the mushrooms, garlic and chilli flakes. Cook until the mushrooms begin to lose their liquid, 3 to 4 minutes. Add the wine (or stock) and the stock and bring to the boil. Reduce the heat to medium-low and simmer until the lamb is tender, 1 to 1¼ hours.

Remove from the heat and stir in the soured cream until evenly distributed. Sprinkle with the parsley (if using).

Makes 4 servings

Per serving: energy 301 cals/1252 kJ; protein 29 g; carbohydrate 5 g (of which 1 g sugars); fat 18 g (of which 5 g saturates); fibre 1 g; sodium 457 mg

Diet Exchanges: 0 milk, 1 vegetable, 0 fruit, 0 bread, 3½ meat, 3½ fat

▶Flavour Tips

You could easily add more vegetables to this dish. Add 1 sliced celery stick and 2 sliced carrots along with the mushrooms. Garnish with chopped fresh basil instead of the parsley.

LAMB KEBABS WITH MUSHROOMS AND TOMATOES

280 calories, 4 g carbs

2½ tablespoons soy sauce

¾ teaspoon sesame oil

½ teaspoon mustard powder

¼ teaspoon garlic powder

½ teaspoon ground ginger

685 g/1½ lb lean lamb, cubed

12–16 cherry tomatoes (170 g/6 oz)

12–16 small mushrooms (115 g/4 oz)

In a bowl, combine the soy sauce, oil, mustard, garlic powder and ginger. Add the lamb, tomatoes and mushrooms, tossing to coat. Cover and refrigerate for up to 10 hours, tossing once or twice.

Coat a grill rack with cooking spray. Preheat the grill. Thread the lamb, tomatoes and mushrooms onto skewers. Place on the rack and cook, turning to brown all sides, until a meat thermometer registers 70°C/160°F for medium, 10 to 14 minutes.

Makes 4 servings

Per serving: energy 280 cals/1164 kJ; protein 39 g; carbohydrate 4 g (of which 0 g sugars); fat 13 g (of which 4 g saturates); fibre 1 g; sodium 630 mg

Diet Exchanges: 0 milk, ½ vegetable, 0 fruit, 0 bread, 5 meat, 1½ fat

▶Flavour Tips

For colour, add thick courgette slices along with the tomatoes and mushrooms. Top each serving with a tablespoon of low-fat natural yoghurt. Serve with cooked wholewheat couscous or brown rice.

Smart-Carb Insider Tip

LOOK YOUR BEST

As you shrink out of them, donate your clothes to a charity or have them altered. As you reach weight-loss milestones, treat yourself to new wardrobe accessories. It's important to look your best each day. If you look good, you will feel good about yourself.

Lamb Chops with Olives

LAMB CHOPS WITH OLIVES
350 calories, 3 g carbs

8 lamb chops (about 100 g/3½ oz each), 2–3 cm/1 in thick

½ teaspoon salt

1 tablespoon chopped fresh oregano or 1 teaspoon dried

¼ teaspoon ground black pepper

2 tablespoons olive oil

8 pitted black olives, chopped

2 tablespoons balsamic vinegar

⅛ teaspoon dried chilli flakes

Season the lamb with the salt, oregano and pepper. Heat 1 tablespoon of the oil in a large, heavy frying pan over medium-high heat. Add the lamb and cook until browned on both sides and a meat thermometer registers 70°C/160°F for medium-rare, 4 to 6 minutes. (If necessary, cook in 2 batches, removing the first batch to a dish and covering loosely with foil while cooking the second.) Remove to a dish.

Pour off the fat. Add the olives, vinegar, chilli flakes and the remaining 1 tablespoon oil. Bring to a simmer over medium heat, stirring and scraping up the browned bits stuck on the bottom of the pan. Pour over the lamb.

Makes 4 servings

Per serving: energy 350 cals/1456 kJ; protein 33 g; carbohydrate 3 g (of which 0 g sugars); fat 24 g (of which 7 g saturates); fibre 1 g; sodium 200 mg

Diet Exchanges: 0 milk, 0 vegetable, 0 fruit, 0 bread, 4½ meat, 1½ fat

▶Flavour Tips

For evenly browned chops, choose a heavy pan, such as cast iron or heavy-gauge aluminium. You can use 2–3 cm/1 in-thick lamb steak cut from the leg. Or use veal or pork chops.

LAMB BURGERS WITH TOMATOES AND FETA CHEESE

347 calories, 6 g carbs

570 g/1¼ lb minced lamb

2 garlic cloves, finely chopped

1 tablespoon chopped fresh rosemary or 1 teaspoon dried and crumbled

½ teaspoon ground black pepper

¼ teaspoon salt

230 g/8 oz tinned chopped tomatoes

Pinch of salt

75 g/2½ oz crumbled feta cheese, at room temperature

In a large bowl, combine the lamb, garlic, rosemary, pepper and salt. Using a fork, break up the meat and mix in the seasonings. Form the mixture into 4 burgers approximately 10 cm/4 in diameter and 2–3 cm/1 in thick.

Heat a large, heavy frying pan over medium-high heat until drops of water skip over the surface. Add the burgers. Cook until the first side has a brown crust, 4 to 5 minutes. Turn and cook until the second side is lightly browned, 1 to 2 minutes. Pour off fat, reduce the heat to low and pour the tomatoes around the burgers (the tomatoes will boil briefly). Cook until a meat thermometer registers 70°C/160°F for medium, about 10 minutes, turning once more. Season the tomatoes with a pinch of salt and spoon over the burgers. Sprinkle with the cheese.

Makes 4 servings

Per serving: energy 347 cals/1443 kJ; protein 30 g; carbohydrate 6 g (of which 2 g sugars); fat 21 g (of which 12 g saturates); fibre 1 g; sodium 486 mg

Diet Exchanges: 0 milk, 1 vegetable, 0 fruit, 0 bread, 3½ meat, 2½ fat

HIDDEN ROADBLOCK to weight loss

LACK OF ACTIVITY

It's no secret that exercise can help you get more fit. But here's why. Increased physical activity helps you maintain or improve your metabolic rate. That means that the more active you are, the more efficient your body becomes at burning calories. Strength-training or other muscle-building activities are especially helpful. Your body will burn additional calories to sustain its increased muscle mass. Keep in mind that if you are weight training, you may not see much change in your weight. That's because muscle weighs more than fat does. However, you should notice a significant difference in your body definition and size. If exercise isn't currently in your life, try to become a little more active each week.

fish & shellfish main dishes

BAKED COD WITH LEMON AND OLIVE OIL 232

BREADED BAKED COD WITH TARTAR SAUCE 234

BAKED SEA BASS WITH SOY SAUCE AND SESAME OIL 235

BETTY'S FISH WITH MUSHROOMS AND SPRING ONIONS 237

MACKEREL BAKED WITH PEPPERS AND CAPERS 238

POACHED HALIBUT WITH HERBED OLIVE OIL 239

BAKED HALIBUT WRAPPED IN LETTUCE LEAVES 241

GRILLED MACKEREL WITH LEMON-MINT BUTTER .242

GRILLED SOLE WITH SPRING ONION-ANCHOVY VINAIGRETTE 243

GRILLED SEA BASS WITH CHILLI-LIME BUTTER 244

SAUTÉED TROUT WITH ALMOND BUTTER SAUCE 245

PAN-FRIED TROUT IN CORNMEAL WITH BACON 246

SHARK BRAISED IN RED WINE WITH TOMATO AND ANCHOVY 247

SAUTÉED TUNA STEAKS WITH GARLIC SAUCE 248

BAKED SALMON WITH OREGANO 250

SALMON SALAD WITH FRESH GINGER 251

GRILLED SALMON WITH MINT-CORIANDER YOGHURT 253

SALMON AND COUSCOUS SALAD WITH VEGETABLES 254

PRAWN SALAD WITH DILL AND ORANGES 255

GRILLED PRAWNS WITH SPICY CABBAGE SALAD 256

SPICY SAUTÉED PRAWNS WITH GARLIC 257

CREOLE-STYLE STEAMED CLAMS 258

SCALLOPS IN TARRAGON CREAM 259

BAKED SCALLOPS WITH HERBS AND WHITE WINE 260

STEAMED MUSSELS WITH ROASTED PEPPERS AND CAPERS 262

BAKED COD WITH LEMON AND OLIVE OIL
154 calories, 0 g carbs

**4 cod fillets (170 g/6 oz each),
   2–3 cm/1 in thick**

1½ tablespoons lemon juice

1 tablespoon olive oil

**2 garlic cloves, finely chopped,
   or ¼ teaspoon garlic powder**

**2 teaspoons chopped fresh thyme or
   ½ teaspoon dried**

Pinch of salt

⅛ teaspoon ground black pepper

**¼ teaspoon sweet Hungarian paprika
   (optional)**

Preheat the oven to 200°C/400°F/gas 6.

   Arrange the fillets in an ovenproof dish.
Drizzle with the lemon juice and oil and
sprinkle with the garlic, thyme, salt and
pepper. Sprinkle with the paprika (if using),
and lightly rub it in. Bake until the flesh is
completely opaque but still juicy, 15 to 20
minutes. Serve with the pan juices spooned
over the top.

Makes 4 servings

Per serving: energy 154 cals/650 kJ; protein 30 g;
carbohydrate 0 g (of which 0 g sugars); fat 4 g (of
which 1 g saturates); fibre 0 g; sodium 228 mg

Diet Exchanges: 0 milk, 0 vegetable, 0 fruit,
0 bread, 4½ meat, ½ fat

▶Flavour Tips

*You can use haddock, hake, red snapper, sole or any
other white fish instead of cod. Serve on a bed of
wholewheat couscous or pasta to soak up the juices.
Bake with 2 tablespoons chopped roasted red peppers.
Serve sprinkled with 1 tablespoon chopped fresh basil.*

Baked Cod with Lemon and Olive Oil

BREADED BAKED COD WITH TARTAR SAUCE

321 calories, 7 g carbs

TARTAR SAUCE

- **115 g/4 oz reduced-fat mayonnaise**
- **1½ tablespoons lemon juice**
- **1 tablespoon finely chopped dill pickles (gherkins)**
- **2 teaspoons mustard**
- **2 teaspoons capers, drained and chopped**
- **2 teaspoons chopped fresh parsley (optional)**

FISH

- **2 slices wholemeal bread, torn**
- **2 eggs**
- **1 tablespoon water**
- **570 g/1¼ lb cod fillet, cut into 4 cm/1½ in pieces**
- **½ teaspoon salt**
- **¼ teaspoon ground black pepper**

To make the tartar sauce: In a small bowl, combine the mayonnaise, lemon juice, pickles, mustard, capers and parsley (if using). Cover and refrigerate.

To cook the fish: Preheat the oven to 200°C/400°F/gas 6. Coat a baking tray with cooking spray.

Place the bread in a food processor and process into fine crumbs. Place in a shallow bowl. In another bowl, beat the eggs with the water. Season the fish with the salt and pepper. Dip into the eggs, then into the bread crumbs. Place on the prepared baking tray. Generously coat the breaded fish with cooking spray. Bake until opaque inside, 10 minutes.

Serve with the tartar sauce.

Makes 4 servings

Per serving: energy 321 cals/1340 kJ; protein 30 g; carbohydrate 7 g (of which 1 g sugars); fat 19 g (of which 3 g saturates); fibre 1 g; sodium 680 mg

Diet Exchanges: 0 milk, 0 vegetable, 0 fruit, 1 bread, 3½ meat, ½ fat

Time-Savers

Cook a few extra pieces of fish, as the leftovers make quick hot or cold meals. Store extra portions in a covered container in the refrigerator for up to 3 days. To reheat, arrange on a baking tray and bake at 200°C/400°F/gas 6 until heated through, 3 to 5 minutes. Or to serve cold, make a sandwich by wrapping the fried fish in lettuce leaves or wholewheat pittas spread with tartar sauce. The tartar sauce can be stored in a covered container in the refrigerator for up to a week.

BAKED SEA BASS WITH SOY SAUCE AND SESAME OIL
176 calories, 1 g carbs

2 tablespoons soy sauce

1 tablespoon rice vinegar

2 teaspoons sesame oil

4 sea bass fillets (170 g/6 oz each), 2–3 cm/1 in thick

⅛ teaspoon ground black pepper

2 spring onions, thinly sliced diagonally

Preheat the oven to 200°C/400°F/gas 6.

In a small bowl, combine the soy sauce, vinegar and oil. Arrange the fish in an ovenproof dish that's large enough to hold the fish comfortably in a single layer. Pour the soy sauce mixture over the fish and turn to coat. Sprinkle with the pepper. Cover and bake until opaque throughout, 18 to 20 minutes.

Serve topped with the pan juices and spring onions.

Makes 4 servings

Per serving: energy 176 cals/743 kJ; protein 31 g; carbohydrate 1 g (of which 0 g sugars); fat 6 g (of which 1 g saturates); fibre 0 g; sodium 572 mg

Diet Exchanges: 0 milk, 0 vegetable, 0 fruit, 0 bread, 4½ meat, 1 fat

▶Flavour Tips

Serve the fish on a bed of brown rice to capture the fragrant juices. Substitute plaice for the sea bass. Plaice is thinner and will cook in 12 to 15 minutes.

Smart-Carb Insider Tip
LEAN ON A FRIEND

Find a friend, relative or colleague with whom you can share your triumphs and setbacks. Better still, find someone else ready to lose some pounds along with you and support each other. It's fun to share recipes, food tips and other slimming ideas.

fish and shellfish main dishes

I D⭐id It!

Betty Carlucci

Betty reached the menopause and started to put on pounds. She adopted a new eating plan, made a commitment to exercise and woke up to a renewed zest for life.

before

'My weight was never much of a problem for me until I reached the menopause. During the 10 or so years of perimenopause, I thought that the 4 to 7-kg/9 to 15-pound fluctuations I experienced were due to fluid retention. But I kept having strong cravings for sugar. It seemed that if I ate anything with even a little sugar in it, I got more and more hungry. And this really put on the pounds . . . 40 of them! My clothes got tighter and I felt like I was losing control of my food choices. This made it a lot harder to cope with the hormonal changes I was going through.

'I tried all kinds of diets. But I knew that to keep my weight off for good, I would have to make long-term changes in my

Weight lost: 19 kg/3 st
Time kept off: 3 years
Weight-loss strategies: avoided refined carbohydrates, ate more vegetables, began exercising again
Weight-maintenance strategies: maintains lower carbohydrate intake, does weight-bearing exercise 3 to 5 times a week

eating habits. After looking closely at my diet, I realised how high my total carbohydrate intake had been. I started avoiding all sweets. I also replaced white flour,

fish and shellfish main dishes

refined cereals and regular pasta with whole grain versions. I concentrated on eating lots of vegetables; getting protein from lean sources like soya foods, eggs, beans and fish; and enjoying fresh fruit now and then. I cut back on dairy products, too, because they seemed to inhibit my weight loss. I supplemented my diet with a multivitamin high in calcium and magnesium.

'My other commitment was to get to the gym for a 1-hour workout three times a week. My exercise was as important to me as my obligation to go to work. After a while, I discovered that the exercise actually gave me *more* energy; and it is impossible to describe how much better I felt mentally.

'The best thing about my lifestyle now is that I feel good in my clothes again, I have the stamina to play with my young grandchildren and I enjoy my food more. I'm truly enjoying the commitment and discipline of taking care of myself. I thank God for my good health at the age of 60 and ask for his blessings and guidance.'

BETTY'S FISH WITH MUSHROOMS AND SPRING ONIONS
232 calories, 1 g carbs

- **45 g/1½ oz butter or 3 tablespoons olive oil**
- **455 g/1 lb sliced mushrooms**
- **8 spring onions, chopped**
- **80 ml/3 fl oz white wine or white wine vinegar**
- **685 g/1½ lb white fish fillets (plaice or cod)**
- **2 tablespoons chopped fresh tarragon or 1 teaspoon dried**
- **¼ teaspoon salt**
- **¼ teaspoon paprika**

Preheat the oven to 180°C/350°F/gas 4. Coat an ovenproof dish with cooking spray.

Warm the butter or oil in a large frying pan over medium heat. Add the mushrooms and spring onions and cook until the mushrooms begin to release their liquid, about 5 minutes. Add the wine or vinegar and cook until the mushrooms are tender, about 5 minutes more.

Place the fish in the prepared ovenproof dish. Stir the tarragon into the mushrooms and spread the mixture over the fish. Sprinkle with the salt and paprika. Bake until the fish just flakes easily when tested with a fork, 15 to 20 minutes.

Makes 4 servings

Per serving: energy 232 cals/975 kJ; protein 32 g; carbohydrate 1 g (of which 1 g sugars); fat 11 g (of which 6 g saturates); fibre 2 g; sodium 369 mg

Diet Exchanges: 0 milk, 1 vegetable, 0 fruit, 0 bread, 4 meat, 2 fat

fish and shellfish main dishes

MACKEREL BAKED WITH PEPPERS AND CAPERS
289 calories, 2 g carbs

2 tablespoons olive oil

2 large red and/or green peppers, thinly sliced

½ small jalapeño chilli, seeded and finely chopped (optional); wear plastic gloves when handling

¼ teaspoon salt

¼ teaspoon ground black pepper

2 tablespoons dry white wine or white wine vinegar

2 teaspoons drained capers

1½ teaspoons chopped fresh thyme or ½ teaspoon dried

4 mackerel fillets (170 g/6 oz each), about 1 cm/½ in thick

Preheat the oven to 200°C/400°F/gas 6.

Heat the oil in a frying pan over medium heat. Add the peppers, jalapeño chilli (if using), ⅛ teaspoon of the salt and ⅛ teaspoon of the black pepper. Cook, stirring occasionally, until the peppers start to soften, 5 to 6 minutes. Stir in the wine or vinegar, capers and thyme, and remove from the heat.

Place the fillets in an ovenproof dish that's large enough to hold the fish comfortably in a single layer and season with the remaining salt and black pepper. Spoon the pepper mixture around and over the fillets, scraping the juices from the frying pan with a rubber spatula. Cover the dish and bake until the fish is opaque throughout, 12 to 15 minutes.

Serve topped with the peppers and pan juices.

Makes 4 servings

Per serving: energy 289 cals/1204 kJ; protein 26 g; carbohydrate 2 g (of which 2 g sugars); fat 19 g (of which 4 g saturates); fibre 1 g; sodium 258 mg

Diet Exchanges: 0 milk, 1 vegetable, 0 fruit, 0 bread, 5 meat, 2 fat

▶Flavour Tips

Substitute other fish fillets, such as sea bass, red snapper, trout or salmon for the mackerel. Use red wine instead of white wine.

POACHED HALIBUT WITH HERBED OLIVE OIL

261 calories, 0 g carbs

I lemon, halved

700 ml/1¼ pints water

600 ml/1 pint semi-skimmed milk

I bay leaf

¼ teaspoon

4 halibut steaks or fillets (230 g/8 oz each), about 2–3 cm/1 in thick

2 tablespoons extra-virgin olive oil

2 tablespoons chopped fresh herbs (such as thyme and tarragon) or 2 teaspoons dried

⅛ teaspoon ground black pepper

Cut 3 thin slices from one lemon half. In a deep frying pan that is large enough to hold the fish in a single layer, combine the water, milk, lemon slices, bay leaf and ¼ teaspoon salt. Bring to a simmer over medium-low heat and cook gently for 5 minutes to blend the flavours. Carefully slide in the fish. (The fish should be just covered by liquid; if not, add just enough hot tap water to cover.) Cook at a gentle simmer until the fish is opaque throughout, 15 to 18 minutes.

Meanwhile, in a small bowl, combine the oil, herbs and a pinch of salt.

Using a slotted spoon, carefully remove the fish to plates. Discard the bay leaf. Sprinkle the fish with the pepper. Drizzle with the herbed olive oil. Cut 4 wedges of lemon and serve with the fish.

Makes 4 servings

Per serving: energy 261 cals/1100 kJ; protein 41 g; carbohydrate 0 g (of which 0 g sugars); fat 11 g (of which 2 g saturates); fibre 0 g; sodium 193 mg

Diet Exchanges: 0 milk, 0 vegetable, 0 fruit, 0 bread, 7 meat, 1½ fat

▶Flavour Tips

Use a fruity extra-virgin olive oil for the best flavour. You can substitute cod or haddock for the halibut steaks. Or substitute salmon steaks or fillets, omitting the milk.

fish and shellfish main dishes

Baked Halibut Wrapped in Lettuce Leaves

BAKED HALIBUT WRAPPED IN LETTUCE LEAVES
228 calories, 2 g carbs

- **8 large soft lettuce leaves**
- **4 skinless halibut fillets (170 g/6 oz each), about 2 cm/¾ in thick**
- **1½ teaspoons chopped fresh thyme or ¾ teaspoon dried**
- **½ teaspoon salt**
- **¼ teaspoon ground black pepper**
- **60 ml/2 fl oz single cream**
- **3 tablespoons dry white wine**
- **15 g/½ oz butter**
- **1 cucumber (170 g/6 oz), peeled, seeded and chopped**

Preheat the oven to 200°C/400°F/gas 6. Coat a large, shallow ovenproof dish (large enough to hold the fillets in one layer) with cooking spray.

Lay 4 lettuce leaves on the bottom of the dish. Season the halibut with the thyme, ¼ teaspoon of the salt and the pepper. Place 1 fillet on each lettuce leaf and top with the remaining 4 leaves. Drizzle with the cream and wine. Dot with the butter.

Bake until the fish is opaque, 15 to 20 minutes. Remove to plates, reserving the pan juices. Pour the juices into a small saucepan. Stir in the cucumber and cook over low heat until slightly thickened and reduced to about 4 tablespoons, about 2 minutes. Season with the remaining ¼ teaspoon salt and spoon over the fish.

Makes 4 servings

Per serving: energy 228 cals/958 kJ; protein 31 g; carbohydrate 2 g (of which 2 g sugars); fat 10 g (of which 4 g saturates); fibre 1 g; sodium 423 mg

Diet Exchanges: 0 milk, ½ vegetable, 0 fruit, 0 bread, 5 meat, 1 fat

Time-Savers

To speed preparation time, omit the lettuce. For quick-fixing lunches or suppers, store leftover fillets in a covered container in the refrigerator for up to 2 days. To reheat, arrange the fillets in an ovenproof dish, cover and bake at 180°C/350°F/gas 4 until heated through, 5 to 8 minutes.

GRILLED MACKEREL WITH LEMON-MINT BUTTER

435 calories, 0 g carbs

30 g/1 oz butter, softened

**1 tablespoon chopped fresh mint or
 1 teaspoon dried**

1½ teaspoons lemon juice

½ teaspoon ground black pepper

**4 skinless mackerel fillets (170 g/6 oz
 each), about 1 cm/½ in thick**

¼ teaspoon salt

Place the grill rack about 8 cm/3 in from the heat source and preheat the grill.

In a small bowl, combine the butter, mint, lemon juice and ¼ teaspoon of the pepper.

Season the fish with the salt and the remaining ¼ teaspoon pepper. Lightly coat a grill pan with cooking spray and arrange the fish on it. Grill, without turning, until the top is lightly browned and the flesh is completely opaque, 5 to 6 minutes. Spread the lemon-mint butter evenly over the fish and serve.

Makes 4 servings

Per serving: energy 435 cals/1802 kJ; protein 32 g; carbohydrate 0 g (of which 0 g sugars); fat 34 g (of which 10 g saturates); fibre 0 g; sodium 423 mg

Diet Exchanges: 0 milk, 0 vegetable, 0 fruit, 0 bread, 5 meat, 2½ fat

Time-Savers

Make the lemon butter ahead. It keeps well in a covered container in the refrigerator for up to 1 week or in the freezer for up to 2 months. Thaw in the refrigerator before using.

To store extra portions of the fish, refrigerate in a covered container for up to 2 days. To reheat, arrange the fish in an ovenproof dish, cover and bake at 190°C/375°F/gas 5 until heated through, 5 to 6 minutes.

GRILLED SOLE WITH SPRING ONION-ANCHOVY VINAIGRETTE

235 calories, 1 g carbs

- **5 anchovy fillets, drained, patted dry and finely chopped**
- **2 spring onions, finely chopped**
- **2 teaspoons lemon juice**
- **2 teaspoons red wine vinegar**
- **1 teaspoon Dijon mustard**
- **3 tablespoons extra-virgin olive oil**
- **¼ teaspoon ground black pepper**
- **4 sole or plaice fillets (170 g/6 oz each)**
- **¼ teaspoon salt**

In a small bowl, combine the anchovies, spring onions, lemon juice, vinegar, mustard, 2 tablespoons of the oil and ⅛ teaspoon of the pepper.

Brush the remaining 1 tablespoon oil over the fish and season with the salt and the remaining ⅛ teaspoon pepper.

Generously coat a grill rack with cooking spray. Preheat the grill. Place the fish, round side down, on the rack and cook until golden, 5 to 6 minutes. Turn and cook until the flesh is completely opaque but still juicy, 2 to 4 minutes more. Serve topped with the spring onion-anchovy vinaigrette.

Makes 4 servings

Per serving: energy 235 cals/987 kJ; protein 32 g; carbohydrate 1 g (of which 0 g sugars); fat 12 g (of which 2 g saturates); fibre 0 g; sodium 366 mg

Diet Exchanges: 0 milk, 0 vegetable, 0 fruit, 0 bread, 4 meat, 3 fat

▶Flavour Tips

Stir 1 small finely chopped garlic clove (or ¼ teaspoon garlic powder) into the anchovy vinaigrette.

GRILLED SEA BASS WITH CHILLI-LIME BUTTER
239 calories, 0 g carbs

45 g/1½ oz butter, softened

Grated zest of 1 lime

1 teaspoon chilli powder

¼ teaspoon salt

4 sea bass fillets (170 g/6 oz each), about 2 cm/¾ in thick

2 teaspoons chopped fresh coriander (optional)

Place the butter, lime zest, chilli powder and salt in a small microwaveable bowl. Microwave on medium power until the butter is melted, 1 minute.

Coat a grill rack with cooking spray. Preheat the grill. Brush the fish on both sides with the chilli-lime butter. Sprinkle with the coriander (if using).

Place on the rack, round side down, and grill until golden, 5 to 6 minutes. Turn and brush again with the butter. Cook until the flesh is completely opaque but still juicy, 3 to 4 minutes more. Drizzle any remaining butter evenly over the fish.

Makes 4 servings

Per serving: energy 239 cals/1004 kJ; protein 30 g; carbohydrate 0 g (of which 0 g sugars); fat 13 g (of which 7 g saturates); fibre 0 g; sodium 373 mg

Diet Exchanges: 0 milk, 0 vegetable, 0 fruit, 0 bread, 4½ meat, 1½ fat

HIDDEN ROADBLOCK to weight loss
GENETICS

When all else fails, perhaps you can blame it on your genes. There is a well-known familial relationship to weight management as well as to body fat distribution. If most of your ancestors had the same body build as you do, it is unlikely that you will be able to change your body shape by changing the foods you eat. That doesn't mean, however, that you should throw in the towel. A study at the University of Utah School of Medicine found that physical activity and environmental factors in the home may be closely related to weight management despite similar genes among siblings. Researchers studied 145 sets of siblings raised under the same roof. In each set of siblings, daily caloric intake differed by more than 350 calories and there was a difference in energy expenditure. It's no surprise that the obese sibling ate more and was less active. The bottom line is that by eating less and exercising more, you can overcome your genetics and lose weight.

SAUTÉED TROUT WITH ALMOND BUTTER SAUCE
345 calories, 8 g carbs

5 tablespoons semi-skimmed milk or unsweetened soya milk

2 tablespoons lemon juice

15 g/1 oz almond butter

½ teaspoon salt

¼ teaspoon ground black pepper

1 large egg

45 g/1½ oz wholemeal flour

4 trout fillets (170 g/6 oz each), about 1 cm/½ in thick

2 tablespoons vegetable oil

4 lemon wedges (optional)

In a bowl, combine 3 tablespoons of the milk, the lemon juice, the almond butter, ¼ teaspoon of the salt and ⅛ teaspoon of the pepper.

Preheat the oven to 130°C/250°F/gas ½. In a shallow bowl, lightly beat the egg and the remaining 2 tablespoons milk. In another shallow bowl, combine the flour, the remaining ¼ teaspoon salt and the remaining ⅛ teaspoon pepper. Dip the fish into the egg mixture, then into the flour, lightly pressing so the flour sticks.

In a large non-stick frying pan, heat 1 tablespoon of the oil over medium heat. Add the fish in two batches, skin side up, and cook until the first side is browned, 2 to 3 minutes. Turn, and cook the second side until the flesh is opaque, 3 to 4 minutes more. Remove to a baking tray and keep warm in the oven. Before adding the next batch of fish, add the remaining 1 tablespoon oil.

Serve with the almond butter mixture and lemon wedges for squeezing (if using).

Makes 4 servings

Per serving: energy 345 cals/1443 kJ; protein 40 g; carbohydrate 8 g (of which 1 g sugars); fat 17 g (of which 4 g saturates); fibre 1 g; sodium 189 mg

Diet Exchanges: 0 milk, 0 vegetable, 0 fruit, ½ bread, 5 meat, 3½ fat

▶Flavour Tips
A variety of nut butters are available in health food shops and supermarkets. Use another nut butter such as macadamia or cashew. You can also replace all or half of the wholemeal flour with soya flour.

Pan-Fried Trout in Cornmeal with Bacon
308 calories, 25 g carbs

2 rashers streaky bacon

1 egg

1 tablespoon water

75 g/2½ oz cornmeal

¼ teaspoon salt

¼ teaspoon ground black pepper

4 skinless trout fillets (145 g/5 oz each), about 1 cm/½ in thick

45 g/1½ oz soya flour

2 tablespoons vegetable oil

4 lemon wedges

Cook the bacon in a large, heavy frying pan over low heat until crisp, 10 to 14 minutes, turning once or twice. Drain on a kitchen paper-lined plate, reserving 1 tablespoon of the fat in the pan.

In a small bowl, lightly beat the egg and water. In another bowl, combine the cornmeal, salt and pepper. Coat the fish with the flour, then dip into the egg mixture and coat with the cornmeal, lightly pressing to help the coating stick. Arrange in a single layer on a large plate and refrigerate for at least 15 minutes or up to 60 minutes to help the coating adhere.

Heat the oil in the same frying pan with the bacon fat over medium heat. Add the fish, round side down, without crowding. Cook until golden brown and crisp on the outside, 3 to 4 minutes. Turn and cook until browned on the outside and opaque inside, 2 to 4 minutes more. (If necessary cook in two batches, keeping the first batch warm in a 130°C/250°F/gas ½ oven on a baking tray lined with kitchen paper.)

Crumble the bacon over the top and serve with the lemon wedges for squeezing.

Makes 4 servings

Per serving: energy 308 cals/1296 kJ; protein 25 g; carbohydrate 25 g (of which 0 g sugars); fat 13 g (of which 3 g saturates); fibre 1 g; sodium 452 mg

Diet Exchanges: 0 milk, 0 vegetable, 0 fruit, 1 bread, 4 meat, 3 fat

▶Flavour Tip
For an easy lunch dish, tuck a fillet (hot or cold) between crisp leaves of romaine lettuce spread with tartar sauce.

SHARK BRAISED IN RED WINE WITH TOMATO AND ANCHOVY

279 calories, 8 g carbs

2 tablespoons olive oil

1 small red onion, thinly sliced

115 g/4 oz tinned chopped tomatoes

1–2 anchovy fillets, finely chopped

¼ teaspoon dried oregano

120 ml/4 fl oz dry red wine

4 shark steaks (170 g/6 oz each), about 2 cm/¾ in thick

¼ teaspoon salt

¼ teaspoon ground black pepper

2 tablespoons wholemeal flour

Preheat the oven to 180°C/350°F/gas 4.

In a large ovenproof pan (large enough to hold the fish in one layer), heat 1 table-spoon of the oil over medium heat. Add the onion and cook, stirring occasionally, until lightly browned, 2 to 3 minutes. Add the tomatoes, the anchovies and the oregano. Cook for 30 seconds, stirring. Pour in the wine, cook for 30 seconds and remove to a bowl.

Season the shark steaks with the salt and pepper. Coat with the flour and pat off the excess.

Heat the remaining 1 tablespoon olive oil in the same pan over medium-high heat. Add the fish and cook until browned on the first side, 3 to 4 minutes. Turn and cook until browned on the second side, 3 to 4 minutes. Remove from the heat and pour the tomato-wine mixture over and around the fish. (The liquid will spatter and boil.) Cover and bake until the fish is opaque throughout, 10 to 12 minutes.

Makes 4 servings

Per serving: energy 279 cals/1180 kJ; protein 42 g; carbohydrate 8 g (of which 2 g sugars); fat 7 g (of which 1 g saturates); fibre 1 g; sodium 705 mg

Diet Exchanges: 0 milk, ½ vegetable, 0 fruit, 0 bread, 5 meat, 3 fat

▶Flavour Tips

Substitute tuna, salmon or swordfish for the shark. Replace the chopped tomatoes with passata.

fish and shellfish main dishes

SAUTÉED TUNA STEAKS WITH GARLIC SAUCE
202 calories, 0 g carbs

2 large garlic cloves, chopped

1½ tablespoons olive oil

1 tablespoon balsamic vinegar

¼ teaspoon salt

⅛ teaspoon ground black pepper

4 tuna steaks (170 g/6 oz each), about 2–3 cm/1 in thick

1½ teaspoons chopped fresh parsley or basil

In a large, heavy non-stick frying pan, cook the garlic in 1 tablespoon of the oil over very low heat, until the garlic's aroma is apparent, 30 to 60 seconds, stirring. Immediately add the vinegar, half of the salt and half of the pepper. Remove to a bowl and cover with foil to keep warm.

Season the fish with the remaining salt and pepper. Heat the remaining ½ tablespoon oil in the same pan over medium heat. Add the fish and cook until browned on the first side, 4 to 5 minutes. Turn and cook until the fish is just opaque throughout, 3 to 4 minutes. Serve topped with the garlic sauce and parsley or basil.

Makes 4 servings

Per serving: energy 202 cals/856 kJ; protein 40 g; carbohydrate 0 g (of which 0 g sugars); fat 5 g (of which 1 g saturates); fibre 0 g; sodium 690 mg

Diet Exchanges: 0 milk, 0 vegetable, 0 fruit, 0 bread, 5½ meat, 2 fat

▶Flavour Tips

Substitute swordfish, salmon or shark for the tuna. If there are leftovers, store them in a covered container in the refrigerator for up to 3 days. For a quick and delicious tuna salad, break the fish into large flakes and toss with a yoghurt or mayonnaise dressing.

Sautéed Tuna Steaks with Garlic Sauce

BAKED SALMON WITH OREGANO
351 calories, 0 g carbs

- **2 teaspoons olive oil**
- **4 skinless salmon fillets (170 g/6 oz each), 2–3 cm/1 in thick**
- **Juice of half a lemon**
- **1 teaspoon dried oregano**
- **½ teaspoon salt**
- **¼ teaspoon ground black pepper**
- **15 g/½ oz butter, cut into small pieces**
- **1 teaspoon chopped fresh parsley (optional)**

Preheat the oven to 190°C/375°F/gas 5.

Use the oil to grease a shallow ovenproof dish that is large enough to hold the fillets in a single layer. Arrange the fish in the dish and turn to coat with the oil. Sprinkle with the lemon juice, oregano, salt and pepper. Dot with the butter and cover with foil.

Bake until the flesh is cooked through but still very juicy, 20 to 24 minutes. Serve topped with the pan juices and parsley (if using).

Makes 4 servings

Per serving: energy 351 cals/1458 kJ; protein 31 g; carbohydrate 0 g (of which 0 g sugars); fat 25 g (of which 6 g saturates); fibre 0 g; sodium 340 mg

Diet Exchanges: 0 milk, 0 vegetable, 0 fruit, 0 bread, 4 meat, 1 fat

Time-Savers

Make this dish ahead or make extra portions for fast meals. Store in a covered container in the refrigerator for up to 3 days. To reheat, arrange the fillets in an ovenproof dish, cover and bake at 180°C/350°F/gas 4 until heated through, 5 to 8 minutes. Or serve the fillets cold or at room temperature mixed with vinegar and oil for a fish salad.

SALMON SALAD WITH FRESH GINGER
336 calories, 1 g carbs

- **I skinless salmon fillet (685 g/1½ lb), 2–3 cm/1 in thick**
- **2 teaspoons groundnut (peanut) oil or vegetable oil**
- **⅛ teaspoon salt**
- **⅛ teaspoon ground black pepper**
- **2 large spring onions, very thinly sliced**
- **I tablespoon grated fresh ginger**
- **2 tablespoons soy sauce**
- **2 teaspoons rice vinegar or cider vinegar**
- **4 large salad or red leaf lettuce leaves (optional)**
- **90 g/3 oz fresh beansprouts**

Preheat the oven to 190°C/375°F/gas 5.

Rub the salmon with 1 teaspoon of the oil and season with the salt and pepper. Place in a shallow ovenproof dish, cover and bake just until cooked through but still very juicy, 20 to 25 minutes. Let cool 5 to 10 minutes.

Meanwhile, in a large bowl, combine the spring onions, ginger, soy sauce, vinegar and remaining 1 teaspoon oil. Flake the salmon into large pieces and add to the bowl. Gently toss to coat.

Arrange the lettuce leaves (if using) on plates and top with the salmon and beansprouts. Serve immediately.

Makes 4 servings

Per serving: energy 336 cals/1396 kJ; protein 32 g; carbohydrate 1 g (of which 1 g sugars); fat 22 g (of which 4 g saturates); fibre 1 g; sodium 597 mg

Diet Exchanges: 0 milk, ½ vegetable, 0 fruit, 0 bread, 4½ meat, ½ fat

Time-Saver

Make the fish for this main course salad ahead if you can. Keep the fish (undressed) in a covered container in the refrigerator for up to 2 days. Don't flake and toss with the sauce until just before serving.

Grilled Salmon with Mint-Coriander Yoghurt

GRILLED SALMON WITH MINT-CORIANDER YOGHURT

418 calories, 3 g carbs

90 g/3 oz low-fat natural yoghurt

2 tablespoons soured cream

1 tablespoon chopped fresh coriander

2 teaspoons chopped fresh mint

¼ teaspoon salt

¼ teaspoon ground black pepper

Pinch of chilli powder (optional)

4 salmon steaks or fillets (200 g/7 oz each), 2–3 cm/1 in thick

2 teaspoons vegetable oil

In a small bowl, combine the yoghurt, soured cream, coriander, mint, salt, ⅛ teaspoon of the black pepper and the chilli powder (if using).

Coat a grill rack with cooking spray. Preheat the grill. Brush the fish with the oil and season with the remaining ⅛ teaspoon black pepper.

Place the salmon on the rack and cook until golden, 5 to 6 minutes. Turn and cook until the flesh is completely opaque but still juicy, 3 to 4 minutes more. Serve topped with the mint-coriander yoghurt.

Makes 4 servings

Per serving: energy 418 cals/1737 kJ; protein 38 g; carbohydrate 3 g (of which 3 g sugars); fat 28 g (of which 6 g saturates); fibre 0 g; sodium 375 mg

Diet Exchanges: 0 milk, 0 vegetable, 0 fruit, 0 bread, 5½ meat, ½ fat

▶Flavour Tips

Substitute red snapper, sea bass or plaice for the salmon. Omit the soured cream and add 2 tablespoons more yoghurt. Add ¼ of a peeled, seeded and finely chopped small cucumber to the sauce.

SALMON AND COUSCOUS SALAD WITH VEGETABLES
443 calories, 32 g carbs

1 skinless salmon fillet (455 g/1 lb), 2–3 cm/1 in thick

3 tablespoons + 1 teaspoon olive oil

¾ teaspoon salt

¼ teaspoon ground black pepper

285 g/10 oz fresh or frozen thin asparagus, thawed if frozen and cut into 1 cm/½ in lengths

1 courgette (170 g/6 oz), halved lengthwise and thinly sliced

1 garlic clove, finely chopped

180 ml/6 fl oz water

145 g/5 oz wholewheat couscous

2–3 teaspoons red wine vinegar or lemon juice

Preheat the oven to 190°C/375°F/gas 5. Rub the salmon with 1 teaspoon of the olive oil and season with ¼ teaspoon of the salt and ⅛ teaspoon of the pepper. Place in a shallow ovenproof dish and bake just until the salmon is cooked through but still juicy, 20 to 25 minutes. Let cool until easy to handle, 5 to 10 minutes. Break into large flakes.

Heat the remaining 3 tablespoons olive oil in a large saucepan over medium heat. Add the asparagus, courgette and garlic. Cook, stirring occasionally, until crisp-tender, 3 to 5 minutes. Add the water, the remaining ½ teaspoon salt and the remaining ⅛ teaspoon pepper. Simmer for 2 to 3 minutes over medium heat. Bring to the boil and stir in the couscous. Cover, remove from the heat and let sit for 5 minutes.

Fluff the couscous with a fork, remove to a large bowl and season with the vinegar or lemon juice. Cool slightly and fold in the salmon. Serve warm, at room temperature or chilled.

Makes 4 servings

Per serving: energy 443 cals/1849 kJ; protein 26 g; carbohydrate 32 g (of which 3 g sugars); fat 24 g (of which 4 g saturates); fibre 2 g; sodium 502 mg

Diet Exchanges: 0 milk, 1 vegetable, 0 fruit, 1½ bread, 3 meat, 2 fat

Time-Saver

Replace the fresh salmon with 340 g/12 oz of tinned salmon. You can also make this salad up to 3 days ahead and store it in a covered container in the refrigerator.

PRAWN SALAD WITH DILL AND ORANGES
291 calories, 8 g carbs

- **685 g/1½ lb medium prawns, peeled and deveined**
- **60 g/2 oz reduced-fat mayonnaise**
- **1 celery stick, finely chopped**
- **2 tablespoons low-fat natural yoghurt**
- **1 tablespoon finely chopped red onion**
- **1 tablespoon chopped fresh dill or ½ teaspoon dried**
- **1 teaspoon lemon juice**
- **¼ teaspoon salt**
- **¼ teaspoon ground black pepper**
- **2 oranges, peeled and segmented**

Bring a large saucepan of water to the boil over high heat. Add the prawns, reduce the heat to medium and cook until curled and opaque, 2 to 3 minutes. Drain and cool under cold running water. Cut into 1 cm/ ½ in pieces.

In a large bowl, combine the mayonnaise, celery, yoghurt, onion, dill, lemon juice, salt and pepper. Add the prawns and toss to coat well. Spoon onto plates and garnish with the oranges. Or chill for 1 to 2 hours before garnishing and serving.

Makes 4 servings

Per serving: energy 291 cals/1221 kJ; protein 40 g; carbohydrate 8 g (of which 8 g sugars); fat 11 g (of which 2 g saturates); fibre 2 g; sodium 400 mg

Diet Exchanges: 0 milk, 0 vegetable, 1 fruit, 0 bread, 2½ meat, 1 fat

▶Flavour Tips

Sprinkle 1 tablespoon drained capers over the salad when serving. Serve on a bed of fresh spinach leaves. Substitute 1 large grapefruit, peeled and segmented, for the oranges. You could also leave the prawns whole if you prefer.

fish and shellfish main dishes

GRILLED PRAWNS WITH SPICY CABBAGE SALAD

286 calories, 4 g carbs

3 tablespoons extra-virgin olive oil or walnut oil

1 tablespoon cider vinegar or distilled white vinegar

1 teaspoon Dijon mustard

½ teaspoon hot-pepper sauce

½ teaspoon salt

¼ teaspoon ground black pepper

½ head (340 g/12 oz total) green cabbage, finely shredded

1 small carrot, grated

685 g/1½ lb large prawns, peeled and deveined

In a large bowl, combine 2 tablespoons of the oil, the vinegar, mustard, pepper sauce, salt and ⅛ teaspoon of the pepper. Add the cabbage and carrot, and toss to coat.

In a medium bowl, combine the remaining 1 tablespoon oil and remaining ⅛ teaspoon pepper. Add the prawns and toss to coat.

Coat a grill rack with cooking spray. Preheat the grill. Thread the prawns onto skewers by pushing the skewer through the back at the thickest part and then through the tail section. Grill the prawns, turning once, until firm and opaque throughout when cut with a knife, 4 to 6 minutes. Serve with the cabbage salad.

Makes 4 servings

Per serving: energy 286 cals/1197 kJ; protein 40 g; carbohydrate 4 g (of which 4 g sugars); fat 12 g (of which 2 g saturates); fibre 2 g; sodium 460 mg

Diet Exchanges: 0 milk, 1½ vegetable, 0 fruit, 0 bread, 2 meat, 2 fat

Time-Saver

Make the cabbage salad ahead and store in a covered container in the refrigerator for up to 4 days. Sprinkle with 1 tablespoon chopped fresh parsley or dill if desired.

SPICY SAUTÉED PRAWNS WITH GARLIC

225 calories, 1 g carbs

- **I tablespoon olive oil**
- **7 g/¼ oz butter**
- **685 g/I ½ lb large prawns, peeled and deveined**
- **⅛ teaspoon salt**
- **⅛ teaspoon ground black pepper**
- **2–3 large garlic cloves, finely slivered or chopped**
- **¼ teaspoon dried chilli flakes**
- **I tablespoon lemon juice**
- **I tablespoon chopped fresh parsley or basil (optional)**

Heat the oil and butter in a large frying pan over medium-high heat until the butter is melted. Add the prawns, salt and black pepper. Cook, stirring frequently, until just slightly translucent inside, 2 to 3 minutes.

Stir in the garlic and chilli flakes and cook, stirring frequently, until the prawns are opaque throughout, 1 to 2 minutes more, lowering the heat if the garlic begins to colour. Remove from the heat and stir in the lemon juice. Serve sprinkled with parsley or basil (if using).

Makes 4 servings

Per serving: energy 225 cals/944 kJ; protein 39 g; carbohydrate 1 g (of which 0 g sugars); fat 7 g (of which 2 g saturates); fibre 0 g; sodium 519 mg

Diet Exchanges: 0 milk, 0 vegetable, 0 fruit, 0 bread, 2 meat, 1 fat

▶Flavour Tip

Serve on a bed of brown rice, wholewheat couscous or wholewheat spaghetti.

CREOLE-STYLE STEAMED CLAMS

129 calories, 4 g carbs

15 g/½ oz butter or 1 tablespoon olive oil

5 spring onions, white part only, finely chopped

1 small green and/or red pepper, finely chopped

½ celery stick, finely chopped

2 garlic cloves, finely chopped

1 tin (400 g/14 oz) chopped tomatoes, with juice

120 ml/4 fl oz white wine or water

Pinch of chilli powder

910 g/2 lb clams, scrubbed

Melt the butter or oil in a large saucepan (twice the volume of the clams) over medium heat. Stir in the spring onions, pepper, celery and garlic. Cook just until the vegetables soften, 6 to 8 minutes, stirring occasionally. Stir in the tomatoes (with juice), wine or water and chilli powder.

Add the clams, raise the heat to medium-high, cover and steam until they open, 5 to 8 minutes. Discard any clams that don't open.

With a slotted spoon, remove the clams to serving bowls and ladle the vegetables and broth on top.

Makes 4 servings

Per serving: energy 129 cals/547 kJ; protein 13 g; carbohydrate 4 g (of which 4 g sugars); fat 5 g (of which 2 g saturates); fibre 1 g; sodium 480 mg

Diet Exchanges: 0 milk, 1½ vegetable, 0 fruit, 0 bread, 1½ meat, 1 fat

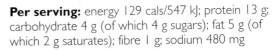

▶Flavour Tips

Sprinkle with 1 tablespoon chopped parsley and 1 tablespoon grated Parmesan before serving. Serve with wholewheat noodles or brown rice to soak up the flavourful juices.

SCALLOPS IN TARRAGON CREAM
237 calories, 1 g carbs

15 g/½ oz butter, softened

685 g/1½ lb fresh or thawed frozen scallops, rinsed and patted dry

1½ teaspoons chopped fresh tarragon or ½ teaspoon dried

¼ teaspoon ground black pepper

120 ml/4 fl oz single cream

1 tablespoon Pernod or 2 tablespoons dry sherry (optional)

2 tablespoons lemon juice

1 tablespoon chopped fresh parsley

Melt the butter in a large frying pan over medium-high heat. When the butter foams, add the scallops, tarragon and pepper. Cook for 2 to 3 minutes, stirring constantly.

Stir in the cream, Pernod or sherry (if using) and lemon juice. Reduce the heat to medium-low and cook until the scallops look opaque throughout and feel slightly springy when lightly pressed, 1 to 2 minutes. Stir in the parsley.

Makes 4 servings

Per serving: energy 237 cals/990 kJ; protein 30 g; carbohydrate 1 g (of which 1 g sugars); fat 12 g (of which 6 g saturates); fibre 0 g; sodium 403 mg

Diet Exchanges: 0 milk, 0 vegetable, 0 fruit, 0 bread, 4 meat, 1 fat

▶Flavour Tips

Both frozen and fresh scallops can have a briny flavour, so don't add salt until you've tasted them. If the sauce in the pan is too thin for your taste, remove the scallops and cook the sauce over medium heat until slightly reduced. Pour over the scallops.

fish and shellfish main dishes

BAKED SCALLOPS WITH HERBS AND WHITE WINE
238 calories, 1 g carbs

45 g/1½ oz butter, softened

685 g/1½ lb fresh or thawed frozen scallops, rinsed and patted dry

1 tablespoon dry white wine

¼ teaspoon ground black pepper

1 tablespoon chopped fresh parsley

1 tablespoon chopped fresh dill

Preheat the oven to 260°C/500°F/gas 10. Grease a shallow ovenproof dish with 15 g/½ oz of the butter and add the scallops. Sprinkle with the wine and the pepper. Dot with the remaining butter.

Bake just until the scallops look opaque throughout and are slightly springy when lightly pressed, 5 to 7 minutes. Remove from the oven and stir in the parsley and dill. Serve immediately with the pan juices.

Makes 4 servings

Per serving: energy 238 cals/992 kJ; protein 30 g; carbohydrate 1 g (of which 1 g sugars); fat 13 g (of which 7 g saturates); fibre 0 g; sodium 447 mg

Diet Exchanges: 0 milk, 0 vegetable, 0 fruit, 0 bread, 4 meat, 2 fat

▶Flavour Tips

Use 1 teaspoon chopped fresh basil or tarragon with 2 teaspoons parsley. Add 60 g/2 oz tinned chopped tomatoes along with the scallops. To make the most of the buttery pan juices, serve the scallops on a bed of brown rice or wholewheat couscous.

HIDDEN ROADBLOCK to weight loss

FLUID RETENTION

Excess water weight may be preventing you from losing those last few pounds. Many people retain fluids if they use too much table salt or eat foods that are high in sodium, especially snack foods. Plus, when the body burns fat, it produces water. And if you don't drink enough water, your body will retain even more water. The bottom line for weight loss is that drinking water helps you lose weight—even water weight. Drink at least 8 glasses of water a day to help flush excess water out of your system. If you think you are retaining fluids, use less table salt and cut back on salty foods such as pickles, mustard, tinned fish, soy sauce, commercial salad dressings and stocks . You can also choose vegetables with natural diuretic properties, such as celery, cucumbers, asparagus and cabbage to help you naturally shed some fluid.

Baked Scallops with Herbs and White Wine

Steamed Mussels with Roasted Peppers and Capers

188 calories, 3 g carbs

2 tablespoons olive oil

1 small onion, finely chopped

2 garlic cloves, finely chopped

60 g/2 oz prepared roasted red peppers, chopped

½ teaspoon dried thyme or oregano

80 ml/3 fl oz dry white wine

1.6 kg/3½ lb mussels, scrubbed, beards trimmed

20 g/¾ oz chopped fresh parsley and/or basil

1 tablespoon drained capers

¼ teaspoon ground black pepper

Heat the oil in a large pan (twice the volume of the mussels) over medium-low heat. Add the onion and garlic and cook, stirring occasionally, until the onion is almost tender, 6 to 8 minutes. Stir in the roasted peppers and the thyme or oregano and cook for 1 minute. Add the white wine.

Add the mussels, cover, raise the heat to high and cook until the mussels open, 3 to 6 minutes. Discard any mussels that don't open. With a slotted spoon, remove the mussels to serving bowls. Stir the parsley and/or basil, capers and pepper into the broth. Ladle over the mussels.

Makes 4 servings

Per serving: energy 188 cals/791 kJ; protein 21 g; carbohydrate 3 g (of which 2 g sugars); fat 9 g (of which 1 g saturates); fibre 1 g; sodium 256 mg

Diet Exchanges: 0 milk, 1 vegetable, 0 fruit, 0 bread, 1 meat, 1½ fat

Time-Savers

To trim mussel beards easily, use small sharp scissors. You could replace the mussels with 4 dozen clams.

casseroles & one-dish dinners

STIR-FRIED CHICKEN AND BROCCOLI 264

CHICKEN AND HAM JAMBALAYA 265

CHICKEN CASSEROLE WITH BUTTERMILK SCONES 266

CHICKEN STEW WITH SWEETCORN AND BUTTERBEANS 268

BEEF AND BARLEY CASSEROLE 269

QUICK PAN SCRAMBLE WITH BEEF, EGGS AND GREENS 270

TEXAS BURRITO 271

AUBERGINE STUFFED WITH SAVOURY BEEF 272

BEEF AND CABBAGE CASSEROLE WITH TOMATO SAUCE 274

BOILED BEEF AND WINTER VEGETABLES 275

CHILLI-CORNBREAD PIE 277

POT ROAST 278

BRAISED BEEF WITH MUSHROOMS 279

TURKEY CHILLI 280

PORK AND PASTA BAKE 283

SAUSAGE, EGG AND VEGETABLE CASSEROLE 284

PORK CHOPS BAKED WITH CABBAGE AND CREAM 286

CANNELLINI BEANS WITH HAM AND SAUSAGE 287

HAM AND LENTIL CASSEROLE 288

AUBERGINE PARMESAN 289

JANET'S ROASTED AUBERGINE AND CHICKPEAS 291

OLD-FASHIONED LAMB STEW 293

LAMB SHANKS WITH RED BEANS 294

SPICY CURRIED VEGETABLES 295

MOUSSAKA 296

SHEPHERD'S PIE 298

STIR-FRIED CHICKEN AND BROCCOLI

317 calories, 17 g carbs

- 120 ml/4 fl oz chicken stock
- 3 tablespoons Chinese oyster sauce
- 2 tablespoons orange juice
- 1½ tablespoons soy sauce
- 2 cloves garlic, finely chopped
- 2 teaspoons finely chopped fresh ginger
- 1 teaspoon sesame oil
- ¼ teaspoon hot-pepper sauce (optional)
- 1 tablespoon cornflour
- 1½ tablespoons cold water
- 3 tablespoons vegetable oil
- 455 g/1 lb boneless, skinless chicken breasts, cut into thin strips
- 1 large bunch (910 g/2 lb) broccoli, cut into small florets
- 5 spring onions, sliced
- 1 teaspoon toasted sesame seeds (optional)

In a small bowl, combine the stock, oyster sauce, orange juice, soy sauce, garlic, ginger, sesame oil and hot-pepper sauce (if using).

In a cup, dissolve the cornflour in the cold water.

Heat the oil in a large wok or frying pan over high heat until the oil just starts to smoke. Add the chicken and cook, stirring continually until no longer pink on the surface, about 30 seconds. Stir in the broccoli and cook, stirring continually, until it turns bright green and the chicken is half-cooked, about 2 minutes. Pour in the stock mixture and cook, stirring frequently, for 2 minutes. Stir in the spring onions and the cornflour mixture. Cook, stirring, until the sauce comes to the boil, thickens and the chicken is cooked through, about 1 minute. Sprinkle with the sesame seeds (if using).

Makes 4 servings

Per serving: energy 317 cals/1318 kJ; protein 34 g; carbohydrate 17 g (of which 4 g sugars); fat 16 g (of which 2 g saturates); fibre 6 g; sodium 600 mg

Diet Exchanges: 0 milk, 3 vegetable, 0 fruit, 0 bread, 4 meat, 2½ fat

▶ Flavour Tips

Replace the chicken with small prawns or slivered pork. Replace half of the broccoli with ½ bunch sliced pak choi or 230 g/8 oz runner beans.

CHICKEN AND HAM JAMBALAYA
290 calories, 23 g carbs

- ½ teaspoon dried thyme
- ½ teaspoon ground black pepper
- ¼ teaspoon salt
- ⅛–¼ teaspoon chilli powder
- 30 g/1 oz butter
- 1 gammon steak (170 g/6 oz), chopped
- 5 skinless, boneless chicken thighs (about 145 g/5 oz each), each cut into eighths
- 1½ large onions, chopped
- 1 large green pepper, chopped
- 3 cloves garlic, finely chopped
- 230 g/8 oz tinned chopped tomatoes
- 350 ml/12 fl oz chicken stock
- 145 g/5 oz long-grain brown rice

Preheat the oven to 180°C/350°F/gas 4.

In a small bowl, combine the thyme, black pepper, salt and chilli powder.

Melt the butter in a large, heavy oven-proof pan over high heat. Add the gammon and chicken and cook until lightly browned, stirring occasionally, about 5 minutes.

Sprinkle the spice mixture over the meat and stir to combine. Add the onions, pepper and garlic. Reduce the heat to medium and cook, stirring frequently, until the vegetables start to soften, about 5 minutes. Stir in the tomatoes and cook for 1 minute. Stir in the stock and rice. Bring to a simmer and cover.

Place in the oven for 45 minutes until the rice is tender, the liquid has been absorbed and the chicken is tender.

Makes 6 servings

Per serving: energy 290 cals/1206 kJ; protein 17 g; carbohydrate 23 g (of which 3 g sugars); fat 10 g (of which 3 g saturates); fibre 2 g; sodium 692 mg

Diet Exchanges: 0 milk, 1 vegetable, 0 fruit, 1½ bread, 2 meat, 1½ fat

Time-Saver

You can make this dish up to 4 days ahead. Keep it in a covered container in the refrigerator. To re-heat, remove from the refrigerator about 45 minutes before cooking, then place in an ovenproof dish, cover and bake at 180°C/350°F/gas 4 until heated through, 20 to 30 minutes.

CHICKEN CASSEROLE WITH BUTTERMILK SCONES
590 calories, 39 g carbs

1.2 litres/2 pints chicken stock

2 bay leaves

1.15 kg/2½ lb boneless skinless chicken breasts

3 parsnips or turnips (340 g/12 oz), chopped

3 large carrots (455 g/1 lb), chopped

2 large celery sticks, sliced

230 g/8 oz pearl (button) onions

240 ml/8 fl oz single cream

1 teaspoon dried thyme

75 g/2½ oz butter, softened

75 g/2½ oz wholemeal flour

1½ teaspoons Worcestershire sauce

¼ teaspoon ground black pepper

285 g/10 oz frozen peas

Dough from Sesame Buttermilk Scones (page 101)

In a large frying pan over medium heat, bring the stock and bay leaves to a simmer. Add the chicken and cook until no longer pink inside, 12 to 14 minutes. Using a slotted spoon, remove the chicken to a dish and let cool. Cut into bite-size cubes.

Increase the heat to medium-high and add the parsnips or turnips, carrots and celery. Cook until tender-firm, 8 to 10 minutes, adding the onions during the last 4 minutes. Using a slotted spoon, remove to a colander.

Discard the bay leaves. If there is more than 700 ml/1¼ pints of stock in the pan, increase the heat and boil until reduced. Reduce the heat to medium and stir in the cream and thyme. Cook until bubbling.

In a small bowl, combine the butter and flour. Gradually whisk into the stock mixture, increasing the heat slightly, until it boils. Remove from the heat and season with the Worcestershire sauce and pepper.

Preheat the oven to 220°C/425°F/gas 7.

In a large bowl, toss together the chicken, peas, vegetable mixture and sauce. Pour into a deep ovenproof dish. Cover with clingfilm, pressing it against the filling.

Prepare the scones and cut them out. Remove the clingfilm from the ovenproof dish and place the scones on top of the filling, about 3 cm/1 in apart.

Place in the oven and bake until the scones are lightly browned and the filling is bubbling, 25 to 30 minutes.

Makes 8 servings

Per serving: energy 590 cals/2454 kJ; protein 40 g; carbohydrate 39 g (of which 5 g sugars); fat 29 g (of which 18 g saturates); fibre 8 g; sodium 580 mg

Diet Exchanges: ½ milk, 1½ vegetable, 0 fruit, 1½ bread, 5 meat, 4 fat

Chicken Casserole with Buttermilk Scones

CHICKEN STEW WITH SWEETCORN AND BUTTERBEANS

480 calories, 20 g carbs

**3 bacon rashers, cut into 2–3 cm/
1 in pieces**

1.8 kg/4 lb skinless chicken joints

½ teaspoon ground black pepper

¼ teaspoon salt

2 tablespoons wholemeal flour

45 g/1½ oz butter

1 large onion, chopped

1 large green pepper, chopped

½ teaspoon dried thyme

½ teaspoon dried sage or marjoram

1 tin (400 g/14 oz) chopped tomatoes

400 ml/14 fl oz chicken stock

**145 g/5 oz frozen or tinned
sweetcorn**

**145 g/5 oz drained tinned
butterbeans**

Preheat the oven to 180°C/350°F/gas 4. Cook the bacon in a large, heavy frying pan over medium-low heat until crisp, 4 to 5 minutes. Remove to a kitchen paper-lined plate. Discard all but 1 tablespoon of the fat in the pan.

Season the chicken with the black pepper and salt and coat with the flour. Add the butter to the pan with the bacon fat and melt over medium-high heat. Add the chicken in batches and cook until browned,

about 12 minutes. Place, meat side up, in an ovenproof dish.

Add the onion, pepper, thyme and sage or marjoram to the pan. Reduce the heat to medium and cook, stirring occasionally, until slightly softened, 6 to 8 minutes. Stir in the tomatoes and stock. Bring to a simmer. Pour over the chicken, cover and place in the oven until the chicken is almost cooked through, about 30 minutes.

Stir in the sweetcorn and butterbeans. Cover and cook until the chicken is tender and a meat thermometer registers 80°C/180°F, 10 to 15 minutes.

Serve with the bacon crumbled over top.

Makes 6 servings

Per serving: energy 480 cals/1996 kJ; protein 45 g; carbohydrate 20 g (of which 3 g sugars); fat 25 g (of which 8 g saturates); fibre 4 g; sodium 700 mg

Diet Exchanges: 0 milk, 4 vegetable, 0 fruit, 0 bread, 6 meat, 3½ fat

▶Flavour Tips

Replace the sweetcorn and butterbeans with 230 g/8 oz of trimmed, sliced okra, adding it during the last 10 minutes of cooking. Stir in 2 teaspoons of lemon juice just before serving. Serve with brown rice to soak up the sauce.

BEEF AND BARLEY CASSEROLE
395 calories, 23 g carbs

2 tablespoons olive oil

**685 g/1½ lb stewing steak,
    cut into cubes**

¼ teaspoon salt

¼ teaspoon ground black pepper

1 onion, chopped

1 large red or green pepper, chopped

700 ml/1¼ pints beef stock

145 g/5 oz pearl barley

115 g/4 oz tinned chopped tomatoes

1 teaspoon ground coriander

1 bay leaf (optional)

115 g/4 oz toasted walnuts, chopped

**Grated zest of 1 large lemon
    (optional)**

Preheat the oven to 180°C/350°F/gas 4.

Heat the oil in a large, deep, ovenproof frying pan over medium-high heat. Add the meat and cook, seasoning with the salt and pepper, until browned, 10 to 12 minutes (work in batches if necessary and remove pieces to a plate as they're done). Reduce the heat to medium.

Return the meat to the pan and add the onion and pepper. Cook until the vegetables begin to soften, 7 to 8 minutes, stirring occasionally. Stir in the stock (reserving 60 ml/2 fl oz), the barley, tomatoes, coriander and bay leaf (if using). Bring to a simmer. Cover and place in the oven until the beef and barley are tender and the stock is absorbed, 1¼ to 1½ hours. Add up to 60 ml/2 fl oz stock if necessary to prevent the mixture from drying out.

Stir in the nuts and lemon zest (if using). Discard the bay leaf before serving.

Makes 4 servings

Per serving: energy 395 cals/1643 kJ; protein 33 g; carbohydrate 23 g (of which 2 g sugars); fat 16 g (of which 4 g saturates); fibre 5 g; sodium 612 mg

Diet Exchanges: 0 milk, 1 vegetable, 0 fruit, 1 bread, 3½ meat, 2 fat

▶Flavour Tips

Substitute 200 g/7 oz of brown rice for the barley and stir in 1 or 2 cloves of garlic, finely chopped, along with the onion and pepper just as the vegetables start to soften. Add ⅛ to ¼ teaspoon cayenne pepper just before baking.

Add 75 g/2½ oz raisins along with the tomatoes.

Top each serving with 1 tablespoon chopped fresh coriander, 3 chopped spring onions, or 45 g/1½ oz grated Parmesan cheese.

QUICK PAN SCRAMBLE WITH BEEF, EGGS AND GREENS

290 calories, 6 g carbs

- **1 large bunch (570 g/1¼ lb) Swiss chard, stemmed and chopped**
- **2 tablespoons olive oil**
- **1 small onion, chopped**
- **1 garlic clove, finely chopped**
- **340 g/12 oz minced beef**
- **¼ teaspoon salt**
- **¼ teaspoon ground black pepper**
- **¼ teaspoon ground allspice**
- **3 large eggs, at room temperature**
- **4–5 drops hot-pepper sauce**
- **30 g/1 oz grated Parmesan cheese or 60 g/2 oz grated Jarlsberg cheese**

Bring a large pan of salted water to the boil. Add the chard and cook just until tender, about 3 minutes. Drain and cool under cold running water. Squeeze dry.

Heat the oil in a large frying pan over medium heat. Add the onion and cook, stirring occasionally, until lightly browned and soft, 8 to 9 minutes. Stir in the garlic and cook, stirring, for 30 seconds. Add the meat and cook, stirring to crumble, just until browned, 5 to 6 minutes. Stir in the chard, salt, pepper and allspice. Cook, stirring frequently, until the meat is no longer pink, 5 to 6 minutes. Reduce the heat to low.

In a small bowl, lightly beat the eggs and hot-pepper sauce. Stir into the beef mixture. Cook, stirring, until the eggs are set but still creamy, 4 to 6 minutes. Remove to a dish and sprinkle with the cheese.

Makes 4 servings

Per serving: energy 290 cals/1206 kJ; protein 29 g; carbohydrate 6 g (of which 1 g sugars); fat 17 g (of which 4 g saturates); fibre 2 g; sodium 633 mg

Diet Exchanges: 0 milk, 1 vegetable, 0 fruit, 0 bread, 3½ meat, 2½ fat

▶Flavour Tip

Substitute spinach, kale, broccoli or cabbage for the chard.

TEXAS BURRITO
600 calories, 50 g carbs

3 tablespoons vegetable oil

**685 g/1½ lb stewing steak,
     cut into 1 cm/½ in cubes**

1 onion, chopped

2 garlic cloves, finely chopped

**1–1½ small jalapeño chillies, seeded
     and finely chopped (wear plastic
     gloves when handling)**

1½ tablespoons chilli powder

2 teaspoons ground cumin

½ teaspoon salt

¼ teaspoon ground black pepper

1 tablespoon tomato puree

**300 ml/10 fl oz hot water or beef
     stock**

8 wholewheat tortillas (15 cm/6 in)

115 g/4 oz Cheddar cheese, grated

4 lettuce leaves, shredded (optional)

1 large ripe tomato, finely chopped

Heat the oil in a saucepan over medium-high heat. Working in batches, add the beef and cook, stirring, until browned, 5 to 8 minutes. Remove to a plate.

Reduce the heat to medium. Return the beef to the pan and stir in the onion, garlic and jalapeño chillies. Cook, stirring occasionally, until the onion starts to soften, about 5 minutes. Stir in the chilli powder, cumin, salt and black pepper.

In a jug, combine the tomato puree and water or stock. Stir into the beef mixture. Reduce the heat to low. Cover and cook, stirring occasionally, for 1 hour. Remove the lid and cook until the beef is tender, 30 minutes.

Meanwhile, preheat the oven to 190°C/375°F/gas 5 and wrap the tortillas in foil. Bake until steaming and pliable, 5 to 10 minutes.

To assemble each burrito, place a tortilla on a work surface and arrange a line of cheese down the centre. Top with the beef mixture, lettuce (if using) and tomato. Fold two opposite sides over the filling, then fold one of the remaining sides over to enclose.

Makes 4 servings (8 burritos)

Per serving: energy 600 cals/2492 kJ; protein 47 g; carbohydrate 50 g (of which 2 g sugars); fat 26 g (of which 10 g saturates); fibre 5 g; sodium 700 mg

Diet Exchanges: 0 milk, 1½ vegetable, 0 fruit, 2 bread, 6 meat, 4 fat

Time-Saver

Make a double batch of the filling and refrigerate or freeze it. Store in a covered container in the refrigerator for up to 5 days or in the freezer for up to 2 months. To reheat, thaw in the refrigerator, then cook in a saucepan over low heat, stirring occasionally, until heated through, about 10 minutes.

AUBERGINE STUFFED WITH SAVOURY BEEF
390 calories, 21 g carbs

2 aubergines (455 g/1 lb each)

3 tablespoons olive oil

1 large onion, chopped

1 red pepper, chopped

2 garlic cloves, finely chopped

455 g/1 lb extra-lean minced beef

1½ teaspoons dried oregano

1½ tablespoons tomato puree

2 anchovy fillets, finely chopped (optional)

1 tablespoon capers, drained and coarsely chopped (optional)

60 g/2 oz Parmesan cheese, grated

¼ teaspoon salt

¼ teaspoon ground black pepper

Preheat the oven to 200°C/400°F/gas 6. Pierce the aubergines in 2 or 3 places and place on a baking tray. Roast, turning once or twice, just until tender when pierced with a fork, 20 to 25 minutes. Leave until cool enough to handle.

Halve the aubergines lengthwise. Scoop out the flesh and leave to drain in a colander, leaving a 2 cm/¾ in shell.

Heat 2 tablespoons of the oil in a large frying pan over medium heat. Add the onion and pepper and cook, stirring occasionally, until tender, 8 to 10 minutes. Add the garlic and beef. Cook, stirring to crumble the beef, until no longer pink, 5 to 6 minutes. Stir in the aubergine flesh, oregano, tomato puree, anchovies (if using) and capers (if using). Reduce the heat to low and cook, stirring occasionally, until thick, 15 to 20 minutes. Stir in 30 g/1 oz of the Parmesan, the salt and black pepper.

Place the aubergine shells on a baking tray and divide the beef mixture among them. Sprinkle with the remaining 30 g/ 1 oz cheese and drizzle with the remaining 1 tablespoon oil. Roast until lightly browned on top, 15 to 20 minutes.

Makes 4 servings

Per serving: energy 390 cals/1622 kJ; protein 29 g; carbohydrate 21 g (of which 3 g sugars); fat 20 g (of which 5 g saturates); fibre 7 g; sodium 352 mg

Diet Exchanges: 0 milk, 4 vegetable, 0 fruit, 0 bread, 4 meat, 3 fat

Flavour Tip
Replace the beef with lamb.

Aubergine Stuffed with Savoury Beef

BEEF AND CABBAGE CASSEROLE WITH TOMATO SAUCE

389 calories, 29 g carbs

2 tablespoons olive oil

1 large onion, chopped

½ small head (340 g/12 oz) green cabbage, shredded

4 garlic cloves, finely chopped

910 g/2 lb extra-lean minced beef or pork

400 ml/14 fl oz beef stock

30 g/1 oz pimento-stuffed green olives, chopped

¾ teaspoon dried oregano

¼–½ teaspoon mace (optional)

90 g/3 oz wholewheat couscous

½ teaspoon ground black pepper

¼ teaspoon salt

1 large red pepper, coarsely chopped

2 tins (400 g/14 oz each) chopped tomatoes

45 g/1½ oz Parmesan cheese, grated

Preheat the oven to 190°C/375°F/gas 5 and coat a 20 × 20 cm/8 × 8 in ovenproof dish with cooking spray.

Heat 1 tablespoon oil in a large, deep frying pan over medium heat. Stir in the onion and cabbage and cook, stirring occasionally, until almost tender, 8 to 10 minutes. Add 2 of the garlic cloves and the meat, stirring, until the meat is crumbled and browned, 5 to 6 minutes. Stir in 350 ml/12 fl oz of the stock, the olives, oregano and mace (if using). Bring to the boil and stir in the couscous, ¼ teaspoon of the black pepper and ⅛ teaspoon of the salt. Immediately reduce the heat to low. Cover and cook for 10 minutes. Uncover, increase the heat to medium-high and cook until the liquid has evaporated, 5 to 6 minutes. Spread the meat mixture in the prepared ovenproof dish and cover to keep warm.

Wipe out the pan, add the remaining 1 tablespoon oil and heat over medium heat. Stir in the red pepper and cook, stirring occasionally, until soft, 8 to 10 minutes. Stir in the remaining 2 garlic cloves and cook, stirring frequently, for 30 seconds. Stir in the tomatoes and season with the remaining ¼ teaspoon pepper and ⅛ teaspoon salt. Cook until thickened, 12 to 15 minutes, stirring occasionally.

Spoon the tomato sauce on top of the beef, cover with foil and place in the oven for 25 minutes. Uncover and sprinkle with the Parmesan.

Makes 6 servings

Per serving: energy 389 cals/1618 kJ; protein 35 g; carbohydrate 29 g (of which 0 g sugars); fat 11 g (of which 4 g saturates); fibre 6 g; sodium 622 mg

Diet Exchanges: 0 milk, 3 vegetable, 0 fruit, 1 bread, 4 meat, 1½ fat

BOILED BEEF AND WINTER VEGETABLES

540 calories, 21 g carbs

3 whole cloves

I large onion

I salt beef, salted silverside or brisket joint (about 1.8 kg/4 lb)

½ bunch parsley, tied with string

I celery stick, halved

½ teaspoon whole peppercorns (optional)

2 bay leaves

3 turnips (230 g/8 oz), peeled and halved

3 parsnips (230 g/8 oz), halved lengthwise

3 carrots (170 g/6 oz), peeled and cut into thirds crosswise

I small head (685 g/1½ lb) green cabbage, cut into 6 wedges

150 ml/5 fl oz Mustard-Horseradish Sauce (page 120)

Insert the cloves into the onion. Place the beef in a large pan and add water to cover by about 8 cm/3 in. Add the onion, parsley, celery, peppercorns (if using) and bay leaves. Bring to the boil over high heat. Immediately reduce the heat to low and skim the foam from the surface. Partially cover the pan and cook until almost tender, 2½ to 2¾ hours.

Discard the onion, celery and parsley. Add the turnips, parsnips, carrots and cabbage. Partially cover and cook until the vegetables are tender, about 15 minutes. Discard the bay leaves. Thinly slice the beef across the grain and serve with the vegetables and the sauce.

Makes 6 servings

Per serving: energy 540 cals/2246 kJ; protein 35 g; carbohydrate 21 g (of which 0 g sugars); fat 33 g (of which 10 g saturates); fibre 7 g; sodium 407 mg

Diet Exchanges: 0 milk, 3 vegetable, 0 fruit, ½ bread, 5 meat, 4 fat

Chilli-Cornbread Pie

CHILLI-CORNBREAD PIE
385 calories, 37 g carbs

2 tablespoons vegetable oil

I onion, chopped

3 garlic cloves, finely chopped

½ small jalapeño chilli, seeded and finely chopped (wear plastic gloves when handling)

455 g/1 lb extra-lean minced beef

I tin (400 g/14 oz) chopped tomatoes

2–3 tablespoons chilli powder

¼ teaspoon salt

¼ teaspoon ground black pepper

¼ teaspoon ground cumin (optional)

I tin (420 g/14½ oz) borlotti, pinto or black-eyed beans, rinsed and drained

145 g/5 oz yellow cornmeal

75 g/2½ oz wholemeal flour

1½ teaspoons baking powder

¼ teaspoon salt

I large egg, at room temperature

240 ml/8 fl oz semi-skimmed milk, at room temperature

3 tablespoons melted butter

Heat the oil in a large frying pan over medium heat. Add the onion, garlic and jalapeño pepper. Cook until soft, stirring occasionally, 8 to 10 minutes. Add the beef and cook, stirring, until crumbled and browned, 5 to 6 minutes. Stir in the tomatoes, chilli powder, salt, black pepper and cumin (if using). Reduce the heat to low and cook for 30 minutes, stirring occasionally. Stir in the beans and cook for 15 minutes. Transfer to a 20 × 20 cm/8 × 8 in ovenproof dish.

Preheat the oven to 200°C/400°F/gas 6.

In a large bowl, combine the cornmeal, flour, baking powder and salt.

In a small bowl, lightly beat the egg, milk and butter. Stir into the cornmeal mixture until smooth. Pour over the meat mixture and spread evenly. Bake until a toothpick inserted in the centre of the cornbread comes out clean, 20 to 30 minutes.

Makes 6 servings

Per serving: energy 385 cals/1601 kJ; protein 27 g; carbohydrate 37 g (of which 2 g sugars); fat 15 g (of which 7 g saturates); fibre 6 g; sodium 600 mg

Diet Exchanges: 0 milk, 1½ vegetable, 0 fruit, 2 bread, 2½ meat, 2½ fat

Time-Saver

Make this dish ahead for quick, satisfying meals. Store it in a covered container in the refrigerator for up to 4 days or in the freezer for up to 2 months. To reheat, thaw in the refrigerator for 12 hours if frozen, then place in an ovenproof dish and bake at 180°C/350°F/gas 4 until heated through, 25 to 30 minutes.

POT ROAST

425 calories, 7 g carbs

- **1½ tablespoons olive oil**
- **1 onion, cut into small wedges**
- **2 garlic cloves, finely chopped**
- **1 boneless beef topside or silverside joint (about 910 g/2 lb)**
- **¼ teaspoon salt**
- **½ teaspoon ground black pepper**
- **1½ teaspoons wholemeal flour**
- **400 ml/14 fl oz beef stock**
- **180 ml/6 fl oz tomato juice or vegetable juice**
- **1 celery stick, quartered**
- **1 teaspoon Worcestershire sauce**
- **½ teaspoon dried thyme**

Preheat the oven to 180°C/350°F/gas 4.

Heat 1 tablespoon of the oil in a large, heavy ovenproof pan over medium heat. Add the onion and garlic. Cover and cook, stirring occasionally, until the onion begins to brown and turn translucent, 5 to 8 minutes. Remove to a plate. Remove the pan from the heat.

Season the meat with the salt and pepper and sprinkle all over with the flour, rubbing it in lightly. Heat the remaining oil in the pan over high heat. Add the meat and cook until browned, 3 to 5 minutes. Reduce the heat to low and return the vegetables to the pan, scattering them over and around the meat. Add the stock, juice, celery, Worcestershire sauce and thyme. Bring to a simmer and cover. Place in the oven until tender, 2 to 2½ hours.

Remove the beef and vegetables to a dish. Pour the pan juices into a glass measuring jug and discard the fat that rises to the surface. Pour the juices over the meat and serve.

Makes 4 servings

Per serving: energy 425 cals/1768 kJ; protein 50 g; carbohydrate 7 g (of which 0 g sugars); fat 15 g (of which 5 g saturates); fibre 1 g; sodium 680 mg

Diet Exchanges: 0 milk, 1 vegetable, 0 fruit, 0 bread, 6½ meat, 1 fat

▶Flavour Tips

Add 285 g/10 oz of sliced mushrooms during the last 45 minutes of cooking. Serve with a side dish of couscous or quinoa to soak up the juices.

BRAISED BEEF WITH MUSHROOMS

340 calories, 8 g carbs

7 g/¼ oz dried wild mushrooms

120 ml/4 fl oz boiling water

910 g/2 lb stewing steak, cut into 4 cm/1½ in cubes

½ teaspoon salt

¼ teaspoon ground black pepper

⅛ teaspoon ground allspice (optional)

2 tablespoons olive oil

285 g/10 oz mushrooms, quartered

1 onion, chopped

1 garlic clove, finely chopped

2 tablespoons wholemeal flour

300 ml/10 fl oz red wine or beef stock

120–240 ml/4–8 fl oz water

1 tablespoon tomato puree

½ teaspoon dried thyme or oregano

Preheat the oven to 180°C/350°F/gas 4.

In a bowl, soak the dried mushrooms in 120 ml/4 fl oz boiling water until softened, about 20 minutes. Using tongs, pluck out the mushrooms and reserve the soaking water. Trim away any dirty sections from the mushrooms and chop any large pieces. Set aside.

Season the meat with the salt, pepper and allspice (if using). Heat the oil in a large, heavy ovenproof pan over medium-high heat. Working in batches, add the meat and cook until browned, 12 to 15 minutes, removing pieces to a plate as they are done.

Reduce the heat to medium and add the fresh mushrooms, rehydrated mushrooms, onion and garlic. Cook, stirring, for 2 minutes. Return the meat to the pan, sprinkle with the flour and cook, stirring, for 1 minute. Carefully pour in the mushroom soaking liquid, leaving behind any grit that has settled to the bottom of the bowl. Add the wine or stock, 120 ml/4 fl oz of the water and the tomato puree. If the mixture is too thick, add up to 120 ml/4 fl oz more water. Bring to the boil and add the thyme or oregano. Cover and place in the oven until the meat is tender, about 1½ hours.

Makes 6 servings

Per serving: energy 340 cals/1414 kJ; protein 33 g; carbohydrate 8 g (of which 2 g sugars); fat 16 g (of which 7 g saturates); fibre 2 g; sodium 250 mg

Diet Exchanges: 0 milk, 1 vegetable, 0 fruit, 0 bread, 4 meat, 2 fat

Time-Saver

Make this richly flavoured dish whenever you have time. Store it in a covered container in the refrigerator for up to 5 days or in the freezer for up to 2 months. To reheat, thaw in the refrigerator for 12 hours if frozen, then place in a pan over low heat, cover and cook until heated through, stirring frequently, for 15 to 30 minutes.

TURKEY CHILLI

312 calories, 27 g carbs

1½ tablespoons vegetable oil

1 large onion, chopped

1 large green pepper, chopped

2 garlic cloves, chopped

600 g/1 lb 5 oz minced turkey

400 ml/14 fl oz chicken stock

3 tablespoons tomato puree

2–3 tablespoons chilli powder

1½ teaspoons dried oregano

1 teaspoon ground coriander

¼ teaspoon salt

½ teaspoon ground cumin

¼ teaspoon ground cinnamon

1 tin (420 g/14½ oz) red kidney beans (with juice)

170 g/6 oz wholewheat spaghetti, broken into short pieces

60 g/2 oz Cheddar or Double Gloucester cheese, grated

Heat the oil in a large, heavy saucepan over medium heat. Add the onion, pepper and garlic. Cook, stirring occasionally, until the onion starts to brown, 8 to 10 minutes. Add the turkey and cook, stirring to coarsely crumble until no longer pink, 8 to 10 minutes. Stir in the stock, tomato puree, chilli powder, oregano, coriander, salt, cumin and cinnamon. Bring to a simmer.

Partially cover and cook, stirring occasionally, until the meat is tender and the stock is slightly thickened, about 30 minutes.

Meanwhile, pour the beans (with juice) into a microwaveable bowl. Microwave on high power for 1 to 2 minutes or until heated through. Drain and cover to keep warm.

Cook the pasta according to the directions on the packet. Drain and divide among 4 bowls. Ladle the chilli over the pasta, top with the beans and sprinkle with the cheese.

Makes 4 servings

Per serving: energy 312 cals/1297 kJ; protein 20 g; carbohydrate 27 g (of which 0 g sugars); fat 12 g (of which 5 g saturates); fibre 6 g; sodium 490 mg

Diet Exchanges: 0 milk, 1 vegetable, 0 fruit, 1½ bread, 2 meat, 1 fat

Time-Saver

Make this chilli ahead of time. The meat portion keeps well in a covered container in the refrigerator for up to 5 days or in the freezer for up to 2 months. Cook the pasta and heat the beans just before serving. To reheat the meat, thaw in the refrigerator for 12 hours if frozen. Place in a saucepan set over low heat and cook, stirring frequently, until heated through, about 15 minutes.

Turkey Chilli

Pork and Pasta Bake

PORK AND PASTA BAKE
351 calories, 25 g carbs

- **145 g/5 oz wholewheat penne or other short pasta**
- **2 tablespoons + 1 teaspoon olive oil**
- **455 g/1 lb boneless pork loin, fat trimmed, halved lengthwise, then sliced crosswise into 5 mm/¼ in strips**
- **1 large red pepper, chopped**
- **1 small onion, chopped**
- **6 large mushrooms (170 g/6 oz), coarsely chopped**
- **3 garlic cloves, finely chopped**
- **1 teaspoon dried oregano**
- **½ teaspoon dried thyme**
- **1 tin (400 g/14 oz) chopped tomatoes**
- **¼ teaspoon salt**
- **¼ teaspoon ground black pepper**
- **1 large ripe tomato, chopped or thinly sliced, slices cut in half (optional)**
- **90 g/3 oz mozzarella cheese, finely chopped**

Preheat the oven to 190°C/375°F/gas 5.

Cook the pasta according to the directions on the packet. Drain and return to the pan. Add 1 teaspoon of the oil and toss to coat.

Heat the remaining 2 tablespoons oil in a large frying pan over medium heat. Add the pork and cook until browned, 3 to 5 minutes. Add the pepper, onion, mushrooms, garlic, oregano and thyme. Cook until the onion is almost soft, 6 to 7 minutes, stirring occasionally. Stir in the tin of tomatoes and cook for 5 minutes. Season with the salt and black pepper.

Add to the pasta, tossing to combine. Pour into a large, shallow ovenproof dish. Top with the fresh tomato (if using) and sprinkle with the cheese. Bake until heated through and the cheese is melted and slightly browned, 20 to 25 minutes.

Makes 4 servings

Per serving: energy 351 cals/1460 kJ; protein 28 g; carbohydrate 25 g (of which 1 g sugars); fat 13 g (of which 4 g saturates); fibre 5 g; sodium 273 mg

Diet Exchanges: 0 milk, 2 vegetable, 0 fruit, 1 bread, 3 meat, 2½ fat

▶Flavour Tips
Replace the pork with chicken, the pepper with courgettes and the mozzarella with 60 g/2 oz grated Parmesan or pecorino cheese. Add 4 tablespoons double cream to the pork and vegetable mixture along with the tomatoes.

SAUSAGE, EGG AND VEGETABLE CASSEROLE

373 calories, 6 g carbs

- **455 g/1 lb fresh pork sausage, cut into 2–3 cm/1 in pieces**
- **1½ tablespoons olive oil**
- **115 g/4 oz young spinach leaves, chopped**
- **2 courgettes (230 g/8 oz), thinly sliced**
- **1 red pepper, chopped**
- **1 small red onion, thinly sliced**
- **¼ teaspoon salt**
- **¼ teaspoon ground black pepper**
- **7 large eggs, at room temperature**
- **120 ml/4 fl oz semi-skimmed milk, at room temperature**
- **30 g/1 oz Parmesan cheese, grated**

Preheat the oven to 180°C/350°F/gas 4. Coat a 20 × 20 cm/8 × 8 in ovenproof dish with cooking spray.

Cook the sausage in a large frying pan over medium-high heat until half-cooked, 6 to 8 minutes, stirring occasionally. Spread over the bottom of the prepared dish. Discard the fat in the pan. Pour the oil into the same pan and stir in the spinach, courgettes, pepper, onion, salt and ⅛ teaspoon of the black pepper. Reduce the heat to medium. Cook, stirring occasionally, until the vegetables are tender and any liquid has evaporated, 8 to 10 minutes. Let cool for 10 minutes and arrange over the sausage.

Meanwhile, in a large bowl, combine the eggs, milk, cheese and remaining ⅛ teaspoon black pepper. Pour over the vegetables. Place in the oven until the eggs are set, 40 to 45 minutes. Cut into squares to serve.

Makes 6 servings

Per serving: energy 373 cals/1551 kJ; protein 25 g; carbohydrate 6 g (of which 4 g sugars); fat 27 g (of which 8 g saturates); fibre 2 g; sodium 612 mg

Diet Exchanges: 0 milk, 1 vegetable, 0 fruit, 0 bread, 3 meat, 3½ fat

▶Flavour Tips

Substitute escarole for the spinach. You could also use kale or broccoli; cook in boiling water for 2 minutes and drain well before adding to the pan with the courgettes and red pepper. Replace the pork sausage with chicken or turkey sausage.

Sausage, Egg and Vegetable Casserole

PORK CHOPS BAKED WITH CABBAGE AND CREAM
490 calories, 11 g carbs

- **1 small head (685 g/1½ lb) green cabbage, cored and finely shredded**
- **4 pork chops (170 g/6 oz each), 2 cm/¾ in thick**
- **½ teaspoon salt**
- **¼ teaspoon ground black pepper**
- **2 teaspoons olive oil**
- **120 ml/4 fl oz single cream**
- **1 teaspoon caraway seeds**
- **½ teaspoon sweet Hungarian paprika**
- **1 teaspoon dried marjoram or thyme**
- **60 g/2 oz Jarlsberg cheese, grated**

Preheat the oven to 180°C/350°F/gas 4.

Bring a large saucepan of salted water to the boil over high heat. Add the cabbage and cook until tender, 4 to 5 minutes. Drain in a colander and dry it well with kitchen paper.

Season the meat with ¼ teaspoon of the salt and the pepper. Heat the oil in a large, heavy ovenproof pan over high heat. Add the meat and cook just until browned, 1 to 2 minutes. Remove to a plate.

Discard any fat in the pan and heat over low heat. Stir in the cabbage, cream, caraway seeds, paprika, marjoram or thyme and the remaining ¼ teaspoon salt. Cook and stir until heated through, about 1 minute. Remove from the heat and arrange the pork over the cabbage, adding any juices accumulated on the plate. Sprinkle with the cheese. Place in the oven until a meat thermometer registers 70°C/160°F, about 25 minutes.

Makes 4 servings

Per serving: energy 490 cals/2038 kJ; protein 50 g; carbohydrate 11 g (of which 0 g sugars); fat 19 g (of which 9 g saturates); fibre 4 g; sodium 403 mg

Diet Exchanges: 0 milk, 2½ vegetable, 0 fruit, 0 bread, 7 meat, 3½ fat

CANNELLINI BEANS WITH HAM AND SAUSAGE
511 calories, 29 g carbs

170 g/6 oz dried cannellini beans, soaked in 850 ml/1½ pints water overnight

2 whole cloves

1 large onion, peeled

4 smoked ham hocks (about 230 g/ 8 oz each) or 1 small bacon joint (about 750 g/1 lb 10 oz)

2 large celery sticks, halved, or ¼ fennel bulb

1 bay leaf

1 tablespoon olive oil

340 g/12 oz mild Italian salami, casing removed and meat cut into 2–3 cm/1 in pieces

3 garlic cloves, finely chopped

½ teaspoon dried rosemary, crumbled

115 g/4 oz tinned chopped tomatoes

¼ teaspoon ground black pepper

30 g/1 oz Parmesan cheese, grated

Drain the beans. Insert the cloves into the onion. In a large pan, combine the beans, onion, ham or bacon, celery or fennel and bay leaf. Add enough water to cover the ingredients by 8 cm/3 in. Bring to the boil, reduce the heat to low and skim the froth from the surface. Cover and cook until the beans are tender but not mushy, 1¼ to 1½

hours. Remove the meat to a plate and let cool. Discard the onion, celery and bay leaf. Drain the beans, reserving 450 ml/15 fl oz cooking liquid.

Remove the meat from the bones and cut into bite-size pieces. Discard the skin, fat and bone.

Rinse out the pan and add the oil. Heat over medium-high heat and add the salami. Cook, stirring occasionally, until browned, 2 to 3 minutes. Stir in the ham, garlic and rosemary and cook for 1 minute. Stir in the tomatoes and cook, stirring occasionally, for 2 minutes. Add the beans and 180 ml/6 fl oz of the reserved cooking liquid (refrigerate any remaining liquid and use it to re-heat leftovers). Cook, stirring occasionally, until thickened, 10 to 12 minutes. Season with the pepper.

Preheat the oven to 220°C/425°F/gas 7. Spoon the mixture into a large, shallow ovenproof dish coated with cooking spray and sprinkle with the cheese. Bake until lightly browned, 15 to 20 minutes.

Makes 4 servings

Per serving: energy 511 cals/2125 kJ; protein 37 g; carbohydrate 29 g (of which 2 g sugars); fat 27 g (of which 9 g saturates); fibre 8 g; sodium 677 mg

Diet Exchanges: 0 milk, 1 vegetable, 0 fruit, 1½ bread, 3½ meat, 3½ fat

HAM AND LENTIL CASSEROLE
307 calories, 26 g carbs

- **2 tablespoons olive oil**
- **I large onion, chopped**
- **2 celery sticks, thinly sliced**
- **I large green pepper, chopped**
- **2 garlic cloves, finely chopped**
- **455 g/I lb boneless smoked or cured ham, cut into 4 cm/I½ in cubes**
- **700 ml/I¼ pints chicken stock**
- **200 g/7 oz dried lentils, rinsed and drained**
- **115 g/4 oz tinned chopped tomatoes**
- **I½ teaspoons Hungarian paprika**
- **I teaspoon dried oregano or thyme**
- **I bay leaf**
- **¼ teaspoon ground black pepper**

Preheat the oven to 180°C/350°F/gas 4.

Heat the oil in a large, heavy ovenproof pan over medium-high heat. Add the onion, celery, pepper and garlic. Cook, stirring occasionally, just until softened, about 5 minutes. Add the ham and cook, stirring occasionally, for 2 minutes. Reduce the heat to medium-low and stir in 600 ml/1 pint of the stock, the lentils, tomatoes, paprika, oregano or thyme, bay leaf and black pepper. Bring to a simmer. Cover and place in the oven until the lentils are tender and almost all of the liquid has been absorbed, 30 to 40 minutes, adding more stock as necessary. Remove the bay leaf before serving.

Makes 6 servings

Per serving: energy 307 cals/1277 kJ; protein 27 g; carbohydrate 26 g (of which 0 g sugars); fat 8 g (of which 2 g saturates); fibre 7 g; sodium 775 mg

Diet Exchanges: 0 milk, I vegetable, 0 fruit, I½ bread, 2½ meat, I½ fat

▶Flavour Tips
Substitute smoked or cured sausage for the ham. Stir in a large handful of coarsely chopped fresh parsley. Top with 45 g/1½ oz crumbled feta or goat's cheese before serving.

AUBERGINE PARMESAN
229 calories, 15 g carbs

2 aubergines (455 g/1 lb each), peeled and sliced lengthwise into 5 mm/¼ in thick slices

3 tablespoons olive oil

½ teaspoon salt

1 tin (400 g/14 oz) chopped tomatoes

1½ tablespoons tomato puree

1 teaspoon dried basil or 3 large fresh leaves, chopped

½ teaspoon dried rosemary, crumbled

¼ teaspoon ground black pepper

115 g/4 oz mozzarella or fontina cheese, grated

60 g/2 oz Parmesan cheese, grated

Preheat the grill.

Place the aubergine slices on a large baking tray and brush both sides with the oil (work in batches if necessary). Sprinkle with ¼ teaspoon of the salt. Grill until just beginning to brown, 2 to 3 minutes each side.

Preheat the oven to 190°C/375°F/gas 5.

In a saucepan, combine the tomatoes, tomato puree, basil and rosemary. Cook over medium-low heat, stirring occasionally, until slightly thickened, about 15 minutes. Season with the remaining ¼ teaspoon salt and the pepper.

Spread a layer of the tomato mixture over the bottom of a large ovenproof dish. Add a layer of aubergine and top with another layer of the tomato mixture. Sprinkle with a thin layer of the mozzarella or fontina and the Parmesan. Continue making 2 more layers with the remaining aubergine, tomato mixture and cheeses, ending with a thick layer of cheeses. Bake until bubbling, 25 to 30 minutes. Let rest for 10 minutes before cutting.

Makes 6 servings

Per serving: energy 229 cals/952 kJ; protein 10 g; carbohydrate 15 g (of which 2 g sugars); fat 15 g (of which 5 g saturates); fibre 4 g; sodium 591 mg

Diet Exchanges: 0 milk, 3 vegetable, 0 fruit, 0 bread, 1 meat, 2 fat

▶Flavour Tips

Substitute 60 g/2 oz grated Jarlsberg for 60 g/2 oz of the mozzarella cheese. For a smooth sauce, puree the tomatoes in a food mill or food processor. Use the aubergines peeled or unpeeled.

I Did It!

Janet Lasky

When a 6-year-old boy came into Janet's life, she turned herself around, made a commitment to health, and lost 70 kg/11 st.

before

'I had a compulsive eating disorder from the age of 5. I constantly ate foods high in fat and sugar. It's no surprise that I was overweight for most of my life. I tipped the scales at over 134 kg/21 st before I turned my life around.

'It wasn't until I adopted a 6-year-old boy that I started down the road to recovery. He came into my life and taught me about love. My desire to live long enough to raise my son pushed me to seek help. The answer to my prayers came from an outpatient eating disorder programme at a nearby hospital. During the 4 years that I participated in the programme, I developed the important foundations of self-love and responsibility that are still a part of my life today. I also became more aware of myself and my eating disorder.

Weight lost: 70 kg/11 st
Time kept off: 8 years
Weight-loss strategies: avoided sugar, wheat, yeast, milk and fermented foods; controlled food sensitivities

Weight-maintenance strategies: maintains low-sugar diet, avoids sensitive foods, walks, takes spinning and aerobics classes several days a week

'When I left the outpatient programme, I wanted to do all that I could to be as healthy as possible. With the assistance of a nutritionist, I was able to identify which foods were best for me. I discovered that I felt best when I avoided wheat, sugar, yeast, milk, fermented products, nuts, dried fruit, corn and a few other foods. Instead, I focused on eating vegetables, lean protein-based foods, beans and occasionally fresh fruit.

'In 8 years, I lost 70 kg/11 st and I now feel wonderful. My doctor has discontinued my blood pressure medication; my blood sugars are within the normal range despite my being diagnosed with diabetes years ago; and unlike the results of earlier readings, my cholesterol is now well within healthy limits.

I owe much of my good health to my new eating habits, but I also exercise about 5 days a week. I take nutritional supplements, get enough sleep, drink plenty of pure water and I play as often as I can. I have a rich spiritual life, too, which helps me to overcome life's challenges in a positive and healthy way.

'What I like best about this new lifestyle is that I don't ever feel deprived. I enjoy preparing and eating a wide variety of foods. I've discovered delicious substitutes for the foods I used to eat. And now I can truly enjoy life with my son.'

JANET'S ROASTED AUBERGINE AND CHICKPEAS
231 calories, 26 g carbs

- **3–4 tablespoons olive oil**
- **1 garlic clove, finely chopped**
- **3 tablespoons tomato-based pasta sauce**
- **1 teaspoon ground cumin**
- **¼ teaspoon salt**
- **¼ teaspoon ground black pepper**
- **1 aubergine (455 g/1 lb), cubed**
- **1 tin (400 g/14 oz) chickpeas, rinsed and drained**
- **1 onion, cut into 2–3 cm/1 in chunks**
- **1 red or yellow pepper, cut into 2–3 cm/1 in chunks**

Preheat the oven to 180°C/350°F/gas 4.

In a large resealable plastic bag, combine 3 tablespoons of the oil, the garlic, pasta sauce, cumin, salt and pepper. Add the aubergine, chickpeas, onion and pepper. Toss to coat evenly. Pour into a large ovenproof dish and bake, stirring occasionally, until the aubergine is soft and the onions are browned, about 45 minutes. If the mixture becomes dry, add 1 tablespoon more oil. Serve warm or at room temperature.

Makes 4 servings

Per serving: energy 231 cals/960 kJ; protein 6 g; carbohydrate 26 g (of which 2 g sugars); fat 12 g (of which 1 g saturates); fibre 7 g; sodium 370 mg

Diet Exchanges: 0 milk, 2 vegetable, 0 fruit, 1 bread, 0 meat, 2 fat

Old-Fashioned Lamb Stew

OLD-FASHIONED LAMB STEW
341 calories, 14 g carbs

- **1½ tablespoons olive oil**
- **1 large onion, chopped**
- **685 g/1½ lb boneless lamb shoulder or neck, trimmed of fat, cut into 4 cm/1½ in cubes**
- **¼ teaspoon salt**
- **¼ teaspoon ground black pepper**
- **2 tablespoons wholemeal flour**
- **1 garlic clove, finely chopped**
- **600–700 ml/1–1¼ pints chicken stock**
- **1 tablespoon tomato puree**
- **1 teaspoon dried thyme**
- **1 teaspoon dried rosemary**
- **1 bay leaf**
- **3 carrots, quartered lengthwise where thick, and then into 2–3 cm/1 in lengths**

Preheat the oven to 180°C/350°F/gas 4.

Heat 1 tablespoon of the oil in a large, heavy ovenproof pan over medium heat. Add the onion and cook, stirring occasionally, until slightly browned, about 5 minutes. Scrape the onion onto a plate and remove the pan from the heat.

Season the lamb with the salt and pepper. Return the pan to the hob and heat the remaining 1½ teaspoons oil over medium-high heat. Add the lamb and cook until browned on all sides, 8 to 10 minutes.

Return the onion to the pan and sprinkle with the flour and garlic. Cook, stirring, for 2 minutes. Stir in 600 ml/1 pint of the stock and the tomato puree, adding more stock as necessary. Bring to the boil and stir in the thyme, rosemary and bay leaf.

Cover and place in the oven for 1 hour. Stir in the carrots. Cover and cook until the meat and vegetables are tender, 30 to 40 minutes. If the sauce seems thick, thin it with 2 to 4 tablespoons hot chicken stock. Remove the bay leaf and serve.

Makes 4 servings

Per serving: energy 341 cals/1418 kJ; protein 33 g; carbohydrate 14 g (of which 2 g sugars); fat 17 g (of which 6 g saturates); fibre 4 g; sodium 740 mg

Diet Exchanges: 0 milk, 1½ vegetable, 0 fruit, 0 bread, 4½ meat, 1½ fat

▶Flavour Tips
Substitute parsnips or chopped turnip for the carrots.
Substitute 120 ml/4 fl oz dry Marsala or Madeira for 120 ml/4 fl oz of the stock.
Add 115 g/4 oz peas (thawed if frozen) or tinned flageolet or haricot beans (rinsed and drained) during the last 3 to 5 minutes of cooking. Serve sprinkled with 1 tablespoon chopped fresh parsley or dill.

Lamb Shanks with Red Beans
580 calories, 22 g carbs

240 ml/8 fl oz red wine or beef stock

2 tablespoons tomato puree

120 ml/4 fl oz hot water

4 lamb shanks (455 g/1 lb each)

½ teaspoon salt

¼ teaspoon ground black pepper

2 tablespoons olive oil

1 large onion, chopped

3 garlic cloves, finely chopped

2 teaspoons chopped fresh thyme or 1 teaspoon dried

2 bay leaves

115 g/4 oz dried red kidney beans, soaked overnight in 500 ml/ 18 fl oz water

700 ml/1¼ pints water

Preheat the oven to 170°C/325°F/gas 3.

In a small saucepan, bring the wine or stock to the boil over medium heat. Cook until reduced to 60 ml/2 fl oz, 8 to 10 minutes. Stir in the tomato puree and water.

Season the lamb with the salt and pepper. Heat 1 tablespoon of the oil in a large, heavy ovenproof pan over high heat. Working in batches, add the meat and cook until browned, 2 to 3 minutes per batch or 10 to 12 minutes total. Remove to a plate as cooking is done.

Pour off the fat and add the remaining 1 tablespoon oil. Reduce the heat to medium and stir in the onion and garlic. Cook, stirring occasionally, just until the onion begins to turn translucent, about 5 minutes.

Return the lamb to the pan. Stir in the wine mixture, thyme and 1 of the bay leaves. Bring to a simmer, cover and cook in the oven, turning the lamb once or twice, until tender, 1½ to 1¾ hours.

Meanwhile, drain the beans, place them in a small saucepan and add the water and the remaining bay leaf. Bring to the boil, reduce the heat, cover and cook just until tender, about 1 hour.

Remove the lamb from the pan. Skim and discard the fat from the surface of the liquid in the pan and discard the bay leaf. Return the lamb to the pan. Drain the beans, remove the bay leaf and add the beans to the meat. Cover and cook 5 minutes more.

Makes 4 servings

Per serving: energy 580 cals/2412 kJ; protein 63 g; carbohydrate 22 g (of which 0 g sugars); fat 19 g (of which 5 g saturates); fibre 7 g; sodium 423 mg

Diet Exchanges: 0 milk, 1 vegetable, 0 fruit, 1 bread, 8½ meat, 3½ fat

SPICY CURRIED VEGETABLES
183 calories, 28 g carbs

2 tablespoons vegetable oil

1 onion, chopped

2 garlic cloves, finely chopped

1 tablespoon finely chopped fresh ginger

¼–½ teaspoon dried chilli flakes

2 teaspoons curry powder

½ teaspoon ground cumin

½ teaspoon ground coriander seeds (optional)

240–350 ml/8–12 fl oz vegetable stock

1 small cauliflower (685 g/1½ lb), cut into 4 cm/1½ in florets

2 small red potatoes (90 g/3 oz each), cut into 2–3 cm/1 in cubes

170 g/6 oz French beans, halved

115 g/4 oz tinned chopped tomatoes

115 g/4 oz low-fat natural yoghurt (optional)

Heat the oil in a deep, large pan over low to medium heat. Stir in the onion, garlic, ginger and chilli flakes. Cook the mixture, stirring occasionally, until the onion is slightly softened, 2 to 3 minutes.

Add the curry powder, cumin and coriander (if using). Cook, stirring, for 30 seconds. Stir in 240 ml/8 fl oz of the stock, the cauliflower, potatoes, beans and tomatoes. Cover and cook over medium heat until the vegetables are tender, stirring occasionally and adding up to 120 ml/4 fl oz stock as needed, 20 to 25 minutes.

There should be 2 to 3 tablespoons of thin sauce in the pan. Remove from the heat and gently stir in the yoghurt (if using).

Makes 4 servings

Per serving: energy 183 cals/761 kJ; protein 6 g; carbohydrate 28 g (of which 3 g sugars); fat 6 g (of which 1 g saturates); fibre 7 g; sodium 412 mg

Diet Exchanges: 0 milk, 3½ vegetable, 0 fruit, ½ bread, 0 meat, 1½ fat

▶Flavour Tips

Top each serving with 1 tablespoon chopped fresh coriander. Add 75 g/2½ oz of frozen peas during the last 5 minutes of cooking time. Substitute turnips for the potatoes. Serve with brown rice.

Moussaka

392 calories, 16 g carbs

1 tablespoon olive oil

1 large onion, chopped

2–3 garlic cloves, finely chopped

750 g/1 lb 10 oz minced lamb

1 tin (400 g/14 oz) chopped tomatoes

1½ teaspoons dried oregano

1 teaspoon ground allspice

1 teaspoon salt

½ teaspoon ground black pepper

2 aubergines (455 g/1 lb each), peeled and sliced lengthwise into 5 mm/¼ in thick slices

3 large eggs, at room temperature

240 ml/8 fl oz single cream, at room temperature

60 g/2 oz feta cheese, finely crumbled

45 g/1½ oz Parmesan cheese, grated

⅛ teaspoon ground nutmeg (optional)

Heat the oil in a large frying pan over medium heat. Add the onion and cook, stirring occasionally, until softened and lightly browned, 6 to 8 minutes. Stir in the garlic and lamb. Increase the heat to medium-high and cook, stirring to crumble, just until no longer pink, 7 to 8 minutes. Drain the excess fat. Stir in the tomatoes, oregano, allspice, ½ teaspoon of the salt and ¼ teaspoon of the pepper. Reduce the heat to very low. Partially cover and cook until very thick, 25 to 30 minutes.

Meanwhile, preheat the grill. Place the aubergine slices on a large baking tray and generously coat both sides with cooking spray (work in batches if necessary). Sprinkle with the remaining ½ teaspoon salt and ⅛ teaspoon of the remaining pepper. Grill until just beginning to brown, 2 to 3 minutes each side.

In a bowl, lightly beat the eggs and cream. Stir in the feta, Parmesan, nutmeg (if using) and the remaining ⅛ teaspoon pepper.

Preheat the oven to 180°C/350°F/gas 4. Arrange a layer of aubergine in a large, shallow ovenproof dish. Top with a layer of the meat mixture. Add another layer of aubergine, another layer of the meat mixture and top with a layer of aubergine. Poke several holes through the layers with a fork. Pour the cream mixture evenly over the top. Bake until the egg is set and lightly browned, 30 to 35 minutes. Let stand 15 to 20 minutes before cutting and serving.

Makes 8 servings

Per serving: energy 392 cals/1630 kJ; protein 27 g; carbohydrate 16 g (of which 1 g sugars); fat 21 g (of which 4 g saturates); fibre 4 g; sodium 574 mg

Diet Exchanges: 0 milk, 3 vegetable, 0 fruit, 0 bread, 3 meat, 3 fat

Time-Saver

This Greek-style dish keeps well. Make it ahead or store extra portions in a covered container in the refrigerator for up to 2 days. To reheat, place in an ovenproof dish, cover and bake at 180°C/350°F/gas 4 until heated through, about 25 minutes.

casseroles and one-dish dinners

SHEPHERD'S PIE

412 calories, 25 g carbs

- **4–5 potatoes (455 g/1 lb), peeled and chopped**
- **2–3 small turnips (230 g/8 oz), peeled and chopped**
- **2 tablespoons olive oil**
- **1 large onion, chopped**
- **2 large garlic cloves, finely chopped**
- **685 g/1½ lb minced lamb**
- **1 tin (400 g/14 oz) chopped tomatoes**
- **120 ml/4 fl oz chicken stock**
- **1½ teaspoons dried thyme or oregano**
- **1 bay leaf**
- **½ teaspoon salt**
- **½ teaspoon ground black pepper**
- **80 ml/3 fl oz semi-skimmed milk**
- **30 g/1 oz butter**
- **30 g/1 oz pecorino cheese, grated (optional)**

Fill a large saucepan with salted water. Add the potatoes and turnips and bring to the boil over high heat. Reduce the heat to medium-low, cover and cook until tender, 15 to 20 minutes.

Meanwhile, heat the oil in a large, heavy ovenproof pan over medium heat. Add the onion and cook, stirring occasionally, until translucent and slightly browned, 5 to 6 minutes. Add the garlic and lamb and cook, stirring to crumble, just until the lamb is no longer pink, 3 to 4 minutes. Drain off and discard the fat from the pan. Stir in the tomatoes, stock, thyme, bay leaf, salt and ¼ teaspoon of the pepper. Reduce the heat to low and cook, stirring occasionally, until very thick, 25 to 30 minutes. Keep warm.

In a small saucepan, combine the milk and butter. Heat over low heat until the butter is melted. Drain the potato-turnip mixture and return it to the pan. Mash, gradually adding the milk mixture, until smooth and fluffy. Season with the remaining ¼ teaspoon pepper.

Discard the bay leaf from the meat mixture. Spread the mashed potatoes over the meat and serve. Or sprinkle with the cheese (if using) and grill until lightly browned, 2 to 3 minutes, before serving.

Makes 6 servings

Per serving: energy 412 cals/1713 kJ; protein 24 g; carbohydrate 25 g (of which 0 g sugars); fat 21 g (of which 10 g saturates); fibre 4 g; sodium 600 mg

Diet Exchanges: 0 milk, 2 vegetable, 0 fruit, 1 bread, 2½ meat, 3 fat

▶Flavour Tips

Substitute minced beef for the lamb. Add thawed frozen peas (285 g/10 oz) to the meat mixture during the last 5 minutes of cooking.

Shepherd's Pie

vegetables
& side dishes

COURGETTES AND RED PEPPERS IN LEMON-HERB BUTTER 302

MUSHROOMS PROVENÇALE 303

BUTTERBEANS WITH BACON 304

BAKED PEPPERS WITH ONION AND TOMATO 305

ASPARAGUS WITH ORANGE-WALNUT VINAIGRETTE 307

ROASTED CAULIFLOWER WITH NUTTY LEMON MUSTARD 308

CABBAGE SALAD WITH APPLES, LIME AND GINGER 309

CREAMED CABBAGE 310

RED CABBAGE WITH APPLES 311

SPINACH SALAD WITH WARM BACON VINAIGRETTE 313

WATERCRESS SALAD WITH GOAT'S CHEESE, PINE NUTS AND PEARS 314

NORMA'S SPINACH SALAD WITH CAJUN CHICKEN 318

TOSSED SALAD WITH GREEN HERB DRESSING 319

TOMATO-ONION SALAD WITH WALNUT VINAIGRETTE 320

CUCUMBER AND RADISH SALAD WITH SESAME-SOY DRESSING 321

SPANISH-STYLE GREEN BEANS 322

FLAGEOLET BEANS WITH SESAME OIL AND GINGER 323

COUSCOUS SALAD WITH LIME-CUMIN DRESSING 324

POLENTA BAKE WITH CHEESE AND CHILLIES 326

QUINOA AND VEGETABLE PILAF 327

BROWN RICE PILAF WITH HAZELNUTS 328

COURGETTES AND RED PEPPERS IN LEMON-HERB BUTTER

109 calories, 6 g carbs

- **6 small courgettes (685 g/1½ lb), sliced 1 cm/½ in thick**
- **½ red pepper, chopped**
- **45 g/1½ oz butter**
- **2 tablespoons chicken stock**
- **¼ teaspoon salt**
- **⅛ teaspoon ground black pepper**
- **2 teaspoons grated lemon zest**
- **1 tablespoon lemon juice**
- **2 tablespoons finely chopped fresh parsley**

In a large frying pan, combine the courgettes, red pepper, butter, stock, salt and black pepper. Cover and cook, over medium heat, until steam comes from the pan, about 3 minutes. Uncover and raise the heat to medium-high. Cook, stirring occasionally, until the vegetables are tender but intact and practically no liquid remains in the pan, 8 to 10 minutes. Stir in the lemon zest and juice. Remove from the heat and stir in the parsley.

Makes 4 servings

Per serving: energy 109 cals/453 kJ; protein 2 g; carbohydrate 6 g (of which 0 g sugars); fat 8 g (of which 2 g saturates); fibre 3 g; sodium 265 mg

Diet Exchanges: 0 milk, 1 vegetable, 0 fruit, 0 bread, 0 meat, 2 fat

▶Flavour Tips

Substitute marrow for the courgettes or use half marrow and half courgettes. Stir in 2 teaspoons chopped fresh basil with the parsley. Or add a pinch of dried chilli flakes.

MUSHROOMS PROVENÇALE
113 calories, 5 g carbs

20 mushrooms, thickly sliced

2 tablespoons olive oil

15 g/½ oz butter

4 spring onions, white part only, finely chopped

2 garlic cloves, finely chopped

2–3 teaspoons lemon juice

¼ teaspoon salt

⅛ teaspoon ground black pepper

2 tablespoons finely chopped fresh parsley

Place the mushrooms in a large frying pan. Cover and cook over medium-high heat until the mushrooms start to give off moisture, 5 to 6 minutes. Uncover and cook until they begin to stick to the pan. Reduce the heat to low and stir in the oil, butter, spring onions, garlic and lemon juice. Cook for 30 seconds, season with the salt and pepper and serve sprinkled with the parsley.

Makes 4 servings

Per serving: energy 113 cals/470 kJ; protein 3 g; carbohydrate 5 g (of which 1 g sugars); fat 9 g (of which 3 g saturates); fibre 2 g; sodium 171 mg

Diet Exchanges: 0 milk, 1 vegetable, 0 fruit, 0 bread, 0 meat, 2 fat

BUTTERBEANS WITH BACON
151 calories, 16 g carbs

2 rashers streaky bacon

I small onion, thinly sliced

I carrot, finely chopped

285 g/10 oz tinned, drained butterbeans

4 tablespoons water

½ teaspoon dried marjoram or thyme

⅛ teaspoon salt

Pinch of ground black pepper

Cook the bacon in a frying pan over medium-low heat, turning occasionally, until browned and crisp, 6 to 8 minutes. Drain on a kitchen paper-lined plate and cover with foil to keep warm. Reserve the bacon fat in the pan.

Add the onion and carrot to the pan. Cover and cook, stirring occasionally, until the onion is lightly golden and almost tender, 6 to 8 minutes. Stir in the beans, water, marjoram or thyme, salt and pepper. Cover and cook until the beans are heated through, 5 minutes. Uncover and, if any water remains in the pan, increase the heat to medium and cook until evaporated, 1 to 2 minutes, stirring once or twice. Serve with the bacon crumbled over the top.

Makes 4 servings

Per serving: energy 151 cals/628 kJ; protein 7 g; carbohydrate 16 g (of which 0 g sugars); fat 6 g (of which 2 g saturates); fibre 5 g; sodium 221 mg

Diet Exchanges: 0 milk, ½ vegetable, 0 fruit, I bread, 0 meat, I½ fat

▶Flavour Tips

Substitute 2 to 3 chopped spring onions for the onion. You could also omit the bacon and use 30 g/1 oz butter in place of the bacon fat.

BAKED PEPPERS WITH ONION AND TOMATO

120 calories, 7 g carbs

2 large red peppers, halved lengthwise and seeded

1 large tomato, cut into 4 slices

1 small red onion, thinly sliced

1 large garlic clove, cut lengthwise into 8 thin slices

2 anchovy fillets, halved (optional)

½ teaspoon dried oregano

¼ teaspoon salt

⅛ teaspoon ground black pepper

3 tablespoons olive oil

Preheat the oven to 220°C/425°F/gas 7.

Place the peppers, hollow side up, on a baking tray. Place a tomato slice in each cavity. Top with 1 or 2 slices of onion, 2 slices of garlic and an anchovy half (if using). Sprinkle with the oregano, salt and black pepper. Drizzle with the oil. Roast just until tender, 25 to 30 minutes. Serve warm or at room temperature and top with any oil left in the pan.

Makes 4 servings

Per serving: energy 120 cals/499 kJ; protein 1 g; carbohydrate 7 g (of which 2 g sugars); fat 9 g (of which 1 g saturates); fibre 2 g; sodium 145 mg

Diet Exchanges: 0 milk, 1½ vegetable, 0 fruit, 0 bread, 0 meat, 2 fat

Time-Saver

Make extra portions and serve for lunch with cheese and rye crackers. Store in a covered container in the refrigerator for up to 3 days and serve at room temperature.

Asparagus with Orange-Walnut Vinaigrette

ASPARAGUS WITH ORANGE-WALNUT VINAIGRETTE
110 calories, 4 g carbs

¼ teaspoon salt

1 bunch (455 g/1 lb) asparagus, ends trimmed

5 teaspoons cider vinegar

2 tablespoons walnut or olive oil

2 teaspoons grated orange zest

⅛ teaspoon ground black pepper

2 tablespoons walnuts, coarsely chopped

Pour water to 1 cm/½ in deep in a large frying pan. Add half of the salt and bring to the boil over high heat. Add the asparagus and cook, until tender-firm, 4 to 7 minutes. Drain in a colander and cool under cold running water. Drain and place on a kitchen paper-lined plate to dry.

In a small bowl, whisk the vinegar, oil, orange zest, pepper and remaining salt. Place the asparagus in a serving dish, spoon the vinaigrette over the top and sprinkle with the nuts. Serve at room temperature or chilled.

Makes 4 servings

Per serving: energy 110 cals/457 kJ; protein 3 g; carbohydrate 4 g (of which 2 g sugars); fat 11 g (of which 1 g saturates); fibre 2 g; sodium 175 mg

Diet Exchanges: 0 milk, 1 vegetable, 0 fruit, 0 bread, 0 meat, 2 fat

▶Flavour Tip
Lightly toast the nuts to bring out their best flavour and texture.

ROASTED CAULIFLOWER WITH NUTTY LEMON MUSTARD

230 calories, 13 g carbs

1 small head cauliflower, cut into small florets

3 tablespoons walnut or olive oil

⅛ teaspoon salt

1 tablespoon lemon juice

1 tablespoon Dijon mustard

80 ml/3 fl oz single cream

90 g/3 oz toasted walnuts, coarsely chopped

⅛ teaspoon ground black pepper

Preheat the oven to 230°C/450°F/gas 8.

In a roasting pan, toss the cauliflower with 2 tablespoons of the oil and the salt. Roast until tender and lightly browned, stirring once or twice, 15 to 20 minutes.

In a large bowl, whisk together the lemon juice, mustard, cream and remaining 1 tablespoon oil. Add the cauliflower, scraping any residual oil into the bowl. Add the nuts and pepper and toss to coat. Serve warm.

Makes 4 servings

Per serving: energy 230 cals/956 kJ; protein 5 g; carbohydrate 13 g (of which 1 g sugars); fat 18 g (of which 3 g saturates); fibre 4 g; sodium 225 mg

Diet Exchanges: 0 milk, 2 vegetable, 0 fruit, 0 bread, ½ meat, 3½ fat

▶Flavour Tips

Replace the walnuts with pecans or hazelnuts. Serve topped with 1 teaspoon of chopped fresh oregano leaves. Or serve on a bed of watercress.

CABBAGE SALAD WITH APPLES, LIME AND GINGER
155 calories, 15 g carbs

- **2 tablespoons rice vinegar**
- **4 tablespoons lime juice**
- **1 teaspoon grated, peeled fresh ginger**
- **4 tablespoons walnut or vegetable oil**
- **½ teaspoon celery seed**
- **¼ teaspoon salt**
- **⅛ teaspoon ground black pepper**
- **230 g/8 oz (about ¼ head) green cabbage, shredded**
- **2 large sweet apples (340 g/12 oz), unpeeled and cut into matchsticks**

In a large bowl, whisk the vinegar, lime juice and ginger. Gradually whisk in the oil, celery seed, salt and pepper. Add the cabbage and apples. Gently toss to coat. Refrigerate for 30 minutes before serving.

Makes 6 servings

Per serving: energy 155 cals/644 kJ; protein 1 g; carbohydrate 15 g (of which 10 g sugars); fat 8 g (of which 2 g saturates); fibre 4 g; sodium 100 mg

Diet Exchanges: 0 milk, ½ vegetable, ½ fruit, 0 bread, 0 meat, 2 fat

Smart-Carb Insider Tip
BE WARY OF SALAD

It's not hard to go astray at a salad bar. A little of this and a little of that and before you know it you may have piled on 30 or 40 grams of carbohydrate. Bacon bits and cheese may be imitation and higher in carbs than you think. Skip the prepared salads. Instead, choose fresh, plain vegetables, olives, nuts, sunflower seeds, beans and chickpeas. Choose an oil and vinegar-style dressing unless the bottles are out and you can read the labels. Remember that low-fat dressings are often higher in sugar content.

CREAMED CABBAGE
109 calories, 8 g carbs

340 g/12 oz (about ½ small head) green cabbage, shredded

80 ml/3 fl oz water

150 ml/5 fl oz single cream

15 g/½ oz butter

½ teaspoon dried dill

¼ teaspoon salt

⅛ teaspoon ground black pepper

Pinch of ground nutmeg

Place the cabbage and water in a large, deep frying pan. Cook over medium-high heat, stirring occasionally, until the cabbage is somewhat softened and the water has evaporated, 12 to 13 minutes.

Reduce the heat to low, stir in the cream, butter and dill. Cover and cook until the cabbage is tender, about 15 minutes, stirring occasionally. Season with the salt, pepper and nutmeg.

Makes 4 servings

Per serving: energy 109 cals/453 kJ; protein 4 g; carbohydrate 8 g (of which 0 g sugars); fat 6 g (of which 3 g saturates); fibre 3 g; sodium 200 mg

Diet Exchanges: 0 milk, 1½ vegetable, 0 fruit, 0 bread, 0 meat, 1½ fat

Time-Saver

Make this dish ahead and store in a covered container in the refrigerator for up to 3 days. To re-heat, place in a pan and add 1 to 2 tablespoons water. Cover and cook over low heat, stirring occasionally, until heated through, 3 to 4 minutes.

RED CABBAGE WITH APPLES
120 calories, 16 g carbs

2 tablespoons walnut oil

340 g/12 oz (about ½ small head) red cabbage, shredded

80 ml/3 fl oz apple juice or cider

1 large Granny Smith or other tart apple, peeled and coarsely chopped

2 tablespoons red wine vinegar or other vinegar

¾ teaspoon dried thyme

¼ teaspoon ground allspice

¼ teaspoon salt

⅛ teaspoon ground black pepper

Heat the oil in a large, deep frying pan over medium-low heat. Stir in the cabbage and cook, stirring occasionally, until it begins to wilt, 5 to 6 minutes. Stir in the apple juice or cider, the apple, vinegar, thyme and allspice. Cover and cook over low heat until the cabbage is very tender, 25 to 30 minutes, stirring occasionally. Season with the salt and pepper.

Makes 4 servings

Per serving: energy 120 cals/499 kJ; protein 2 g; carbohydrate 16 g (of which 5 g sugars); fat 6 g (of which 1 g saturates); fibre 4 g; sodium 156 mg

Diet Exchanges: 0 milk, 1 vegetable, ½ fruit, 0 bread, 0 meat, 1½ fat

Time-Saver

Make this German-style dish ahead and store in a covered container in the refrigerator for up to 5 days. To reheat, place in a saucepan and add 1 to 2 tablespoons water. Cover and cook over low heat, stirring occasionally, until heated through, 3 to 4 minutes.

Spinach Salad with Warm Bacon Vinaigrette

Spinach Salad with Warm Bacon Vinaigrette
210 calories, 7 g carbs

- **3 rashers streaky bacon**
- **2–3 tablespoons walnut or olive oil**
- **2 tablespoons red wine vinegar or other vinegar**
- **1 teaspoon Dijon mustard (optional)**
- **1 small garlic clove, finely chopped**
- **⅛ teaspoon salt**
- **⅛ teaspoon ground black pepper**
- **285 g/10 oz young spinach leaves**
- **1 eating apple (115 g/4 oz), peeled and cut into 1 cm/½ in pieces**
- **20 g/¾ oz Parmesan or pecorino cheese, shaved**

Cook the bacon in a frying pan over medium-low heat, turning occasionally until crisp and browned, 8 to 10 minutes. Drain on a kitchen paper-lined plate and keep warm. Measure the fat in the pan (there should be 2 to 3 tablespoons). Add enough oil to equal 5 tablespoons of total fat in the pan. Whisk the vinegar, mustard (if using), garlic, salt and pepper into the fat in the pan. Keep warm.

In a large bowl, combine the spinach and apple. Spoon the warm bacon vinaigrette over the spinach and apple. Toss to coat. Divide among 4 plates, crumble the bacon over the spinach and top with the cheese.

Makes 4 servings

Per serving: energy 210 cals/873 kJ; protein 5 g; carbohydrate 7 g (of which 2 g sugars); fat 17 g (of which 5 g saturates); fibre 2 g; sodium 350 mg

Diet Exchanges: 0 milk, ½ vegetable, ½ fruit, 0 bread, ½ meat, 3 fat

▶Flavour Tips
The cheese on this salad tastes best when cut into thin shavings rather than grated over the top. To cut a shaving of Parmesan or pecorino cheese, drag a vegetable peeler or cheese slicer along the broad side of the block of cheese to create thin slices about 2–3 cm/1 in wide and 5 cm/2 in long.
To make a main course salad, garnish each serving with 2 or 3 wedges of tomato, a few slices of hard-boiled egg and a slice of red onion. Or add cold, cooked chicken.

WATERCRESS SALAD WITH GOAT'S CHEESE, PINE NUTS AND PEARS

163 calories, 7 g carbs

90 g/3 oz log-type goat's cheese

1 tablespoon olive or walnut oil

2–3 tablespoons semi-skimmed milk

1 tablespoon lemon juice

⅛ teaspoon salt

⅛ teaspoon ground black pepper

2 large heads chicory, leaves separated and cut into 2–3 cm/ 1 in diagonal slices

1 large bunch watercress, chopped

2 tablespoons toasted pine nuts

½ large pear, cut into 1 cm/½ in cubes

Per serving: energy 163 cals/678 kJ; protein 7 g; carbohydrate 7 g (of which 1 g sugars); fat 11 g (of which 5 g saturates); fibre 2 g; sodium 203 mg

Diet Exchanges: 0 milk, 0 vegetable, ½ fruit, 0 bread, 1 meat, 2 fat

▶Flavour Tips

Substitute young spinach leaves or 1 large bunch rocket for the chicory. Substitute 2 kiwifruits for the pear. Keep the dressing refrigerated in a covered container for up to 5 days. Bring to room temperature before using.

In a blender, combine the cheese, oil, 2 tablespoons of the milk, the lemon juice, salt and pepper. Process until thickened and creamy, adding up to another tablespoon milk if too thick.

Place the chicory and watercress in a large salad bowl, add the cheese mixture and toss to combine. Divide among 4 plates. Sprinkle with the nuts and pear.

Makes 4 servings

Watercress Salad with Goat's Cheese, Pine Nuts and Pears

I Did It!

Norma Gates

Norma had been gaining 4.5 kg/10 lb a year. Before she knew it, she weighed 109 kg/17 st and wore a size 26. When her request for gastric bypass surgery was turned down, Norma became focused, ate a sensible low-carb diet, and lost nearly 20 kg/3 st in 8 months.

before

'With a steady weight gain of 4.5 kg/10 lb per year, I added larger- and larger-size clothes to my wardrobe each season. Before I knew it, I was wearing a size 26. I had gained 48 kg/ 7½ st over the course of 12 years.

'When I had only 13 kg/ 2 st to lose, I used to mentally beat myself up for not getting hold of my problem. After gaining 48 kg/7½ st, I desperately wanted a resolution. I even went to a surgeon with hopes that a gastric bypass,

Weight lost: 20 kg/3 st
Time kept off: 3½ years
Weight-loss strategies: reduced carb intake, reduced portion sizes, ate more slowly, stopped eating when full, walked regularly
Weight-maintenance strategies: maintains lower carb intake and smaller portion sizes, eats more slowly, stops eating when full, accepts gradual weight loss and continues to walk 3–5 days a week

which would cause food to bypass most of my stomach, would change my life. When the doctor told me I was not a surgical candidate because I didn't have any other medical problems, I was heartbroken.

'I remember how embarrassed I was while watching a video taken of me sitting in our garden. Sadly, even that didn't motivate me enough to start watching my food intake. I was overwhelmed by cravings for food. Even when I was away from home, I would count the minutes until I could get back to my refrigerator.

'Not understanding my carb "addiction" at that time, I could almost relate it to a person going through withdrawal from cigarette smoking.

'There came a point when I knew I'd have to do something about my eating behaviour. Psychological counselling didn't help. Finally, I consulted a dietitian.

'My dietitian took a comprehensive medical and diet history and immediately placed my 109-kg/17-st body on a low-carbohydrate eating plan. As soon as I started reading food labels, I realised what massive amounts of sugars and starches I was consuming. About 90 per cent of my diet was carbohydrate!

'Within 2 weeks of eating fewer carbs, I'd lost 5 kg/11 lb. A few weeks later – and 9.6 kg/1½ st lighter – I felt like I had broken my carbohydrate addiction. The food cravings finally subsided. I had more energy and I started walking five times a week for 2 to 3 miles each time.

'Over the next 5 months, I lost another 9.6 kg/1½ st. It is incredible how much better I felt. I can remember getting teary-eyed as I stood in front of a full-length mirror in my favourite department store admiring myself in a size 20 instead of a size 26. Extra attention from my husband and friends reinforced the excitement of being on the road to successful weight loss. Dropping below the 90-kg/14-st mark was another milestone.

'I no longer shop in the outsize departments. I can't even begin to tell someone what that feels like!

'My husband and I almost always split meals when we go out. It not only saves us calories (and carbs, especially in the breads and pastas that are so popular in restaurants), but it saves us money as well.

'If by chance I am not at my 68 kg/10 st 10 lb goal weight as you read this, it's OK with me – as long as I have not regained the weight. I have learned to accept my body at every stage along the way to my goal. My expectations are realistic. I do not have to be in a hurry. I am eating a variety of healthy and delicious foods, I have control over my portions, I have plenty of energy, and I have new-found pleasures in life besides just food.'

(continued)

vegetables and side dishes

I Did It! (cont.)

NORMA'S SPINACH SALAD WITH CAJUN CHICKEN

399 calories, 9 g carbs

**4 boneless, skinless chicken breasts
(170 g/6 oz each)**

1 tablespoon Cajun seasoning

2 rashers streaky bacon

**455 g/1 lb fresh spinach, washed and
torn**

½ cucumber, chopped

2 hard-boiled eggs, chopped

60 g/2 oz feta cheese, crumbled

30 g/1 oz wholewheat croutons

3 tablespoons sliced black olives

**2 tablespoons pecans, chopped,
or sunflower seeds**

**4 tablespoons bottled Italian vinai-
grette or other dressing**

Preheat the grill to high. Coat the grill rack
with cooking spray.

Place the chicken in a resealable bag.
Add the seasoning and shake to coat.
Transfer to the prepared grill rack and grill,
turning once, until the juices run clear and
a meat thermometer registers 70°C/160°F,
8 to 10 minutes. Cut into strips and set
aside.

Meanwhile, cook the bacon in a frying
pan over medium-low heat, turning
occasionally, until browned and crisp,
6 to 8 minutes. Drain on a kitchen paper-
lined plate.

When cool enough to handle, crumble
the bacon into a large bowl with the spinach.
Add the cucumber, eggs, feta, croutons,
olives and pecans or seeds. Pour in the
dressing and toss to coat. Divide among four
salad plates and top with the chicken.

Makes 4 servings

Per serving: energy 399 cals/1659 kJ; protein 48 g;
carbohydrate 9 g (of which 1 g sugars); fat 18 g (of
which 5 g saturates); fibre 3 g; sodium 979 mg

Diet Exchanges: 0 milk, 1 vegetable, 0 fruit,
½ bread, 6 meat, 2½ fat

Time-Savers

*If you're in a hurry to whip up this main course
salad, you can replace the bacon with real bacon
pieces (not imitation) from your supermarket. Or
omit the bacon altogether, which will reduce the
sodium in this dish.*

TOSSED SALAD WITH GREEN HERB DRESSING
140 calories, 4 g carbs

115 g/4 oz young spinach leaves

30 g/1 oz parsley leaves

15 g/½ oz fresh dill

4 tablespoons walnut or olive oil

**2 tablespoons chicken
or vegetable stock**

4 teaspoons cider vinegar

¼ teaspoon salt

⅛ teaspoon ground black pepper

455 g/1 lb mixed salad greens

Combine the spinach, parsley, dill, oil, stock, vinegar, salt and pepper in a blender or food processor. Process, scraping the sides of the blender once or twice, until smooth and slightly thickened.

Place the salad greens in a large bowl, drizzle the spinach mixture over the top and toss gently to coat.

Makes 4 servings

Per serving: energy 140 cals/582 kJ; protein 2 g; carbohydrate 4 g (of which 0 g sugars); fat 15 g (of which 2 g saturates); fibre 3 g; sodium 231 mg

Diet Exchanges: 0 milk, 1 vegetable, 0 fruit, 0 bread, 0 meat, 1½ fat

▶Flavour Tips

Sprinkle 1 tablespoon of chopped pecans or walnuts over the salad when serving. Garnish with slices of ripe tomato. Substitute grapeseed or flaxseed oil for the walnut or olive oil. The dressing will keep in a covered container in the refrigerator for up to 3 days.

Tomato-Onion Salad with Walnut Vinaigrette

172 calories, 5 g carbs

4 tablespoons walnut oil

1–1½ tablespoons lemon juice

1 small garlic clove, finely chopped

2 teaspoons chopped fresh tarragon or ½ teaspoon dried

⅛ teaspoon salt

⅛ teaspoon ground black pepper

4 tomatoes (115 g/4 oz each), sliced

1 red onion, thinly sliced

2 tablespoons chopped walnuts

Per serving: energy 172 cals/715 kJ; protein 1 g; carbohydrate 5 g (of which 1 g sugars); fat 17 g (of which 1 g saturates); fibre 1 g; sodium 91 mg

Diet Exchanges: 0 milk, 1 vegetable, 0 fruit, 0 bread, 0 meat, 3 fat

Time-Saver

Make the dressing ahead; it stores well in a covered container in the refrigerator for up to 3 days.

In a small bowl, whisk the oil, lemon juice, garlic, tarragon, salt and pepper.

On individual plates or a serving dish, overlap the tomato and onion slices in an alternating pattern until all the slices have been used. Drizzle with the tarragon-garlic mixture. Top with the walnuts.

Makes 4 servings

HIDDEN ROADBLOCK to weight loss

TRIGGER FOODS

If you eat many of the same foods day after day, there is a good chance that these are your trigger foods. Do you eat cereal every morning? Lots of pasta for dinner? The foods you eat most frequently are usually the foods that can trigger you to overeat. To manage your trigger foods, be sure to eat a wide variety of foods. Break out of old eating habits by making a point of trying something new every day. To find out more about identifying and managing your trigger foods, see page 31.

Cucumber and Radish Salad with Sesame-Soy Dressing

115 calories, 14 g carbs

3 tablespoons rice vinegar

2 tablespoons soy sauce

1½ tablespoons orange juice

1 tablespoon sesame oil

1 teaspoon grated, peeled, fresh ginger or ½ teaspoon ground

1 garlic clove, crushed

⅛ teaspoon hot-pepper sauce (optional)

1 cucumber (340 g/12 oz), peeled and thinly sliced

8 radishes, thinly sliced

½ small red onion, halved and thinly sliced

2 teaspoons toasted sesame seeds

In a large bowl, whisk together the vinegar, soy sauce, juice, oil, ginger, garlic and hot-pepper sauce (if using). Add the cucumber, radishes, onion and sesame seeds. Toss well and serve at room temperature or chilled.

Makes 4 servings

Per serving: energy 115 cals/478 kJ; protein 2 g; carbohydrate 14 g (of which 0 g sugars); fat 4 g (of which 1 g saturates); fibre 2 g; sodium 300 mg

Diet Exchanges: 0 milk, 2 vegetable, 0 fruit, 0 bread, 0 meat, 1½ fat

▶Flavour Tip

Top with 1 tablespoon chopped fresh coriander before serving.

Spanish-Style Green Beans
170 calories, 12 g carbs

- **455 g/1 lb green beans, trimmed and cut into 5 cm/2 in lengths**
- **3 tablespoons olive oil**
- **1 onion, chopped**
- **1 small green pepper, chopped**
- **1 tomato (115 g/4 oz), peeled, seeded and coarsely chopped**
- **2 garlic cloves, finely chopped**
- **¼ teaspoon salt**
- **⅛ teaspoon ground black pepper**
- **2–3 tablespoons coarsely chopped, pitted kalamata or other purple olives**
- **2 teaspoons drained capers (optional)**

Combine the beans, oil, onion, green pepper, tomato, garlic, salt and black pepper in a saucepan over medium heat. Cook, stirring, until the vegetables start to sizzle, 2 to 3 minutes. Reduce the heat to low, cover and cook, stirring occasionally, until the beans are very tender but not falling apart, 20 to 25 minutes. Stir in the olives and capers (if using) and heat 1 minute. Serve warm, at room temperature or chilled.

Makes 4 servings

Per serving: energy 170 cals/707 kJ; protein 2 g; carbohydrate 12 g (of which 0 g sugars); fat 13 g (of which 2 g saturates); fibre 5 g; sodium 218 mg

Diet Exchanges: 0 milk, 2½ vegetable, 0 fruit, 0 bread, 0 meat, 2½ fat

FLAGEOLET BEANS WITH SESAME OIL AND GINGER
160 calories, 10 g carbs

- **1 tin (420 g/14½ oz) flageolet or cannellini beans**
- **2 tablespoons water**
- **1 tablespoon soy sauce**
- **2–3 teaspoons finely chopped, peeled fresh ginger**
- **2 teaspoons sesame oil**
- **Pinch of chilli powder (optional)**
- **Pinch of salt (optional)**
- **1 tablespoon chopped fresh coriander (optional)**

In a saucepan, combine the beans, water, soy sauce and ginger. Bring to the boil over high heat, stirring once or twice. Reduce the heat to low, cover and cook for 2 minutes. Uncover and cook until the beans are tender and the liquid evaporates, 2 to 4 minutes more.

Remove from the heat, stir in the sesame oil, chilli powder (if using) and salt (if using). Serve hot, sprinkled with the coriander (if using).

Makes 4 servings

Per serving: energy 160 cals/707 kJ; protein 12 g; carbohydrate 10 g (of which 0 g sugars); fat 9 g (of which 1 g saturates); fibre 4 g; sodium 235 mg

Diet Exchanges: 0 milk, 2 vegetable, 0 fruit, 0 bread, 1 meat, 1 fat

▶Flavour Tips

Substitute 340 g/12 oz frozen peas for the beans. If you ever see fresh green soya beans (also called by their Japanese name, edamame) in an oriental food shop, they make the ideal ingredient for this dish. If using soya beans, increase the cooking time to 6 minutes covered and a further 6 to 8 minutes uncovered. For a milder flavour, use freshly ground black pepper instead of the chilli powder.

COUSCOUS SALAD WITH LIME-CUMIN DRESSING

209 calories, 31 g carbs

- **3 tablespoons groundnut (peanut) or olive oil**
- **½ large red pepper, chopped**
- **170 g/6 oz wholewheat couscous**
- **300 ml/10 fl oz hot vegetable stock or chicken stock**
- **3 tablespoons lime juice**
- **1 teaspoon ground cumin**
- **3–4 drops hot-pepper sauce**
- **45 g/1½ oz pine nuts (optional)**
- **1 spring onion, finely chopped**

Heat 1 tablespoon of the oil in a small saucepan over medium-high heat. Add the pepper and cook, stirring occasionally, until tender-firm, 3 to 4 minutes. Add the couscous and stir for 30 seconds. Add the stock. Bring to the boil and stir once. Cover tightly, remove from the heat and let stand for 5 minutes.

Meanwhile, in a bowl, whisk the lime juice, the remaining 2 tablespoons oil, the cumin and hot-pepper sauce.

Fluff the couscous with a fork and add it to the lime dressing. Toss to combine. Add the pine nuts (if using) and spring onion and toss. Serve warm or at room temperature.

Makes 6 servings

Per serving: energy 209 cals/869 kJ; protein 5 g; carbohydrate 31 g (of which 0 g sugars); fat 9 g (of which 1 g saturates); fibre 5 g; sodium 223 mg

Diet Exchanges: 0 milk, 0 vegetable, 0 fruit, 2 bread, 0 meat, 1½ fat

Time-Savers

Use 1½ finely chopped bottled roasted peppers instead of the fresh pepper. This dish keeps well for later meals — and improves with age. Keep it in a covered container in the refrigerator for up to 3 days and serve at room temperature.

Couscous Salad with Lime-Cumin Dressing

POLENTA BAKE WITH CHEESE AND CHILLIES

240 calories, 21 g carbs

700 ml/1¼ pints water

480 ml/16 fl oz semi-skimmed milk

½ teaspoon salt

170 g/6 oz quick-cooking polenta

60 g/2 oz butter

115 g/4 oz mature Cheddar cheese, grated

2 large eggs, lightly beaten

2–4 tablespoons bottled, roasted, chopped chillies

⅛ teaspoon ground black pepper

Preheat the oven to 180°C/350°F/gas 4. Grease a large, shallow ovenproof dish.

In a large saucepan, combine the water, half of the milk and the salt. Bring to the boil over high heat. Reduce the heat to medium-low and gradually stir in the polenta. Cook, stirring, until very thick, 8 to 10 minutes. Remove from the heat and stir in the butter, cheese and the remaining milk. Gradually stir in the eggs. Stir in the chillies and pepper.

Spoon into the prepared dish and bake until the top is browned and a toothpick inserted in the centre comes out clean, about 1 hour.

Makes 8 servings

Per serving: energy 240 cals/998 kJ; protein 8 g; carbohydrate 21 g (of which 1 g sugars); fat 14 g (of which 7 g saturates); fibre 1 g; sodium 321 mg

Diet Exchanges: ½ milk, 0 vegetable, 0 fruit, 1 bread, ½ meat, 2 fat

Time-Saver

This recipe can be halved if you'd like to make less. But leftovers make a wonderful light supper or lunch. Store in a covered container in the refrigerator for up to 4 days. To reheat, let stand at room temperature for an hour, place in an ovenproof dish, cover and bake at 170°C/325°F/gas 3 until heated through, 30 to 35 minutes.

QUINOA AND VEGETABLE PILAF
132 calories, 19 g carbs

- **15 g/½ oz butter**
- **1 small onion, finely chopped**
- **1 small carrot, finely chopped**
- **1 celery stick or ½ small fennel bulb, finely chopped**
- **90 g/3 oz quinoa, rinsed until the water runs clear, and drained**
- **180 ml/6 fl oz chicken or vegetable stock**
- **⅛ teaspoon salt**
- **⅛ teaspoon ground black pepper**
- **2 teaspoons chopped fresh parsley (optional)**

Melt the butter in a saucepan over medium-low heat. Stir in the onion, carrot and celery or fennel. Cook, stirring occasionally, until the vegetables are almost tender, 6 to 7 minutes. Stir in the quinoa, increase the heat to medium-high and cook until lightly toasted, stirring frequently, about 3 minutes. Stir in the stock, salt and pepper.

Reduce the heat to low, cover and cook until the grains are tender-chewy and all the liquid is absorbed, 15 minutes. Serve sprinkled with the parsley (if using).

Makes 4 servings

Per serving: energy 132 cals/549 kJ; protein 5 g; carbohydrate 19 g (of which 0 g sugars); fat 3 g (of which 1 g saturates); fibre 3 g; sodium 309 mg

Diet Exchanges: 0 milk, 1 vegetable, 0 fruit, 1 bread, 0 meat, ½ fat

Time-Saver

Make extra portions and store in a covered container in the refrigerator for up to 4 days. To reheat, place in an ovenproof dish, cover and bake at 180°C/350°F/gas 4 until steaming, about 15 minutes.

Brown Rice Pilaf with Hazelnuts
170 calories, 22 g carbs

- **20 g/¾ oz butter**
- **3 large mushrooms, coarsely chopped**
- **1 small onion, chopped**
- **100 g/3½ oz brown rice**
- **60 g/2 oz hazelnuts, coarsely chopped**
- **300 ml/10 fl oz chicken stock**
- **½ teaspoon dried thyme**
- **½ teaspoon grated lemon zest**

Melt the butter in a saucepan over medium heat. Stir in the mushrooms and onion. Cook, stirring occasionally, until the mushroom liquid evaporates, 8 to 10 minutes. Stir in the rice and nuts and cook, stirring frequently, for 2 minutes. Stir in the stock, thyme and lemon zest. Bring to a simmer. Cover, reduce the heat to low and cook until the rice is tender, about 45 minutes.

Fluff the rice with a fork before serving.

Makes 4 servings

Per serving: energy 170 cals/707 kJ; protein 4 g; carbohydrate 22 g (of which 0 g sugars); fat 8 g (of which 1 g saturates); fibre 2 g; sodium 374 mg

Diet Exchanges: 0 milk, 1 vegetable, 0 fruit, 1 bread, 0 meat, 1½ fat

▶Flavour Tips
Replace the hazelnuts with walnuts, pine nuts or pecans. For best results, avoid stirring the rice while it cooks.

biscuits, cakes, puddings & fruit desserts

PEANUT BUTTER COOKIES 330

CHOCOLATE-ALMOND MERINGUE BISCUITS 331

ORANGE-WALNUT BISCOTTI 333

GINGERBREAD CAKE WITH PEACH WHIPPED CREAM 334

STRAWBERRY CREAM CAKE 336

CHOCOLATE HAZELNUT FLOURLESS CAKE 338

COURGETTE–CHOCOLATE CHIP SNACK CAKE 340

DOUBLE CHOCOLATE CUSTARD 341

GENE'S LEMON JELLY WHIP 343

CHOCOLATE CUSTARD CUPS 344

BREAD AND BUTTER PUDDING 346

CHOCOLATE-RASPBERRY DIP AND FRESH FRUIT 347

BAKED PANCAKE WITH BERRIES AND CINNAMON 348

CANTALOUPE SORBET 349

RASPBERRY-ALMOND TARTE 350

WARM BUTTERED FRUIT COMPOTE 352

DRIED APRICOT FOOL 353

GRILLED PINEAPPLE WITH GINGER-YOGHURT SAUCE 354

BAKED BANANAS WITH RUM SAUCE 355

APRICOT-ORANGE CLAFOUTIS 356

PEACH SOUFFLÉ WITH BLUEBERRIES 357

PEANUT BUTTER COOKIES (photo on page 332)
106 calories, 8 g carbs

- **90 g/3 oz unsalted butter, softened**
- **115 g/4 oz unsweetened smooth peanut butter, at room temperature**
- **50 g/1¾ oz light brown sugar**
- **4 tablespoons Splenda**
- **1 large egg, at room temperature, lightly beaten**
- **1 teaspoon vanilla essence**
- **170 g/6 oz plain flour, sifted**
- **¼ teaspoon baking powder**
- **3 tablespoons salted peanuts, chopped**

Place an oven rack in the middle position and preheat the oven to 180°C/350°F/gas 4.

In a large bowl, beat together the butter and peanut butter until very smooth, about 1 minute. Add the sugar and Splenda and beat until well-combined and light in colour, 1 to 2 minutes. Gradually beat in the egg and vanilla, beating until very smooth and a little fluffy, 1 to 2 minutes. Mix in the flour and baking powder, beating until a moist but cohesive dough forms. Stir in the peanuts.

Drop by the tablespoon about 5 cm/ 2 in apart on non-stick baking trays. Using the prongs of a fork dampened in cold water, flatten each in a cross-hatch pattern until 5 cm/2 in in diameter. Bake until golden brown, 22 to 25 minutes. Remove to a rack to cool.

Makes 24

Per biscuit: energy 106 cals/443 kJ; protein 3 g; carbohydrate 8 g (of which 3 g sugars); fat 7 g (of which 3 g saturates); fibre 1 g; sodium 62 mg

Diet Exchanges: 0 milk, 0 vegetable, 0 fruit, ½ bread, ½ meat, 1 fat

▶Flavour Tips

Stir 3–4 tablespoons of currants into the mixture. Use chunky peanut butter and omit the peanuts. For a sweeter, more crunchy biscuit, use brown sugar and omit the Splenda (this will add about 2 grams carbohydrate per biscuit). Or for fewer carbs per biscuit, use 8 level tablespsoons Splenda and omit the brown sugar. Store the biscuits in a tightly closed container at room temperature for up to 5 days.

CHOCOLATE-ALMOND MERINGUE BISCUITS *(photo on page 332)*
77 calories, 11 g carbs

- **75 g/2½ oz blanched almonds**
- **5 tablespoons sugar**
- **3 egg whites, at room temperature**
- **¼ teaspoon cream of tartar**
- **2 tablespoons unsweetened cocoa powder**
- **90 g/3 oz raspberry or strawberry jam**

Preheat the oven to 130°C/250°F/gas ½. Line a baking tray with greaseproof paper or aluminium foil.

In a food processor, process the almonds with 2 tablespoons of the sugar until finely ground. Set aside.

In a large, clean bowl, beat the egg whites and cream of tartar until frothy. Gradually add the remaining 3 tablespoons sugar and beat until stiff peaks form when the beaters are lifted. Gently fold in the cocoa powder and almond mixture.

Spoon the meringue into 4 cm/1½ in mounds on the prepared baking tray. Using the back of a spoon, depress the centres and build up the sides of each meringue to form a shallow cup.

Bake for 1 hour. Do not open the oven door. Turn off the oven and let the meringues cool in the oven. Store in an airtight container. When ready to serve, fill each with jam.

Makes 16

Per biscuit: energy 77 cals/325 kJ; protein 2 g; carbohydrate 11 g (of which 10 g sugars); fat 3 g (of which 1 g saturates); fibre 1 g; sodium 35 mg

Diet Exchanges: 0 milk, 0 vegetable, 0 fruit, ½ bread, 0 meat, ½ fat

Peanut Butter Cookies (page 330), Chocolate-Almond Meringue Biscuits (page 331) and Orange-Walnut Biscotti

ORANGE-WALNUT BISCOTTI
65 calories, 5 g carbs

75 g/2½ oz walnuts

50 g/1¾ oz sugar

170 g/6 oz wholemeal plain flour

45 g/1½ oz cornmeal

1 teaspoon baking powder

¼ teaspoon salt

60 g/2 oz butter, softened

4 tablespoons Splenda

2 eggs

2 teaspoons grated orange zest

½ teaspoon orange essence

In a food processor, combine the walnuts and 2 tablespoons of the sugar. Process until the walnuts are coarsely ground but not made into a paste. Transfer to a large bowl and add the flour, cornmeal, baking powder and salt. Stir until combined.

In a large bowl, using an electric mixer, beat the butter, Splenda and remaining 2 tablespoons sugar until light and fluffy. Beat in the eggs, orange zest and orange essence. Gradually beat in the flour mixture until smooth and thick. Divide the dough into two equal-size pieces. Refrigerate for 30 minutes, or until firm.

Preheat the oven to 180°C/350°F/gas 4. Coat a baking tray with cooking spray.

Shape each piece of dough into a 30 cm/12 in-long log and place both on the prepared baking tray. Bake for 25 to 30 minutes, or until golden. Remove the logs to wire racks to cool.

Cut each log on a slight diagonal into 1 cm/½ in-thick slices. Place the slices, cut side down, on the baking tray and bake for 5 minutes. Turn the slices over and bake 5 minutes more, or until dry. Remove to wire racks to cool.

Makes 24

Per biscotto: energy 65 cals/270 kJ; protein 1 g; carbohydrate 5 g (of which 2 g sugars); fat 5 g (of which 2 g saturates); fibre 0 g; sodium 69 mg

Diet Exchanges: 0 milk, 0 vegetable, 0 fruit, ½ bread, 0 meat, 1 fat

▶Flavour Tip

Replace the walnuts with pine nuts and the orange zest and orange essence with lemon zest and lemon essence. For a sweeter, more crunchy biscuit, use 100 g/3½ oz sugar and omit the Splenda (this will add about 2 grams carbohydrate per biscuit). Or for fewer carbs per biscuit, omit the sugar and use 8 level tablespoons Splenda.

GINGERBREAD CAKE WITH PEACH WHIPPED CREAM

311 calories, 46 g carbs

200 g/7 oz oat flour, sifted

100 g/3½ oz wholemeal flour

2 teaspoons baking powder

I teaspoon ground ginger

I teaspoon ground cinnamon

½ teaspoon ground cloves

Pinch of salt

4 tablespoons black treacle

80 ml/3 fl oz vegetable oil

300 ml/10 fl oz hot water

I teaspoon bicarbonate of soda

I large egg + I yolk, at room temperature, lightly beaten

4 tablespoons Splenda

120 ml/4 fl oz double cream

3 tablespoons peach fruit spread, at room temperature

Preheat the oven to 180°C/350°F/gas 4. Coat a 20 cm/8 in round cake tin or 20 × 20 cm/8 × 8 in tin with cooking spray.

In a medium bowl, combine the flours, baking powder, ginger, cinnamon, cloves and salt.

In a large bowl, combine the treacle and oil. In a measuring jug, combine the water and bicarbonate of soda. Whisk into the molasses-oil mixture.

Gradually whisk the dry ingredients into the molasses mixture. Whisk in the egg, yolk and Splenda. Pour into the prepared tin and bake until a toothpick inserted in the centre comes out clean, about 30 minutes.

Cool in the tin on a rack for 10 minutes. Remove to the rack and cool completely.

In a large bowl, whip the cream and fruit spread together until soft peaks form. Serve wedges of cake topped with a spoonful of the peach cream.

Makes 10 servings

Per serving: energy 311 cals/1307 kJ; protein 4 g; carbohydrate 46 g (of which 23 g sugars); fat 13 g (of which 5 g saturates); fibre 1 g; sodium 77 mg

Diet Exchanges: 0 milk, 0 vegetable, 0 fruit, 1½ bread, 0 meat, 2½ fat

▶Flavour Tips

Replace the peach fruit spread with apricot, raspberry or cherry. Stir 60 g/2 oz fruit spread and ½ teaspoon vanilla essence into 230 g/8 oz Soft Yoghurt Cheese (page 107) and use instead of the whipped cream. For a more moist cake, replace the Splenda with 50 g/1¾ oz sugar (this will add about 6 grams of carbohydrate per serving). This gingerbread cake (minus the cream topping) keeps well in a resealable bag at room temperature for 1 day or in the freezer for 1 month. The whipped cream will keep in a covered container in the refrigerator for 1 day.

Gingerbread Cake with Peach Whipped Cream

STRAWBERRY CREAM CAKE
273 calories, 21 g carbs

CAKE

- **100 g/3½ oz wholemeal flour, sifted**
- **100 g/3½ oz plain or oat flour, sifted**
- **1 tablespoon baking powder**
- **115 g/4 oz butter, slightly softened**
- **50 g/1¾ oz light brown sugar**
- **4 tablespoons Splenda**
- **2 egg yolks + 3 whites, at room temperature**
- **180 ml/6 fl oz semi-skimmed milk, at room temperature**
- **1 teaspoon vanilla essence**

TOPPING

- **180 ml/6 fl oz double cream**
- **4 tablespoons strawberry fruit spread**
- **285 g/10 oz strawberries, hulled and sliced**

To make the cake: Preheat the oven to 180°C/350°F/gas 4. Butter and flour a 20 cm/8 in round cake tin or 20 × 20 cm/ 8 × 8 in tin.

In a small bowl, combine the flours and the baking powder.

In a large bowl, using an electric mixer on medium speed, beat the butter, sugar and Splenda until creamy, about 2 minutes. Add the egg yolks, one at a time, beating until the mixture is somewhat fluffy, 3 to 4 minutes.

Beat in the flour mixture alternately with the milk in 3 additions. Beat in the vanilla essence.

In a clean, large bowl, beat the 3 egg whites until they form stiff but moist peaks, about 1 minute. Spoon ⅓ of the whites on top of the egg yolk mixture and gently fold in. Fold in the remaining whites. Spoon into the prepared tin and bake until a tooth-pick inserted in the centre comes out clean, 35 to 40 minutes.

Cool in the tin on a rack for 10 to 15 minutes. Turn out and cool completely.

To make the topping: In a clean, large bowl, whip the cream until soft peaks form and refrigerate.

Melt the fruit spread in a small frying pan over very low heat, stirring, about 15 seconds. To make a layer cake, split the completely cooled cake horizontally into 2 layers. Spread ⅓ of the fruit spread over the cut side of the bottom layer. Cover with ⅓ of the berries and ⅓ of the whipped cream. Top with the remaining layer and coat with the remaining fruit spread and whipped cream. Arrange the remaining berries over the top.

Makes 10 servings

Per serving: energy 273 cals/1137 kJ; protein 6 g; carbohydrate 21 g (of which 8 g sugars); fat 19 g (of which 11 g saturates); fibre 2 g; sodium 281 mg

Diet Exchanges: 0 milk, 0 vegetable, ½ fruit, 1 bread, ½ meat, 3½ fat

Strawberry Cream Cake

CHOCOLATE HAZELNUT FLOURLESS CAKE
185 calories, 20 g carbs

- **30 g/1 oz unsalted butter**
- **3 tablespoons unsweetened cocoa powder**
- **75 g/2½ oz blanched hazelnuts or almonds**
- **8 tablespoons sugar**
- **90 g/3 oz plain chocolate**
- **115 g/4 oz soured cream**
- **2 egg yolks**
- **1 tablespoon Frangelico or amaretto (optional)**
- **1 teaspoon vanilla essence**
- **½ teaspoon cinnamon**
- **5 egg whites, at room temperature**
- **¼ teaspoon salt**
- **Fresh sliced strawberries (optional)**

Preheat the oven to 180°C/350°F/gas 4. Generously coat a 20–23 cm/8–9 in springform cake tin with one third of the butter and dust with 1 tablespoon of the cocoa powder (don't tap out excess cocoa; leave it in the tin).

In a food processor, process the nuts with 1 tablespoon of the sugar until finely ground.

In the top of a double boiler over barely simmering water, melt the chocolate and the remaining butter, stirring occasionally, until smooth.

Remove from the heat. Place the chocolate mixture in a large bowl. Add the nut mixture, sour cream, egg yolks, Frangelico or amaretto (if using), vanilla essence, cinnamon, 5 tablespoons of the remaining sugar and the remaining 2 tablespoons cocoa powder. Stir until well blended.

In another large bowl, with an electric mixer on high speed, beat the egg whites and salt until foamy. Gradually add the remaining 2 tablespoons sugar, beating, until the whites hold stiff peaks when the beaters are lifted.

Stir ¼ of the beaten whites into the chocolate mixture to lighten it. Gently fold in the remaining whites. Spoon into the prepared cake tin. Gently smooth the top.

Bake for 30 minutes or until the cake has risen, is dry on the top and a toothpick inserted in the centre comes out with a few moist crumbs. Cool on a rack until warm. The cake will fall dramatically. Loosen the edges of the cake with a knife and remove the cake tin sides. Serve with the strawberries (if using).

Makes 12 servings

Per serving: energy 185 cals/773 kJ; protein 3 g; carbohydrate 20 g (of which 19 g sugars); fat 11 g (of which 4 g saturates); fibre 1 g; sodium 114 mg

Diet Exchanges: 0 milk, 0 vegetable, 0 fruit, 1 bread, 0 meat, 2 fat

Chocolate Hazelnut Flourless Cake

COURGETTE-CHOCOLATE CHIP SNACK CAKE
157 calories, 22 g carbs

250 g/9 oz wholemeal plain flour

1½ teaspoons baking powder

½ teaspoon bicarbonate of soda

1½ teaspoons ground cinnamon

¼ teaspoon salt

2 eggs

65 g/2¼ oz light brown sugar

115 g/4 oz low-fat natural yoghurt

80 ml/3 fl oz rapeseed oil

2 teaspoons vanilla essence

170 g/6 oz courgette, grated

115 g/4 oz mini plain chocolate chips

Preheat the oven to 180°C/350°F/gas 4.

Line a 20 × 20cm/8 × 8 in baking tin with aluminium foil, leaving extra foil over 2 opposite edges to use as handles after the cake is baked. Coat the foil with cooking spray.

In a large bowl, combine the flour, baking powder, bicarbonate of soda, cinnamon and salt.

In a medium bowl, with a wire whisk, beat the eggs, sugar, yoghurt, oil and vanilla until smooth. Stir in the courgette and chocolate chips.

Add the courgette mixture to the flour mixture and stir just until blended. Scrape into the prepared tin. Bake for 40 minutes or until the cake is springy to the touch and a toothpick inserted in the centre comes out clean.

Let the cake cool in the tin on a rack for 30 minutes. Remove from the tin using the foil handles. Discard the foil and cool completely on the rack.

Makes 16 servings

Per serving: energy 157 cals/660 kJ; protein 3 g; carbohydrate 22 g (of which 9 g sugars); fat 7 g (of which 2 g saturates); fibre 1 g; sodium 170 mg

Diet Exchanges: 0 milk, 0 vegetable, 0 fruit, 1 bread, 0 meat, 1½ fat

▶Flavour Tips

For a more spicy cake, replace ½ teaspoon of the cinnamon with ½ teaspoon ground allspice and/or cloves.

DOUBLE CHOCOLATE CUSTARD
169 calories, 28 g carbs

65 g/2¼ oz light brown sugar

5 tablespoons Splenda

30 g/1 oz unsweetened cocoa powder

2 tablespoons cornflour

450 ml/15 fl oz whole milk or unsweetened soya milk

30 g/1 oz plain chocolate

1 teaspoon vanilla essence

In a medium saucepan, whisk together the sugar, Splenda, cocoa and cornflour until smooth. Whisk in the milk over medium heat. Cook until thickened and bubbly, 2 minutes. Remove from the heat and stir in the chocolate and vanilla. Stir until the chocolate melts.

Pour into 4 custard cups or small serving dishes. Cover with clingfilm and chill for 2 hours before serving.

Makes 6 servings

Per serving: energy 169 cals/714 kJ; protein 4 g; carbohydrate 28 g (of which 18 g sugars); fat 5 g (of which 3 g saturates); fibre 1 g; sodium 95 mg

Diet Exchanges: ½ milk, 0 vegetable, 0 fruit, 1 bread, 0 meat, ½ fat

▶Flavour Tips

For mocha custard, add 1 teaspoon instant espresso or coffee granules along with the milk. Cook and stir until dissolved. For the taste of chocolate cream pie, crumble a digestive biscuit into the bottom of each dish, then add the custard. If you prefer, replace the Splenda with 65 g/2¼ oz brown sugar (this will add about 12 grams carbohydrate per serving).

HIDDEN ROADBLOCK to weight loss

HIGH EXPECTATIONS

Whenever you set a weight-loss goal, be realistic. Losing 6.4 kg/1 st in 1 week is not very realistic. It's possible, but that sudden loss would be difficult to sustain. To minimise frustration, set goals that you know you can stick to. If everything points to the fact that you are in excellent health despite the fact that you still weigh more than you want to or you don't look as slim as you'd like to, don't sweat it. You are making progress. Accept yourself the way you are, feel good about your good health and get on with your life. Just keep making the right choices when you face a food decision (with occasional indulgences, of course) and stay physically active. And be patient. It may take time for your body weight and shape to balance out to what is ideal for your particular physical makeup.

biscuits, cakes, puddings and fruit desserts

I Did It!

Gene Newman

As Gene got older, he went from 83 kg/13 st to over 98 kg/15½ st. He decided to avoid breads, sweets and soft drinks and lost 19 kg/3 st.

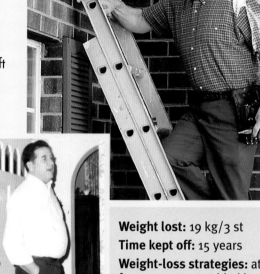

before

'Weight loss was never a real concern for me until I started getting a little older, spending more time behind a desk and having a greater desire for ice cream and bananas as a late-night snack.

'I was on the podgy side in my early teens. That's because my family ate a lot of fried foods – mostly chicken and pork chops – lots of biscuits and big portions. At 13, I weighed 60 kg/9½ st and was nicknamed Butterball. But then I started playing football, and by 16 I had trimmed down a bit and weighed 70 kg/11 st. At 18, after Army basic training, I weighed 83 kg/ 13 st and had an 80-cm/32-inch waist.

'I started gaining weight in the mid-1970s. It became more difficult to bend

Weight lost: 19 kg/3 st
Time kept off: 15 years
Weight-loss strategies: ate fewer sweets; avoided bread; ate more vegetables, lean protein foods and 'good' fats; increased physical activity
Weight-maintenance strategies: eats fewer sweets; avoids bread; eats more lean protein foods; eats whole grains instead of refined ones; eats sensible portions; maintains physical activity

over and tie my shoes and get into the size 34 trousers that I had worn since my mid-twenties. By the early 1980s, I weighed over 98 kg/15½ st and had trouble buttoning a

biscuits, cakes, puddings and fruit desserts

42 cm/17-inch collar. It wasn't long before I had to buy a new suit and discovered that I needed a size 38! And that *really* caused me to take a hard look at what was happening.

'I tried the grapefruit diet, a no-fat diet, a low-fat diet – I even attempted several times to just reduce the amount of food that I ate. None of these approaches worked. I kept looking for an eating style that would satisfy my hunger and be healthy enough to sustain for the rest of my life.

'Finally, I decided to cut out breads and sweets, including fizzy drinks and ice cream. Within 8 months, my weight had dropped back down to below 83 kg/13 st. I was always fairly active, so all of this

extra weight was due to my eating habits.

'Over the next 15 years, I tried low-fat eating plans but I immediately started to regain the weight. Now I eat a small amount of starches, mostly in the form of high-fibre whole grains, plenty of vegetables and lots of fish and poultry. I rarely eat cakes, sweets or fizzy drinks with sugar. Occasionally I eat beef, pork and lamb. My current weight is around 80 kg/12½ st and I fit into size 34 trousers. My cholesterol level is well within the healthy range. I still stay active by walking and doing DIY on weekends, but I'm planning to get to the gym more often to stay fit. I feel so much better not lugging the extra weight around!'

GENE'S LEMON JELLY WHIP
61 calories, 2 g carbs

2 packets sugar-free lemon jelly

450 ml/15 fl oz boiling water

240 ml/8 fl oz cold water

90 g/3 oz low-fat crème fraîche

90 g/3 oz ricotta cheese

90 g/3 oz light cream cheese

½ teaspoon lemon essence

Dissolve the jelly in the boiling water. Stir in the cold water, cover and refrigerate until firm.

In a blender, combine the crème fraîche, ricotta, cream cheese and lemon essence.

Blend on high speed until light and fluffy. Cut the jelly into sections and add to the mixture in the blender. Blend on high speed until smooth and frothy like a milkshake, about 3 to 4 minutes. Pour into individual serving dishes or small containers with lids. Cover and refrigerate for at least 1 hour or overnight.

Makes 6 servings

Per serving: energy 61 cals/253 kJ; protein 4 g; carbohydrate 2 g (of which 2 g sugars); fat 4 g (of which 3 g saturates); fibre 0 g; sodium 64 mg

Diet Exchanges: ½ milk, 0 vegetable, 0 fruit, 0 bread, 1½ meat, 0 fat

CHOCOLATE CUSTARD CUPS
185 calories, 18 g carbs

**8 wholemeal crepes
(from recipe on page 94)**

**240 ml/8 fl oz whole milk or
unsweetened soya milk**

**1 packet (30 g/1 oz) sugar-free
instant chocolate custard powder**

**115 g/4 oz cream cheese, softened
and cut into pieces**

**455 g/1 lb strawberries, sliced,
or raspberries**

8 fresh mint leaves (optional)

Preheat the oven to 200°C/400°F/gas 6.

Invert eight 170-g/6-oz custard cups or coffee mugs over a baking tray. Coat the outside of the cups with cooking spray. Drape each crepe, browned side down, over each cup. Coat the crepes with cooking spray. Bake for 20 minutes. Turn the oven off and let the crepes sit in the oven until they are crisp, 30 minutes more. Carefully lift the crepe cups from the moulds and cool on a wire rack.

Pour the milk into a food processor or blender. Add the custard powder, cover and process until blended. Add the cream cheese. Cover and process until smooth.

Place each crepe cup right side up on a dessert plate. Spoon a layer of berries in the bottom of each. Spoon some of the cream cheese filling over the berries. Top with additional berries and the mint leaves (if using). Serve immediately.

Makes 8 servings

Per serving: energy 185 cals/773 kJ; protein 6 g; carbohydrate 18 g (of which 4 g sugars); fat 10 g (of which 5 g saturates); fibre 2 g; sodium 166 mg

Diet Exchanges: 0 milk, 0 vegetable, 1 fruit, 1 bread, ½ meat, 1½ fat

Time-Saver

Use shop-bought crepes (they will be somewhat higher in carbohydrates). To make this dessert ahead, prepare the crepes and filling, cover each separately and refrigerate for up to 24 hours before assembling.

Chocolate Custard Cups

Bread and Butter Pudding
316 calories, 35 g carbs

- **50 g/1¾ oz raisins**
- **4 tablespoons whisky or 1 teaspoon rum essence**
- **450 ml/15 fl oz semi-skimmed milk**
- **80 ml/3 fl oz double cream**
- **170 g/6 oz peach or apricot fruit spread**
- **2 teaspoons vanilla essence**
- **¾ teaspoon ground cinnamon**
- **Pinch of salt**
- **4 large eggs + 3 yolks, at room temperature**
- **8 slices (about 40 g/1¼ oz each) dried light wholemeal bread**
- **45 g/1½ oz unsalted butter, softened**
- **1 tablespoon icing sugar (optional)**

In a microwaveable cup or mug, combine the raisins and whisky or rum essence. Microwave on high power until hot, 15 to 20 seconds. Cover to keep warm.

In a large saucepan, combine the milk, cream, fruit spread, vanilla essence, cinnamon and salt. Cook over low heat until tiny bubbles appear around the edge of the pan, 8 to 10 minutes, stirring occasionally to incorporate the fruit spread.

Meanwhile, in a large bowl, whisk the eggs and yolks together. Gradually whisk 120 ml/4 fl oz of the milk mixture into

the eggs. Quickly whisk in the remaining milk mixture. Strain the raisin-whisky mixture over the egg mixture, reserving the raisins.

Coat a 20 × 20 cm/8 × 8 in baking tin with cooking spray. Spread 1 side of each bread slice with the butter. Cut the bread into cubes and arrange in the bottom of the prepared tin in an even layer. Scatter the raisins over the bread and pour the milk-egg mixture over the top. Press a piece of clingfilm directly onto the surface of the mixture and let sit until the bread is thoroughly soaked, 30 to 40 minutes, occasionally pressing down on the clingfilm to keep the bread submerged.

Meanwhile place a rack in the middle position in the oven and preheat the oven to 180°C/350°F/gas 4. Discard the clingfilm and bake until a wooden skewer inserted in the centre comes out clean, 45 to 50 minutes. Serve warm or at room temperature. Dust with the icing sugar (if using).

Makes 8 servings

Per serving: energy 316 cals/1327 kJ; protein 10 g; carbohydrate 35 g (of which 23 g sugars); fat 16 g (of which 8 g saturates); fibre 2 g; sodium 294 mg

Diet Exchanges: ½ milk, 0 vegetable, ½ fruit, 1½ bread, ½ meat, 2½ fat

CHOCOLATE-RASPBERRY DIP AND FRESH FRUIT
142 calories, 19 g carbs

90 g/3 oz raspberry fruit spread

2 tablespoons unsweetened cocoa powder

2 tablespoons semi-skimmed milk

115 g/4 oz soured cream

2 teaspoons vanilla essence

2 teaspoons raspberry liqueur (optional)

1½–2 tablespoons Splenda

1 tablespoon chopped walnuts

1 large navel orange, peeled and segmented

1 pear, cut lengthwise into 1 cm/½ in slices

1 apple, cut lengthwise into 1 cm/½ in slices

145 g/5 oz strawberries, with stems left on

In a small saucepan, mix the fruit spread, cocoa and milk. Cook over low heat, stirring occasionally, until the cocoa has dissolved and the fruit spread has melted, 1 to 2 minutes. Remove to a bowl, cover and let cool to room temperature.

Place the soured cream in a serving bowl and gradually stir in the cocoa mixture, vanilla essence, liqueur (if using) and Splenda. Sprinkle with the nuts and place on a platter. Arrange the orange, pear, apple and strawberries around the bowl.

Makes 6 servings

Per serving: energy 142 cals/593 kJ; protein 2 g; carbohydrate 19 g (of which 19 g sugars); fat 7 g (of which 3 g saturates); fibre 2 g; sodium 36 mg

Diet Exchanges: ½ milk, 0 vegetable, 1 fruit, 0 bread, 0 meat, 1 fat

▶Flavour Tip

The raspberry flavour in this chocolate dip becomes more pronounced after a day or two. To make the dip ahead, store in a covered container in the refrigerator for up to 5 days. Let come to room temperature before serving. To keep the dip warm, place the bowl in a larger bowl filled with boiling water and replenish the hot water as needed.

BAKED PANCAKE WITH BERRIES AND CINNAMON

269 calories, 22 g carbs

4 large eggs

120 ml/4 fl oz semi-skimmed milk

45 g/1½ oz plain flour

Pinch of salt

45 g/1½ oz unsalted butter, softened

⅛–¼ teaspoon ground cinnamon

3 tablespoons raspberry or blueberry fruit spread, warmed
or 3 tablespoons fresh berries

In a blender, combine the eggs, milk, flour and salt. Process until smooth, about 15 seconds. Remove to a medium bowl, cover and let rest for 45 to 60 minutes at room temperature. Meanwhile, preheat the oven to 190°C/375°F/gas 5.

Heat 30 g/1 oz of the butter in a 23 cm/9 in ovenproof frying pan over medium heat and cook until frothy. Pour in the egg-flour mixture. Place in the oven and bake until puffy and set, 14 to 16 minutes.

Remove from the oven and sprinkle with the cinnamon. Spread the fruit spread or berries over the pancake and dot with the remaining butter. Using a spatula, fold the pancake in half (or roll it up) and slide it onto a platter. Slice into 4 pieces.

Makes 4 servings

Per serving: energy 269 cals/1125 kJ; protein 10 g; carbohydrate 22 g (of which 14 g sugars); fat 16 g (of which 8 g saturates); fibre 0 g; sodium 228 mg

Diet Exchanges: 0 milk, 0 vegetable, 0 fruit, 1 bread, 1 meat, 2½ fat

▶Flavour Tips

Use any fruit spread you like for this recipe. You could also arrange 1 thinly sliced banana over the fruit spread before folding. Top each serving with a dollop of unsweetened whipped cream and sprinkle with cinnamon or nutmeg.

CANTALOUPE SORBET
40 calories, 9 g carbs

455 g/1 lb frozen cantaloupe melon, slightly thawed

1 frozen banana, sliced

4 tablespoons Splenda

1 tablespoon crème de menthe liqueur (optional)

1 tablespoon lime juice

2 teaspoons grated lime zest

⅛–¼ teaspoon ground cinnamon

In a food processor, combine the cantaloupe, banana, Splenda, liqueur (if using), lime juice, lime zest and cinnamon. Process until smooth.

Scrape into a shallow metal tin. Cover and freeze for 4 hours or overnight. Using a knife, break the mixture into chunks. Process briefly in a food processor before serving.

Makes 6 servings

Per serving: energy 40 cals/170 kJ; protein 1 g; carbohydrate 9 g (of which 9 g sugars); fat 0 g (of which 0 g saturates); fibre 1 g; sodium 6 mg

Diet Exchanges: 0 milk, 0 vegetable, 1 fruit, 0 bread, 0 meat, 0 fat

►Flavour Tips

Frozen cantaloupe saves time in this recipe, but fresh will have more flavour. Use the flesh of 1 small cantaloupe, cut into chunks. For a sweeter sorbet, replace the Splenda with 4 tablespoons sugar (this will add about 8 grams carbohydrate per serving). Serve with toasted almonds for an extra shot of flavour — and to reduce the overall glycaemic index of the dessert.

RASPBERRY-ALMOND TARTE
156 calories, 24 g carbs

CRUST

- **75 g/2½ oz rolled oats**
- **75 g/2½ oz wholemeal flour**
- **1 tablespoon sugar**
- **1 teaspoon ground cinnamon**
- **¼ teaspoon bicarbonate of soda**
- **2 tablespoons rapeseed oil**
- **2–3 tablespoons low-fat natural yoghurt**
- **60 g/2 oz plain chocolate chips (optional)**

FILLING

- **4 tablespoons raspberry fruit spread**
- **¾ teaspoon almond essence**
- **340 g/12 oz raspberries**
- **2 tablespoons sliced almonds**

Preheat the oven to 190°C/375°F/gas 5. Coat a baking tray with cooking spray.

In a medium bowl, combine the oats, flour, sugar, cinnamon and bicarbonate of soda. Stir in the oil and 2 tablespoons of yoghurt to make a soft, slightly sticky dough. If the dough is too stiff, add the remaining 1 tablespoon yoghurt.

Place the dough on the prepared baking tray and, using lightly oiled hands, pat evenly into a 25 cm/10 in circle. Place a 23 cm/9 in cake tin right side up on the dough and trace around the bottom of the tin with a sharp knife, being careful only to score the surface of the dough. With your fingers, push up and pinch the dough around the outside of the tin to make a 23 cm/9 in crust with a rim 5 mm/¼ in high. Remove the cake tin. Bake for 12 minutes on the baking tray. Scatter the chocolate chips (if using) evenly over the surface of the crust and bake until the chocolate is melted and the crust is firm and golden, 3 to 4 minutes more. Remove from the oven and spread the chocolate over the crust to make an even layer. Set aside to cool.

In a small, microwaveable bowl, combine the fruit spread and almond essence. Microwave on high power for 10 to 15 seconds, or until melted. Brush a generous tablespoon evenly over the crust. Arrange the raspberries evenly over the crust. Brush the remaining spread evenly over the berries, making sure to get some of the spread between the berries to secure them. Sprinkle with the almonds.

Refrigerate for at least 30 minutes, or until the spread has jelled.

Makes 8 servings

Per serving: energy 156 cals/659 kJ; protein 4 g; carbohydrate 24 g (of which 10 g sugars); fat 6 g (of which 1 g saturates); fibre 2 g; sodium 17 mg

Diet Exchanges: 0 milk, 0 vegetable, ½ fruit, ½ bread, 0 meat, 1 fat

Raspberry-Almond Tarte

WARM BUTTERED FRUIT COMPOTE
111 calories, 19 g carbs

- 320 ml/11 fl oz apple juice
- 150 ml/5 fl oz dry white wine or white grape juice
- 2 teaspoons lemon juice
- 1 teaspoon vanilla essence
- 6 dried peach slices (90 g/3 oz), cut into 2 cm/¾ in pieces
- 2 Granny Smith or other tart apples, peeled and cut into 2 cm/ ¾ in-thick wedges
- 2 cooking pears, peeled and cut into 2–3 cm/1 in cubes
- 15 g/½ oz butter
- 4 sprigs fresh mint (optional)

In a wide saucepan, combine the apple juice, wine or grape juice, lemon juice and vanilla essence. Cook over low heat for 5 minutes. Add the peaches, partially cover and cook until tender, 8 to 10 minutes. Add the apples and pears. Partially cover and cook until tender-firm, 5 to 6 minutes, stirring occasionally.

Remove from the heat, stir in the butter and serve warm, garnished with the mint (if using).

Makes 6 servings

Per serving: energy 111 cals/468 kJ; protein 1 g; carbohydrate 19 g (of which 19 g sugars); fat 2 g (of which 1 g saturates); fibre 3 g; sodium 25 mg

Diet Exchanges: 0 milk, 0 vegetable, 1½ fruit, 0 bread, 0 meat, 1 fat

▶Flavour Tips

Serve with slices of Raisin Spice Quick Bread (page 100) or with the crepes in Wholemeal Crepes with Banana and Kiwifruit (page 94). Garnish each serving with a dollop of plain yoghurt instead of the butter. Or drizzle each serving with a teaspoon of double cream and sprinkle with a pinch of nutmeg.

Smart-Carb Insider Tip
KEEP TREATS ON HAND

If you have a sweet tooth, make the biscuits or desserts in this book that keep well so that they are ready when you need them. Keep sugar-free jelly in the refrigerator and top with a couple of squirts of real whipped cream. Or look in your local supermarkets or health food shops for low-carbohydrate chocolate snack bars, biscuits, cake mixes, milkshakes and beverages.

DRIED APRICOT FOOL
295 calories, 21 g carbs

- **170 g/6 oz dried apricots**
- **180 ml/6 fl oz orange juice**
- **1 teaspoon lemon juice**
- **1 teaspoon grated orange zest**
- **1½ tablespoons rum or ½ teaspoon rum essence (optional)**
- **120 ml/4 fl oz double cream**
- **3 tablespoons slivered or sliced almonds, toasted**
- **⅛ teaspoon ground nutmeg**

Combine the apricots and orange juice in a saucepan over low heat. Bring to a simmer, partially cover and cook until the fruit is very tender, about 15 minutes. Pour the fruit and liquid into a food processor and process until smooth, 2 to 3 minutes. Remove to a large bowl, stir in the lemon juice, orange zest and rum or essence (if using) and let cool.

In a large bowl, whip the cream to firm but not stiff peaks. Stir one-quarter of the cream into the apricot mixture. Gently fold in the rest until evenly incorporated. Remove to a serving bowl and chill for at least 3 hours or up to 3 days. Serve sprinkled with the almonds and nutmeg.

Makes 4 servings

Per serving: energy 295 cals/1227 kJ; protein 5 g; carbohydrate 21 g (of which 21 g sugars); fat 22 g (of which 10 g saturates); fibre 4 g; sodium 23 mg

Diet Exchanges: 0 milk, 0 vegetable, 2 fruit, 0 bread, 0 meat, 2 fat

▶Flavour Tip
Replace the apricots with prunes, dried mangoes or other dried fruit.

GRILLED PINEAPPLE WITH GINGER-YOGHURT SAUCE
144 calories, 21 g carbs

- **115 g/4 oz low-fat natural yoghurt**
- **1½ teaspoons chopped crystallised ginger**
- **1 teaspoon vanilla essence**
- **1 teaspoon grated orange zest**
- **2 tablespoons butter**
- **1½ tablespoons lime juice**
- **2 tablespoons unsweetened peach or apricot fruit spread**
- **½ cored, peeled pineapple, cut into wedges 4 cm/1½ in thick**

Place a grill rack 10 cm/4 in from the heat source and preheat the grill.

In a small bowl, combine the yoghurt, ginger, vanilla and orange zest. Cover and set aside.

In a small frying pan, combine the butter, lime juice and fruit spread. Cook over low heat until the butter and fruit spread are melted. Place the pineapple in a 28 × 18 cm/11 × 7 in baking tin. Pour the butter mixture over the wedges and toss to coat. Arrange in a single layer.

Grill, turning once, until lightly browned on both sides, 5 to 7 minutes, shaking the tin occasionally so the juices don't burn. Remove the wedges and juices to 4 bowls and serve hot or warm topped with the yoghurt sauce.

Makes 4 servings

Per serving: energy 144 cals/607 kJ; protein 2 g; carbohydrate 21 g (of which 21 g sugars); fat 7 g (of which 4 g saturates); fibre 1 g; sodium 84 mg

Diet Exchanges: 0 milk, 0 vegetable, 1 fruit, 0 bread, 0 meat, 1½ fat

BAKED BANANAS WITH RUM SAUCE
349 calories, 54 g carbs

5 tablespoons orange juice

**3 tablespoons dark rum or
1½ teaspoons rum essence**

**3 tablespoons plum or blueberry
fruit spread**

30 g/I oz butter

1½ tablespoons lemon juice

⅛ teaspoon ground nutmeg

**4 bananas (685 g/1½ lb), halved
lengthwise**

**3 tablespoons coarsely chopped
pecans**

Preheat the oven to 200°C/400°F/gas 6.

In a small saucepan, combine the orange juice, rum or essence, fruit spread, butter, lemon juice and nutmeg. Bring just to the boil over medium heat, stirring. Immediately remove from the heat.

Arrange the bananas, flat side down, in a single layer in a shallow ovenproof dish. Pour the butter mixture over the bananas and sprinkle with the pecans. Bake until the bananas are tender and the sauce has thickened slightly, 12 to 15 minutes.

Makes 4 servings

Per serving: energy 349 cals/1466 kJ; protein 3 g; carbohydrate 54 g (of which 50 g sugars); fat 12 g (of which 5 g saturates); fibre 2 g; sodium 62 mg

Diet Exchanges: 0 milk, 0 vegetable, 2½ fruit, 0 bread, 0 meat, 2½ fat

▶Flavour Tips

Substitute apricot, cherry or raspberry fruit spread for the plum or blueberry spread.
Sprinkle with 1 tablespoon toasted coconut.

APRICOT-ORANGE CLAFOUTIS
165 calories, 25 g carbs

50 g/1¾ oz granulated sugar

320 ml/11 fl oz semi-skimmed milk or unsweetened soya milk

100 g/3½ oz plain flour or wholemeal plain flour

4 tablespoons Splenda

3 eggs

2 teaspoons grated orange zest

½ teaspoon grated ginger

½ teaspoon vanilla essence

230 g/8 oz (about 10) pitted and sliced apricots

¼ teaspoon ground cinnamon

Preheat the oven to 200°C/400°F/gas 6. Coat a 23 cm/9 in deep-dish pie plate or quiche dish with cooking spray and dust with 1 teaspoon of the granulated sugar.

In a large bowl, whisk together the milk, flour, remaining sugar, Splenda, eggs, orange zest, ginger and vanilla essence.

Pour half of the batter into the prepared dish. Arrange the apricots evenly over the batter, then top with the remaining batter. Sprinkle with the cinnamon.

Bake for 40 minutes, or until puffed, browned and firm. Cool on a rack for at least 15 minutes.

Makes 6 servings

Per serving: energy 165 cals/699 kJ; protein 8 g; carbohydrate 25 g (of which 14 g sugars); fat 5 g (of which 1 g saturates); fibre 2 g; sodium 73 mg

Diet Exchanges: ½ milk, 0 vegetable, ½ fruit, ½ bread, ½ meat, ½ fat

Time-Saver

Replace the fresh apricots with 230 g/8 oz frozen and thawed sliced apricots or peaches. Pat the fruit dry before using.

For fewer carbohydrates, replace the sugar with 4 tablespoons Splenda (this will reduce each serving by about 8 grams carbohydrate).

PEACH SOUFFLÉ WITH BLUEBERRIES
71 calories, 6 g carbs

170 g/6 oz frozen peaches, thawed and patted dry

2 tablespoons sugar

2 tablespoons Splenda

2 egg yolks

1 tablespoon lemon juice

½ teaspoon ground nutmeg

5 egg whites, at room temperature

½ teaspoon cream of tartar

⅛ teaspoon ground cinnamon

60 g/2 oz blueberries

Preheat the oven to 180°C/350°F/gas 4.

In a blender or food processor, puree the peaches. Transfer to a medium bowl and stir in the sugar, Splenda, egg yolks, lemon juice and nutmeg. Set aside.

In a large, clean bowl, using an electric mixer, beat the egg whites at medium speed until foamy. Add the cream of tartar and beat on high speed until stiff peaks form.

Stir one-quarter of the egg-white mixture into the peach mixture to lighten it. Gently fold the peach mixture back into the remaining egg white mixture.

Scrape into a 1.5 litre/2½ pint soufflé or ovenproof dish and sprinkle with the cinnamon. Place the dish in a larger dish or baking tin, then place on the bottom rack of the oven. Pour 2–3 cm/1 in of hot water into the larger dish or tin. Bake for 50 to 60 minutes, or until puffed and lightly browned. Do not open the oven door during baking. Serve immediately with the blueberries. The soufflé will fall as it cools.

Makes 4 servings

Per serving: energy 71 cals/299 kJ; protein 6 g; carbohydrate 6 g (of which 6 g sugars); fat 3 g (of which 1 g saturates); fibre 1 g; sodium 81 mg

Diet Exchanges: 0 milk, 0 vegetable, 1 fruit, 0 bread, 0 meat, ½ fat

▶Flavour Tips

Replace the peaches with apricots and the cinnamon with ⅛ teaspoon ground nutmeg.
For fewer carbohydrates per serving, replace the sugar with 2 tablespoons Splenda (this will reduce each serving by about 6 grams carbohydrate).

biscuits, cakes, puddings and fruit desserts

index

Note: <u>Underscored</u> page references indicate boxed text. **Bold** page references indicate photographs.

a

Alcohol, 7, 11, <u>14</u>
Almonds, <u>27</u>
  Chocolate-Almond Meringue Biscuits, 331, **332**
  nutrients in, 72
  Porridge with Ricotta, Fruit and Nuts, 102
  Raspberry-Almond Tarte, 350, **351**
  Roast Pork Tenderloin with Sherry, Cream and
    Almonds, **220**, 221
Amaranth flour, 71
Anchovies
  Grilled Sole with Spring Onion-Anchovy Vinaigrette,
    243
  Shark Braised in Red Wine with Tomato and Anchovy,
    247
Appetisers and snacks
  Avocado with Black Bean Salad, **112**, 113
  Cannellini Beans with Cheese and Basil, 114, **115**
  Cheese, Apple and Nut Butter Roll-Ups, 106
  Chicory with Aubergine, Olives and Pine Nuts, **116**,
    117
  Courgette Chips, 108
  Courgette-Stuffed Mushrooms, 122
  Cracked Wheat Salad with Spinach, 111
  Crudités with Spicy Peanut Dipping Sauce, 118
  Curried Eggs with Horseradish and Spring Onions,
    110
  healthy choices for, 77–78, <u>108</u>
  high-GI snacks, 7, 9
  low-GI snacks, 7, 9
  Mini Aubergine Pizzas, 119
  Prawns in Mustard-Horseradish Sauce, 120, **121**
  Roasted Mixed Nuts, 109
  Soft Yoghurt Cheese, 107
  Soft Yoghurt Cheese with Olives, 107

Apple juice, 9
  Hot Apple Juice with Ginger, 124
Apples, 9
  Baked Apples, 83
  Cabbage Salad with Apples, Lime and Ginger, 309
  Cheese, Apple and Nut Butter Roll-Ups, 106
  Chocolate-Raspberry Dip and Fresh Fruit, 347
  Red Cabbage with Apples, 311
  Spinach Salad with Warm Bacon Vinaigrette, **312**,
    313
  Turkey Drumstick Curry, 192
  Turkey Sandwich with Jarlsberg and Apple, **146**, 147
  Warm Buttered Fruit Compote, 352
Apricots, 9
  Apricot-Orange Clafoutis, 356
  Baked Apples, 83
  Dried Apricot Fool, 353
  Turkey Drumstick Curry, 192
Artificial sweeteners, 30, 60–61, <u>152</u>
Asparagus
  Asparagus and Goat's Cheese Omelettes, 91
  Asparagus with Orange-Walnut Vinaigrette, **306**, 307
  Salmon and Couscous Salad with Vegetables, 254
Aubergine
  Aubergine Parmesan, 289
  Aubergine Stuffed with Savoury Beef, 272, **273**
  Chicory with Aubergine, Olives and Pine Nuts, **116**,
    117
  Janet's Roasted Aubergine and Chickpeas, <u>291</u>
  Mini Aubergine Pizzas, 119
  Moussaka, 296–97, **297**
  Poached Eggs on Tomato-Aubergine Beds, 93
Avocados
  Avocado with Black Bean Salad, **112**, 113
  Crisp Tortilla with Avocado, Beans and Cheese,
    159

b

Bacon
  Bacon-Mushroom Melt, 154, **155**
  Butterbeans with Bacon, 304
  Pan-Fried Trout in Cornmeal with Bacon, 246
  Spinach Salad with Warm Bacon Vinaigrette, **312**, 313
Bananas, 9
  Baked Bananas with Rum Sauce, 355
  Bananas, Dates and Walnuts in Yoghurt Sauce, 84
  Cantaloupe Sorbet, 349
  Wholemeal Crepes with Banana and Kiwifruit, 94, **95**
Barley, 8
  Beef and Barley Casserole, 269
  Lamb and Barley Soup, 134, **135**
Beans
  Avocado with Black Bean Salad, **112**, 113
  for breakfast, 75
  Butterbeans with Bacon, 304
  Cannellini Beans with Cheese and Basil, 114, **115**
  Cannellini Beans with Ham and Sausage, 287
  Chicken Stew with Sweetcorn and Butterbeans, 268
  Chilli-Cornbread Pie, **276**, 277
  Crisp Tortilla with Avocado, Beans and Cheese, 159
  dried, 65–66
  Flageolet Beans with Sesame Oil and Ginger, 323
  GI scores for, 8–9
  Grilled Pork Steaks with Spicy Lentils, 219
  Ham and Lentil Casserole, 288
  health benefits from, 65
  Hearty Country Vegetable Soup, 130
  Italian Bean Soup with Chard and Mushrooms, 140
  Janet's Roasted Aubergine and Chickpeas, 291
  Lamb Shanks with Red Beans, 294
  Lentil Soup with Cauliflower and Yoghurt, 137
  in minced beef recipes, 56
  soaking, 67
  soya bean products, 67–68
  Spanish-Style Green Beans, 322
  Spicy Curried Vegetables, 295
  storing, 67
  tinned, buying, 65
  Turkey Chilli, 280

White Bean Soup with Sausage, 128, **129**
Beef
  Aubergine Stuffed with Savoury Beef, 272, **273**
  Beef and Barley Casserole, 269
  Beef and Cabbage Casserole with Tomato Sauce, 274
  Beef Kebabs with Yoghurt and Spices, **210**, 211
  Boiled Beef and Winter Vegetables, 275
  Bolognese Sauce for Pasta, 214, **214**
  Braised Beef with Mushrooms, 279
  Braised Beef with Turnips, 206, **207**
  buying lean cuts of, 26
  Chilli-Cornbread Pie, **276**, 277
  Cuban-Style Beef Picadillo, 208
  Fillet Steaks with Tomatoes and Rosemary, 204
  Grilled Fillet Steak with Mustard Sauce, **202**, 203
  Italian-Style Beef Burgers, 213
  Meat Loaf with Walnuts, 212
  Pan-Fried Steak with Mushrooms, 200
  Pot Roast, 278
  Quick Pan Scramble with Beef, Eggs and Greens, 270
  Roast Beef with Onion Pan Juices, 201
  Roast Beef Sandwich with Mustard-Horseradish Mayonnaise, 145
  Spicy Meatballs with Coconut Milk, 209
  Texas Burrito, 271
  Topside of Beef Marinated in Soy Sauce and Mustard, 205
Beverages
  Buttermilk Fruit Shake, 125, **146**
  Hot Apple Juice with Ginger, 124
  Iced Orange-Coconut Drink, 123, **123**
  Mint-Infused Darjeeling Tea, 125
  Peach-Pear Smoothie, 126
  Strawberry Protein Shake, 124
Biscuits
  Chocolate-Almond Meringue Biscuits, 331, **332**
  Orange-Walnut Biscotti, **332**, 333
  Peanut Butter Cookies, 330, **332**
Black beans
  Avocado with Black Bean Salad, **112**, 113
Blood sugar levels
  high, risks from, 7, 10–11
  high-GI foods and, 7, 10–11
  insulin and, 7, 10–11
  soluble fibre and, 3
Blueberries
  All-Purpose Fruit Syrup, 82

Baked Pancake with Berries and Cinnamon, 348, **348**
Breakfast Berry Sundaes, 82
Buttermilk Fruit Shake, 125, **146**
Peach Soufflé with Blueberries, 357
Wholemeal Pancakes with Berry Cream Syrup, **96**, 97
Borlotti beans, 9
Chilli-Cornbread Pie, **276**, 277
Crisp Tortilla with Avocado, Beans and Cheese, 159
Breads *see also* Sandwiches; Tortillas
Bread and Butter Pudding, 346
high-GI breads, 7, <u>8</u>
low-GI breads, 7, <u>8</u>
Pecan Muffins, 99, **99**
Raisin Spice Quick Bread, 100
for sandwiches, 76
Sesame Buttermilk Scones, **86**, 101
whole grains in, 69
Breakfast foods
All-Purpose Fruit Syrup, 82
Asparagus and Goat's Cheese Omelettes, 91
Baked Apples, 83
Baked Eggs with Cheese and Courgettes, **86**, 87
Bananas, Dates and Walnuts in Yoghurt Sauce, 84
Breakfast Berry Sundaes, 82
Cherry Porridge, 104
Courgette and Mushroom Frittata, 90
Creamy Quinoa, 103
creative ideas for, 74–75
Fried Eggs with Vinegar, 85
Kamut Crepes with Cottage Cheese and Fruit, 98
Pecan Muffins, 99, **99**
Poached Eggs on Tomato-Aubergine Beds, 93
Porridge with Ricotta, Fruit and Nuts, 102
Puffy Frittata with Ham and Green Pepper, 88, **89**
Raisin Spice Quick Bread, 100
Scrambled Eggs with Sausage and Spring Onions, 92
Sesame Buttermilk Scones, **86**, 101
Wholemeal Crepes with Banana and Kiwifruit, 94, **95**
Wholemeal Pancakes with Berry Cream Syrup, **96**, 97
Broccoli
Creamy Broccoli Soup with Chicken, 131
Stir-Fried Chicken and Broccoli, 264
Buckwheat, GI score for, <u>8</u>
Buckwheat flour, 71
Wholemeal Pancakes with Berry Cream Syrup, **96**, 97
Bulgar wheat, <u>8</u>
Cracked Wheat Salad with Spinach, 111

Burgers
Italian-Style Beef Burgers, 213
Lamb Burgers with Tomatoes and Feta Cheese, 230
Turkey Burgers Stuffed with Chillies and Cheese, 196, **197**
Burritos
Texas Burrito, 271
Butter, buying, 28
Butterbeans, 9
Butterbeans with Bacon, 304
Chicken Stew with Sweetcorn and Butterbeans, 268
Buttermilk
Buttermilk Fruit Shake, 125, **146**
Sesame Buttermilk Scones, **86**, 101

C

Cabbage
Beef and Cabbage Casserole with Tomato Sauce, 274
Boiled Beef and Winter Vegetables, 275
Cabbage Salad with Apples, Lime and Ginger, 309
Creamed Cabbage, 310
Grilled Prawns with Spicy Cabbage Salad, 256
Hearty Country Vegetable Soup, 130
Pork Chops Baked with Cabbage and Cream, 286
Pork Stew with Cabbage, 223
Red Cabbage with Apples, 311
Two-Cheese Pitta Melt, 153
White Bean Soup with Sausage, 128, **129**
Cakes
Chocolate Hazelnut Flourless Cake, 338, **339**
Courgette-Chocolate Chip Snack Cake, 340
Gingerbread Cake with Peach Whipped Cream, 334, **335**
Strawberry Cream Cake, 336, **337**
Calcium, 29, 72
Cancer
dietary factors and, 23–24
high insulin levels and, 7
meat consumption and, 19–20, 56
Cantaloupe, 9
Cantaloupe Sorbet, 349
Capers
Breaded Baked Cod with Tartar Sauce, 234

Chicken Scallopini with Sage and Capers, 166, **167**
Cuban-Style Beef Picadillo, 208
Mackerel Baked with Peppers and Capers, 238
Pork Medallions with Lemon-Caper Sauce and Dill, 215
Smoked Salmon and Cream Cheese on Rye
    Crispbread, 151
Steamed Mussels with Roasted Peppers and Capers,
    262
Tuna Salad in Lettuce Wraps, 160
Carbohydrates, 3
  in healthy diet, 2, 156
  refined, 2
  in sugar-added products, 15–17
  unrefined, 2–3
Carrots, 9
  Boiled Beef and Winter Vegetables, 275
  Chicken Casserole with Buttermilk Scones, 266, **267**
  Hearty Country Vegetable Soup, 130
  Old-Fashioned Lamb Stew, **292**, 293
Cashews, 27, 72
Casseroles and one-dish dinners
  Aubergine Parmesan, 289
  Aubergine Stuffed with Savoury Beef, 272, **273**
  Beef and Barley Casserole, 269
  Beef and Cabbage Casserole with Tomato Sauce, 274
  Boiled Beef and Winter Vegetables, 275
  Braised Beef with Mushrooms, 279
  Cannellini Beans with Ham and Sausage, 287
  Chicken Casserole with Buttermilk Scones, 266, **267**
  Chicken and Ham Jambalaya, 265
  Chicken Stew with Sweetcorn and Butterbeans, 268
  Chilli-Cornbread Pie, **276**, 277
  Ham and Lentil Casserole, 288
  Janet's Roasted Aubergine and Chickpeas, 291
  Lamb Shanks with Red Beans, 294
  Moussaka, 296–97, **297**
  Old-Fashioned Lamb Stew, **292**, 293
  Pork Chops Baked with Cabbage and Cream, 286
  Pork and Pasta Bake, **282**, 283
  Pot Roast, 278
  Quick Pan Scramble with Beef, Eggs and Greens, 270
  Sausage, Egg and Vegetable Casserole, 284, **285**
  Shepherd's Pie, 298, **299**
  Spicy Curried Vegetables, 295
  Stir-Fried Chicken and Broccoli, 264
  Texas Burrito, 271
  Turkey Chilli, 280

Cauliflower
  Chickpea Pancakes with Spicy Vegetables, 158
  Lentil Soup with Cauliflower and Yoghurt, 137
  Roasted Cauliflower with Nutty Lemon Mustard, 308
  Spicy Curried Vegetables, 295
Celery
  for healthy snacks, 77, 108
  Soft Yoghurt Cheese with Olives, 107
Cereals
  Cherry Porridge, 104
  Creamy Quinoa, 103
  GI scores for, 7, 8
  Porridge with Ricotta, Fruit and Nuts, 102
Chard
  Italian Bean Soup with Chard and Mushrooms, 140
  Quick Pan Scramble with Beef, Eggs and Greens, 270
Cheese
  Asparagus and Goat's Cheese Omelettes, 91
  Aubergine Parmesan, 289
  Aubergine Stuffed with Savoury Beef, 272, **273**
  Bacon-Mushroom Melt, 154, **155**
  Baked Eggs with Cheese and Courgettes, **86**, 87
  Cannellini Beans with Cheese and Basil, 114, **115**
  Cheese, Apple and Nut Butter Roll-Ups, 106
  Chicken Breasts with Mozzarella, Peppers and
      Olives, **164**, 165
  Chicken Tetrazzini, 182
  cottage cheese, for breakfast, 75
  Courgette-Stuffed Mushrooms, 122
  Crisp Tortilla with Avocado, Beans and Cheese,
      159
  Gene's Lemon Jelly Whip, 343
  for healthy snacks, 108
  Italian Chicken, 180, **181**
  Italian-Style Beef Burgers, 213
  Kamut Crepes with Cottage Cheese and Fruit, 98
  Lamb Burgers with Tomatoes and Feta Cheese,
      230
  Lynne's On-the-Go Chicken, 174
  Mini Aubergine Pizzas, 119
  Moussaka, 296–97, **297**
  Norma's Spinach Salad with Cajun Chicken, 318
  Pesto Chicken Sandwich with Roasted Peppers, 156,
      157
  Polenta Bake with Cheese and Chillies, 326, **326**
  Pork Chops Baked with Cabbage and Cream, 286
  Pork and Pasta Bake, **282**, 283

Porridge with Ricotta, Fruit and Nuts, 102
Soft Yoghurt Cheese, 107
Soft Yoghurt Cheese with Olives, 107
Texas Burrito, 271
Turkey Burgers Stuffed with Chillies and Cheese, 196, **197**
Turkey Escalopes with Ham and Provolone, **190**, 191
Turkey Sandwich with Jarlsberg and Apple, **146**, 147
Two-Cheese Pitta Melt, 153
Watercress Salad with Goat's Cheese, Pine Nuts and Pears, 314, **315**
Chicken
   Becky's Tropical Chicken Salad in Lettuce Wraps, 150
   buying low-fat parts, 26
   Chicken Breasts with Mozzarella, Peppers and Olives, **164**, 165
   Chicken Breasts with Roasted Peppers and Thyme, 162
   Chicken Breasts in Sherry Sauce with Grapes and Cucumbers, 163
   Chicken Casserole with Buttermilk Scones, 266, **267**
   Chicken Drumsticks Roasted with Herbs, 185
   Chicken Gumbo, **132**, 133
   Chicken and Ham Jambalaya, 265
   Chicken Scallopini with Sage and Capers, 166, **167**
   Chicken Stew with Sweetcorn and Butterbeans, 268
   Chicken Tetrazzini, 182
   Chicken Thighs with Lemon-Pepper Sauce, 168
   Creamy Broccoli Soup with Chicken, 131
   Curried Chicken with Coconut, **170**, 171
   Ginger-Soy Chicken Wings, 178
   Grilled Chicken Diavolo, 187
   Grilled Chicken with Mango Salsa, 188, **189**
   Grilled Lemon-Thyme Chicken Thighs, 183
   Grilled Marinated Chicken Kebabs, 184
   Grilled Orange-Rosemary Chicken, 175
   Italian Chicken, 180, **181**
   Lynne's On-the-Go Chicken, 174
   Norma's Spinach Salad with Cajun Chicken, 318
   Pan-Fried Chicken with Peppery Cream Sauce, 179
   Pesto Chicken Sandwich with Roasted Peppers, 156, **157**
   Roast Chicken with Vegetable and Soya Stuffing, 186
   Roasted Chicken Breasts with Lemon and Mustard, 169
   Sautéed Chicken with Shallots and White Wine, 176, **177**

Stir-Fried Chicken and Broccoli, 264
Chickpeas, 9
   Chickpea Pancakes with Spicy Vegetables, 158
   Janet's Roasted Aubergine and Chickpeas, 291
Chicory
   Chicory with Aubergine, Olives and Pine Nuts, **116**, 117
   Watercress Salad with Goat's Cheese, Pine Nuts and Pears, 314, **315**
Chilli
   Turkey Chilli, 280
Chilli peppers
   Chilli-Cornbread Pie, **276**, 277
   Crisp Tortilla with Avocado, Beans and Cheese, 159
   Crudités with Spicy Peanut Dipping Sauce, 118
   Polenta Bake with Cheese and Chillies, 326, **326**
   Texas Burrito, 271
   Turkey Burgers Stuffed with Chillies and Cheese, 196, **197**
Chocolate
   Chocolate-Almond Meringue Biscuits, 331, **332**
   Chocolate Custard Cups, 344, **345**
   Chocolate Hazelnut Flourless Cake, 338, **339**
   Chocolate-Raspberry Dip and Fresh Fruit, 347
   Courgette-Chocolate Chip Snack Cake, 340
   Double Chocolate Custard, 341
Cholesterol, 18–19
Chowder
   Clam Chowder with Greens, **138**, 139
Clams, 25
   Clam Chowder with Greens, **138**, 139
   Creole-Style Steamed Clams, 258, **258**
Coconut
   Curried Chicken with Coconut, **170**, 171
   Iced Orange-Coconut Drink, 123, **123**
   Spicy Meatballs with Coconut Milk, 209
Cod
   Baked Cod with Lemon and Olive Oil, 232, **233**
   in batter, 25
   Breaded Baked Cod with Tartar Sauce, 234
Cornmeal, 8
   Chilli-Cornbread Pie, **276**, 277
   Pan-Fried Trout in Cornmeal with Bacon, 246
Cottage cheese
   breakfast ideas with, 75
   Kamut Crepes with Cottage Cheese and Fruit, 98

Courgettes
    Baked Eggs with Cheese and Courgettes, **86**, 87
    Chickpea Pancakes with Spicy Vegetables, 158
    Courgette Chips, 108
    Courgette-Chocolate Chip Snack Cake, 340
    Courgette and Mushroom Frittata, 90
    Courgettes and Red Peppers in Lemon-Herb Butter, 302
    Courgette-Stuffed Mushrooms, 122
    Grilled Marinated Chicken Kebabs, 184
    Hearty Country Vegetable Soup, 130
    Mexican-Style Courgette Soup, 144
    Salmon and Couscous Salad with Vegetables, 254
    Sausage, Egg and Vegetable Casserole, 284, **285**
Couscous, 8
    Beef and Cabbage Casserole with Tomato Sauce, 274
    Couscous Salad with Lime-Cumin Dressing, 324, **325**
    Salmon and Couscous Salad with Vegetables, 254
Crabsticks, 25
Cracked wheat (bulgar), 8
    Cracked Wheat Salad with Spinach, 111
Crackers, for healthy snacks, 78
Crepes
    Chocolate Custard Cups, 344, **345**
    Kamut Crepes with Cottage Cheese and Fruit, 98
    Wholemeal Crepes with Banana and Kiwifruit, 94, **95**
Cucumbers
    Chicken Breasts in Sherry Sauce with Grapes and Cucumbers, 163
    Chilled Cucumber, Spring Onion and Yoghurt Soup, 142, **143**
    Cucumber and Radish Salad with Sesame-Soy Dressing, 321
Curry
    Curried Chicken with Coconut, **170**, 171
    Roasted Mixed Nuts, 109
    Spicy Curried Vegetables, 295
    Turkey Drumstick Curry, 192

d

Dairy products see also specific kinds
    GI scores for, 9
    healthy, choosing, 29
    serving sizes of, 38

Dates
    Bananas, Dates and Walnuts in Yoghurt Sauce, 84
    Creamy Quinoa, 103
Desserts see also Biscuits; Cakes
    Apricot-Orange Clafoutis, 356
    Baked Bananas with Rum Sauce, 355
    Baked Pancake with Berries and Cinnamon, 348, **348**
    Cantaloupe Sorbet, 349
    Chocolate-Raspberry Dip and Fresh Fruit, 347
    Dried Apricot Fool, 353
    Grilled Pineapple with Ginger-Yoghurt Sauce, 354
    Peach Soufflé with Blueberries, 357
    Raspberry-Almond Tarte, 350, **351**
    Warm Buttered Fruit Compote, 352
Diabetes, 7
Diet exchanges, 79
Dinner ideas, simple, 77
Dips and spreads
    Cannellini Beans with Cheese and Basil, 114, **115**
    Chocolate-Raspberry Dip and Fresh Fruit, 347
    Crudités with Spicy Peanut Dipping Sauce, 118
    Soft Yoghurt Cheese, 107
    Soft Yoghurt Cheese with Olives, 107
Drinks see Beverages

Eggs
    Asparagus and Goat's Cheese Omelettes, 91
    Baked Eggs with Cheese and Courgettes, **86**, 87
    Bread and Butter Pudding, 346
    Courgette and Mushroom Frittata, 90
    Curried Eggs with Horseradish and Spring Onions, 110
    Fried Eggs with Vinegar, 85
    nutrients in, 26, 103
    Peach Soufflé with Blueberries, 357
    Poached Eggs on Tomato-Aubergine Beds, 93
    Puffy Frittata with Ham and Green Pepper, 88, **89**
    quick meal ideas with, 75, 76, 103
    Quick Pan Scramble with Beef, Eggs and Greens, 270
    Sausage, Egg and Vegetable Casserole, 284, **285**
    Scrambled Eggs with Sausage and Spring Onions, 92
Exercise, 36–37, 230

f

Fatigue, 17–18

Fats
in healthy diet, 17, 106, 187
healthy types of, 25–28, 61, 64–65
heart disease and, 18–19
hydrogenated, 27–28
omega-3 fatty acids, 26–27
saturated, 27, 187
serving size of, 38
trans fats, 187
unsaturated, 27

Feta cheese
Lamb Burgers with Tomatoes and Feta Cheese, 230
Moussaka, 296–97, **297**
Norma's Spinach Salad with Cajun Chicken, 318

Fibre, 3, 6, 20

Fish *see also* Shellfish
Baked Cod with Lemon and Olive Oil, 232, **233**
Baked Halibut Wrapped in Lettuce Leaves, **240**, 241
Baked Salmon with Oregano, 250
Baked Sea Bass with Soy Sauce and Sesame Oil, 235
Betty's Fish with Mushrooms and Spring Onions, 237
Breaded Baked Cod with Tartar Sauce, 234
carbohydrates in, 25
Grilled Mackerel with Lemon-Mint Butter, 242
Grilled Salmon with Mint-Coriander Yoghurt, **252**, 253
Grilled Sea Bass with Chilli-Lime Butter, 244
Grilled Sole with Spring Onion-Anchovy Vinaigrette, 243
healthy fats in, 26
Mackerel Baked with Peppers and Capers, 238
Pan-Fried Trout in Cornmeal with Bacon, 246
Poached Halibut with Herbed Olive Oil, 239
Salmon and Couscous Salad with Vegetables, 254
Salmon Salad with Fresh Ginger, 251
Sautéed Trout with Almond Butter Sauce, 245
Sautéed Tuna Steaks with Garlic Sauce, 248, **249**
Shark Braised in Red Wine with Tomato and Anchovy, 247
Smoked Salmon and Cream Cheese on Rye Crispbread, 151
Tuna Salad in Lettuce Wraps, 160

Flageolet beans
Flageolet Beans with Sesame Oil and Ginger, 323

Flavouring foods, 64, 73–74

Flours, wholegrain, 69–71

Fluid retention, 260

Food product labels, 22, 29, 61, 66

French beans
Hearty Country Vegetable Soup, 130
Spanish-Style Green Beans, 322
Spicy Curried Vegetables, 295

Frittatas
Courgette and Mushroom Frittata, 90
Puffy Frittata with Ham and Green Pepper, 88, **89**

Fruit *see also specific kinds*
All-Purpose Fruit Syrup, 82
Chocolate-Raspberry Dip and Fresh Fruit, 347
for healthy snacks, 77
high-GI fruits, 7, 9
in low-carb diet, 23–25
low-GI fruits, 7, 9, 29–30
serving size of, 38
Warm Buttered Fruit Compote, 352

g

Genetics, 11, 244

GI *see* Glycaemic index

Ginger
Beef Kebabs with Yoghurt and Spices, **210**, 211
Cabbage Salad with Apples, Lime and Ginger, 309
Chickpea Pancakes with Spicy Vegetables, 158
Cucumber and Radish Salad with Sesame-Soy Dressing, 321
Flageolet Beans with Sesame Oil and Ginger, 323
Ginger-Soy Chicken Wings, 178
Grilled Marinated Chicken Kebabs, 184
Hot Apple Juice with Ginger, 124
Salmon Salad with Fresh Ginger, 251
Stir-Fried Chicken and Broccoli, 264

Glucose, 3, 7, 10 *see also* Glycaemic index (GI)

Glycaemic index (GI), 3–7, 8–9
high-GI foods, 6–7
low-GI foods, 6–7, 22, 29–30

Goat's cheese
Asparagus and Goat's Cheese Omelettes, 91
Watercress Salad with Goat's Cheese, Pine Nuts and
Pears, 314, **315**
Grains
Beef and Barley Casserole, 269
Beef and Cabbage Casserole with Tomato Sauce,
274
in breakfast cereals, 74–75
Brown Rice Pilaf with Hazelnuts, 328
Cherry Porridge, 104
Chicken and Ham Jambalaya, 265
Chilli-Cornbread Pie, **276**, 277
Couscous Salad with Lime-Cumin Dressing, 324,
325
Cracked Wheat Salad with Spinach, 111
Creamy Quinoa, 103
in minced beef recipes, 56
high-GI grains, 7, 8
Lamb and Barley Soup, 134, **135**
in low-carb diet, 21–23, 68–70
low-GI grains, 7, 8, 22
Mushroom and Kasha Soup, 136
Pan-Fried Trout in Cornmeal with Bacon, 246
Polenta Bake with Cheese and Chillies, 326, **326**
Porridge with Ricotta, Fruit and Nuts, 102
Quinoa and Vegetable Pilaf, 327
Raspberry-Almond Tarte, 350, **351**
Roast Chicken with Vegetable and Soya Stuffing,
186
Salmon and Couscous Salad with Vegetables, 254
Turkey Loaf, 194, **195**
wholegrain flours, 69–71
Wholemeal Crepes with Banana and Kiwifruit, 94,
95
Wholemeal Pancakes with Berry Cream Syrup, **96**,
97
Grapes, 9
Becky's Tropical Chicken Salad in Lettuce Wraps,
150
Chicken Breasts in Sherry Sauce with Grapes and
Cucumbers, 163
slicing, 163
Greens see also specific kinds
Clam Chowder with Greens, **138**, 139
Quick Pan Scramble with Beef, Eggs and Greens,
270

Tossed Salad with Green Herb Dressing, 319
Watercress Salad with Goat's Cheese, Pine Nuts and
Pears, 314, **315**
Gumbo
Chicken Gumbo, **132**, 133

h

Halibut
Baked Halibut Wrapped in Lettuce Leaves, **240**, 241
Poached Halibut with Herbed Olive Oil, 239
Ham
Cannellini Beans with Ham and Sausage, 287
Chicken and Ham Jambalaya, 265
Chicken Gumbo, **132**, 133
Ham and Lentil Casserole, 288
Ham and Soft Yoghurt Cheese on Rye Crispbread,
152
Poached Eggs on Tomato-Aubergine Beds, 93
Puffy Frittata with Ham and Green Pepper, 88, **89**
Turkey Escalopes with Ham and Provolone, 190, 191
Hazelnuts, 27
Brown Rice Pilaf with Hazelnuts, 328
Chocolate Hazelnut Flourless Cake, 338, **339**
HCAs see Heterocyclic amines
Heart disease
dietary factors and, 23–24
dietary fats and, 18–19, 26–28
insulin levels and, 7
Herbs see also specific kinds
Baked Scallops with Herbs and White Wine, 260, **261**
for boosting flavours, 64, 73
Chicken Drumsticks Roasted with Herbs, 185
Poached Halibut with Herbed Olive Oil, 239
Roast Turkey Breast with Herb Rub and Pan Juices,
193
Tossed Salad with Green Herb Dressing, 319
Herring, rollmop, 25
Heterocyclic amines (HCAs), 56
Horseradish
Curried Eggs with Horseradish and Spring Onions,
110
Prawns in Mustard-Horseradish Sauce, 120, **121**
Roast Beef Sandwich with Mustard-Horseradish
Mayonnaise, 145

i

Insoluble fibre, 3
Insulin levels, 7, 10–11

j

Jarlsberg
    Baked Eggs with Cheese and Courgettes, **86**, 87
    Cheese, Apple and Nut Butter Roll-Ups, 106
    Lynne's On-the-Go Chicken, 174
    Pork Chops Baked with Cabbage and Cream, 286
    Turkey Sandwich with Jarlsberg and Apple, **146**, 147
    Two-Cheese Pitta Melt, 153

k

Kebabs
    Beef Kebabs with Yoghurt and Spices, **210**, 211
    Grilled Marinated Chicken Kebabs, 184
    Lamb Kebabs with Mushrooms and Tomatoes, 227
Kamut flour, 70
    Kamut Crepes with Cottage Cheese and Fruit, 98
Kasha
    Mushroom and Kasha Soup, 136
Kidney beans, 8, 9
    Lamb Shanks with Red Beans, 294
    Turkey Chilli, 280
Kidney damage, 18
Kiwifruit, 9
    Wholemeal Crepes with Banana and Kiwifruit, 94, **95**

l

Lamb
    buying lean cuts of, 26
    Lamb and Barley Soup, 134, **135**

    Lamb Burgers with Tomatoes and Feta Cheese, 230
    Lamb Chops with Olives, **228**, 229
    Lamb with Garlic and Mushrooms, 226
    Lamb Kebabs with Mushrooms and Tomatoes, 227
    Lamb Shanks with Red Beans, 294
    Moussaka, 296–97, **297**
    Old-Fashioned Lamb Stew, **292**, 293
    Shepherd's Pie, 298, **299**
Leftovers, planning, 36, 76
Lemons
    Baked Cod with Lemon and Olive Oil, 232, **233**
    Breaded Turkey Escalopes with Oregano and Lemon, 198
    Chicken Thighs with Lemon-Pepper Sauce, 168
    Courgettes and Red Peppers in Lemon-Herb Butter, 302
    Gene's Lemon Jelly Whip, 343
    Grilled Chicken Diavolo, 187
    Grilled Lemon-Thyme Chicken Thighs, 183
    Grilled Mackerel with Lemon-Mint Butter, 242
    Pork Medallions with Lemon-Caper Sauce and Dill, 215
    Roasted Cauliflower with Nutty Lemon Mustard, 308
    Roasted Chicken Breasts with Lemon and Mustard, 169
Lentils, 9
    Grilled Pork Steaks with Spicy Lentils, 219
    Ham and Lentil Casserole, 288
    Lentil Soup with Cauliflower and Yoghurt, 137
Lettuce
    Baked Halibut Wrapped in Lettuce Leaves, **240**, 241
    Becky's Tropical Chicken Salad in Lettuce Wraps, 150
    as sandwich wrappers, 75
    Tuna Salad in Lettuce Wraps, 160
Limes
    Cabbage Salad with Apples, Lime and Ginger, 309
    Couscous Salad with Lime-Cumin Dressing, 324, **325**
    Grilled Sea Bass with Chilli-Lime Butter, 244
Low-carb cooking
    boosting flavours, 64
    browning meats, 53, 56
    healthy oils for, 61, 64–65
    stocking foods for, 54–55
    sugar alternatives for, 57, 60–61
Low-carb diet, 1, 2, 10–11, 14, 17
    daily menus for, 45–51

food pyramid for, 42
low-carb food substitutions, 62–63
questions about, 17–20
research on, 14–15
Lunch ideas, 75–76

Mackerel
Grilled Mackerel with Lemon-Mint Butter, 242
Mackerel Baked with Peppers and Capers, 238
Main courses
  beef
    Beef Kebabs with Yoghurt and Spices, **210**, 211
    Bolognese Sauce for Pasta, 214, **214**
    Braised Beef with Turnips, 206, **207**
    Cuban-Style Beef Picadillo, 208
    Fillet Steaks with Tomatoes and Rosemary, 204
    Grilled Fillet Steak with Mustard Sauce, **202**, 203
    Italian-Style Beef Burgers, 213
    Meat Loaf with Walnuts, 212
    Pan-Fried Steak with Mushrooms, 200
    Roast Beef with Onion Pan Juices, 201
    Spicy Meatballs with Coconut Milk, 209
    Topside of Beef Marinated in Soy Sauce and
      Mustard, 205
  chicken
    Chicken Breasts with Mozzarella, Peppers and
      Olives, **164**, 165
    Chicken Breasts with Roasted Peppers and Thyme,
      162
    Chicken Breasts in Sherry Sauce with Grapes and
      Cucumbers, 163
    Chicken Drumsticks Roasted with Herbs, 185
    Chicken Scallopini with Sage and Capers, 166, **167**
    Chicken Tetrazzini, 182
    Chicken Thighs with Lemon-Pepper Sauce, 168
    Curried Chicken with Coconut, **170**, 171
    Ginger-Soy Chicken Wings, 178
    Grilled Chicken Diavolo, 187
    Grilled Chicken with Mango Salsa, 188, **189**
    Grilled Lemon-Thyme Chicken Thighs, 183
    Grilled Marinated Chicken Kebabs, 184
    Grilled Orange-Rosemary Chicken, 175
    Italian Chicken, 180, **181**

Lynne's On-the-Go Chicken, 174
Pan-Fried Chicken with Peppery Cream Sauce, 179
Roast Chicken with Vegetable and Soya Stuffing,
  186
Roasted Chicken Breasts with Lemon and
  Mustard, 169
Sautéed Chicken with Shallots and White Wine,
  176, **177**
  fish
    Baked Cod with Lemon and Olive Oil, 232, **233**
    Baked Halibut Wrapped in Lettuce Leaves, **240**, 241
    Baked Salmon with Oregano, 250
    Baked Sea Bass with Soy Sauce and Sesame Oil, 235
    Betty's Fish with Mushrooms and Spring Onions,
      237
    Breaded Baked Cod with Tartar Sauce, 234
    Grilled Mackerel with Lemon-Mint Butter, 242
    Grilled Sea Bass with Chilli-Lime Butter, 244
    Grilled Sole with Spring Onion-Anchovy
      Vinaigrette, 243
    Grilled Salmon with Mint-Coriander Yoghurt, **252**,
      253
    Mackerel Baked with Peppers and Capers, 238
    Pan-Fried Trout in Cornmeal with Bacon, 246
    Poached Halibut with Herbed Olive Oil, 239
    Salmon and Couscous Salad with Vegetables, 254
    Salmon Salad with Fresh Ginger, 251
    Sautéed Trout with Almond Butter Sauce, 245
    Sautéed Tuna Steaks with Garlic Sauce, 248, **249**
    Shark Braised in Red Wine with Tomato and
      Anchovy, 247
  lamb
    Lamb Burgers with Tomatoes and Feta Cheese, 230
    Lamb Chops with Olives, **228**, 229
    Lamb with Garlic and Mushrooms, 226
    Lamb Kebabs with Mushrooms and Tomatoes, 227
  one-dish dinners
    Aubergine Parmesan, 289
    Aubergine Stuffed with Savoury Beef, 272, **273**
    Beef and Barley Casserole, 269
    Beef and Cabbage Casserole with Tomato Sauce, 274
    Boiled Beef and Winter Vegetables, 275
    Braised Beef with Mushrooms, 279
    Cannellini Beans with Ham and Sausage, 287
    Chicken Casserole with Buttermilk Scones, 266,
      267
    Chicken and Ham Jambalaya, 265

Chicken Stew with Sweetcorn and Butterbeans, 268
Chilli-Cornbread Pie, **276**, 277
Ham and Lentil Casserole, 288
Janet's Roasted Aubergine and Chickpeas, 291
Lamb Shanks with Red Beans, 294
Moussaka, 296–97, **297**
Old-Fashioned Lamb Stew, **292**, 293
Pork Chops Baked with Cabbage and Cream, 286
Pork and Pasta Bake, **282**, 283
Pot Roast, 278
Quick Pan Scramble with Beef, Eggs and Greens, 270
Sausage, Egg and Vegetable Casserole, 284, **285**
Shepherd's Pie, 298, **299**
Spicy Curried Vegetables, 295
Stir-Fried Chicken and Broccoli, 264
Texas Burrito, 271
Turkey Chilli, 280
Pork
Barbecued Spareribs, 222
Grilled Pork Steaks with Spicy Lentils, 219
Pork Chops with Cider, Walnuts and Prunes, 216, **217**
Pork Chops in Mustard-Wine Sauce, 218
Pork Medallions with Lemon-Caper Sauce and Dill, 215
Pork Stew with Cabbage, 223
Roast Pork Loin with Orange Juice and White Wine, 224, **224**
Roast Pork Tenderloin with Sherry, Cream and Almonds, **220**, 221
shellfish, 25
Baked Scallops with Herbs and White Wine, 260, **261**
Creole-Style Steamed Clams, 258, **258**
Grilled Prawns with Spicy Cabbage Salad, 256
Prawn Salad with Dill and Oranges, 255
Scallops in Tarragon Cream, 259
Spicy Sautéed Prawns with Garlic, 257
Steamed Mussels with Roasted Peppers and Capers, 262
turkey
Breaded Turkey Escalopes with Oregano and Lemon, 198
Roast Turkey Breast with Herb Rub and Pan Juices, 193
Turkey Burgers Stuffed with Chillies and Cheese, 196, **197**
Turkey Drumstick Curry, 192
Turkey Escalopes with Ham and Provolone, **190**, 191
Turkey Loaf, 194, **195**
venison
Peppered Venison Fillets, 225
Mangoes, 9
Grilled Chicken with Mango Salsa, 188, **189**
Margarine, buying, 28
Meat see also Beef; Lamb; Pork; Venison
browning, 53, 56
cancer risks and, 19–20, 56
lean cuts of, 26
Meatballs
Spicy Meatballs with Coconut Milk, 209
Meat loaf
Meat Loaf with Walnuts, 212
Turkey Loaf, 194, **195**
Melon, 9
Cantaloupe Sorbet, 349
Chilled Melon Soup with Basil, 141
Milk
GI scores for, 9
serving size of, 38
soya, 67–68
sugars in, 29
Mint
Grilled Mackerel with Lemon-Mint Butter, 242
Grilled Salmon with Mint-Coriander Yoghurt, **252**, 253
Mint-Infused Darjeeling Tea, 125
Mozzarella cheese
Aubergine Parmesan, 289
Chicken Breasts with Mozzarella, Peppers and Olives, **164**, 165
Italian Chicken, 180, **181**
Mini Aubergine Pizzas, 119
Pesto Chicken Sandwich with Roasted Peppers, 156, **157**
Pork and Pasta Bake, **282**, 283
Two-Cheese Pitta Melt, 153
Muffins
Pecan Muffins, 99, **99**
Mushrooms
Bacon-Mushroom Melt, 154, **155**

Betty's Fish with Mushrooms and Spring Onions, 237
Braised Beef with Mushrooms, 279
Chicken Tetrazzini, 182
Courgette and Mushroom Frittata, 90
Courgette-Stuffed Mushrooms, 122
Grilled Marinated Chicken Kebabs, 184
Italian Bean Soup with Chard and Mushrooms, 140
Lamb with Garlic and Mushrooms, 226
Lamb Kebabs with Mushrooms and Tomatoes, 227
Mushroom and Kasha Soup, 136
Mushrooms Provençale, 303
Pan-Fried Steak with Mushrooms, 200
Pork and Pasta Bake, **282**, 283
Mussels
Steamed Mussels with Roasted Peppers and Capers, 262
Mustard
Grilled Fillet Steak with Mustard Sauce, **202**, 203
Pork Chops in Mustard-Wine Sauce, 218
Prawns in Mustard-Horseradish Sauce, 120, **121**
Roast Beef Sandwich with Mustard-Horseradish Mayonnaise, 145
Roasted Cauliflower with Nutty Lemon Mustard, 308
Roasted Chicken Breasts with Lemon and Mustard, 169
Topside of Beef Marinated in Soy Sauce and Mustard, 205

n

Nut butters, 73
Cheese, Apple and Nut Butter Roll-Ups, 106
Crudités with Spicy Peanut Dipping Sauce, 118
Peanut Butter Cookies, 330, **332**
for quick snacks, 108
Sautéed Trout with Almond Butter Sauce, 245
Turkey Sandwich with Jarlsberg and Apple, **146**, 147
Nuts *see also* Almonds; Hazelnuts; Nut butters; Pecans; Pine nuts; Walnuts
buying and storing, 72
calories and carbohydrates in, 27
creative uses for, 72–73
healthy fats in, 26–27
for healthy snacks, 77, 108

nutrients in, 72
Roasted Mixed Nuts, 109
serving size of, 27, 38
toasting, 72

O

Oat flour, 70
Gingerbread Cake with Peach Whipped Cream, 334, **335**
Raisin Spice Quick Bread, 100
Strawberry Cream Cake, 336, **337**
Oats
Cherry Porridge, 104
GI score for, 6, 8
Porridge with Ricotta, Fruit and Nuts, 102
Raspberry-Almond Tarte, 350, **351**
soluble fibre in, 6
Obesity, 17
Oils, healthy, 61, 64–65
Olives
Chicken Breasts with Mozzarella, Peppers and Olives, **164**, 165
Chicory with Aubergine, Olives and Pine Nuts, **116**, 117
Cuban-Style Beef Picadillo, 208
Lamb Chops with Olives, **228**, 229
Soft Yoghurt Cheese with Olives, 107
Spanish-Style Green Beans, 322
Omega-3 fatty acids, 26–27
Omelettes
Asparagus and Goat's Cheese Omelettes, 91
Oranges, 9
Apricot-Orange Clafoutis, 356
Asparagus with Orange-Walnut Vinaigrette, **306**, 307
Chocolate-Raspberry Dip and Fresh Fruit, 347
Dried Apricot Fool, 353
Grilled Orange-Rosemary Chicken, 175
Iced Orange-Coconut Drink, 123, **123**
Orange-Walnut Biscotti, **332**, 333
Prawn Salad with Dill and Oranges, 255
Roast Pork Loin with Orange Juice and White Wine, 224, **224**
Strawberry Protein Shake, 124
Osteoporosis, 19, 24
Overeating, 23

p

Pancakes
    Baked Pancake with Berries and Cinnamon, 348, **348**
    Chickpea Pancakes with Spicy Vegetables, 158
    Wholemeal Pancakes with Berry Cream Syrup, **96**, 97
Parmesan cheese
    Aubergine Parmesan, 289
    Aubergine Stuffed with Savoury Beef, 272, **273**
    Cannellini Beans with Cheese and Basil, 114, **115**
    Chicken Tetrazzini, 182
    Courgette-Stuffed Mushrooms, 122
    Lynne's On-the-Go Chicken, 174
    Moussaka, 296–97, **297**
Parsnips, 9
    Boiled Beef and Winter Vegetables, 275
    Chicken Casserole with Buttermilk Scones, 266, **267**
Pasta
    Bolognese Sauce for Pasta, 214, **214**
    Chicken Tetrazzini, 182
    GI scores for, 7, 8
    Pork and Pasta Bake, **282**, 283
    Turkey Chilli, 280
Peaches, 9
    Peach-Pear Smoothie, 126
    Peach Soufflé with Blueberries, 357
    Porridge with Ricotta, Fruit and Nuts, 102
    Warm Buttered Fruit Compote, 352
Peanut butter
    Crudités with Spicy Peanut Dipping Sauce, 118
    Peanut Butter Cookies, 330, **332**
    unsweetened, buying, 73
Pears, 9
    Chocolate-Raspberry Dip and Fresh Fruit, 347
    Kamut Crepes with Cottage Cheese and Fruit, 98
    Peach-Pear Smoothie, 126
    Warm Buttered Fruit Compote, 352
    Watercress Salad with Goat's Cheese, Pine Nuts and Pears, 314, **315**
Pecans, 72
    Pecan Muffins, 99, **99**
    Roasted Mixed Nuts, 109
Peppers *see also* Chilli peppers
    Baked Peppers with Onion and Tomato, 305
    Beef and Barley Casserole, 269
    Beef and Cabbage Casserole with Tomato Sauce, 274
    Beef Kebabs with Yoghurt and Spices, **210**, 211
    Chicken Breasts with Mozzarella, Peppers and Olives, **164**, 165
    Chicken Breasts with Roasted Peppers and Thyme, 162
    Chicken Gumbo, **132**, 133
    Chicken and Ham Jambalaya, 265
    Chicken Stew with Sweetcorn and Butterbeans, 268
    Courgettes and Red Peppers in Lemon-Herb Butter, 302
    Couscous Salad with Lime-Cumin Dressing, 324, **325**
    Creole-Style Steamed Clams, 258, **258**
    Cuban-Style Beef Picadillo, 208
    Curried Chicken with Coconut, **170**, 171
    Italian Bean Soup with Chard and Mushrooms, 140
    Mackerel Baked with Peppers and Capers, 238
    Pesto Chicken Sandwich with Roasted Peppers, 156, **157**
    Pork and Pasta Bake, **282**, 283
    Puffy Frittata with Ham and Green Pepper, 88, **89**
    Sausage, Egg and Vegetable Casserole, 284, **285**
    Spanish-Style Green Beans, 322
    Steamed Mussels with Roasted Peppers and Capers, 262
Pies
    Chilli-Cornbread Pie, **276**, 277
    Shepherd's Pie, 298, **299**
Pilaf
    Brown Rice Pilaf with Hazelnuts, 328
    Quinoa and Vegetable Pilaf, 327
Pineapple, 9
    Becky's Tropical Chicken Salad in Lettuce Wraps, 150
    Grilled Pineapple with Ginger-Yoghurt Sauce, 354
Pine nuts
    Baked Apples, 83
    calories and carbohydrates in, 27
    Chicory with Aubergine, Olives and Pine Nuts, **116**, 117
    for healthy snacks, 108
    Italian-Style Beef Burgers, 213
    protein in, 72
    Watercress Salad with Goat's Cheese, Pine Nuts and Pears, 314, **315**

Pitta bread, 8
    Two-Cheese Pitta Melt, 153
Plums, 9
    Porridge with Ricotta, Fruit and Nuts, 102
Polenta Bake with Cheese and Chillis, 326, **326**
Pork *see also* Bacon; Ham
    Barbecued Spareribs, 222
    Bolognese Sauce for Pasta, 214, **214**
    buying lean cuts of, 26
    Cannellini Beans with Ham and Sausage, 287
    Grilled Pork Steaks with Spicy Lentils, 219
    Pork Chops Baked with Cabbage and Cream, 286
    Pork Chops with Cider, Walnuts and Prunes, 216, **217**
    Pork Chops in Mustard-Wine Sauce, 218
    Pork Medallions with Lemon-Caper Sauce and Dill, 215
    Pork and Pasta Bake, **282**, 283
    Pork Stew with Cabbage, 223
    Roast Pork Loin with Orange Juice and White Wine, 224, **224**
    Roast Pork Tenderloin with Sherry, Cream and Almonds, **220**, 221
    Sausage, Egg and Vegetable Casserole, 284, **285**
    White Bean Soup with Sausage, 128, **129**
Portion sizes, 30–31
Potatoes, 9
    Shepherd's Pie, 298, **299**
    Spicy Curried Vegetables, 295
Poultry *see* Chicken; Turkey
Prawns, 25
    Grilled Prawns with Spicy Cabbage Salad, 256
    Prawns in Mustard-Horseradish Sauce, 120, **121**
    Prawn Salad with Dill and Oranges, 255
    Spicy Sautéed Prawns with Garlic, 257
Prescription medications, 175
Protein
    lean choices for, 25–28
    in low-carb diet, 18–19
    low-GI protein foods, 7
    protein bars and powders, 74
    serving size of, 38
    varying, in weekly menu, 77
Provolone cheese
    Baked Eggs with Cheese and Courgettes, **86**, 87
    Turkey Escalopes with Ham and Provolone, **190**, 191
Prunes
    Baked Apples, 83
    Pork Chops with Cider, Walnuts and Prunes, 216, **217**

Puddings
    Bread and Butter Pudding, 346
    Chocolate Custard Cups, 344, **345**
    Double Chocolate Custard, 341
    Gene's Lemon Jelly Whip, 343

q

Quinoa
    Creamy Quinoa, 103
    flour, 71
    Quinoa and Vegetable Pilaf, 327
    Turkey Loaf, 194, **195**

r

Radishes
    Cucumber and Radish Salad with Sesame-Soy Dressing, 321
Raisins, 9
    Bread and Butter Pudding, 346
    Cuban-Style Beef Picadillo, 208
    Raisin Spice Quick Bread, 100
Raspberries
    All-Purpose Fruit Syrup, 82
    Baked Pancake with Berries and Cinnamon, 348, **348**
    Chocolate-Raspberry Dip and Fresh Fruit, 347
    Raspberry-Almond Tarte, 350, **351**
Restaurant menus, 23, 76
Rice
    Brown Rice Pilaf with Hazelnuts, 328
    Chicken and Ham Jambalaya, 265
    GI scores for, 8
    whole grain, buying, 69
Ricotta cheese
    Gene's Lemon Jelly Whip, 343
    Porridge with Ricotta, Fruit and Nuts, 102
Rye crispbread, 8
    Ham and Soft Yoghurt Cheese on Rye Crispbread, 152
    Smoked Salmon and Cream Cheese on Rye Crispbread, 151

S

Salads
Avocado with Black Bean Salad, **112**, 113
Becky's Tropical Chicken Salad in Lettuce Wraps, 150
Cabbage Salad with Apples, Lime and Ginger, 309
Couscous Salad with Lime-Cumin Dressing, 324, **325**
Cracked Wheat Salad with Spinach, 111
creative ideas for, 75
Cucumber and Radish Salad with Sesame-Soy
Dressing, 321
Grilled Prawns with Spicy Cabbage Salad, 256
Norma's Spinach Salad with Cajun Chicken, 318
Prawn Salad with Dill and Oranges, 255
from salad bars, 309
Salmon and Couscous Salad with Vegetables, 254
Salmon Salad with Fresh Ginger, 251
Spinach Salad with Warm Bacon Vinaigrette, **312**,
313
Tomato-Onion Salad with Walnut Vinaigrette, 320
Tossed Salad with Green Herb Dressing, 319
Tuna Salad in Lettuce Wraps, 160
Watercress Salad with Goat's Cheese, Pine Nuts and
Pears, 314, **315**
Salmon
Baked Salmon with Oregano, 250
Grilled Salmon with Mint-Coriander Yoghurt, **252**,
253
Salmon and Couscous Salad with Vegetables, 254
Salmon Salad with Fresh Ginger, 251
Smoked Salmon and Cream Cheese on Rye
Crispbread, 151
Sandwiches
Bacon-Mushroom Melt, 154, **155**
Becky's Tropical Chicken Salad in Lettuce Wraps, 150
Chickpea Pancakes with Spicy Vegetables, 158
Crisp Tortilla with Avocado, Beans and Cheese, 159
Ham and Soft Yoghurt Cheese on Rye Crispbread,
152
healthy breads for, 76
Pesto Chicken Sandwich with Roasted Peppers, 156,
157
Roast Beef Sandwich with Mustard-Horseradish
Mayonnaise, 145
Smoked Salmon and Cream Cheese on Rye
Crispbread, 151

Tuna Salad in Lettuce Wraps, 160
Turkey Sandwich with Jarlsberg and Apple, **146**, 147
Two-Cheese Pitta Melt, 153
Saturated fats, 27, 38
Sauces
Bolognese Sauce for Pasta, 214, **214**
Breaded Baked Cod with Tartar Sauce, 234
Crudités with Spicy Peanut Dipping Sauce, 118
Grilled Fillet Steak with Mustard Sauce, **202**, 203
Prawns in Mustard-Horseradish Sauce, 120, **121**
Sausage
Cannellini Beans with Ham and Sausage, 287
Sausage, Egg and Vegetable Casserole, 284, **285**
Scrambled Eggs with Sausage and Spring Onions, 92
White Bean Soup with Sausage, 128, **129**
Scallops, 25
Baked Scallops with Herbs and White Wine, 260,
261
Scallops in Tarragon Cream, 259
Scampi, 25
Scones
Sesame Buttermilk Scones, **86**, 101
Sea bass
Grilled Sea Bass with Chilli-Lime Butter, 244
Baked Sea Bass with Soy Sauce and Sesame Oil, 235
Serving sizes, 27, 30–31, 38
Shark
Shark Braised in Red Wine with Tomato and Anchovy,
247
Shellfish
Baked Scallops with Herbs and White Wine, 260,
261
carbohydrates in, 25
Clam Chowder with Greens, **138**, 139
Creole-Style Steamed Clams, 258, **258**
Grilled Prawns with Spicy Cabbage Salad, 256
Prawns in Mustard-Horseradish Sauce, 120, **121**
Prawn Salad with Dill and Oranges, 255
Scallops in Tarragon Cream, 259
Spicy Sautéed Prawns with Garlic, 257
Steamed Mussels with Roasted Peppers and Capers,
262
Side dishes
Asparagus with Orange-Walnut Vinaigrette, **306**, 307
Baked Peppers with Onion and Tomato, 305
Brown Rice Pilaf with Hazelnuts, 328
Butterbeans with Bacon, 304

Cabbage Salad with Apples, Lime and Ginger, 309
Courgettes and Red Peppers in Lemon-Herb Butter, 302
Couscous Salad with Lime-Cumin Dressing, 324, **325**
Cucumber and Radish Salad with Sesame-Soy Dressing, 321
Creamed Cabbage, 310
Flageolet Beans with Sesame Oil and Ginger, 323
Mushrooms Provençale, 303
Norma's Spinach Salad with Cajun Chicken, 318
Polenta Bake with Cheese and Chillies, 326, **326**
Quinoa and Vegetable Pilaf, 327
Red Cabbage with Apples, 311
Roasted Cauliflower with Nutty Lemon Mustard, 308
Spanish-Style Green Beans, 322
Spinach Salad with Warm Bacon Vinaigrette, **312**, 313
Tomato-Onion Salad with Walnut Vinaigrette, 320
Tossed Salad with Green Herb Dressing, 319
Watercress Salad with Goat's Cheese, Pine Nuts and Pears, 314, **315**
Snacks see Appetisers and snacks
Sole
    Grilled Sole with Spring Onion-Anchovy Vinaigrette, 243
Soluble fibre, 3, 6
Sorbet
    Cantaloupe Sorbet, 349
Soufflés
    Peach Soufflé with Blueberries, 357
Soups see also Stews
    Chicken Gumbo, **132**, 133
    Chilled Cucumber, Spring Onion and Yoghurt Soup, 142, **143**
    Chilled Melon Soup with Basil, 141
    Clam Chowder with Greens, **138**, 139
    Creamy Broccoli Soup with Chicken, 131
    Hearty Country Vegetable Soup, 130
    Italian Bean Soup with Chard and Mushrooms, 140
    Lamb and Barley Soup, 134, **135**
    Lentil Soup with Cauliflower and Yoghurt, 137
    Mexican-Style Courgette Soup, 144
    Mushroom and Kasha Soup, 136
    White Bean Soup with Sausage, 128, **129**
Soya beans, 9
    buying and cooking, 323
    health benefits from, 67

Soya flour, 68
    Pecan Muffins, 99, **99**
    Sesame Buttermilk Scones, **86**, 101
Soya milk, 9, 67–68
Soya mince, 68
    Roast Chicken with Vegetable and Soya Stuffing, 186
Soy sauce
    Baked Sea Bass with Soy Sauce and Sesame Oil, 235
    Crudités with Spicy Peanut Dipping Sauce, 118
    Cucumber and Radish Salad with Sesame-Soy Dressing, 321
    Flageolet Beans with Sesame Oil and Ginger, 323
    Ginger-Soy Chicken Wings, 178
    Grilled Marinated Chicken Kebabs, 184
    Lamb Kebabs with Mushrooms and Tomatoes, 227
    Salmon Salad with Fresh Ginger, 251
    Topside of Beef Marinated in Soy Sauce and Mustard, 205
Spices, for flavouring, 64, 73
Spinach
    Cracked Wheat Salad with Spinach, 111
    health benefits from, 75–76
    Lynne's On-the-Go Chicken, 174
    Norma's Spinach Salad with Cajun Chicken, 318
    Roast Beef Sandwich with Mustard-Horseradish Mayonnaise, 145
    Sausage, Egg and Vegetable Casserole, 284, **285**
    Spinach Salad with Warm Bacon Vinaigrette, **312**, 313
    Tossed Salad with Green Herb Dressing, 319
Splenda, 60–61
Spreads see Dips and spreads
Starches, 22–23, 38
Stews
    Chicken Stew with Sweetcorn and Butterbeans, 268
    Old-Fashioned Lamb Stew, **292**, 293
    Pork Stew with Cabbage, 223
Strawberries, 9
    All-Purpose Fruit Syrup, 82
    Buttermilk Fruit Shake, 125, **146**
    Chocolate Custard Cups, 344, **345**
    Chocolate-Raspberry Dip and Fresh Fruit, 347
    Strawberry Cream Cake, 336, **337**
    Strawberry Protein Shake, 124
Strokes, diet and, 24
Stuffing
    Roast Chicken with Vegetable and Soya Stuffing, 186

Sugar
  addiction to, 11
  alternatives to, 57, 60–61
  cravings, 30
  daily recommendations for, 16
  in low-fat food products, 16, 29
  in milk, 29
  in soft drinks, 15
  in specific foods, 16, 28
  limiting, 28–30, 57, 60–61
Sugar substitutes *see* Artificial sweeteners
Sweetcorn, 9
  Chicken Stew with Sweetcorn and Butterbeans, 268
Syrups
  All-Purpose Fruit Syrup, 82
  Wholemeal Pancakes with Berry Cream Syrup, **96**, 97

T

Tartar sauce
  Breaded Baked Cod with Tartar Sauce, 234
Tartes
  Raspberry-Almond Tarte, 350, **351**
Tea
  Mint-Infused Darjeeling Tea, 125
Tofu, 68
Tomatoes, 9
  Aubergine Parmesan, 289
  Bacon-Mushroom Melt, 154, **155**
  Baked Peppers with Onion and Tomato, 305
  Beef and Cabbage Casserole with Tomato Sauce, 274
  Bolognese Sauce for Pasta, 214, **214**
  Chicken and Ham Jambalaya, 265
  Chicken Gumbo, **132**, 133
  Chilli-Cornbread Pie, **276**, 277
  Chicken Stew with Sweetcorn and Butterbeans, 268
  Creole-Style Steamed Clams, 258, **258**
  Cuban-Style Beef Picadillo, 208
  Curried Chicken with Coconut, **170**, 171
  Fillet Steaks with Tomatoes and Rosemary, 204
  Ham and Soft Yoghurt Cheese on Rye Crispbread, 152
  Italian Chicken, 180, **181**
  Lamb Burgers with Tomatoes and Feta Cheese, 230
  Lamb Kebabs with Mushrooms and Tomatoes, 227

  Mini Aubergine Pizzas, 119
  Moussaka, 296–97, **297**
  Poached Eggs on Tomato-Aubergine Beds, 93
  Pork and Pasta Bake, **282**, 283
  Pork Stew with Cabbage, 223
  Sautéed Chicken with Shallots and White Wine, 176, **177**
  Shark Braised in Red Wine with Tomato and Anchovy, 247
  Shepherd's Pie, 298, **299**
  Spanish-Style Green Beans, 322
  Spicy Curried Vegetables, 295
  Tomato-Onion Salad with Walnut Vinaigrette, 320
  White Bean Soup with Sausage, 128, **129**
Tortillas, 8
  Crisp Tortilla with Avocado, Beans and Cheese, 159
  Pesto Chicken Sandwich with Roasted Peppers, 156, **157**
  Texas Burrito, 271
Trans fats, 27–28
Trigger foods, 31–33, 36, 320
Trout
  Pan-Fried Trout in Cornmeal with Bacon, 246
  Sautéed Trout with Almond Butter Sauce, 245
Tuna
  Sautéed Tuna Steaks with Garlic Sauce, 248, **249**
  Tuna Salad in Lettuce Wraps, 160
Turkey
  Bacon-Mushroom Melt, 154, **155**
  Breaded Turkey Escalopes with Oregano and Lemon, 198
  buying low-fat parts, 26
  Roast Turkey Breast with Herb Rub and Pan Juices, 193
  Scrambled Eggs with Sausage and Spring Onions, 92
  Turkey Burgers Stuffed with Chillies and Cheese, 196, **197**
  Turkey Chilli, 280
  Turkey Drumstick Curry, 192
  Turkey Escalopes with Ham and Provolone, **190**, 191
  Turkey Loaf, 194, **195**
  Turkey Sandwich with Jarlsberg and Apple, **146**, 147

U

Undereating, 60

V

Vegetables *see also specific kinds*
  buying, 24
  Crudités with Spicy Peanut Dipping Sauce, 118
  Hearty Country Vegetable Soup, 130
  high-GI vegetables, 7, 9
  in low-carb diet, 23–25
  low-GI vegetables, 7, 9, 24–25
  Quinoa and Vegetable Pilaf, 327
  Roast Chicken with Vegetable and Soya Stuffing, 186
  serving size of, 38
  starchy, limiting, 23
Venison
  Peppered Venison Fillets, 225

W

Walnuts, 72
  Asparagus with Orange-Walnut Vinaigrette, **306**, 307
  Bananas, Dates and Walnuts in Yoghurt Sauce, 84
  calories and carbohydrates in, 27
  Creamy Quinoa, 103
  Meat Loaf with Walnuts, 212
  Orange-Walnut Biscotti, **332**, 333
  Pork Chops with Cider, Walnuts and Prunes, 216, **217**
  Roasted Cauliflower with Nutty Lemon Mustard, 308
  Roasted Mixed Nuts, 109
  Smoked Salmon and Cream Cheese on Rye Crispbread, 151
  Tomato-Onion Salad with Walnut Vinaigrette, 320
Water, daily recommendations for, 33, 260
Watercress
  Turkey Sandwich with Jarlsberg and Apple, **146**, 147
  Watercress Salad with Goat's Cheese, Pine Nuts and Pears, 314, **315**
Weight loss
  roadblocks
    alcohol, 14
    artificial sweeteners, 152
    fluid retention, 260
    genetics, 244
    hidden carbohydrates, 84
    high expectations, 341
    lack of activity, 230
    lack of dietary fats, 106
    overeating, 23
    prescription medications, 175
    rapid weight-loss diets, 14
    trigger foods, 320
    undereating, 60
  slow, coping with, 37–39
Weight-loss strategies *see also* Low-carb cooking
  choosing healthy fats, 25–28
  choosing lean proteins, 25–28
  choosing plan for, 39–43
  controlling portion sizes, 30–31
  eating vegetables and fruits, 23–25
  eating whole grains, 21–23
  increasing physical activity, 36–37
  limiting added sugars, 28–30
  managing trigger foods, 31–33, 36
White beans
  Cannellini Beans with Cheese and Basil, 114, **115**
  Cannellini Beans with Ham and Sausage, 287
  Hearty Country Vegetable Soup, 130
  Italian Bean Soup with Chard and Mushrooms, 140
  White Bean Soup with Sausage, 128, **129**
Whole grains
  breakfast cereals, 74–75
  flour, 69–71
  in low-carb diet, 21–23, 68–71
Wholemeal flour, 70

Y

Yoghurt, 9
  Bananas, Dates and Walnuts in Yoghurt Sauce, 84
  Beef Kebabs with Yoghurt and Spices, **210**, 211
  Breakfast Berry 'Sundaes', 82
  Grilled Pineapple with Ginger-Yoghurt Sauce, 354
  Chilled Cucumber, Spring Onion and Yoghurt Soup, 142, **143**
  Grilled Salmon with Mint-Coriander Yoghurt, **252**, 253
  Soft Yoghurt Cheese, 107
  Soft Yoghurt Cheese with Olives, 107
  Strawberry Protein Shake, 124

stockists

■ **Kamut flour.** For your nearest stockist of organic kamut flour, telephone Infinity Foods, 01273 424060.

■ **Oat flour.** Available from Carblife Foods, 8 Badger Way, North Cheshire Trading Estate, Prenton, Wirral, Cheshire CH43 3HQ; telephone: 0151 608 9162; www.carblife.co.uk
You can also make oat flour at home by running whole rolled oats (porridge oats) through your food processor until finely ground. Begin with slightly more than the amount called for in the recipe, and sift the flour to remove any remaining larger pieces of oats.

■ **Sugar-free pancake syrup.** With a flavour close to maple syrup, but with 0 carbohydrate, this product is not widely available outside the US, but can be ordered from Carblife Foods, 8 Badger Way, North Cheshire Trading Estate, Prenton, Wirral, Cheshire CH43 3HQ; telephone: 0151 608 9162; www.carblife.co.uk

■ **Nitrate-free bacon.** Nitrates and nitrites have, for many centuries, been used to preserve cured meats, and scientists are still researching their effects on the human body. Some, but not all, organic meat products avoid the use of nitrates and nitrites; check with your supplier. Nitrate- and nitrite-free bacon is available from Park Farm Shop, Park Farm, Heckfield, Hampshire RG27 0LD; telephone: 0118 932 6650; www.parkfarmorganics.co.uk